Explanation in Social History

For my Mother and Father:
Nancy and Barney Lloyd

Explanation
in Social History

CHRISTOPHER LLOYD

Basil Blackwell

First published 1986

Basil Blackwell Ltd
108 Cowley Road, Oxford OX4 1JF, UK

Basil Blackwell Inc.
432 Park Avenue South, Suite 1505,
New York, NY 10016, USA

British Library Cataloguing in Publication Data

Lloyd, Christopher, *1950–*
    Explanation in social history.
    1. Social history——Historiography
    I. Title
    901   HN8
    ISBN 0-631-13113-2

Library of Congress Cataloging in Publication Data

Lloyd, Christopher, 1950–
    Explanation in social history.

    Bibliography: p.
    Includes index.
    1. Social history——Philosophy. 2. Social history——
Methodology. 3. Structuralism. 4. Criticism
(Philosophy) 5. Social structures. 6. Social change.
I. Title.
HN28.L58 1985   301'.09   85-13359
ISBN 0-631-13113-2

Typeset by Freeman Graphic, Tonbridge, Kent
Printed in Great Britain by T. J. Press Ltd, Padstow

Contents

Preface

This is a book which aims to explicate, clarify, and criticise the philosophical and methodological framework in which social historical discourse is conducted. It is not primarily a work of theory construction, although some theoretical ideas are discussed.

> *Theory* is concerned with constructing concepts and models and with making general but detailed explanations of certain types of events and processes which can be used to explain the causes of actual events and processes.
>
> *Methodology* is concerned with the frameworks of general concepts, categories, models, hypotheses, and procedures which are employed in theory construction and testing.
>
> *Philosophy* is concerned with the epistemological, ontological, and semantical assumptions (often tacit) about the general nature of knowledge and the general structure of the world which underpin and infuse the methodologies and theories of particular discourses.

The muddling of these aspects of analysis is a major cause of misunderstanding and confusion in the social studies today. They are dependent on each other but logically distinct. This work is concerned with the two more abstract and general aspects of methodology and philosophy.

Another way to conceptualise these aspects of a discourse is to picture them as two concentric 'shells' around a central core of the empirical subject matter as conceptualised and dealt with by a particular discourse. In this case the core is the events and processes of social history. Surrounding the core is a shell of methodologies, theories, and procedures that are tacitly or explicitly employed by practitioners of the discourse, i.e. by social historians, when they conceptualise and study the events and processes. The outer shell consists of metatheoretical and philosophical reflections and criticisms about what ontologies, methodologies, types of logical arguments, concepts, and theories are or should be employed in the discourse. All academic disciplines or discourses exhibit this structure and so contain examples of critical methodological and philosophical writings about the nature of the discourse. Social history is no exception.

Thus this work is an example of a small but growing genre concerned with understanding and criticising, as a complex entity, the explanatory framework of particular social science discourses. Recent examples have included Rom Harré and Paul Secord's *The Explanation of Social Behaviour*, David Harvey's *Explanation in Geography*, Peter McClelland's *Causal Explanation and Model Building in History, Economics, and the New Economic History*, Mark Blaug's *The Methodology of Economics*, and Jon Elster's *Explaining Technical Change*. (There have also been many recent works on the explanation of history, including those of W. H. Dray, Patrick Gardiner, Murray Murphey, R. F. Atkinson, and Maurice Mandelbaum.) All of these, as their titles indicate, have attempted to carry out aims similar to those of the present work in relation to their fields of enquiry. Social history has so far lacked such a detailed analysis, although recently there has been a profusion of much smaller manifesto-like works purporting to outline the methodological basis of social history. While general history and sociology have been the subjects of many detailed analyses, these have not been much concerned with the new social history. This volume offers some clarifications and criticisms as a contribution to filling this gap.

However, clarification and criticism are not the ultimate end of such an enquiry: that must always be the construction of better empirical explanations. To put it in somewhat unfashionable terminology, the general aim must always be to try to move closer to truthful explanations of the causes of social phenomena and processes. While we may never achieve the ultimate truth (because it is ultimately unachievable), the search for it can serve as a powerful regulative principle of our scientific researches and arguments, as Popper has cogently argued. Clarification and criticism of philosophical and methodological foundations can help the search.

During the four years it took to write this book I have had valuable help from the following colleagues at Wolfson College, whom I warmly thank but absolve from any responsibility for the final product: Ken Kierans, Giorgio Gagliani, Harvey Shoolman, and Sam Lee. Kay Cornish provided invaluable help with the bibliography and household logistics for which I am very thankful. John Torrance has read the entire manuscript and made many valuable suggestions. I am very grateful to him but have not been able to accept all his advice or incorporate all his suggestions.

Of the utmost importance to me has been the constant emotional, intellectual, editorial, and secretarial support of my wife, Linley Lloyd, to whom I owe a great deal. And the birth of our daughter Tamsin in March 1983 gave me an even greater reason for pressing on. Her joy of life is truly inspiring in a foreboding time! My deepest thanks go to them for sustaining me.

Oxford   Christopher Lloyd

Acknowledgements

The author and publisher would like to thank the following for permission to reproduce figures and diagrams in this book: University of Minnesota Press for a diagram from H. Feigl, 'The "Orthodox" View of Theories: Remarks in Defence as Well as Critique', in M. Rudner and S. Winokur (eds), *Minnesota Studies in the Philosophy of Science*, IV, 1970 (figure 1); Macmillan, London and Basingstoke, for a diagram from Mary Hesse, *Theory and Observation: The Structure of Scientific Inference*, 1974 (figure 3); Routledge & Kegan Paul for a diagram from T. Parsons and N. Smelser, *Economy and Society*, 1956 (figure 9); The American Sciological Association for a diagram from T. Parsons, 'Pattern Variables Revisited: A Response to Robert Dubin', *American Sociological Association*, vol. 25, 1960 (figure 10). Figure 11 is from Jackson Toby, 'Parsons' Theory of Societal Evolution', in *The Evolution of Societies*, © 1977, p. 10, and is reproduced by permission of Prentice-Hall, Inc., Englewood Cliffs, NJ; and figure 12 is from Norbert Elias, *What is Sociology?*, and is reproduced by permission of Hutchinson Books Ltd.

Five Themes

HISTORY AND THE SOCIAL SCIENCES

History, from Thucydides to Michelet, was of course included in the humanities. And then along came the 'third culture', unobtrusively at first, but soon becoming visible to all: the social sciences. For a long time, they coexisted quite cheerfully with the historian: in the line running from Marx to Weber, Durkheim and Freud, there was a constant exchange of concepts and much crossing of frontiers between the two. More recently, however, old Chronos came under attack. The social sciences, wishing to preserve a reputation for hardness and purity, began to operate a closed shop against history, which was accused of being a 'soft' science. The attack was characterised by a great deal of ignorance and not a little gall on the part of the attackers, who affected to forget that since Bloch, Braudel and Larousse, history too had undergone a scientific transformation. Clio had stolen the clothes of the social sciences while they were bathing, and they had never noticed their nakedness. Today at any rate, the move to exclude history seems to be almost over, since it is becoming clear that it has no future. Everyone has eventually bowed to the obvious: it is no more possible to build up a human science without the extra dimension of the past, than it is to study astrophysics without knowing the ages of the stars or galaxies. History was, for a few decades of semi-disgrace, the Cinderella of the social sciences, but it has now been restored to its rightful place. Indeed, it now appears to have chosen just the right moment to withdraw, refusing to become a narcissistic mental activity, rotting away in self-absorption and self-congratulation; while the death of history was being loudly proclaimed in certain quarters, it had simply gone through the looking-glass, in search not of its own reflection, but of a new world.

Emmanuel Le Roy Ladurie *The Territory of the Historian*, 1981, pp. 26–7

SOCIAL HISTORY AS THE HISTORY OF STRUCTURES

Narrative history always claims to relate 'things just as they really happened'. Ranke deeply believed in this statement when he made it. In fact, though, in its own covert way, narrative history consists in an interpretation, an authentic philosophy of history. . . . It is precisely our task to get beyond this first stage of history. The social realities must be tackled *in themselves and for themselves*. By social realities I mean all the major forms of collective life, economies, institutions, social structures, in short and above all, civilizations – all aspects of reality which earlier historians have not exactly overlooked, but which with a few outstanding exceptions have all too often been regarded as a backdrop, there only to explain or as if intended to explain the behaviour of the exceptional individuals on whom the historian so complacently dwells.

Fernand Braudel *On History*, 1980, pp. 11–12

THE NEED FOR CRITICAL PHILOSOPHY

The fact is . . . we are all making ferocious or lofty epistemological faces, but most of us, especially in Britain, are the merest novices in philosophy. A training by way of Althusser (who himself makes gross logical blunders) or by way of a critique of Althusser is not an adequate substitute for a more rigorous preparation. . . . The historical discipline (its 'discourse of the proof') presupposes that an encounter with objective evidence is what is at issue: and particular techniques and a particular disciplinary logic have been devised to that end. But I concede also that the historian, in every moment of his or her work, is a value-formed being, who cannot, when proposing problems or interrogating evidence, in fact operate in this value-free way.

E. P. Thompson 'The Politics of Theory', 1981, p. 407

THE IMPORTANCE OF STRUCTURAL TRANSFORMATION

We live at a time when we can see the interdependence of the political, the economic and the cognitive transformations; a time also when transformation has gathered enormous speed and has come to embrace the whole of humanity. Its understanding is certainly the first task of thought. We only possess fragments of such an understanding – enough for a reassurance that understanding is possible, if not much more. But systems of thought that are constitutionally unable even to perceive the change, let alone to understand it, are worthless.

Ernest Gellner *Thought and Change*, 1964, p. 219

TOWARDS A STRUCTURATIONIST METHODOLOGY FOR HISTORY

Historians must structure their field, simply because they cannot (except for reasons of pure technical convenience or necessity) select from among the totality of all human activities in the past which is their subject. Even when historians, for whatever reason, choose to concentrate on certain human activities and to neglect others, it is always in terms of a conscious or unconscious judgement of analytical priorities. Traditional historians concentrated on kings and cabinets, wars and diplomacy, because they considered the actions of decision-makers among the ruling groups as the most important motive forces in history. All historians, whatever their view of the central forces of history, know that they have to bring them into some systematic relation with the other phenomena of the past – economic, political, cultural, religious or whatever – within their field of vision, and however restricted that field of vision may be by the standards of other historians, it always implies the synthesis of phenomena which, outside history, would be treated separately and without relation to each other. Newtonian physics 'belongs' to natural science, Hobbes and Locke to philosophy, debates on the balance of trade to economics. Milton is a subject for literary critics and the massacre of Glencoe would today be part of a field report by social anthropologists on kinship systems in Scottish clan society. But all historians of Great Britain in the late seventeenth century must fit all these into their accounts. If all history is thus obliged to structure the totality of human activities and to establish relationships between the subject-matter of various specialized disciplines, some kinds of history (such as Marx's) do so systematically and consciously. In doing so they are not only forced into conceptual clarifications, but also assist in structuring the field of the social sciences. That is why the most fruitful approaches to social science – classical political economy of the eighteenth-century kind, Marx, Weber – have operated in an essentially historical framework, even when their practitioners were not themselves primarily historians.

E. J. Hobsbawm, 'The Contribution of History to Social Science',
1981, pp. 638–9

Introduction and Overview

The discourse of social history, as its name implies, deals with the history of society and as such is in a sense both one of the oldest and one of the newest branches of the social studies. Although it could be claimed that the first systematic social enquiries were of a political-constitutional kind, such as by Hobbes and Locke in the seventeenth century, in fact the foundations that these men had for their ideas consisted of general theoretical conceptions about the structure of society and how it related to politics over time. Without at least a tacit belief that society is an ordered and historical entity there would be no point in making an enquiry into its nature, its relationship to action, or the causes of its transformations. Many of the great social scientists of the eighteenth and nineteenth centuries, such as Montesquieu, Ferguson, Smith, Tocqueville, Marx, Sombart, and Weber combined an interest in abstraction and theory building about social structure in general with a concern to grasp the real history of society, and so they were both sociologists and historians. However, from the late nineteenth century a rift gradually developed between abstraction and concrete enquiry such that sociology and history became increasingly separate fields of enquiry. The work of Ranke and of the late-nineteenth-century German neo-Kantian philosophers, especially Windelband and Rickert, and the uncritical borrowing by many historians of a simplified empiricist epistemology, all helped to legitimise this growing division between supposedly general and theoretical (i.e. nomothetic) and particular (i.e. idiographic) discourses.

But the rift was never complete, and since World War II the Marxists and the French Annalistes (especially) have inspired a growing *rapprochement* between abstract social theory and concrete history. The

1

situation has now been reached where there is a veritable welter of discussion about how history and social theory can be reunited to provide the basis for a new social history or historical sociology. That the history of society should somehow form the basis for all social enquiry is now also advocated. But how the new social history should conceive of its object, and what methodological framework it should use to explain it, are matters for great disagreement.

The concept of 'social history' is a problematical one and the range of work done under its rubric is now very wide indeed. It ranges from 'microscopic' 'people's history', such as that carried out under the auspices of the British *History Workshop* and *Oral History* movements, and Ladurie's imaginative reconstructions of historical episodes (all based upon detailed personal testimony); through the studies of class consciousness and class interaction of writers such as Edward Thompson, Harold Perkin, R. S. Neale, and Charles Tilly; to 'macroscopic' long-run structural enquiries such as those by Barrington Moore, Eric Hobsbawm, Immanuel Wallerstein, Perry Anderson, Norbert Elias, and Fernand Braudel. Faced with such an array of focal lengths it may seem at first glance an impossible task to find a sufficiently comprehensive viewpoint from which to criticise all the explanatory modes adopted by social historians.

Indeed, one response to this variegated scene would be to declare: let a thousand flowers bloom! And there is something to recommend that since it seems to be a possible way of avoiding dogma, reduction, and even 'epistemological terrorism'. On the other hand, many historians and social scientists do claim to be trying to offer *factual* reconstructions and at least fairly *objective* explanations, and see themselves as making some *progress* in understanding their designated processes and in solving empirical problems. Social historians often see their explanations as being *superior* to those of traditional historians, and among social historians there are heated debates about the explanatory merits of different theories and methodologies. Furthermore, some social historians are political activists, drawing a direct link between historical understanding and contemporary social criticism. Thus one cannot avoid *evaluative* questions about the explanations being offered since certain claims are often made for the veracity of these explanations. I believe such claims to be, at least in part, *philosophical* in nature.

Indeed, fundamentally important questions about the aims, objectivity, rationality, verisimilitude, truthfulness, and commensurability of explanations are present at the very heart of any empirical-explanatory discourse or research project. Moreover, these matters have a vital bearing upon action since beliefs about the reliability of both personal and scientific knowledge influence all action and especially political action.

As soon as socio-historical explanations are examined, compared, and evaluated the issue of explanatory unity between the humanities and the natural sciences also arises. Are there or should there be certain *a priori* standards and approaches to explanation derived perhaps from natural or social science, which if made explicit and adhered to would improve explanation? Or should social history be considered a *sui generis* interpretive (i.e. hermeneutical) discourse attempting to construct a *circle* of understanding linking observers with actors and epochs in a self-validating insightful manner? Most importantly of all, by what standards and by whom should explanations be judged and compared? Should there be publicly stated criteria available so that good explanations can be separated from bad or spurious ones? Or should social historians themselves be the sole judges of what should be considered acceptable and progressive explanations and reconstructions? I believe strongly that there must be a role for critical philosophy in resolving such methodological disputes.

BASIC QUESTIONS AND AIMS

Despite (or perhaps because of) the flourishing of social historians in recent years and a good deal of discussion about problems of disciplinary delineation and explanation, many differences of opinion and some confusion still exist among practitioners as to what their objects of enquiry should be and about the status of its results. I shall address myself to six questions about these problems:

1 What should be the object of study for those describing themselves as 'social historians'?
2 How should social history relate to other branches of social and historical enquiry?
3 What should be the mode and structure of explanation employed by social historians?
4 Is it possible for them to develop objective causal explanations?
5 Can social history be a science?
6 What methodologies are appropriate for studying the history of society?

These questions are clearly philosophical in nature, being about general aspects of reality (ontological questions), knowledge (epistemological questions), and methodology. Unfortunately, however, the discourses of philosophy, history, and social science are still more or less self-contained academic worlds that have little intercourse with each other. Even philosophers of social science and history, who have made many attempts in recent years to break down the frontier barriers, have had little impact on the work and ideas of empirical researchers in history, economics, sociology, and politics (although philosophical arguments *have* become central to anthropology). Social *theory* of all kinds has, of course, always had a close relationship with speculative and analytical philosophical thinking, but theory has not had the impact upon concrete historical explanation that its producers would have liked. Two of the possible reasons for this are, firstly, that many historical researchers believe themselves to be sufficiently equipped with common-sense psychological and social knowledge, perhaps by virtue of their place in the society they are studying. (Anthropologists usually cannot have this security.)

Secondly, to acquire the confidence of an adequate knowledge of explicit philosophical/theoretical work which can be systematically used is a long and difficult task, requiring great sacrifices of time and effort. Such knowledge is usually thought to be unnecessary by many historians since they are happy to operate within a largely tacit general framework of theories, concepts, and procedures (often centring upon a common-sense empiricism and behaviourism) which their peers and betters hold to be sufficient and which do not seem to contain glaring contradictions or inadequacies. Only when contradictions and inadequacies do become glaringly obvious, for whatever reason – perhaps because of empirical weaknesses or economic and socio-cultural change – are tensions produced. These tensions may in turn produce academic realignments and/or the search for new approaches. Such a period of change began in the late 1960s and its manifestations have included a turn to philosophy by many social theorists and a turn to theory by many social historians. (A similar phenomenon occurred in Germany and Austria in the 1880s and 1890s.)

The current period of crisis and realignment has affected all the social studies and to a lesser extent history. There has been a good deal of discussion about the use of social theory but little about philosophical problems associated with this development. The recent debates carried on in *History Workshop* and *Past and Present*, for instance, show both the desire and need for philosophical clarification and assistance, as Edward Thompson acknowledged in the passage quoted as one of my five themes.

Therefore this book has been written primarily for an audience of social historians, who wish to gain an insight into some of the philosophical and methodological ideas which are of relevance to them in attempting to clarify and answer certain fundamental questions about scope and explanation. It may also be of interest to others who wish to gain an overview and insight into the nature of the foundations of modern social history. It has not been written primarily for professional philosophers. Consequently I have tried to adopt a method that combines exegesis and criticism, since I believe exegesis to be necessary in this context, at the risk of its being tedious in various places to some philosophers, historians, and social theorists.

My main aim is *not* primarily one of describing in detail the history of methodologies and approaches to explanation in social history, although I have had to do a limited amount of that (and I hope to make it the subject of a separate volume at a later date). Rather, one of my main aims is to criticise contemporary methodological approaches to explaining historical social change in the light of a prior argument about general questions of ontology and epistemology. My procedure is essentially one of moving from the philosophy of explanation to the discourse of social change, and not the reverse. This particular way of proceeding has been made possible by developments within philosophy of explanation in the past decade or so and this volume is partly an attempt to employ these developments in a critical capacity.

This book is thus a defence of the importance of philosophical argument to empirical enquiry. While I have been, and still consider myself to be, a social scientist rather than a philosopher, I have become convinced of the importance of philosophical reasoning in helping to solve problems of social scientific research and explanation. Like Imre Lakatos I believe that the establishment of better methodological 'statute laws', rather than a reliance upon 'case laws', is essential to further progress in the immature sciences, since without explicit statutes the cases may be inconsistent and inappropriate to the quest for successful discoveries. *Rational criticism* of existing practices requires a firm shared basis of ontological, epistemological, and methodological concepts.

THE PROBLEMS OF SOCIAL HISTORY

Social historians, by so describing themselves, usually wish to establish their partial (at least) independence from their institutional parents – sociology, political history, and economic history – and sometimes wish to supersede those disciplines. As their name obviously implies and as they often point out, the history of *society* is their object of enquiry. However, the chief problems of disciplinary delineation and explanation arise in establishing just what society is and how it could have a history. The general form in which an object of enquiry is ontologically specified will strongly influence the forms of research and explanation employed in studying it.

Modern problems of social ontology and epistemology have long antecedents. With the development of modern social thought from the early eighteenth century there came an awareness by some thinkers of (1) the possible real existence of such entities as patterns of mass social behaviour and social relational structures, and (2) the importance of conceptualising and studying them. This awareness led to attempts at theorising and studying social change or the history of such patterns and structures. In turn this helped to give rise, from the mid nineteenth century, to the gradual institutionalisation of separate branches of

academic enquiry concerned exclusively with such matters: the 'disciplines' of economic and social history and social change. The members of
these 'disciplines' came to see themselves as dealing with special problems of explanation, and were concerned to delineate the boundaries of
their problems and to label themselves as separate from the other, related
human studies of history, economics, and sociology. Overlapping somewhat with this development was a parallel movement in the human
studies to establish them as being scientific in a manner similar to the
more successful sciences of nature. This led to the twin phenomena of
claims about the possibility of 'scientific' study of social change and
history, and of attempts to write such histories.

These two developments of the emergence of institutionalised disciplines of economic and social history and of some attempts to make such
history a science must be seen partly against a background of the history
of debates within the philosophies of natural science, social science, and
history. The human and social studies have always been more influenced
than the natural sciences by philosophical/methodological discussions
(though not necessarily carried out by professional philosophers or in an
immediately recognisable academic-philosophical mode). Innovations in
their logic, conceptual frameworks, and orientations have sometimes
occurred as a consequence of abstracting and applying developments
made in other discourses, as well as from internal problems of empirical
enquiry.

Nevertheless, despite two and a half centuries of discussion, there still
is considerable disagreement over these questions of delineation and
explanation of social history and a wide spectrum of opinion has
developed among modern practitioners. At one extreme is the individualist view of Trevelyan and Cobb, for instance, who see social history as
being primarily an interpretive reconstruction of the observable lives of
ordinary people and as such being different from traditional history only
by virtue of the sort of people it deals with. This position is still rather
influential. Opposed to this interpretivist view but helping to make up the
same end of the spectrum is empiricist quantitative history, epitomised by
Fogel, which places great emphasis upon the 'scientific' counting of
individual events. Both these approaches tend to see their object in
atomistic terms, as consisting of the aggregation of a host of discrete
individual social or economic actions or lives. At the other end of the
spectrum is a view which sees social history as being concerned with
long-term (and probably gradual) changes in macro structures. The
structures can be cultural, geographical, economic, social, and so on, and
they are thought of as having an existence virtually independnt of human
behaviour. Functionalist evolutionists, some members of the Annales
School, and some Marxists fall into this group.

Leaving aside for the moment the problem of conceptualisation of
structures, action, and behaviour, it can be said that most practitioners

and thinkers about these questions claim to be somewhere between. They wish to study both structures and action, and see such a study either as the basis of other sociological and historical discourses, or as a totalising discourse. Perhaps the clearest expression by a practising historian of the importance of examining, through the use of theory, the interconnection between structure and action was given by Eric Hobsbawm (1971b), who said that economic and social history was concerned not only with 'structures and their mechanisms of persistence and change and with the general possibilities and patterns of their transformations' but also with what 'actually happened'. Therefore, he believed, the history of society, is 'a collaboration between general models of social structure and change and the specific set of phenomena which actually occurred' (p. 9). I believe this is broadly correct but it needs philosophical clarification and support.

General philosophical and theoretical questions about the nature and interrelationship of structures and action have not been much discussed by historians. I wish to try to offer some clarification and criticism of these issues of scope and knowledge by thinking through the problems again rather than by making original philosophical innovations. My thinking through has been made possible at this time by what I believe to be indeed some genuine innovations in the philosophies of the sciences made by thinkers in the neo-realist tradition. I have used their work as a critical perspective since I believe they have developed important arguments about the *possibility* of *objective* socio-historical knowledge based upon accounts of the *relatively independent and enduring reality* of social structures and the mechanisms of their history. That is, they offer solutions to the problems of both scope and knowledge by first making an argument about the fundamental nature of the social world and in turn of how we could have knowledge of it.

TOWARDS A CAUSAL SCIENCE OF SOCIAL HISTORY

I hope to show that social history should be primarily concerned with the *causal explanation* of the history of the recurrent *relational structures* of social life (i.e. the relatively enduring small- and large-scale structures of organised human relationships such as families, institutions, and economies) and not with particular individual or group acts or lives. However, social historical explanations must use observations of and theories about the relationship of group and patterned behaviour and cultural expressions to social structures over time. But conceptualisations of the nature and form of social structures and of how they could have a history do differ a good deal and often suffer from vague and possibly outmoded ontological and epistemological arguments. I believe that some realist philosophies and theories collectively offer valuable help towards solutions of the philosophical and theoretical questions facing social historians, and this book is partly an attempt to begin to apply their arguments in a critical role, both in relation to the existing accounts of the nature of social historical discourse and to existing claims about the scientific nature of that discourse.

The question of *causation* is basic to the philosophy of scientific explanation but is a very contentious concept. Like all the human and social studies, social historians are divided on this issue into three broad camps. Firstly there are those who see their task not as seeking for causes but primarily as imaginative reconstruction, description, and interpretation of part of the past, using a narrative method of presentation. They attempt to develop a hermeneutical understanding of motives for action and the meanings that actors give to social processes. Secondly, there are those who wish primarily to study causation but who see historical social processes as having their own peculiar causal relationships requiring research methods and explanatory procedures different from other discourses. And thirdly there are a few who see social history as being, potentially at least, a causal science broadly akin to that of nature, having a similar methodological and explanatory structure but different subject matter and less precision.

I wish to defend the third view, and in order to do so I will try to specify the concept of 'causation' in a non-Humean, realist manner, which rejects the necessity of regular mechanical connection between events in favour of the idea of the essential causal powers of kinds of things. It is then possible to see the legitimate (but relative) distinctiveness of social history as arising not from having philosophical foundations radically different from other sciences but mainly from the nature of its object of enquiry. The social scientific viewpoint does not deny that there can be imaginative interpretation and reconstruction of the past but sees such work as ancillary to or a facet of causal explanation. Unfortunately, many 'traditional' historians tend mistakenly to deny any validity to the possibility of scientific historical explanation.

The possibility of scientific explanation in history and the social studies *is* still on the agenda, despite attempts by some historians and philosophers to reject it. But unfortunately some of its main defenders within the history discipline, such as Fogel, have adopted the unpromising point of view of vulgar empiricism, which tends to equate scientific explanation simply with (doubtfully) accurate measurement of 'given' observable events. Against empiricism, some structuralists, such as Parsons, Braudel, and Althusser, have attempted to confine historical science to the study of the supposedly impersonal 'structural causality' of structural processes.

The problem of the possibility of social science can be transformed by rejecting the old dichotomy of positive physical science and subjective humanities. The positivist-physicalist account of science and the relativist-hermeneutical account of the humanities have bedevilled the social studies, since they have led on the one hand to a simplistic, reductionist, and unattractive argument for a scientific approach, or on the other to a misleading account of the mechanisms of human action and belief and therefore of the possibility of an objective explanation of them. A realist framework not only is able to do greater justice to the actual situation in the advanced sciences but points the way to how a progressive and successful social science could be constructed.

Science as a mode of explanation should not be characterised by empiricist epistemology, or by technical methods such as quantification and experimentation, but by the structure of its logical inferences; the rational, critical, and public nature of its results; and the importance to explanation of philosophically-based coherent traditions or frameworks of research. Moreover, to avoid the weaknesses of relativistic accounts of science, it is essential to grasp what it is about *the ordered real structure of the natural world* that makes the mature sciences so successful in corroborating theories, solving empirical and conceptual problems, and having their solutions applied in open systems. Nature, in short, is characterised by universal, atemporal, structures. Thus any defence of the possibility of a socio-historical science similar to that of nature must first address the question of whether and how there could exist real and relatively atemporal *social* structures such that there could be objective and progressively successful discoveries and explanations of them. The idea of scientific social history can be rescued from its individualist and hermeneuticist enemies as well as its empiricist and holist friends by basing itself in the first instance upon a prior argument about the necessary interconnections between observed human expressions and actions, and *real social structures*. Furthermore, it must be accepted that there is an interaction between theoretical specifications of the objects of enquiry and observational evidence about them. But this does not mean that there cannot be progress towards truthful explanation, only that the progress is not simply linear. This is shown markedly by the history of the natural sciences, which are also partly characterised by the interpenetration of theories and data but in addition by long-run progress in making discoveries.

The prior argument about social reality should operate, then, as a framework for research and as a regulative principle akin to the principle of truth. That is, it is hypothesised that there are historical but relatively enduring regular patterns in social behaviour and culture, which have real and relatively enduring structural mechanisms (biological, environmental, psychological, and sociological), and that there can be progress towards the discovery of these patterns and structures. Recent work by some realist philosophers and social theorists has succeeded, to my mind, in showing the possibility of such a science of society by developing a philosophical and theoretical framework which links observable patterns of behaviour and expressions to social structures through the vital

notions of *human agency* and *intentionality*. It is by paying full attention
to the importance of these concepts that the earlier insights of the
'scientific structuralism' of Marx and Lévi-Strauss can be built upon and
transcended. Moreover, unlike some physical sciences, social science
must have as its basic aim the explanation of social *transformation*. That
makes for a major difference in its theoretical foundations, but certainly
not one which necessitates the abandonment of scientificity. Indeed,
some natural sciences such as cosmology, geology, and evolutionary
biology are just as historical as social history and just as scientific as
physics. It is not physics that should be our model, or geology, but the
idea of science as a quest for truth about causality – a quest that proceeds
through a complex process of reasoning, theory, observation, and
constant criticism.

TOWARDS THE UNIFICATION OF SOCIAL SCIENCE

One of the main themes running through my critical re-examination is an
attempt to defend the old argument that social explanation and historical
explanation should be parts of the one discourse; that there should not
be, in other words, a form of explanation and knowledge which is
peculiar to the study of history, whether history is seen as 'total',
'political', 'social', 'economic', or whatever. History and the social
studies (including economics) should *not* remain as separate discourses
(idiographic versus nomothetic) but should be related aspects of one
science – a science which must embody a concern to study actual and
possible human acts, behaviour, events, processes, and structures, using a
combination of theoretical and empirical methods.

Resolution of the divisions in the social sciences, firstly between studies
of action and studies of structure, and secondly between determinist and
agential approaches to action and structure, is still the key problem for
social historians as well as psychologists and sociologists. How action
relates to the structure of social order over time has been conceptualised
and theorised from many points of view ever since systematic thought on
the nature of society began in the early nineteenth century. I shall argue
that a basic requirement is a model of humans as agential and social
beings, who structure the world through intentional action and have
their action structured by the social world.

Unification of the socio-historical studies has thus to be based upon a
coherent general theoretical foundation which links together persons and
structures in such a way that action is explainable by its structural and
psychological imperatives and constraints, and structure and its history
are explainable as the intended and unintended consequences of individual actions and patterned mass behaviour over time. Action and
structure cannot be explained without each other; nevertheless, different

questions requiring different answers can be asked about the history of each of them, and that gives rise to the possibility of a *division of labour* between studies of actions and structures.

Many modern social historians do see their work as the basis for a unified socio-historical discourse but this of course contrasts with the recent development (i.e. of about the last century) of orthodox historical writing and the bulk of the philosophy of history as branches of both metaphysics and epistemology. Historians as individuals and as a profession have on the whole resisted arguments about their lack of uniqueness as a discipline. They have usually seen themselves as being concerned with separate problems and using different methodologies from those of the social studies. Indeed, sociology emerged as a separate discipline or mode of discourse partly because historians, especially in England and Germany, were so unsympathetic towards sociological reasoning (although in recent years the barriers have begun to dissolve a little, owing largely to the insistence of sociologists). Caught in the middle of this essentially philosophical debate are the historians of economy and society. I believe they should accept the philosophical nature of the issues and seek first to resolve them on the plane of the philosophy of the sciences.

In short, the *general aims* of this book are the following:

1 To survey and discuss the philosophical and methodological resources relevant to solving problems of disciplinary explanation and delineation.
2 To develop my own argument that social history should be primarily concerned with the causal explanation of the history of structures of social relations within a context of underlying unity in the socio-historical studies. This argument will thus answer the first five of the six questions posed earlier in this chapter.
3 To survey and analyse the problems of and the range of methodological resources available for explaining historical structural change.
4 To develop my own argument, in response to question six, that a structurationist framework for explaining structural change is the best because it is able to show how human agency and social action relate dialectically to social structures over time.

In order to achieve these aims the book has the following structure:

Part I: Social History and Philosophy In chapter 1 I briefly raise the philosophical and methodological problems that face social historians in explaining their object and delineating their discourse from other discourses. In chapter 2 I show how analytical philosophical reasoning is relevant to clarifying problems and concepts and offering hypotheses to empirical discourses struggling with such problems.

Part II: Explanation in Science and the Humanities This part contains a detailed discussion and defence of the realist argument introduced above. I survey and discuss the recent debates in the philosophy of explanation in the following way. In chapter 3 the positivist orthodoxy of the 1950s and 1960s is summarised. Chapter 4 surveys some arguments for and reactions against positivism in philosophy of history. In chapter 5 I discuss holist and conventionalist reactions against positivism in the philosophy of science. In chapter 6 the hermeneutical and idealist approaches to explanation in the humanities are briefly discussed. Chapter 7 contains a detailed defence of the realist philosophy of explanation in the context of the foregoing chapters. Finally, chapter 8 shows why I believe realism and structurism are relevant to explanation in the social studies.

Part III: Action, Structure, and History: Approaches to Structural Change This part is about the appropriate methodology for social historians and it defends the structurist approach by elaborating it in the context of alternative approaches. Chapter 9 discusses in a general way the sorts of methodological and theoretical problems that are involved in studying the history of social structures. In chapters 10, 11, and 12 I discuss determinist methodologies that try to explain structural change by causes external to the agency powers of persons. Lastly, chapters 13 and 14 discuss various sorts of non-determinist, agential approaches of which structurationism is the most recent and synthetic example.

PART I

Social History and Philosophy

1

The Explanatory Problems of Social History

Social history as a recognisable academic discourse, with its own institutional arrangements of chairs, courses, textbooks, journals, and so on, is a fairly new invention in Anglophone countries, being only about thirty years old. In some other countries, notably France and Germany, where the division between sociology and history has not been so marked and where the strength of empiricism has been much weaker, the study of the history of society in the forms of historical sociology and historical economics has had a much longer history, stretching back into the mid nineteenth century at least. In the Anglophone countries historical writing was dominated by a concern with politics and the state until after World War II, when a growing number of historians began to see that the focus of historical writing was too narrow. They took comfort and support from a similar feeling that was growing within the older economic history discipline. This led directly to the separate institutional-isation of social history – that is, as an offshoot largely from history and not from sociology. For this reason, the problem of the general nature of the object of enquiry was not raised by many historians. Their problem was, rather than historical writing was simply too narrow; it concentrated on the 'top' of society and ignored the 'bottom'. It was only later when an older, submerged tradition of historical sociology began to reappear in Anglophone thought and when the relevance of sociological theories began to be explored by historians that philosophical questions about their discourse became of more concern to them.

Even now when we look at the wide field that contains all those who claim to be studying the history of society – a scene whose outlines are blurred but in which a great variety of activities is occurring – we can still distinguish at first these two broad types of people: the empirical social historians who think of themselves as historians first and foremost, and the historical sociologists who see themselves as social scientists. The first wish to establish particular 'truths', the second general 'truths'. But if we look closer at the field we can also see that there are some there who are trying to be both, and it is they who, armed with appropriate methodologies and theories, are usually producing the best results. It is necessary from the point of view of the quality of explanation that more practitioners do likewise.

History and sociology both suffer if they are divorced, and I believe it is in the true interests of both historians and sociologists that their explanations of particular social events and processes, whether past or present, be improved by merging their methodologies. But this raises many problems to do with the scope of their discourse, how they should explain their objects, and how their discourse relates to other branches of the socio-historical studies. Social historians are right to be sceptical about the models and theories of many sociologists, just as in turn sociologists are right to see the common-sense empiricism of some historians as philosophically and theoretically naïve and inadequate. But theory and models are indispensable, whether historians like it or not, and there are some very useful theories and models available. And attention to the philosophical foundations of socio-historical explanation can greatly aid the construction of better empirical explanations.

Both social historians and historical sociologists say they wish to explain the history of society *qua society*.[1] The basic methodological problems of the discourse are thus to do mainly with defining the three key terms of 'society', 'history', and 'explanation', and with delineating the relationship that the discourse has with other branches of the socio-historical studies.

DEFINING THE 'SOCIAL'

Society can be conceptualised in many ways and there is little agreement about the matter, unlike in say economics, geography, chemistry, or physics where there is a broad consensus on what the object is in general terms. As a first approximation, it can be said that there are three main ways to conceptualise society – aggregational, structurist, and holist – and social historians have collectively adopted all three. However, their adoptions have often been more tacit than explicit, and some have even conflated aspects of these three conceptions.

An *aggregational* conception sees society as a collection of discrete

[1] For recent general discussions of and points of view about the nature of social history and historical sociology, see Abrams :1980, 1982), Braudel (1980), Cahnman (1976), Eley (1979), Henretta (1979), Hobsbawm (1971b, 1981a), Judt (1979), Neale (1981, Introduction), Perkin (1962, 1976), Stearns (1976, 1980), Thomas (1963), Vann (1976).

atomistic individuals in more or less accidental relationship with each other. 'Society' is then a wholly instrumental term which is used to describe this theoretically constructed entity but which does not refer to a real thing that exists independently of the individual people that constitute it. It is a taxonomic collective, in Harré's phrase (1981, p. 140). It is doubtful whether any social historian or sociologist ever actually fully subscribes to this extreme reductionist viewpoint, but sometimes some cliometricians and other so-called 'quantificatory historians' have written as if they found it attractive.[2] In fact, if they were actually to adopt it they would cease to be social historians, because surely the minimum required to be one is a concern to explain the history of society *qua* society and not just individual action. However, we shall see that the aggregational approach has sometimes been constructed in such a way as to save the concept 'society' and employ the term rather than to reject it altogether. With such reductionists there is, then, an obvious gap between the apparent indispensability of the term and the supposed non-existence of the entity.

The concept of 'structure' is widely used in the social sciences to refer to either all of society or some part or level of it.[3] Its uses and meanings differ a great deal, although they are united on the general idea that structure has an existence independent of collections of individuals. It is not reducible simply to persons. Similarly, there are many versions of 'structuralism' – general theories that purport to be about structure. The main ones are those developed by Francophone linguists, anthropologists and philosophers (e.g. Saussure, Lévi-Strauss and Althusser); Francophone historians (e.g. Braudel); American structural-functional sociologists (e.g. Merton, Parsons, and Smelser); the Swiss psychologist and epistemologist Piaget; the American linguist Chomsky; the American network theorists such as James Coleman and Peter Blau; and of course various sorts of Marxists (see bibliography for references).

It is possible to divide all conceptions of non-reducible structure and structuralist theories into two broad types, which I shall call structurism and holism.

A *structurist* conception sees society as an ordered, independent but *loosely integrated,* constantly changing set of relations, rules, and roles that holds a collectivity of individual persons together. It transcends and has an existence independent of any individual but not all (or a significant proportion) of those individuals. It is not simply constituted of individuals but has an organisation, properties, and powers of its own, which are emergent from the collective actions, personalities, and

---

[2] On cliometrics and quantitative history, see, for example, Clubb (1980), Fogel (1975, 1982), Kousser (1980), Meyer and Conrad (1957), Scheuch (1980).

[3] For general discussions and examples of the range of meanings of the concept, see chapters 9 and 10, and Blau (1974, 1976b, 1981), Boudon (1971), Burke (1980), Mayhew (1980–1), Merton (1976), Murdock (1949), Piaget (1971b), Rossi (1982).

motives of many individuals over time. In order to go on existing it must be collectively reproduced by those individuals and it has a strong potential to be transformed into a different structure by their actions.

A *holist* conception goes beyond the structurist to conceive of society as a *very tightly integrated* historical entity with an existence, character, needs, spirit, and even self-activating powers of its own. Now it is possible that, as with the aggregational conception, this construct is seen as wholly theoretical, not meant to be a description of an actual entity. Nevertheless, as with the other two cases, such a conception has powerful effects upon historical explanation, as can be seen, for instance, in the work of the systemic functionalists Parsons and Smelser and the French structuralist Braudel, who characterised and explained their objects as having holistic powers: the system or structure, as an entity, supposedly causes its own history.

Their work can be contrasted with the bulk of social historical writing which, in effect, adopts the structurist conception, sometimes in a tacit and underdeveloped form. Examples include the British empiricist social historians Perkin and Stone; the behaviourist Blau; the Marxists Hobsbawm, Thompson, and Moore; the institutionalists North and Olson; the Weberians Hirschman, Bendix, and Gellner; and the structurationist Touraine (see bibliography). All of these conceive of social history as having to deal with the central problem of the relationship of the structures of society to individual and collective action over time. I believe they are right to do so, but many other problems arise once this basic conception has been adopted.

ACTION/STRUCTURE/CULTURE INTERRELATIONSHIPS

The second basic problem of the discourse is thus to conceptualise in general theoretical terms the relationship of human action to social structure and culture. This can also be seen as the micro/macro problem and the problem of social order. How is it that an entity such as society, which neither is constituted by individuals nor has holistic powers, can develop some emergent properties and powers of its own? How do those properties and powers relate to the properties and powers of persons? Is constant individual and collective consciousness and action necessary to their continuance? Will society disintegrate if people stop acting in the required ways? What is the relationship between culture and action? Are some types of action and culture more important for social creation, social order, and social change?

An aggregationalist/individualist approach to these questions concentrates on the problem of describing and/or explaining action only, perhaps partly by reference to sociological concepts. Most 'ordinary' non-social historians see their task as dealing with specific actions and events, but individualist social historians are apparently concerned with the collective behaviour of individuals. The classic statement of this approach was made by Trevelyan, who saw the task of social history as studying 'the daily life of the inhabitants of the land in past ages' (1942, p. 111), and its ideal sum total would be the biographies of all those who ever lived. More recently, Theodore Zeldin has written that his approach to social history is to try to avoid preconceptions about groups and instead to decompose them into their individual constituents. 'My solution has been to try to keep the individual as the central character. . . . I have looked at the world through his eyes, instead of working the other way and studying a multitude of disconnected forces.' (Zeldin, 1976, p. 244)

But both Trevelyan and Zeldin were in methodological difficulty because they were forced to concede immediately that the social context is also of concern to the social historian. Individualists have usually been afraid that if they concede too much about the existence of society *as an entity* they will become holists, something to be avoided at all costs. Holists have similarly been afraid that any weakening of their conception of the indivisibility of the social entity will lead to the charges of reductionism and/or empiricism, which are anathema. But they too must concede that without people acting they have nothing to study. Even a supposedly holistic society has to be 'borne' by social actors and societies cannot leave evidence of themselves except through the utterances and actions of persons.

Methodological individualism, which is what Trevelyan and Zeldin in effect argue for, is not necessarily incompatible with ontological structurism. That is, the adoption of an individualist methodology does not logically imply reductionism. This has been recently argued from different standpoints by George Homans, a behaviourist (1964a, 1964b, 1967b, 1982), and John Elster, a Marxist (1982b). They have tried to show that a study of individual behaviour is the proper foundation for social theory and social history. In practice, however, they and others who argue for methodological individualism seem to be unable to avoid secreting structurist concepts and methodologies within their work. The point here is that any sociological and historical discourse has to come to terms with the general relationship of individual action to social structure, something that radical individualists and holists fail to do. I shall be arguing that structurism is the only viable ontology *and* methodology.

The role of culture in society and action is fundamental to the problem of social order. Social order grows out of collective action over time and is institutionalised, but the form it takes, how it relates to action, and how it is understood are all dependent on the institutionalised cultural forms that develop with it, legitimise it, and articulate it. Some theorists even come close to arguing that society *is* culture (e.g. Harré, 1975, 1978, 1979; Lévi-Strauss, 1953). Such cultural reductionism can be made the basis for an interpretive anthropological approach to social history, but in the end it is unable to provide a genuinely explanatory account of society and its history. Social explanation depends upon drawing distinctions between action, structure, and culture. If structure is not seen as a relatively independent entity but is collapsed either into the realm of ideas about such things or into patterns of human action then I believe, and will try to show later, that incoherence and vacuousness result.

HISTORICAL/TEMPORAL/STRUCTURAL RELATIONSHIPS

The divide between historical and sociological perspectives on society is often seen in terms of change and uniqueness versus continuity and generality. The historian supposedly studies only the rich, individualistic complexity of particular past lives, events, and processes, while the social scientist supposedly compares and contrasts the general structures and cultures of present society, seeing individual actions and events as instances of general categories and as data to be used for testing theories.[4]

We do seem to need to make distinctions between structures, processes, actions, and events, but how they relate to each other is a matter of much contention. Structures, in order to be such, do have relatively fixewd, temporal continuity and are the 'containers', or the constraints, of processes, actions, and events. But processes, actions, and events also exist through time. Indeed, actions and events can be seen as theoretically postulated slices of processes. Alternatively, processes can be seen as theoretical colligations of discrete actions and events. Some sociologists and historians believe that structure is also a theoretically postulated pattern of actions and events and not something separate from them.

In any case, all life and organisation, and perhaps all nature, is in constant process. The processes may take different forms at different times, proceed at different speeds, change to new processes, and so on. Processes always have form, which is given to them by their structures. The natural and social worlds are fundamentally structurally ordered, and ordered process is inherent within all structures. (Perhaps some structures also have chaotic and random processes.) So, distinctions between actions, events, and processes should always be theoretical. Nevertheless they are heuristically very useful and, moreover, seemingly necessary to our thought and communication. We have to divide up the

---

[4] This distinction is a very old one and was given a canonical formulation by the late-nineteenth-century neo-Kantian philosophers in Germany, notably Windelband (1980). For recent discussions and defences of the history/social science distinction, see Antoni (1959), Berlin (1960), Mink (1965, 1973), Perkin (1962), Thompson (1963, Postscript), Trevor-Roper (1980).

world in certain relatively arbitrary but useful ways in order to comprehend any part of it, but the ubiquity of ordered structures and processes should not be forgotten. However, drawing a line between past and present seems to be entirely arbitrary and pointless. The 'present' is always becoming the 'past' and processes continually exist in both dimensions.

All this means that the historical/structural and present/past distinctions are meaningless. All entities and processes are structured and historical in the senses of both change and relative uniqueness. The only useful divisions should be of processes into time slices and phases and of structures into levels and aspects.

Nevertheless, it is a major empirical problem to explain the causes of particular social structural processes. Understanding that all society is in process does not help much in explaining particular examples of change and transformation. Not all change is transformation, and it is the latter that is of prime interest because it is relatively 'unnatural'.

EXPLANATORY METHODOLOGY

Should social historians see their task as causal explanation or should they try to interpretively understand their object? Whatever decision is made, further problems arise. If they believe they should and can causally explain social events and processes, should they attempt to do so in a social scientific manner? If so, what would that entail, and if not, what other explanatory processes are appropriate?

Those who have seen themselves as being historians rather than sociologists have, on the whole, rejected the notion of science; even some Marxists have done so, in spite of Marx's claim to be a social scientist. But there are some notable exceptions to this, especially among empiricist quantificatory historians who have seen the route to scientific knowledge as lying through the precision of careful counting of discrete events and actions and inductive generalisations. They then make claims about social change in terms of changes in statistical aggregates (see references in footnote 2 of this chapter).

The debate over the scientificity of the socio-historical studies has been bedevilled by inadequate understandings of scientific methodology. Several examples of this – by Fogel, Berlin, Homans, Trevor-Roper, and Shapiro[5] – show how an inadequate conception of science leads to a misunderstanding of what a scientific social history could be like. All of them, whether arguing for or against the possibility of scientific history, have explicitly or implicitly, and certainly uncritically, borrowed the once-standard empiricist account given by philosophers such as Braithwaite

---

[5] Berlin (1960), Fogel (1975, 1982), Homans (1967b), Shapiro (1976), Trevor-Roper (1980).

(1953), Hempel (1942, 1962b, 1963), and Nagel (1961). The question for these historians is then simply one of whether history can be like science as described by these empiricists.

The philosophers, social historians, and sociologists who reject the possibility of a scientific explanation of change in a social totality in effect argue one or both of the following:

1 The social totality does not exist or change in such a way as to make it amenable to a systematic objective enquiry into its genesis, composition, operation, and effects (i.e. a structural-causal enquiry).

2 Although the social totality may exist in a form as to make it amenable to a structural-causal enquiry, such an enquiry cannot be scientific.

Those in the holistic-hermeneutical tradition of thought (to be discussed in chapter 6), including Berlin (1960) and Trevor-Roper (1980), claim that the task of historians is to interpretively understand the *meanings* of actions, events, processes, and social wholes. For them society is a whole which can only be comprehended through empathetic understanding. To attempt to analytically deconstruct a social whole is to destroy its essential character. Although social wholes have components they cannot be reduced to those components. These writers thus usually subscribe to the first option given above.

However, many historians, whether they deal with acts, events, structures, or social totalities, believe that their task is to seek for the *causation* of their designated phenomena. But they usually reject the possibility of doing so scientifically because they believe science is a method which is appropriate only to the study of universal, unchanging regularities, as revealed by constant conjunctions of events, and only in nature do such relationships occur. Thus science supposedly cannot account for personal dispositions, unique intentions, social norms, social rules, meanings, or patterns of behaviour. They therefore subscribe to the second option.

But I shall be arguing (especially in chapters 7 and 8) not only that empiricism is a poor account of science but also that social explanation can be scientific because science is the mode of enquiry that concentrates on the uncovering of causal mechanisms. Science is not restricted to employing either reductionist physicalist explanations or statistical probability explanations or to accounting for every act and events by a universal determinist model.

THEORY/OBSERVATION RELATIONSHIP

This leads directly to the fifth problem, one already touched upon. Whatever view one takes of the possibility of a science of social history, there still has to be faced the question of the relationship of theories of various sorts to observational evidence. If 'theory' is taken to mean not just causal hypotheses but also definitions of terms, sets of models, categories, and concepts about kinds of entities and processes, then theory is indispensable to social enquiry of any sort. But how these theoretical constructs should be arrived at and what role they play in enquiry is hotly disputed. Traditionally historians, especially in Anglophone countries, have been dismissive of theory, preferring the evidence to somehow speak for itself (cf. Elton, 1967, pp. 52–6). This of course avoids the question of how evidence can have meaning and significance independent of particular questions, problems, concepts, and theories. It cannot, but common-sense empiricism, even if not actually practised, does influence the types of accounts and explanations historians give. Usually in such cases a kind of unexamined, often incoherent and certainly inadequate behaviourist psychological explanation is given of actions and social processes. People supposedly act out of simply defined self-interest which in turn may be taken to be the result of conditioning or perhaps of innate human nature.

DISCIPLINARY DELINEATION

The final methodological problem that the discourse faces is of how to delineate itself from other related branches of the socio-historical studies. There are two dimensions to this problem, to do with the subject matter and with methodology. I have touched upon the first in relation to the structural/historical problem. Many historians, whether social or not, prefer to believe that their discourse is *sui generis*, dealing with a realm of subject matter and having methods quite distinct from any other discourse. Many philosophers of history, notably R. G. Collingwood, W. H. Walsh, W. B. Gallie, W. Dray, M. Oakeshott, Isaiah Berlin, and Michael Scriven (see bibliography) have supported this intuition and developed detailed defences of historical understanding. Their methodological position has been based upon the idea that the explanation of past events and actions requires a form of interpretive understanding of their meaning and motivation as 'unique' occurrences.

This idea that history is a *sui generis* discourse unrelated to other social and psychological studies I shall call *historicialism*, a somewhat barbarous term but one, I hope, that serves to distinguish the concept from 'historicism'. The latter term already has two meanings: one is to do with the idea that all the world is in constant historical process and must be understood accordingly; the other is Popper's idiosyncratic definition in which the process is taken to be a deterministic one. Historicalists are usually opposed to historicism.

A concomitant of historicalism is antiquarianism – the study of the past because of its intrinsic interest, rarity, and importance as a humanistic cultural enquiry rather than for any knowledge it may teach us about the present or about human action and society in general.

In brief, historicalists draw a sharp line between history and social science and between present and past. Social historians have a peculiar problem in this regard because they study *processes* which exist through time and which can often straddle past and present. If they claim to be historicalists they have to eschew sociological reasoning, which they sometimes do, preferring to see a historical perspective on social change as somehow providing insights and knowledge which social science cannot, even if the processes they study continue into the present. They sometimes also, with even greater difficulty, claim to be antiquarian in their historical interest, having no interest in explaining the structures and processes of present society. In this case they would have to restrict their attention to societies and processes which no longer exist.

Of course many historians, social and non-social, are neither historicalists nor antiquarians. Radicals and Marxists of various sorts have always believed that a study of the past not only illuminates the present but is essential to its understanding (cf. Hobsbawm, 1981b). The related historicist movement of the nineteenth century, born in Germany and receiving its strongest manifestation in historical economics both there and in Britain and America, was based upon the idea of the essentially evolutionary nature of all society. Social evolutionism, in fact, always held that past and present were bound together by universal stages and laws and only a positivist science could explain the process. There is currently a great deal of discussion about how social history and sociology could be united.[6] I believe they should be. As Philip Abrams cogently expressed it:

> Sociological explanation is necessarily historical. Historical sociology is thus not some special kind of sociology; rather, it is the essence of the discipline. All varieties of sociology stress the so-called 'two-sidedness' of the social world, presenting it as a world of which we are both the creators and the creatures, both makers and prisoners; a world which our actions construct and a world that powerfully constrains us. The distinctive quality of the social world for the sociologist is, accordingly, its *facticity* – the way in which society is experienced by individuals as a fact-like system, external, given, coercive, even while individuals are busy making

[6] On the history/sociology relationship see, for example, Abrams (1980, 1982), Bonnell (1980), Braudel (1980), Burke (1980), Cahnman (1976), Cahnman and Boskoff (1964), Chirot (1976), Hobsbawm (1981a), Hughes (1960), Jones (1976), Knapp (1984), Laslett (1968; 1971, Introduction), Lipset (1968), Skocpol and Somers (1980), Smith (1982), Stinchcombe (1978), Stone (1976), C. Tilly (1970, 1980a, 1980b).

and re-making it through their own imagination, communication and action. Thus the central issue for sociological analysis can be said, by Berger and Luckmann (1966), to be the resolution of the 'awesome paradox' discovered in turn by each of the founding fathers in concluding that there is only one way in which that paradox can be resolved: namely, historically. The two-sidedness of society, the fact that social action is both something we choose to do and something we have to do, is inseparably bound up with the further fact that whatever reality society has is an historical reality, a reality in time. (Abrams, 1982, p. 2)

I shall be attempting to develop (especially in chapters 8 and 14) a methodological basis for constructing a unified socio-historical discourse.

Having outlined these problems, my task now is to present an argument in the next chapter as to why the place to begin to solve them is through analytical philosophical reasoning.

2

The Importance of Critical Philosophy

EXPLANATORY CHANGE: THE TASKS OF
CLARIFICATION AND CRITICISM

To someone who is not a philosopher or historian of explanation it may seem rather strange that there is a large and rapidly growing debate among philosophers about the nature of scientific explanation and what it should be. Science as an institution tends to project an image, which many scientists themselves believe, of obvious success; a success apparently flowing from the relatively simple application of so-called 'scientific method'. This method is often assumed to be unproblematical and universally shared by scientists. Science is often taken to be a linear process of accumulating true factual knowledge about nature by the use of correct methods and empirical observations. Against this the humanities, especially history, are looked upon as in a state of flux, without fixed methods or objective results. Their explanations are constantly revised and there is a lack of agreement about goals. Everyone's opinion carries equal, if little, weight.

But of course even a moment's close inspection of the natural sciences and their history reveals widespread disagreement there too. It soon becomes obvious that the great fact about the empirical discourses – physics as much as history – is that *methods, theories, explanations, and even laws change and conflict*. The history of all discourses is marked by methodological disputes, competition, and explanatory change.[1] This fact gives both the history and philosophy of explanation their first *raison d'être* since it permits the asking of two basic questions: why and how do methodologies and explanations change; and are there better and

[1] On the problem of explanatory change, see Toulmin (1972, ch. 1).

worse explanations? In other words, do methodologies and explanations change for rational or irrational reasons; can we discover these reasons and their antecedants; and is there *progress* in explanation? The external, socio-historical problem is closely related to the internal philosophical/ normative one about if and how we should judge between explanations.

In this light, it is my view that the basic tasks of philosophy of explanation[2] are twofold. The first is *explication and clarification* – trying to extract and describe what are and have been the structures of methodology, concepts, and explanation of particular discourses. That is, what are the logical, ontological, epistemological, and conceptual tenets which form a framework for theory construction, theory appraisal, empirical enquiry, and explanation? These frameworks and tenets may not be well articulated or closely adhered to; consequently the answering of this question is not a matter of simply describing a surface pattern of concepts, practices, and rules. Rather, the framework has to be abstracted and reconstructed by the enquirer using some pre-existing methodology designed for the task, as in all research. Furthermore, the *conceptions* of methodology held by practitioners of a discourse may differ from the actual rules and practices *followed* in research and from the structures of explanatory arguments employed in *presenting* the results of research.

These discrepancies and the second-order empirical-methodological problems that philosophy encounters are the main reasons why it is essential for philosophy to have a second, *critical,* task. It must not only uncover philosophies, methodologies, and explanatory structures but point out their *contradictions,* and their *effects* upon research. Moreover, it must adopt a critical attitude towards its own methodologies and practices. Philosophy of explanation, as an explicatory discourse dealing with the question of explanatory structure and change in other discourse, reflects the general situation of change, competition, and contention. Philosophy must be critically reflexive about its own assumptions, procedures, and arguments in a way that no other discourse is. This thus gives philosophy the meta-task of also studying *philosophical* attitudes, debates, and change.

Most importantly, philosophy should attempt to answer a critical-normative question about what *should be* the preferred structure of explanation of a discourse, perhaps by reference to some set of assumptions, concepts, standards, principles, or guidelines (whether universal or convention) which can be used to demarcate between appropriate and inappropriate methodologies and good, bad, and spurious explanations. Without definitions, explicit assumptions, principles, and standards it

---

[2] For general critical discussions of the nature of philosophy of explanation, see Berlin (1962), Gellner (1964, ch. 8), Kekes (1980), Sellars (1962), J. J. C. Smart (1963, ch. 1), Toulmin (1972, general introduction).

may be impossible to discuss coherently what is an explanation or methodology, let alone questions about types of theoretical coherence, rationality, and acceptability; and certainly not problems of theory *choice* and *progress*.

Without a critical function, philosophy becomes at best merely auxiliary to the history and sociology of beliefs. While self-perceptions are an important source of evidence about methodologies, practitioners can be deluded, muddled, and influenced by inappropriate and perhaps dangerous methodological attitudes. The influence of vulgar empiricism (or scientism), for example, upon the social studies has had very deleterious effects, blinding many researchers to the existence of a whole range of causal mechanisms and relational structures. Philosophical criticism is essential to overcoming such influences. The historical study of explanation is partly relevant to such a task since it provides a basis for the testing of hypotheses about methodological and explanatory progress and effectiveness.

But philosophy conceived as criticism is not directly concerned with the social, psychological, and rational *origins* of beliefs, theories, and actions, important as these questions are.[3] It is concerned, rather, with the *structure, content, coherence, influence,* and *effectiveness* of methodologies and explanations. Of course, it is true that the influence that methodologies have is also partly a matter of social context and psychological predisposition, especially in the short term; but more important in the long term is the power of theories and laws to affect our control and manipulations of the world. And that depends upon our ability to understand the real nature of the world. The ultimate criticism that can be made of a theory is in relation to its effectiveness in solving empirical problems about and in the world.

The relevance of philosophy to criticising methodologies and explanations is hotly disputed, especially by many practitioners in empirical discourses. This provides a further *raison d'être* for philosophy in uncovering and articulating those sometimes tacit attitudes – i.e. a meta-meta-task. This is in fact the proper place to begin in defending the importance of critical philosophy.

ATTITUDES TO THE RELEVANCE OF PHILOSOPHY

Using the set of categories developed by Imre Lakatos in a posthumously published article (Lakatos, 1978), it can be said that there are three main schools of thought on the *possibility* of judging different forms of explanation, of separating good from bad theories, and hence of estab-

---

[3] On the relationship of the history and philosophy of science, see Giere (1974), Kuhn (1977b, 1980), Lakatos (1971a), Laudan (1977b), Shapere (1977).

lishing the criteria for progress. They are: scepticism, demarcationism, and elitism.[4]

Scepticism denies superiority to any particular form of explanation, whether it be modern science, or earlier forms of science, or history, or religion, or witchcraft, or whatever, seeing each (as Paul Feyerabend does) as equally legitimate (or dogmatic) ways of comprehending the world. There should be no *a priori* standard for appraising theories and explanations or for reconstructing the history of explanations since all philosophers and historians have their own biases and value systems. The watchphrase for some radical sceptics is: do your own thing! The only studies of explanatory discourses which are apparently licensed are of a historical, sociological, or anthropological kind (see Barnes, 1974, 1981; Bloor, 1976, 1981; Feyerabend, 1975a). However, even those sceptics who engage in such studies do see a role for a descriptive, articulating meta-discourse which attempts to uncover the structures of explanation of different belief systems. It follows that they also see a role for various categories such as 'logic', 'rationality', 'concept', 'explanation', 'coherence', and so on, in order to examine the socio-historical origins of belief systems. Indeed, any socio-historical enquiry into beliefs must first undertake what is in fact the philosophical task of enquiring into the *structure, content,* and *coherence* of beliefs. And furthermore, the proponents of scepticism usually feel the need to engage in *critical philosophical* arguments against their demarcationist and elitist opponents! So, while sceptics can eschew criticism of a first-order kind, they cannot avoid a second-order form of critical philosophy. Furthermore, even sceptics would accept that even though they may believe no world view to be superior to another, there is at least a need to *choose* courses of action and sets of beliefs within particular world views, especially within the intellectual-empirical discourses, and such choices should surely be based upon good reasons rather than mere whim or coercion. Scepticism, if pursued to its logical conclusion, reduces to nihilism, vacating the plane of argument and leaving it open perhaps to unargued, amoral, force.

Demarcationists do attempt to develop standards to separate better from worse knowledge and to define progress. They differ markedly, however, over the units of appraisal, and the criteria of appraisal used to draw the line of demarcation between good and bad. The units of appraisal range from specific empirical causal theories, to research programmes and paradigms, to research traditions, and ultimately to world views. In order to try to develop criteria for demarcation they must make a separation between the cognitive value of a framework or theory and its psychological influence on people's minds. The explanatory value of a framework or theory is partly independent of beliefs, understand-

---

[4] For a similar, but more discursive, and very stimulating discussion of this whole problem, see Gellner (1974, passim).

ings, and commitments. Demarcationists lay down 'statute laws' (in Lakatos's terminology), which can be used to judge particular cases, but there are many different bases for statutes – such as the autonomy of observational and empirical tests; or conventions about meaning, content, and basic statements; or problem-solving ability; and so on. The criteria adopted also determine the nature of the reconstructions of the history of science made by demarcationists, since such reconstructions are written from a normative point of view rooted in those criteria.

Elitists also wish to separate science from pseudo-science and non-science. But they do not adopt universal standards. Rather, in their view, science can only be judged by 'case law' and the only judges are scientists themselves. They reject the normative or critical roles of philosophy altogether. Academic autonomy is sacrosanct and scientists are the only authorities. This has to be, so the elitist argument goes, because much of science is inarticulable, or tacit. Philosophers or laymen thus cannot judge science without first becoming scientists and so able to share in science's self-understandings and ways of knowing. The history of attempts to construct universal public statutes serves to reinforce them in their belief that there cannot be such, since each standard seems to be short lived and dogmatic.

Lakatos restricted his thoughts to natural science, where elitism is the dominant attitude held by practitioners. It is also prelevant in the humanities, where there is widespread suspicion of attempts to construct methodological statutes and, furthermore, a current of subjectivism, which says that each person forms an elite of one in forming and judging explanations. There is also a corresponding tendency to adhere to theories for pre-rational, intuitive 'reasons'.

Moreover, as Lakatos pointed out, elitism is closely related to several 'abhorrent' doctrines. The first is what he called *psychologism* and/or *sociologism,* which holds that theories are preferable only if the elite prefers them, so it is then important to know who is a member of the elite and why. While demarcationists employ critical philosophy to judge standards of explanation, elitists simply claim that only members of the elite can give good explanations. Thus elitists psychologically and sociologically appraise the producer, not the product. If a theory is produced by a member of the scientific elite it must be scientific. But Lakatos rightly pointed out that they in fact must use some *independent* criteria for demarcating the superiority of scientific elites or groups from non-scientific ones, such as religious communities. (For a critique of sociologism, see Harré, 1983b, postscript.)

The second is *authoritarianism*: elitists are authoritarian within their own group, arguing that science necessarily takes place within a totalitarian sub-society. Thomas Kuhn and others claimed that this is, in fact, and should be, the case. To admit the possibility of conflict raises the spectre for them of scepticism and perhaps of methodological anarchism. But, as Lakatos said, since the elitist believes in rationality and the superiority of his science but not in universal appraisal, he must invoke either the authority of internal consensus or, in the case of conflict, that of Great Scientific Archbishops or the Cunning of Reason to restore order.

The third of his abhorrent doctrines is *pragmatism,* which he said denies the existence of an objective world of ideas and sees knowledge and truth as a state of mind or relative to a pattern of behaviour. Theories differ only in their practical uses and so are better or worse according to practical criteria relative to persons or communities. Theories are better if they work better, or have more 'cash value'. But for Lakatos this pragmatism was akin to the appeal to force, as Bertrand Russell had argued. Truth for (some) pragmatists is based not upon propositions or reason but upon beliefs, or activities, or popularity. Many elitists, he believed, easily slip into pragmatism, and this would certainly seem to be so in the human studies. (On pragmatism see also Gellner, 1979b.)

This article of Lakatos's is valuable in underlining the importance of critical philosophy to explanation in the humanities. The potential evils of elitism are perhaps even greater there than in the natural sciences (although the imperviousness of many scientists to calls for reasoned social accountability is obvious). Elitism can be overcome only through (1) a strong defence of the necessity of *independent* rational and critical standards of explanation, and (2) the grounding of those standards partly in the need for human democratic and socialised freedom as well as in more abstract principles of logic and ontology.

Demarcationism does not have to result, as some may suppose, in a different form of dogmatic authoritarianism. Methodological standards have to be argued for in a rational and critical manner and supported by appeals to logic, history, and social order. Rational demarcationists are not necessarily absolutists. They must be circular in their reasoning, i.e. they must be at all times reflexive – responding to critical arguments and tolerating alternatives. But the goals of knowledge and progress must not be lost sight of. The barren hopelessness of scepticism and relativism and the dangers of elitism demand reflexive, critical, arguments if we are to have good reasons not only for living our lives but for enriching them, partly through coming to know and thus control the power that nature and oppressive social situations and individuals can have over us and partly through sharing understandings of the richness, complexity, and beauty of the universe.

CONCEPTIONS OF PHILOSOPHY

Philosophy, then, in my view has the important tasks of *description* and *prescription.* But this critical epistemological view is not shared by all philosophers, let alone by all empirical researchers. It is only one of three main ways in which it is possible to conceive of what philosophy should be.

Firstly, summarising and building upon what I have argued so far, we can think of philosophy as an *analytical meta-discourse*. Philosophy transcends other discourses, its tasks being to discuss general principles or standards of rationality, logic, meaning, ontology, knowledge, and truth. (Good examples are the works of Hume, Kant, Popper, Nagel, and Sellars.) There are three subsidiary sets of dimensions to be considered within this conception:

1 A *descriptive/prescriptive dimension* Philosophy can be seen either as just the description of the conceptual, logical, semantical, etc. foundations of particular discourses such as physics, sociology, history, art, religion, and of everyday understanding and speech; or as also embodying a *critical* concern to go beyond description to prescribing what these foundations should be.

2 An *internal/external dimension* Philosophical and methodological concepts exist within and as a necessary part of each particular discourse. They are the explanatory principles actually used by that discourse and are perhaps unarticulated by practitioners, in which case the task of philosophers is to articulate them. In addition, philosophy is also external to each and all discourses, providing overarching *a priori* principles which can be used to evaluate these internal concepts. The idea that each discourse adopts its own peculiar philosophical principles, which usually goes with the internal notion, unfortunately neglects the external dimension.

3 A *methodological/ontological dimension* The problems of either method or existence are seen as primary and the more fundamental task of philosophical reasoning. That is, do solutions to problems of existence in general determine solutions to problems of method, or vice versa, when theories and explanations are developed? The answer given to this will determine approaches to problems of the nature and structure of theories, and questions about realism and objectivity versus instrumentalism and relativism, evaluation of research techniques, and justification of solutions.

Secondly, we can think of philosophy as a *metaphysical world view*, being an all-encompassing outlook upon the world, providing the basis for answers to problems of meaning, existence, understanding, morality, and life conduct. It is an *a priori* holistic view of the task of philosophy. This is also a meta conception, but one which goes much further than the analytical conception, which restricts itself to a critical and analytical role. (Examples of holistic philosophers are Hegel and Whitehead.)

The third conception is a rather radical view of philosophy, seeing its proper task in neither of the traditional meta ways but rather as *dialectic* or *conversation*. It opposes the view of philosophy as meta-discourse with a behavioural notion – a notion of *practice* rather than form, of critique rather than construction. Philosophy in this conception is something that is *done*, with an argumentative and/or poetic attitude. (Probably the best example is the later Wittgenstein. For a defence of philosophy as edification, see Rorty, 1980.)

All three of these descriptions apply to sections of existing philosophical discourse in that there is little agreement about what the tasks of philosophising should be. As I have indicated, in this book I wish to adopt and employ the first (analytical) view, but I believe it is possible to retain at the same time an idea of philosophy as world view, providing we are clear about what this entails. Indeed, many of the philosophers I shall discuss share a world view ideal, often with attendant notions of relativism. But world view conceptions and relativism do not necessarily imply each other and so a weak or partial world view notion can be retained in conjunction with a *rationalist* and *progressive* outlook upon empirical explanation.

Within the first conception I see the task of philosophy as both descriptive and critically prescriptive of explanatory foundations, as external to particular discourses, and, furthermore, as providing *general ontological hypotheses*. Indeed, ontology is crucial to my criticism of social historical explanation since a quasi-metaphysical realist hypothesis about the nature of social structural reality is the 'starting place' for my criticism of existing practices and explanations.

Of course this starting point has not been arrived at arbitrarily but is the result of many years of thought and enquiry by philosophers of the social sciences. Nevertheless the ontological starting point is still a general *hypothesis*; it must be vindicated or rejected and the theories developed from it must be corroborated or abandoned. It is not enough to retain this ontology solely on the grounds of its fruitfulness in generating theories and solutions to problems, although that is important to begin with. In the end it must be judged for its verisimilitude to reality as revealed through a progressive research programme undertaken within its ambit. The hypothesis thus plays the role of providing a partial world view in which research and criticism are given a foundation. It is not a metaphysical foundation in the bad (purely speculative) sense but the foundation of a research tradition, setting one of the parameters and operating as a regulative (and revisable) principle of research.

Philosophy is thus closely related to science, being continuous with it. Philosophy cannot solve empirical problems but it does overlap with theory. Empirical enquiry, in turn, can help solve ontological problems.

This is, of course, a controversial view and one which, in a general sense, this whole volume seeks to defend. And the defence gains powerful support from (among others) the work of Quine (1960, 1969, 1980),

Mandelbaum (1964), Sellars (1962, 1968 ch. 1), Lakatos (1970), and Piaget (1972b). As Sellars has rightly said,

> There are, of course, many who would say that it is the business of science to introduce hypothetical entities, and *therefore* not the business of philosophers to do so. The pragmatically useful division of intellectual labour, reflected in the proliferation of academic departments and disciplines, has been responsible for many necessary evils, but none more pernicious than this idea. Philosophy may perhaps be the chaste muse of clarity, but it is also the mother of hypotheses. Clarity is not to be confused with insight. It is the latter which is the true final cause of philosophy, and the insight which philosophy seeks and which always eludes its grasp is total insight. If the maxim *hypotheses non fingo* had captured classical and medieval philosophy there would have been abundance of clarity but no science, and, in particular, no theoretical science as we know it today.
>
> Unless a purely instrumentalist account of the language game of hypothetical entities is to be taken for granted, philosophers must concern themselves with the ways in which these entities are related to the more familiar objects of everyday life. (Sellars, 1968, pp. 11–12)

In short, philosophy is not interested only in categorising, describing, and analysing the methodologies and explanatory procedures of empirical discourses and philosophy. It has inherently the tasks of *evaluating* the ontological and epistemological foundations which exist within those discourses, using first a process of abstract reason and logic, and of suggesting *clarifications* and *alterations* to those foundations. The idea that the 'philosopher kings' have little to say to practical research workers must be resisted. Those most mature of sciences – particle physics and astrophysics – constantly employ *philosophical* notions about the nature of the universe in general and the appropriate logic of enquiry and justification, and many of their most striking advances have come from thinking in such ways. The work of Einstein on relativity is a classic case of a great advance arising from *explicitly* philosophically recasting the *ontological* basis of cosmology. Developing new ways of conceptualising and classifying entities is often a means to new advances in comprehending the complexity of the structures of nature and society. Moreover, as Popper has written,

> We all have our philosophies, whether or not we are aware of this fact, and our philosophies are not worth very much. But the impact of our philosophies upon our actions and our lives is often devastating. This makes it necessary to try to improve our philosophies by criticism. This is the only apology for the continued existence of philosophy which I am able to offer. (Popper, 1972c, p. 33)

Philosophies must be seen as existing partly independently of us as individuals, influencing our ideas and actions. The more consciously and rationally they are held the better we are able both to control them and to ameliorate their effects.

THE IMPORTANCE OF REALISM

In order to defend a modified naturalist approach to social history on the basis of realist ontology and epistemology, it is essential first to uphold a realist conception of natural science as being the best account of what it is about the world that makes natural science successful and progressive in the discovery and application of results in natural situations. Realism also shows how the potential unity of all forms of explanation could be based upon a similarity in the form of their structures of reasoning and their explanatory methodologies. This argument will be presented in detail in chapters 7 and 8. Here I shall outline it in simplified form in order to give some some direction to chapters 1–6.

Realists argue that although particular phenomena can be described and understood in various ways – mathematical, artistic, religious, scientific – it is the task of science alone to reveal the *general,* and perhaps hidden, *structural* features of phenomena, and the underlying *mechanisms* of their becoming. Science is not on the whole concerned with supposedly unique features of phenomena, whether they be particular particles, atoms, molecules, cells, organisms, animals, persons, or social or natural systems. Science is primarily concerned, rather, with universals, i.e. with the general defining characteristics, modes of being and causes of types, classes, and patterns of phenomena. Without a notion of real types of entities, which have discoverable, relatively fixed dispositions, powers, and potentialities, there can be no scientific enquiry, since such enquiry consists fundamentally of uncovering such properties and in showing how actual phenomena relate to those properties.

Science must operate with a concept of *multi-layered* depth – i.e. the observable behaviour of entities has to be explained by uncovering the innate shared nature of those entities, as well as by uncovering the relationships in which entities exist and have their being. Therefore, without a theory of the real and relatively enduring nature of *social* entities and mechanisms, it is impossible to see how there could be a 'naturalistic' science of society, which was not reducible either to a science of behaviour or to a purely hermeneutical study of intentions, reasons, actions, and (perhaps) social wholes.

Against relativists and instrumentalists realists argue that it is at least theoretically possible to progress towards objectively truthful knowledge of the hidden structures and causation of enduring real and irreducibly social entities. They agree with the positivists that explanation in history and social science must be of the same general logical structure as natural science but disagree about the specification of what it is that scientific methods have to explain; and they disagree also with some positivists about what precisely the logical structure should be. The realists agree with structurists that it is structure and not just the phenomena of the social world that must be studied. But there are internal disagreements about the relationship of structure to action: some locating the source of structural change in the structuring consequences of action and others in the structure itself. Realists do not, furthermore, deny the importance of quantification, but hold, rather, that it is only an important tool of research, not a defining method or ontological doctrine. In the end the basic question concerns the *possibility* of rational, shared, truthful, causal explanation, and that in turn depends upon our ability to attempt to discover the reality of the social world. What should be the logic of *discovery* is the crucial issue, and the importance of distinguishing scientific from non-scientific approaches is not to privilege the former but to defend it as the only discourse that aims at discovering the real but hidden structural processes of society.

However, realism gives rise to a major problem of *epistemic access* which is not faced by empiricists or hermeneuticists. These latter both remain on the level of phenomena, whether the phenomena are seen as objective actions and events or as meaningful and value-laden actions, utterances, and products. But if reality is layered and some layers are not available to sense perception, and so must be modelled before being known, then the question of how we move from our base in the sensory world to uncover these hidden layers must be of central concern to scientists of all kinds. In the case of the social sciences the problem is compounded by the nature of some of the phenomena with which it must deal – i.e. meaningful intentions and actions. But it also deals with relatively objective entities – structures of various sorts. Society, as I shall argue, does have a real and relatively enduring structural existence and can be the object of a scientific enquiry, but one that must take account of intentions, reasons, and meanings, although not restricting itself to them. Indeed, they must be *criticised* by science. Realism does not deny the importance of the investigation of reasons and intentionality, or of emotional and 'irrational' motivations for behaviour. They too must be investigated in a scientific (psychological and social) manner, using general theories, hypotheses, and empirical investigation. The adoption of a scientific methodology does not entail subscribing to a theory of action as physically determined.

Furthermore, it is not the case that scientific history or sociology must dispense with creative imagination in favour of some supposedly wholly inductive or deductive method. Imaginative conjectures, metaphors, analogies, and intuitive leaps seem to be necessary in all sciences, especially for the framing of new hypotheses and models. In history, where only retrospective explanation and not accurate prediction is possible, and where the general theories available are not yet very powerful, imaginative and metaphorical thinking are indispensable. But they are by no means the only or basic method – being rather an essential part of scientific method itself. In the final analysis, the scientificity of a discourse should not primarily be judged by its ability to explain or predict every act or event, but by general results and methods and those methods have to be tied squarely, via general theory, to a clear onto-logical conception of the (relative) space-time invariance of mechanisms.

Persons and societies are highly complex but determinate entities requiring for the explanation of their actions, compositions, and trans-formations an order of enquiry which must go beyond pre-theoretical knowledge. The use of explicit general theory is as indispensable to historical explanation as it is to natural science. While all observation, interpretation, and understanding of the world takes place through cognitive frameworks containing concepts, categories, analogies, rules, paradigm cases, and so on, they are often unconsciously or semi-consciously adopted – even by practising historians – and are often internally muddled, not to say seriously defective. They need to be brought out into the open, available for public inspection and criticism, if knowledge is to be shared, more firmly based, and advanced. This is not to say that ordinary persons do not have a good deal of insight, intuitive understanding, and cultural knowledge about their own immediate situation. But they can also be seriously deluded. It is only through critical, reflexive, and theoretically directed research that the opaque structures of everyday social life, which spread out to encompass ultimately the whole world, can be made known. I believe those structures to be real, enduring, and causative. But this is a controversial view and needs to be presented with care if it is to be upheld against those who would reduce social science to psychology or some form of social atomism. Thus the chief targets of a defence of the scientificity of social history are the doctrines of sociological empiricism and sociological hermeneutics. A structurist methodology is required to explain social structure, social action, and social change in a scientific manner.

METHODOLOGICAL STRUCTURISM

Realism is only one of four modes of explanation employed in the social and historical studies, the others being empiricist, intentionalist, and functionalist. These in turn have employed, in no necessary relationships, individualist, holist, and structurist methodologies when approaching their objects of enquiry. All these will be discussed in detail in chapter 8 but here I want to continue my proposal for a scientific social history by outlining and supporting structurism. I believe this to be the methodology that does the most justice to the realist scientific emphasis upon causal mechanisms.

Methodological individualism argues that social entities and processes have to be explained by reference to individual motivations and actions. Methodological holism argues that society should be explained somehow by reference to the social whole. I believe that the former doctrine overemphasises human autonomy while the latter wrongly imputes agency powers to social entities – i.e. it reifies them.

Methodological structurism tries to tie the micro and macro levels of social analysis together by giving an account of how human personality, intentions, and action interact with culture and structure to causally determine each other and social transformations. In order to do this it is essential that there be a model of man as a social agent. Agential persons have innate causal powers to intentionally and unintentionally affect their own actions and bring about changes in the world. Action is thus socially structuring. But structure pre-exists individual actions. However, the generality of action through time is necessary for the creation and continued reproduction of structure. Time is essential to the structurist methodology. Both methodological individualism and holism tend to ignore it.

Action always takes place within structures of relations, rules, roles, and classes. But structures are not agents in the way that some functionalists and holists seem to believe. They do have powers of a *conditioning* kind, which set parameters for the exercising of human agential action, but they cannot cause themselves to change. This means that humans are not pure agents because their power is limited and constrained both internally and externally and it also means that individual and collective human action is the fundamental agent of history. Thus methodological structurism is not reductionist, holding that explanations of mechanisms have to be given on both the micro and macro levels.

PART II

Explanation in Science and the Humanities

Introduction to Part II

The philosophy of explanation has been dominated ever since the seventeenth century, and especially since the Enlightenment of the eighteenth century, by the paradigm case of natural science, especially physics and astronomy. Before that time epistemology drew its main inspiration from other discourses and ways of knowing, including literature, art, and religion. The dominance of the philosophy of natural science reached its peak in the 1940s and 1950s. That period was marked by many attempts to systematically abstract, formalise, and reconstruct the logic of scientific inference and to generalise the results to all explanatory empirical enquiry, especially to psychology, sociology, economics, and history. This logical, empiricist, and positivist phase has proved to be only the first in a three-phase movement in post-war philosophy of explanation.

The second phase, although having some roots at least as long as positivism, began in the 1950s and flowered in the 1960s. It was characterised by a widespread attack upon the positivist tradition, by some who sought only to modify certain aspects, and by more radical critics who supported versions of holism, conventionalism, and relativism. The radicals sought to reject altogether the autonomy of facts and the abstract and formaliisng programme of the earlier tradition and to replace it with a historical, sociological, and relativist account of explanation. In the 1970s a third phase began in which a critique of both earlier approaches has been made by realists who oppose the descriptive, the normative, and the historical attitudes to explanation of both positivists and relativists.[1] But the philosophy of natural science has

[1] For helpful overviews of modern philosophy of science see Achinstein (1969), Harré (1972), Hooker (1975), Losee (1980), McMullin (1970), Newton-Smith (1981), Nickles (1980), Shapere (1969), Suppe (1977a, 1977b).

continued to hold a central place in the epistemological scene, largely because certain natural sciences have retained their perceived pre-eminence as successful discourses. However, the claims of the non-science discourses to develop good explanations can now be better evaluated and the differing standpoints of the positivists and relativists can be given a critical comparison.

In comparisons between explanation in different types of discourse, the problem that has exercised people's minds the most has been that of *demarcation*. On what grounds are we to separate scientific explanation from non-scientific? Should we in fact even attempt to do so? If they are different, should they remain so; and what does it matter if they are? The philosophy of science has been very interested in this problem, usually attempting to isolate what it is that makes scientific explanation different; but in recent times there has been a strong movement to reject such questions as ill conceived, as we shall see.

My aims in the next six chapters are twofold. Firstly, I try to show how the answers given to these questions by philosophers are of relevance to social historians. I do this by giving a critical introduction to debates in the philosophies of natural and social science, the analytical philosophy of history, and the hermeneutical philosophy of the humanities. Chapters 3 to 6 contain brief introductions to positivist and relativist approaches to explanation in science, history, and the humanities. Chapters 7 and 8 contain more detailed criticisms of these positions and defences of the realist alternative.

My second aim is to draw out philosophical support for my two basic arguments, viz.:

1 That social history should conceive of its object as the history of real social relational structures, and
2 That it can become a discourse logically (but not ontologically) similar to that of the more successful sciences of nature if it founds itself upon realist philosophical principles.

Thus the upholding of the possibility of a realist and objectivist science of the history of society – the crucial task of my criticism of post-war debates – is supported in part II through a criticism of empiricism and relativism, individualism and holism, and a defence of realist epistemology and ontological and methodological structurism. But the main defence of structurism is left to part III, where I propose a potential solution to methodological problems of explaining social history.

3

Empiricist Positivism

'Positivism' is probably the most abused concept in methodological and theoretical discussions in the social studies today. It has often been used as a pejorative label to attach to any argument that a critic wishes to denigrate. These critics have included some Marxists, Popperians, Parsonians, phenomenologists, and hermeneuticists, and they have sometimes attached the label to each other! Thus in this dispute, as is usually the case with polemics, there is an inverse ratio between its heat and its clarity of light. But what it also indicates is that the term 'positivism' has tended to change in meaning, although it has maintained a small core of meaning ever since it was invented in the early nineteenth century by the French sociologists Saint-Simon and Comte. That core is the idea that positive, objective knowledge is to be had only by the method of natural science and that method is empiricism. All metaphysics, subjectivism, and speculation are to be excluded. Any discourse that wishes to produce positive knowledge has to become like natural science, especially like physics and chemistry. 'Positivism' is thus an account of scientific explanation and a programme for applying it to other discourses in order to improve them.

THE VIENNA CIRCLE

Modern philosophy of explanation can be said to have originated in Vienna and Berlin in the late 1920s with the rise of the logical-empiricist movement (sometimes called logical positivist) which centred on the Vienna Circle of philosophers, chief among whom were Moritz Schlick, Rudolf Carnap, Otto Neurath, Herbert Feigl, Hans Hahn, and Friedrich Waismann. The chief influences on their all-embracing attempt to refound philosophy, free of metaphysics, were the empiricist and positivist tradition leading from Locke to Hume to Mach; the analytical and logical thought of Leibnitz, Frege, and Russell; and the early linguistic philosophy of Wittgenstein.[1] In their manifesto of 1929 they emphasised the importance of these aspects of their position:

> First, it is empiricist and positivist: there is knowledge only from experience, which rests on what is immediately given. This sets the limit for the content of legitimate science. Second, the scientific world-conception is marked by application of a certain method, namely logical analysis. The aim of scientific effort is to reach the goal, unified science, by applying logical analysis to the empirical material. (Hahn, Neurath and Carnap, 1929, p. 309)

Although their influence has waned in recent decades, the logical empiricists had great influence in the middle decades of this century. They were responsible for a reorientation in the philosophy of the sciences since their work constituted a complete break with Germanic idealist and neo-Kantian ideas (see Suppe, 1977a); and they inspired logical-analytical enquiry into the foundations of all the empirical discourses. All philosophy of explanation has been forced to grapple with the trains of thought they set in motion and which were propelled with an exemplary clarity of thought. But there were considerable disagreements among them.

The logical empiricists were much in the tradition of the greatest of the British empiricists, David Hume, who wrote that if any book contains no abstract reasoning about quantity or number or experimental reasoning about facts or existence then it contains nothing but sophistry or illusion (Ayer, 1959, p. 10). The analytical/synthetic distinction that this view rests upon became the means whereby the logical empiricists, building upon Wittgenstein's *Tractatus Logico-Philosophicus* (1921), claimed to be able to separate meaningful from meaningless statements. The only propositions that were considered meaningful were either those that are analytically true because of the tautological or definitional meanings of terms and words (i.e. logic and mathematics) or which assert empirically testable factual claims about the world. Thus empiricism aided by logic enabled them to make what they believed were considerable advances on the earlier empiricist and positivist traditions in epistemology. Indeed, they saw themselves as having revolutionary aims, as having inaugurated a new 'turning point', in Moritz Schlick's phrase. Their basic aim was to put an end to the hitherto apparently endless process of each great

---

[1] For discussions of the Vienna Circle positivists, see Ayer (1946, 1959), Bergmann (1967), Feigl (1956, 1969), Halfpenny (1982), Hanfling (1981), Joergensen (1951), Kolakowski (1972), Shapere (1969).

thinker refounding philosophy anew. Against the 'anarchy' of philosophical opinions and systems, Schlick expressed his conviction that the logical methods now existed to end the fruitless conflict of ideas. All that was required was their resolute application (Schlick, 1930, p. 54).

The new insights into the nature of the logical forms of language revealed, he believed, that all knowledge is such only by virtue of its form; it represents the facts through its form. But the form itself cannot be represented. This insight had, for Schlick, the very greatest consequences:

> Above all, it enables us to dispose of the traditional problems of 'the theory of knowledge'. Investigations concerning the human 'capacity for knowledge', in so far as they do not become part of psychology, are replaced by considerations regarding the nature of expression, of representation, i.e. concerning every possible 'language' in the most general sense of the term. Questions regarding the 'validity and fruits of knowledge' disappear. Everything is knowable which can be expressed, and this is the total subject matter concerning which meaningful questions can be raised. There are consequently no questions which are in principle insoluble. What have been considered such up to now are not genuine questions, but meaningless sequences of words. (Schlick, 1930, pp. 55–6)

The logical empiricists were resolutely opposed to all metaphysics on the general grounds that such statements are meaningless and can be shown to be so through the logical analysis of language. For them, the only way of giving meaning to a sentence was to indicate the rules of how it was to be used – that is, the facts which would confirm or deny its truth must be describable. A sentence becomes a proposition if it is in principle, even if not in practice, empirically verifiable. In short, 'the meaning of a proposition is its method of verification', in Schlick's words; and so, 'whenever we assert anything we must, at least in principle, be able to say how the truth of our assertion can be tested; otherwise we do not know what we are talking about; our words do not form a real proposition at all, they are mere noises without meaning.' (Schlick, 1938, pp. 34–5) Metaphysical statements do not lend themselves to such verification. *This* is their problem, not that they are speculative or fairy tales, since such statements could be formulated in such a way that their truth conditions could be stated. Neither are they analytic statements, i.e. they are not true or false by virtue of their form (Carnap, 1932, p. 72).

The method of logical analysis enabled the logical empiricists to apparently jettison many doctrines (including realism and idealism) and a great deal of what had traditionally passed as philosophical thinking. The positive task of philosophy was to be reduced to the clarification of meaningful concepts and propositions that constitute the logical foundations for empirical science and mathematics (Carnap, 1932). In doing this the relationship between sense experience (empirical data), language, and meaning was obviously fundamental. At first they tended to hold to the Russellian position that all personal experience could be analysed into raw sense data which could be expressed as supposedly incorrigible elementary statements or facts. But the problem was how such experience could be shared. Schlick argued that it was only structure or form, not content (i.e. not particular facts about the natural world) which could be expressed and so communicated by language. Although the same proposition could be expressed in many ways by different languages it would always have the same logical structure. There can be, the argument goes, an intersubjective understanding of the structure of the world but not of each personal experience of it (Schlick, 1938, pp. 131–3).

Carnap and Neurath rejected such a position, arguing that the elementary statements of an empirical science must themselves be intersubjective. Science rested, for them, on a system of *shared basic protocol statements,* which were derived from direct experience and controlled the system of experimental verification. The protocol language from which they were drawn was a language of direct experience referring to the given physical world. This physical language of experience could in turn serve as the basis for theories (Carnap, 1934, pp. 152–5; Neurath, 1932, pp. 160–8).

Carnap and Neurath were the strongest defenders of physicalist reductionism, i.e. the thesis that the terms of all empirical science can be reduced to a language which contains only logico-mathematical terms and physical terms. This became perhaps the dominant position among the logical empiricists. Carnap argued that all scientific terms belong either to physical or biological languages and that basic to both these as well as to everyday pre-scientific language is a *physical thing-language,* which is used to refer to the properties of observable things in the world. These observable properties he called observable *thing-predicates.* He believed that terms referring to the dispositions or substances of organic or inorganic things could all be reduced by definition or experiment to physical thing-predicates. This applied, he held, to psychology and sociology as well. All psychology could be reduced to behaviourist methods and laws and in turn to biological science, and all social science could be reduced to psychology and then ultimately to biology (Carnap, 1938, pp. 114–26). This was because, he said,

> any investigation of a group of men or other organisms can be described in terms of the members, their relations to one another and to their environment. Therefore the conditions for the application of any term can be formulated in terms of psychology, biology, and physics, including the thing-language. Many terms can even be defined on that basis, and the rest is certainly reducible to it.
> (Carnap, 1938, p. 126)

In keeping with this position, the hallmarks of Neurath's scientific sociology were the rejection of all supposedly metaphysical presuppositions, and the consequent adoption of a physicalist ontology, i.e. a simple behaviourist and materialist approach to society. He criticised the entire hermeneutical-*Verstehen* tradition beginning with Dilthey, and including Windelband, Rickert, and Weber, for its metaphysics and separation of the human from the natural sciences. Empathy (or *Verstehen*), he said, may *help* with research, but it entered the totality of scientific statements 'as little as does a good cup of coffee which also furthers a scholar in his work' (Neurath, 1973, p. 357). Although he believed Weber had made important advances in empirical sociology through, for instance, his enquiries into religion, he thought he had gone seriously astray when discussing such things as 'rational economic ethos' or the 'achievement of Protestantism', as if Protestantism were a reality that acted upon people. On the contrary, wrote Neurath,

> in a strictly scientific sociology one can describe only the behaviour of men at a certain time, their habits, their way of life, their processes of production, etc., in order then to raise the question of how new habits arise by the joint effect of these observed habits and other circumstances. There are Protestants but there is no Protestantism. Physicalistically speaking, one can only note that men who have a certain mode of life and use certain words in cults (and otherwise) begin at a certain point in time to exhibit a different behaviour and perhaps to use different words. (Neurath, 1973, p. 358)

In general, Neurath's sociology was a rather artificial outgrowth of a radical empiricist epistemology. He paid little systematic attention to problems of the logic of historical or sociological explanation, and his attempt to discuss the ontological status of society as a structure was considerably inferior to Durkheim's. Nevertheless, the (rather crude) attack upon so-called metaphysics, the desire to unify all sciences, and the wish to save society through science were important counterpoints to a world of increasing irrationalism in economy, society, and politics in the 1930s.

MODERN EMPIRICIST POSITIVISM

In the 1930s most of the Austrian and German positivists moved to Britain and the United States, where the work of Hans Reichenbach, Rudolf Carnap, Herbert Feigl, Carl Hempel, Ernest Nagel, and others contributed to the development of the tradition. The influence of Karl Popper, although oblique, was also important. This 'school' has been the target of a good deal of misunderstanding, not to say denigration, in recent years by over-simplifying and ill-informed critics from opposed traditions, especially in the social sciences. The empiricists have often been mistakenly taken to subscribe to 'vulgar empiricism', the idea that all knowledge is a simple recording of sense impressions; and have sometimes been labelled as reactionaries supporting right-wing political and social philosophies. Radical social historians have been particularly strong in their condemnation but correspondingly weak in their understanding.

The modern empiricist-positivist movement, although far from being monolithic and in fact containing divergent views on many philosophical issues, especially from the 1960s onwards, is based upon three main doctrines (cf. McMullin, 1974):

1 *Logicism (or formalism)* This is the idea that the goal of the philosopher of science is to uncover and redescribe in a logically formal way the structure of reasoning in science. There must be a distinction, then, between the procedures that scientists employ to make discoveries and the formal structure by which they justify their knowledge – i.e. a historical/philosophical distinction in the study of science as a discourse. If knowledge cannot be reconstructed as conforming to either inductive or deductive logic then it cannot be considered scientific.

2 *Empiricism (or foundationalism)* That scientific knowledge has a rock-bottom foundation in sensory experience. There must be a distinction between empirical observations and theoretical/ methodological statements and frameworks such that theories are to be considered good or bad, confirmed or disproved, according to how they relate to empirical data. The task of science is to try to empirically verify theoretical explanations and predictions.

3 *Positivism* That only knowledge conforming to the previous two canons is objective and that any discourse that adopts them can become a positive science like that of physics. In principle any causal empirical enquiry is potentially a science.[2]

THE STRUCTURE OF LAWS

For all positivists, explanation is concerned with causation and there can be no ascription of causation without the use of laws. Two of the seminal works of the mature movement are Hempel's *Aspects of Scientific Explanation* (1965b) and Carnap's *The Philosophical Foundations of Physics* (1966), which together constitute a clear statement of the

[2] Empiricist positivism is discussed by Feigl (1970, 1974), Hempel (1965a), Hesse (1969), McMullin (1974), Newton-Smith (1981), Shapere (1969), Suppe (1977a, 1977b).

dominant conception of scientific explanation at that time. In these works, the stress upon nomological (i.e. lawful) explanation is paramount.

Scientists, Carnap said, begin by observing single facts from which they establish regular correlations. Regularities are called laws and no fact is explainable without a law, which asserts a causal correlation, no matter whether the law is arrived at inductively as a generalisation from instances or is deduced from a set of more general laws or theories. Universal laws also make precise predictions possible because of their form, which can be given the notation as follows (Carnap, 1966, p. 4):

1 $(x)\,(Px \supset Qx)$
2 Pa
3 Qa

This means:

> 1 *For all cases of* x, if x has the property P then it also has the property Q. (The symbol $\supset$ means 'if . . . then' or 'is implied by'.) This is the statement of a universal law.
> 2 Thus, if a has the property P, we can deduce that
> 3 It must have the property Q.

Laws are either universal, as in this case, or statistical, in which case a different form of logical reasoning is needed, i.e. induction. The problem of induction, which is a very old and troublesome one, is that an inductive conclusion or generalisation can never be justified completely since it always relies upon known particular cases and cannot say anything with absolute certainty about the unknown. Unlike a deductive conclusion, which is true if its premises are true, it is logically incorrect to say, for instance, 'the sun has always risen in the east, therefore it will rise in the east tomorrow.' The premise is not a universal law, only an observation of a regular occurrence. But if the sun has always risen in the east then there is a very high *probability* that it will rise in the east tomorrow. Carnap had been concerned throughout his career with the problem of justifying such probable inductions and giving them a precisely quantifiable expression, which he called 'degree of confirmation'. He believed the logic of statistical explanation to be no different from the logic of probability and on that basis predictions of a certain probability could be made.

Hempel has done most to explicate these two forms of lawful (i.e. nomological or covering-law) explanation. The first, which relies upon universal laws, he called *deductive-nomological* (D–N).[3] (Other writers

---

[3] D-N (or N-D) reasoning has a long history, numbering among its early adherents N. Campbell (1921), Karl Popper (1972b, originally 1934), and R. B. Braithwaite (1953). See the discussion in Laudan (1977b).

sometimes call this N–D reasoning.) As its name indicates, the explanation is arrived at by deducing it from statements about general laws and initial conditions. It has the following logical structure. The phenomenon to be explained is called the *explandum phenomenon*. Its occurrence is to be expected in virtue of a combination of particular factual conditions (called C_1, C_2, ..., C_k) and general laws which are the expression of uniformities (called L_1, L_2, ..., L_r). Together these are called the *explanans* statement (or set of statements) and their combination as premises allows a deductive conclusion called the *explanandum* (Hempel, 1965a, p. 336).

If the explanans is true, the explanandum must be true. But D–N explanation can have this logical structure and still be false, or perhaps be only a partially supported argument, or be true only potentially. It all depends upon the character of the evidence supporting the explanans sentences about facts and laws. To have a D–N explanation it is only necessary to have *law-like* sentences of a universal conditional kind about uniformities. The question of the status of the laws themselves (i.e. whether they are theoretical or empirical) and their truthfulness are separate matters involving further nomological-deductive reasoning and empirical observations of regularities (Hempel, 1965a, pp. 338–46).

The second form of covering-law explanation is that which Carnap has been most concerned with – *statistical*. These are of less stringency than the universal conditional type of the form (x) $(Px \supset Qx)$, which attribute, truly or falsely, a certain characteristic to all members of a class. Statistical laws only do so to a specified proportion of its members. They have the form

$$p(G, F) = r$$

where the statistical probability of an event of kind F to be also of kind G is r, i.e. a ratio of one to the other, in the long run.

Hempel argued that these laws could be used for deductive as well as inductive explanation since, especially if well confirmed, they will allow a deduction of the *probability* of an event occurring in a specified frequency and hence of the proportion of that event that does in fact occur in a large number of oservations (Hempel, 1965a, pp. 380–6). Their veracity depends upon repeated observations of regularities, of course, and both Hempel's essay and Carnap's book provide discussions of the several attempts to construct a non-ambiguous mathematical logic for the justification of such laws. A fundamental problem they face is that since they are only probable in form (not universal) even if true they cannot explain every event, only the predicted proportion of a particular kind of event. But Hempel believed this criticism adopted too restricted a view of actual natural and social scientific explanations which make quite explicit use of such laws and offer only at best highly probable conclusions about the outcome of processes or experiments. The 'epistemic ambiguity' which science often faces when attempting to decide between alternative statistical laws to explain phenomena could be overcome, he believed, by adopting the principle of always attempting to offer the maximal specificity for a law from the available evidence. There would then be seen to be more support for one conclusion as against another. Statistical explanation is thus always relative to the given knowledge situation at that time (pp. 391–402).

LAWS AND CAUSALITY

As direct inheritors of the Humean regularity concept of causation, the logical empiricists hold that nomological explanation and causal explanation are synonymous. As Hempel wrote, in order to describe event a as the effect of event b they have to be viewed as instances of certain *kinds* of events A and B, which are linked by a causal law. Then, to say a causes b is to say that under certain particular circumstances an instance of A is invariably followed by an instance of B. If a statement of the causation of a singular event does not mention the antecedent conditions then, in Hempel's view, this means that the causal law is either as yet unknown or simply left unstated. In the former case the place of the law can be taken by a working hypothesis which may give direction to the search for a causal law (Hempel, 1965a, pp. 349–50). He claims this is the situation for much scientific work; it is based upon a *hypothetico-deductive* (H–D) procedure from which certain candidate explanations are derived for testing.

Hempel went to some length to reject the claims made by some opponents of nomological explanation, such as Ryle, Scriven, and Dray (discussed in the next chapter) to the effect that causal explanations need not involve covering laws. Both he and Carnap were careful to point out that natural laws did not imply strict necessity (à la Laplace) or a rejection of conditional arguments regarding causality, as is sometimes thought.

THEORIES, OBSERVATIONS, AND NON-OBSERVABLES

For the logical empiricists theories are hypotheses or laws about the status and effects of *non-observable* entities, such as electromagnetic fields or sub-atomic particles. They differ from empirical laws not by necessarily having a lesser degree of confirmation but by having terms referring to non-observables. They cannot be developed as empirical inductions through observations of regularities but must begin as general hypotheses from which empirical laws would then be indirect confirmation of theoretical laws. The more new empirical observations and laws a theory can predict, the more valuable it is. In short, for the logical empiricists (at least in the early 1960s) there were two kinds of entities – observables and non-observables, each requiring its own terms of reference (Carnap, 1966, ch. 23; Hempel, 1965b, ch. 8). These two levels correspond roughly to two different stages in the history of a scientific procedure in Hempel's view. Theories can only be constructed after a body of knowledge about empirical regularities has been developed:

> A theory then aims at providing a deeper understanding by construing those phenomena as manifestations of certain underlying processes governed by laws which account for the uniformities previously studied, and which, as a rule, yield corrections and refinements of the putative laws by means of which those uniformities had been previously characterised. (Hempel, 1970, p. 142)

By the early 1960s the logical empiricists had more or less collectively developed and agreed upon a precise logico-analytical model of what has become known as the 'standard conception' or 'received view' of scientific theories. Chief earlier proponents of a similar view had been N. R. Campbell and Hans Reichenbach, and contemporary adherents included Braithwaite, Carnap, Nagel, and Feigl (but not Hempel after the mid 1950s) (see Suppe, 1977a).

This conception was meant to be a statement of the logical structure only of theories and not of their historical and psychological origins. It was based upon the observable/non-observable distinction and was designed to present a viable means of linking them. Clearly the main problem was how to define and give meaning to theoretical terms referring to unknown entities which could not be simply described using empirical terms. In order to overcome this they held that a theory should contain three basic kinds of statements:

1 Theoretical statements about postulated entities, processes, and laws;
2 Observation statements about empirical observables; and
3 Bridge principles or correspondence rules which enabled a link to be made between observables and non-observables.

These principles or rules were conventions decided upon beforehand by the community of scientists.

The theoretical/observational distinction is further closely related, as one would expect, to another fundamental principle of the logical empiricists – the analytic/synthetic distinction, which separates statements having purely formal or logical meaning and those having empirical or descriptive meaning about the world. The problem here was how

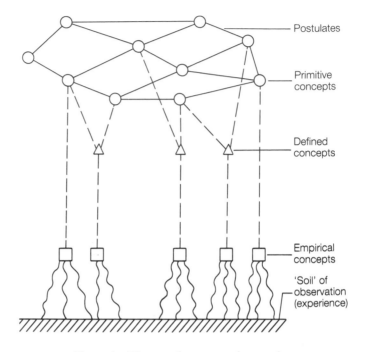

Figure 1   The net of correspondence rules

these two kinds of statements were to be divided and brought into a relationship within a scientific theory.

The received view characterised theories, therefore, as couched in a language employing terms and sentences of an observational, theoretical, and logical kind. The theoretical terms consist of a system of axiomatic postulates about assumed basic entities, such as electrons or fields. These postulates are connected to the empirically known facts by the 'correspondence rules' (Carnap) or 'coordinative definitions' (Reichenbach) consisting of primitive concepts, experimental procedures, derived definitions, and logical rules of deductive inference between the level of pure postulate and observation. But the axioms always remain partially undefined.

Feigl's diagram (figure 1) (Feigl, 1970, p. 6) sums up the situation in a conveniently simple way. For empiricists, the meaning of the theoretical postulates is purely axiomatic, but the meaning of the deduced primitive and defined concepts, i.e. the heart of what the theory is attempting to specify, is one of the fundamental issues in the philosophy of science. Two opposed views see them either as referring to real but as yet undiscovered entities or mechanisms (realism), or as merely very useful fictions or instruments for deriving empirically testable statements (instrumentalism). The question of ontology is thus of crucial importance.

THE PROBLEM OF ONTOLOGY

As Carnap wrote in 1950, and as their name obviously implies, empiricists are like nominalists when it comes to talking about abstract entities, i.e. they reject a specification of them as real. The early Vienna Circle logical positivists usually adopted the doctrine of phenomenalism, which rules out the idea of ascribing reality to non-observable entities. While most of the later empiricists did hold firmly to the view that there was a fundamental distinction between theoretical and empirical entities, in Carnap's view the nature of reality was a question that could be posed only within a semantical framework and it made little sense to discuss the reality or otherwise of abstract entities (Carnap, 1950a, pp. 220–1). The attempt to found all scientific knowledge upon an *incorrigible* basis of sense experience alone was abandoned in the late 1930s or 1940s. But, as Feigl later argued, although sense data are far from purely given they are not a fictional construct or theory dependent. The temporal sequence of impressions and the repeated observations of regular relationships among events, i.e. the more or less lawful relationships among our impressions of the world, do furnish for empiricists the independent corroborating evidence for explanations. Empirical laws are not wholly incorrigible but nevertheless, as Feigl rightly stated, they are quite different from theories and do form an approximately correct foundation for scientific knowledge. In fact, the position of the later empiricists can be characterised as one of critical *empirical realism* since they had abandoned phenomenalism and the empirical testability criterion of meaningfulness in favour of a view of knowledge, as we have seen, as a network of concepts and propositions about both observables and non-observables – the latter being, moreover, non-observable in *principle* (Feigl, 1956, pp. 16–22). This of course seems to ignore the difficulty of what to say about entities which were once unobservable, such as viruses, but which became observable after the development of new technology such as the electron microscope. And in a sense even the fundamental forces of nature such as electromagnetism can be observed in a way similar to temperature, i.e. through a precise gauge. If the temperature of a physical object can be considered by the empiricists as an observable property, should not magnetism also be so considered? The question of the theoretical/observational distinction is of crucial importance in the debates over the received view of theories of the 1960s and 1970s, as we shall see.

MODELS OF EXPLANATION AND ACTUAL PRACTICE

The empiricists have always wished to draw a distinction between (1) the historical, sociological, and psychological contexts of discoveries and (2) the logical structure of justification of explanations, i.e. a historical/ epistemological distinction. That the how and the why of the *origins* of explanations should be distinguished for analytical purposes from the explication or reconstruction of the *structure* of those explanations seems clear enough (but of course not always understood or distinguished, as we shall see in chapter 5). However, the more contentious and important issue concerns the relationship between their models of theories and explanation and how explanations are actually arrived at and justified by practising scientists, sociologists, historians, or whoever. The critics of the applicability to history of Hempel's covering-law account, such as Dray and Scriven, were of the view that it was irrelevant as a description of actually existing historical explanation and furthermore that such explanation simply could not comply with it (see the next chapter).

Hempel was careful to point out that his covering-law models of explanation were not meant to describe practice accurately. Rather, they were abstractions from and logical schematizations about practice (i.e. idealised or rational reconstructions). They were like the concepts of mathematical proof, and not meant to exclude other uses of the word 'explanation'. But each use of the word has a different logical character. With objective scientific explanation of events and uniformities, how- ever, his analytical models should serve, he believed, as a standard; and they could, like mathematical proofs, be the basis for developing new results about probability, decidability, definability, and ontology (Hempel, 1965a, pp. 412–15).

Of course it is relevant to this issue of verisimilitude to know the degree of explanatory incompleteness in science or history due to elliptical or partial formulations. Hempel claimed that many expla- nations are elliptically presented while being, perhaps, tacitly in keeping with his idealised models (p. 415). Partial explanations deviate consider- ably more in that the explanans does not account for the explanandum phenomenon with the degree of specificity actually claimed for it, owing to inadequately formulated generalisations from which deductions are made. History and psychoanalysis were cited as disciplines containing such incomplete explanations, although still being examples of D–N reasoning (pp. 415–16). Statistical explanations might also be thought to be incomplete, but Hempel believed that D–N reasoning employing statistical rather than universal laws is formally coherent and complete since it assigns only a *logical probability* to the explanandum event. Such statistical laws are furthermore now thought to be basic laws of nature owing to a certain indeterminacy at the fundamental quantum level of matter (p. 418).

The structure of explanation of individual concrete singular events (such as are often thought of by historians to be unique occurrences) is also relevant in this regard. The general standpoint of the empiricists was that scientific explanation is made on the basis of establishing the laws connecting classes of events.

The orthodox empiricist consensus on the nature of the logical structure of theories began to break up in the 1960s. This was due to the impact of criticisms from 'within' the consensus made by Hempel, among others (see Hempel, 1970, 1973; Feigl, 1974; McMullin, 1974; Suppe, 1977a, 1977b). There were also of course many 'external' critics, as we shall see in the following chapters. Occupying a position somewhere between the internal and external critics was Karl Popper. His ideas were not of the orthodox positivist sort but he did have an affinity for their programme of scientific unity.

POPPER'S CRITICAL FALSIFICATIONISM

Karl Popper was a close contemporary of the original Vienna Circle of philosophers and had considerable contact with them. But from the beginning of his philosophical work he was critical of their phenomenalism and inductivism. Since then he has become one of the most influential philosophers of the century. But his position is difficult to categorise because it incorporates elements of empiricism, conventionalism, and realism in a non-eclectic manner.[4]

In *The Logic of Scientific Discovery* (1972b, first published 1934) he rejected the idea of separating the context of scientific discovery from the context of justification and denied the possibility of finding an absolutely incorrigible foundation for scientific explanation. The distinction he saw as being more important was that between the origin of a new idea and the process of examining it. He argued that the logic of scientific reasoning was hypothetico-deductive: an initial conjecture or hypothesis or general theory about a problem is developed, from which theoretical conclusions are deduced. They are in turn tested in four ways: by logical comparison among the conclusions; by examining the logical form of the theory to see that it is not tautological but open to empirical testing; by comparison with other theories to see if it says anything new; and by empirical testing (pp. 32–3).

The early logical empiricists used the notion of *empirical verifiability* as both the criterion of meaningfulness and the method of separating scientific from metaphysical discourses. Popper was opposed completely to this doctrine, which was based upon induction. The problem of

---

[4] There is a vast literature on Popper's work. See, for example, Albert (1978), Lakatos (1974), Lakatos and Musgrave (1970), Lieberson (1982), Magee (1973), O'Hear (1982), Putnam (1974), Radnitzky (1981), Watkins (1974, 1978a, 1978b).

induction, as Hume had argued, was that universal statements drawn from singular experiences could never be considered proven completely true (pp. 28–9). Against this Popper proposed the notion of *falsifiability* as a demarcation of science: it must in principle be possible for an empirical scientific system to be falsified by experience (pp. 40–4). Thus science should be characterised by its methods of enquiry. But where do those methods come from? He believed that science relied upon a set of conventions or decisions about methods which were not themselves part of science. The logical empiricists had been opposed to the notion that non-scientific statements could be meaningful but Popper thought it impossible for scientists to develop their methods of empirical enquiry from empirical enquiry itself (pp. 52–3).

Logical empiricism was based upon the idea of a theory/observation distinction. But Popper believed that observations were always made in the light of theories. He held that theories, as we have seen, were hypothetico-deductive in structure, giving a causal explanation of an event by deducing a statement which describes it from premises consisting of (1) universal natural laws and (2) singular statements about the initial conditions of the event (pp. 59–60). Once a conclusion about the causation of an event is deduced in this way it can then be empirically tested and perhaps thereby falsified. It could be corroborated but never verified as completely true because such an inductive generalisation can never be logically warranted. Until falsified, a theory remains as tentatively correct or simply provisionally accepted.

Popper's concept of falsifiability rested upon a realist view of nature and theories. For a theory to be falsifiable there must be a level of reality against which it can be compared. The point of view known as instrumentalism, to which most of the logical empiricists subscribed at the time, held that theories were not putative pictures or descriptions of nature but were, rather, logical constructions of axiomatic laws which could not be falsified by observation (p. 79). They were *conventions* adopted by scientists as a framework for determining what counts as an observation. But Popper himself conceded that a certain type of conventionalism was necessary to science, although it was confined to decisions about methods and a class of statements he described as 'basic' (p. 84). His realist alternative rested upon this class of basic statements. They were singular statements of fact about the world which could be used to falsify or corroborate theories; but he conceded that since the world is multilayered in reality the level at which basic statements about it were pitched was a matter for *decision* (p. 104).

Neurath and Carnap had made much of their protocol sentences about observations as the rock-bottom intersubjectively acceptable basis for science. Popper's basic statements were not direct observations of particular events but were statements of an existential kind about the dispositional nature of particular events, which were then open to observation (pp. 102–3). A decision is made in every empirical enquiry to stop at some basic statement about the world. This does not imply that testing can go no further, only that it has been decided not to do so. Such statements are agreed upon as basic by the community of scientists, for not to do so would be to lead to an infinite regress. These statements are a form of dogma but accepted as such for the time being (p. 105). Thus one theory is acceptable as opposed to another which is not on the grounds of its corroboration by basic statements about the reality of the world, which are arrived at in turn by extra-scientific decisions. This does not mean that they are false, only primordial since, in Popper's view,

> the empirical basis of objective science has nothing 'absolute' about it. Science does not rest upon solid bedrock. The bold structure of its theories rises, as it were, above a swamp. It is like a building erected on piles. The piles are driven down from above into the swamp, but not down to any natural or 'given' base; and if we stop driving the piles deeper, it is not because we have reached firm ground. We simply stop when we are satisfied that the piles are firm enough to carry the structure, at least for the time being. (Popper, 1972b, p. 111)

He criticised both (1) the idea that science aims at, and ideally succeeds in, uncovering and describing the essences of the world in an ultimately truthful manner, and (2) the converse instrumental idea that theories do not attempt to describe the world, but are merely instruments for guiding experiments and making calculations (Popper, 1972a, ch. 3). He did not wish to deny either that there are unexplained and hidden realities or that theories are sometimes used as instruments, but said that science does not aim at ultimate explanation and so a belief in essences is obscurantist. Science aims, rather, at testing and refuting theories in order to move closer to truth. His alternative is to conceive of theories as *conjectures* – serious attempts to discover the truth about the various layers of reality of the world. These conjectures can be falsified but never shown to be completely true.

Until Popper discovered Tarski's work in the late 1930s he hesitated to speak about 'truth' and 'falsity' in science (see Popper, 1972b, p. 274). But Tarski had shown how the notion of 'truth' as being applicable to statements which correspond to facts could be saved by speaking of both statements and facts in a metalanguage, which specifies the conditions under which statements do correspond to facts. For example, 'the statement "snow is white" corresponds to the facts if and only if snow is indeed white.' This is an expression in metalanguage. Popper believed Tarski had thus shown that an *objective* idea of truth was possible and so it licensed a *search for truth*. This could then be a regulative principle of scientific practice because, although we do not know what the truth is in advance, we are able to have criteria of progress towards it. Subjectivist theories of truth can play no such role. The regulative idea of truth as objective correspondence to the facts was compared with a mountain peak wrapped in clouds:

> A climber may not merely have difficulties in getting there – he may not know when he gets there, because he may be unable to distinguish, in the clouds, between the main summit and a subsidiary peak. Yet this does not affect the objective existence of the summit; and if the climber tells us 'I doubt whether I reached the actual summit', then he does, by implication, recognise the objective existence of the summit. The very idea of error, or of doubt (in its normal straightforward sense) implies the idea of an objective truth which we may fail to reach.... Thus while coherence, or consistency, is no criterion of truth, simply because even demonstrably consistent systems may be false in fact, incoherence or inconsistency do establish falsity; so, if we are lucky, we may discover the falsity of some of our theories. (Popper, 1972a, p. 226)

Testing and fruitful critical discussion depend upon a shared background of knowledge. While this background may not be unproblematical, most of it remains tacitly unquestioned, although certain parts may be challenged. It is never challenged as a whole – a point on which Popper clashes with the holistic position of thinkers such as Duhem, Kuhn, and Feyerabend, as we shall see in chapter 5.

4

Positivist and Intentionalist Explanations of History

Perhaps the fundamental problem for the philosophy of historical explanation concerns the objectivity and reliability of historical knowledge, especially when viewed from the standpoint of the natural sciences, which have usually been taken to be objective and reliable discourses. But of course many historians and philosophers have rejected this comparison, seeing history as a *sui generis* discourse with its own peculiar methodologies and standards. Thus the two poles of this long-running debate are the positions of naturalism, which argues that history should and could be like natural science, and historicalism, which argues that history is unique as an explanatory discourse. That is, the two extreme positions argue for either a complete identity of explanation in natural science, social science, and history on objectivist grounds, or a complete separation of history from other modes of explanation on indeterminist and relativist grounds. The positivist position is, however, only one possible version of naturalism and there have been several attempts to argue that historians in fact employ a combination of theoretical generalisations and interpretive understanding to arrive at their explanations of events. Max Weber, for example, believed both to be essential, but his generalisations were not universal laws, being rather of a less precise, heuristic kind.

Within the analytical philosophical debate over the nature of historical explanation, therefore, it is important to realise that there are four related but separate issues:

1 The relationship of scientific and historical explanation.
2 The nature of scientific explanation.

3 The role of laws and other generalisations in historical explanation.
4 The role of intentionality in historical explanation.

MANDELBAUM'S EMPIRICAL REALISM

Relativism dominated the philosophy of history from the 1880s until
the 1930s, and was epitomised by Dilthey, Croce, and Collingwood.
From the late 1930s objectivist critics began to attack this prevailing
orthodoxy. In *The Problem of Historical Knowledge* (1938) Maurice
Mandelbaum attempted to defend the possibility of objectivity on the
grounds of the existence of an external ordered reality of historical events
and thus of the correspondence theory of truth. He claimed that in fact
historians did indeed adopt an objectivist methodology (pp. 185–6)
which asserted a correspondence between statements about facts and the
facts themselves. To be truthful, statements had to be in accord with the
recorded factual observations about events (pp. 180–6).

This argument rests upon an empirical realist ontology which holds
that the events of the world not only are given to (or discovered by) the
historian, but exist in a specific pattern or order, which is also given in
reality (p. 200). In short, according to Mandelbaum, there is an order of
events in the social world independent of cognition of them.

On the basis of this empirical realism Mandelbaum was able to argue
that causation is the prime concern of historical enquiry since causal
relationships are inherent in the given ordered relationship which exists
between real events. While the task of science is to formulate laws, those
laws are not wholly causal in character. It is history that is supposedly
concerned with the *concrete causal description* of particular events
(pp. 237–9). Those events share the same characteristics as natural
events, i.e. they endure through time, and they contain sub-events which
have an existential relation to them, and which are contemporaneous
with them (p. 254). To show the existential relationship is the task of
causal enquiry, but clearly, as Mandelbaum knew, such a bond is often
unclear. Social and psychological theory is essential to uncover causal
connections. Nevertheless Mandelbaum believed that social theory and
social analysis were necessarily distinct practices:

History ... depends for the furtherance of its analysis upon
principles which only sociology and the other theoretical social
sciences can disclose; sociology depends upon historical investigation for the material upon which it works, examining and
comparing historical instances in order to discover the laws which
may be implicit in them. Such mutual dependence again demonstrates that historical analysis is causal in character, for if it were

not the sociologist could never generalise from historical data, setting up laws which hold of the historical process. (p. 265)

Certain unresolved problems stand out from Mandelbaum's discussion which were of central importance for the subsequent debate. Firstly, there is the relationship of general theories and laws to particular concrete descriptions. Mandelbaum's argument was a little ambiguous on this, since it was not completely clear whether general laws were to be distinguished from theoretical hypotheses, or whether laws and theories were established deductively or inductively. Were particular descriptions to be deduced from laws and/or theories, or were events to be read off in a theory-neutral manner, with theories then being inductively generalised from particular instances? And to say that causation is *inherent* in the order of the world was a controversial view. These issues were to be of central concern to the later positivists.

Secondly, the nature of the external social reality that Mandelbaum argued existed was unclear. He seemed to be at times unable to go beyond phenomenalism in his ontological specification of the historical process; yet at other times he approached a transcendental position which specified the structure of social order itself as a transfactually real entity. On the whole, he subscribed to the former view, which accounts for his inadequate theory of structure and consequently for the lack of a theory of agency. To say that social order is just patterns of events is to avoid the question of the existence of real relations, thus allowing the physicalist individualist to argue that supposedly social entities are in fact not real but ideal. Empirical realism is not a viable philosophy for social science any more than for natural science since it is unable to give an account of *non-phenomenal* generative mechanisms, as I shall further argue in a moment.

HEMPEL'S COVERING-LAW MODELS

Carl Hempel argued in a famous paper of 1942 that methodologically there should be no difference between explanation in natural science and history and, indeed, that in effect there was none. In any branch of empirical enquiry, he argued (as we saw in the previous chapter), scientific explanation of events could be achieved only by the subsumption of those events under suitable general hypotheses, theories, or laws. This was a causal explanation *deducing* the occurrence of an event from the existence of determining conditions and general laws of which those conditions were instances. Historical explanation, he said, like that in natural science, does aim to make such causative connections, yet many historians deny the possibility of referring to the operation of general laws in history (Hempel, 1942, p. 349). He believed this denial could be accounted for by the tacit and perhaps ambiguous adoption of universal hypotheses of a vague and probabilistic kind. They constitute an 'explanation sketch', which needs 'filling out', requiring further empirical research. Thus historians, too, attempt to offer explanations of a positivistic nature (pp. 349–52).

Hempel was fully aware that this account of historical method differed a good deal from what he called the 'familiar view' that natural and social studies were based upon contrasting procedures, that social studies employed empathetic understanding of the situation and motives of action. However, he claimed that this hermeneutical procedure did not produce explanations of events; it was in reality a heuristic device which seemed to suggest psychological hypotheses, which could in turn be used as explanatory principles (p. 352).

His argument also contrasted with Mandelbaum's view that historical explanation, while being objective, differed from natural science in that it was not nomological-deductive but employed a *causal-descriptive* inductive orientation to individual events and their relationship to other individual events. Hempel believed that such an argument had been refuted by Hume and that it was impossible to explain the causal relationship between events without reference to similar cases and general regularities.

Hempel's regularity (or nomological-deductive) theory had in fact been anticipated by Popper in his (German language) book *Logik der Forschung* of 1934 but it had attracted very little attention at that time. Hempel made no reference to it in his 1942 article and it was not until Popper published (in English) the second volume of *The Open Society and its Enemies* in 1945 that his close similarity with Hempel became apparent (Popper, 1966, vol. 2, pp. 262–3). Therefore the argument must be correctly labelled the Popper-Hempel theory.

Hempel's argument went through a series of refinements during the 1950s (Hempel, 1950, 1952, 1962a, 1962b), some prompted by critics, until being stated in its clearest form in his seminal article of 1963. In it he restated his two models (or theoretical idealisations) of the logic of scientific explanation, both of which were nomological: deductive and probabilistic. They were outlined in the previous chapter. Hempel claimed that both these models could be used to understand explanation as it actually appeared in the natural sciences, and went on to argue that historical explanation, despite claims to the contrary, was also necessarily in keeping with these models, although perhaps being often elliptical or only partially nomological. In this way he strongly supported the positivist claim of methodological unity between all the sciences, whether they studied natural phenomena or human action (pp. 123–4).[1]

[1] For discussions of the applicability of the Popper-Hempel theory to history, see Brodbeck (1962), Danto (1968, ch. 10), Donagan (1964), Dray (1957, 1963, 1964), Fales (1980), Gardiner (1952), Mandelbaum (1961), Murphey (1973, ch.. 3), Scriven (1959, 1966), Weingartner (1961).

Philosophical opposition to the relevance of covering laws and empiricism to the human studies has come from three main sources: intentionalist analytical philosophers (discussed in this chapter), phenomenological and hermeneutical philosophers (discussed in chapter 6), and realist analytical philosophers (discussed in chapters 7 and 8). The first and third of these agree with the positivists to the extent of wishing to establish the structure of *causal* enquiry into actions and events. The second group wish to restrict the human studies to interpretive understanding rather than causality.

THE INTENTIONALIST APPROACH TO HISTORY

A fundamental fact about human action, which it does not share with any other type of event, is its *intentional* character. Humans act for reasons, to achieve consciously established goals. They are able to monitor their actions and to evaluate them, and then to monitor their monitorings. This has long been realised, of course, and has been the basis for the rejection by many philosophers, psychologists, social theorists, and historians of any similarity between the natural and human studies. The neo-Kantian philosophers of late-nineteenth-century Germany, such as Dilthey, Rickert, and Windelband, whom Mandelbaum and Hempel reacted against, held that only an idiographic rather than a nomothetic form of enquiry was appropriate to human action (see especially Windelband, 1980). This was supported by idealists such as Croce and Collingwood. In England the neo-Wittgensteinian Ryle (1949) also defended such a position, believing that 'thick description' was the task of the human studies (Ryle, 1968, p. 221), and Isaiah Berlin (1960) also followed this line in his attack upon the possibility of scientific history.

Perhaps the leading recent critic of positivism within analytical philosophy of history has been W. H. Dray, whose historicalist argument for a radical separation of history from natural and social science has been in the spirit of Windelband, Collingwood, and Ryle. He sees history as indeed a different 'universe of discourse', whose *sui generis* nature is made possible in two ways. The first is by a different orientation or presupposition by the historian towards the social world so that history is concerned fundamentally with individuality (Dray, 1957, pp. 48–50). The second is by the supposed indeterminism of human action. History as an existing discourse, he believed, embodied a conception of explanation which did not entail deductive determinism. He did not wish to reject the validity of N–D reasoning in science, only to argue that the two methodologies are concerned with separate questions. History is concerned, in his view, with the reconstruction of the lives of individual people at other times and places; science with the attempt to regularise and predict. Thus he sees the covering-law doctrine as a barrier to understanding and evaluating human life from the standpoint of agency (Dray, 1963, p. 89). In his book *Laws and Explanation in History* (1957), he attempted to demonstrate this *sui generis* nature of existing historical reasoning and to argue that it required a 'practical and rational' method of causal analysis, rather than a subsumption of entities under general categories and laws (pp. 48–50).

Dray believed that the historian's typical problem is to weigh counter-factually a set of miscellaneous factors that contributed to a particular result, and which cannot be deduced from general laws (1957, p. 56). It is sufficient to show a *practical* connection (pp. 96–7). The historian asks, counterfactually and *inductively*, if a supposedly causal condition was really necessary to the particular effect in question, since his task is to answer not 'what causes *y*s?', but 'what is the cause of this *y*?' (p. 98) His judgement of the crucial causal conditions in the situation is pragmatic (p. 100). This judgement requires no *a priori* theoretical or experimental knowledge (p. 106).

In general, Dray's attitude towards the causal analysis of historical events was typical of most historians: they reject laws in favour of a *descriptive narrative*. In Dray's words:

> Finding the cause of a historical event is thus no substitute for knowing exactly what happened – which Oakeshott rightly regards as an essential mark of historical enquiry. Indeed, it involves a judgement which depends on knowing just that.
>
> It is true that in the explanatory statement which arises out of this detailed knowledge, one or a few conditions are picked out as 'the cause'. But this does not amount to opening a 'lacuna'; nor does it confer upon the causal conditions any mysterious onto-logical priority. It merely satisfies certain pragmatic criteria of importance which are superimposed upon, but do not replace, the inductive requirement that the causal condition be a necessary one.
> (Dray, 1957, p. 114)

Turning to the causation of individual human *actions*, Dray defended the necessity of a *rational* mode of explanation based upon eliciting an agent's *reasons* for action. If action can be thought to be at all purposive, he said, then there must have been a calculation by the actor, which is then made the basis for a rational explanation, which aims at showing 'what was done was the thing to have done for the reasons given, rather than merely the thing that is done on such occasions, perhaps in accordance with certain laws (loose or otherwise).' (p. 124) The historian attempts to 'work' the agent's calculation by taking account of his beliefs, purposes and principles (p. 125), as revealed by empirical evi-dence (p. 129). Dray rejected the characterisation of such an empathetic method as relying upon mere imagination.

His theory of rational or intentionalist explanation was not the same as a dispositional analysis, since dispositions do not reveal anything about motives. Dispositions may tell the historian about the conditions of forms of behaviour but not about particular acts (pp. 148–9). Dispositional characteristics may indeed be causes but so can be reasons. Therefore there is no important difference between saying of the action of a rational agent, '*A*'s reason for doing *x* was *y*' and saying 'the cause of *A*'s doing *x* was *y*.' The difference was simply one of approach (p. 154).

While the critics of Hempel have not agreed with his argument for the necessity of universal empirical laws, many of them (such as Gardiner) have supported the necessity for other kinds of law-like knowledge or generalisations of a weaker kind in the explanation of events. Dray himself argued more explicitly in a 1959 article for the importance of *summative generalisations* of a non-lawful kind in reconstructing historical sequences (Dray, 1959, pp. 406–7). He was clearly indebted in this to an earlier argument of W. H. Walsh that general *colligatory concepts* which held together such sequences were essential to historians (Walsh, 1942, pp. 133–5; and see also Walsh, 1967a, and 1967b, pp. 24–5).

A similar argument has been developed in greater detail by Michael Scriven who, together with Dray, has been one of the most persistent critics of the Hempelian theory (for main works, see bibliography). He attempted to draw a distinction between explanations and their deductive justifications: 'explanations are practical context-bound affairs', he wrote, 'and they are merely converted into something else when set out in full deductive array . . . i.e. into a justification of an explanation (and usually no longer explain but demonstrate).' (Scriven, 1959, p. 450) Thus there can be explanations without their being deduced from laws. His view was that there is a family of explanation types, each of which may require a different type of justification (p. 451). Moreover, he attacked the possibility of nomological-deductive explanation in *any* field of enquiry because he believed that there are in fact no universally true hypotheses, and without them deduction must also be abandoned (p. 457). The model must be then replaced by an essentially *inductive* one using what he called 'normic statements'. This was a 'hybrid' category of general statements,

> with some universal features and some statistical features, from which alone can be selected the role-justifying grounds for good explanations of individual events. It includes truisms . . ., many natural laws, some tendency statements and probability statements, and – in other areas less relevant to explaining – rules, definitions, and certain normative statements in ethics. The crucial common property of these statements is best illustrated by examples, but can be described as norm-defining; they have a *selective immunity* to apparent counter-examples. (Scriven, 1959, p. 464)

These statements are *guarded generalisations,* which say that 'everything falls into a certain category except those to which certain special conditions apply.' (p. 466) They are thus somewhere between universal hypotheses and statistical statements and are the basis for historical explanations, serving to locate and explain every particular event.

Scriven assimilated the rationalist account of the explanation of actions to his normic theory by arguing that the grounds for reasons/ explanations include the general truism that intelligent humans do act for what they say are good reasons when the matter is of importance and time for deliberation is available (Scriven, 1963, p. 351). Thus in order to show that such a truism does account for an action there need to be grounds for supposing that no other likely generalisation, whether a truism or a law, is present – 'and we need those grounds anyway, whether we have a loose truism or a precise general law.' (p. 354) Scriven believed this to be the key logical point of historical methodology:

> The strength that a general law has by comparison with a possibility statement is logically redundant for explanatory purposes. And hence we can have good historical explanations without having good predictive laws: from (1) 'Y is a possible explanation of X and was present' and (2) 'No other plausible explanation of X appears to have been present', it follows that Y is *the* (most plausible) explanation of X, subject to the usual assumption that there is an explanation for everything. (Scriven, 1963, p. 354)

Thus both Dray and Scriven, and other intentionalist philosophers, recognise that the question of causation is crucial and Scriven supports the use of weak generalisations. But do human phenomena have a special kind of causation which requires a non-scientific methodology, or can history and science be brought together on a basis other than positivism?

CAN SCIENTIFIC AND INTENTIONALIST METHODOLOGIES BE COMBINED?

In order to show that there can be some *logical* similarity between explanation in natural science, social science, and history it is essential to show that the causal structures of human action and social relations are not radically different from those in nature. If the wholly empiricist account of natural causation and the wholly intentionalist account of human causation could both be shown to be false, then the way would be clear for a rapprochement.

It is possible to be a critic of the Hempelian N–D thesis while still supporting the necessity of generalisation-governed explanation in history. Morton White (1943) and Patrick Gardiner (1952) have presented versions of this argument, and Maurice Mandelbaum (1955, 1957, 1961) has more recently supported the cause of unifying all the empirical studies, but around a different version of scientific method. Part of his defence has been on the grounds of the possibility of historical laws about *mechanisms* within the operation of real social structures. (More on this in a moment.) The critics of nomological reasoning considered so far have usually concentrated on simply denying the existence of historical laws. While they may have referred to the *conditions* of historical events as the bases of explanations they have seen humans as essentially autonomous and free rational beings making history under freely chosen conditions and giving accurate accounts of their personal motivations. Like ordinary-language philosophers generally (in the tradition of Ryle and Wittgenstein), they have seen their main task as elucidating the ordinary practices and linguistic usages of existing historians rather than offering a general critique from an ontological or epistemological standpoint. I believe this to have been a mistake because this approach has blinded them to the possibility that there may be laws of the mechanism kind operating in the both the natural and social world requiring a different conception of scientific laws from that of the empiricists.

Obviously, the existence of (so-called) 'unique' motives and conscious intentions of particular individual human actions is a problem for any serious covering-law theorist, although the positivist tradition has generally tended to reject the existence of, let alone any independent role for, consciousness or free will, as can be seen, for instance, in the cases of Buckle, Neurath, and Skinner. Gardiner attempted to show that what can be taken to be genuine differences in the logic of explanation by scientists and historians should be accounted for not by *sui generis* arguments, as supposed by idealists, or by mistaken methodologies, as Hempel argued, but by different *purposes* of research and explanation (Gardiner, 1952, pp. 32–3). There are not different realms of causes – material and mental – requiring different methodologies; rather, he believed, there are different types of explanation which complement each other (pp. 136–7). The problem is to bring the two approaches to explanation together; i.e. there are general psychological, sociological, and physiological causal conditions as well as individual consciousness to take account of. In Gardiner's view it was on this point that the scientist and the historian diverged, since the former was not interested in conscious motivation, and the historian's generalisations were of a less precise form, being rather guides to understanding (pp. 59–61). Hempel's attitude to such an argument was that the historian's generalisations were explanation sketches of a putative hypothetico-deductive form. But the role of consciousness was conspicuously absent from his account. On the other hand, the intentionalists and idealists placed all their weight upon it.

Any examination of historical writings will show that while historians do usually wish to establish causality, empiricist causal laws are very difficult to establish for historical events. The inductive approach of generalising laws from particular instances of supposedly given causal connections is logically flawed, and both it and Hempel's covering-law method always risk missing *hidden* mechanisms in the causal situation. On the other hand, the fundamental question that must be asked of the intentionalists is: how is it possible to gain an understanding and explanation of intentional actions without reference to general social/ psychological/linguistic causes? In other words, explanation and under-standing by reference to intentions alone may not be possible. I believe it is these general predicates that need greater elaboration on the basis of a *realist* ontology and epistemology of causal mechanisms. But before I say something more about that, it is important to dispose of the idea that human and social phenomena are radically indeterminate.

THE PROBLEM OF DETERMINISM

It is crucial to my basic argument that there is in fact only one ultimately telling argument on behalf of the realist scientific approach to the explanation of human action and against the intentionalist-hermeneutical-historicalist view that history is a *sui generis* discourse. Given a stubborn insistence by either or both sides not to agree on the meaning of key concepts there is no way in which an appeal to an argument about the true logic of explanation, no matter how consistent, will finally separate the two views since there is no compelling necessity for agreement on the meaning of 'explanation'. Of course this must be the first line of attack but, having failed, only an *ontological* argument about what is the *general* nature of humans and social structures can show why a unified *realist* scientific methodology is necessary. And that must partly involve showing that human action and the social word are *determinate*.

As Ernest Nagel (1960, pp. 347–9) pointed out, it is crucial to separate completely the doctrine of determinism from that of historical inevit-ability, which holds that humans are impotently caught up in an inexorable historical process.[2] Rather, determinism can be said to exist where the variables in a system stand in definite relations of interdepen-dence so that the value of a variable at a given time is determined by the values of the other variables at that time. The system itself is determinis-tic if its state at any particular time is the result of a previous state and if the value of each variable at any time is the result of a definite state of the system at a prior time (pp. 351–2). Nagel warned against three possible misunderstandings about this doctrine. Firstly, it did not imply that states

---

[2] These two doctrines were confused by Isaiah Berlin (1969) who argued that determinist beliefs denied individual responsibility. For an excellent discussion of the problem, see the essays in Lehrer (1966).

of a deterministic system were necessarily wholly predictable, although it is likely that rather accurate laws can *in principle* be formulated about them. Systems could in fact be deterministic without the fact being known or if their laws had not been discovered. Secondly, while a system may be deterministic with respect to one set of properties it may not be so to another set. Thirdly, the doctrine of universal determinism can only be asserted as a general guiding principle (pp. 352–4). As a positivist, Nagel was in general committed to the basic postulate that the universe was a determinate system, but that could not be conclusively proved or disproved.

The opposite of the doctrine of inevitability is that of radical indeterminism. Versions of this doctrine have been held by all those in the long tradition which has been opposed to the possibility of a science of social life and which includes Dray and Scriven, as we have just seen. Nagel's article contains a convincing rebuttal of the main arguments against determinism. The chief weaknesses of these arguments are, firstly, that they confuse determinism with inevitability or with the claim of accurate prediction of all future events; secondly, that they mistake 'chance' events for undetermined events; and thirdly, that they mistake the possibility of rational choice for indeterminism.

A determinist does not claim that all the conditions of events are known accurately, or that genuinely novel ideas, modes of behaviour, and so on do not arise. Emergence is not incompatible with determinism. The fact that historians are not able to explain or predict all events does not indicate that they are unable to uncover the main and perhaps crucial conditions, perhaps using, as Nagel conceded, a non-nomological method (pp. 366–7).

The argument for free will and moral responsibility can similarly be shown to be compatible with determinism since the existence of biological, psychological, and social *conditions* for action does not prevent choice and hence moral behaviour. Choice is always possible, within certain parameters, but it seems absurd to deny that there are external and internal *imperatives* as well as *limits* to individual action. In explaining acts and behaviour we need to examine their complex conditioning situations as well as the agency powers of persons. This last point is crucial because human action is intentional and humans are agents in a way that no other kind of entity is so to place all our explanatory weight upon the conditions of action (external or psychological) is to make an important mistake, as I argue at greater length in Part III.

TOWARDS A REALIST AND STRUCTURIST SOLUTION

The fundamental error of the positivist account of historical explanation was their Humean and logicist (i.e. N–D) formulation of the naturalist programme. Scientific explanation is not restricted to formulating universal laws from which deductions are made, although it is clear that the explanation of particular events and actions must use law-like generalities of a less precise kind. And the 'laws' should not be of the empiricist kind which attempt to link together only actual observed sequences of events. Rather, the 'laws' employed should be ones which state uniform connections between the types of forces, powers, and propensities that are contained *within* complex events and processes and these events and processes. In other words, they should be 'laws' about *real mechanisms* rather than about regular observable temporal connections.

Many philosophers and theorists now agree that historians cannot avoid using general statements of the mechanism type to establish the causes of each action and event. Explanation of particular events involves knowledge of the general laws of several sciences. An example which recurs in the literature is that of explaining the seizing up of a car engine. The Hempelian theory would indicate that the explanation must be subsumed under a law of engine seizures. Dray's response would be to trace, rather, a continuous series of sub-events, explaining the total process inductively using colligatory concepts. The realist argument is that the continuous series can only be constructed using prior knowledge of the physical mechanisms involved in the sub-processes and micro relationships of an engine – i.e. laws about friction, the flow of liquids, the behaviour of gases, and so on.

The implication of this criticism (and as indicated a moment ago) is that the explanation of human actions, involves the use of generalisations about behaviour and social structures as well as knowledge of conscious intentions. Now, it is often argued that precisely stated general predicates about human behaviour and social structures are not necessary to historical explanation since what is being explained are particular acts; the general predicates can thus be taken for granted, at least, and usually are. But just what it is that is being taken for granted by historians is often unclear, sometimes contradictory, and sometimes false. Historical explanations undoubtedly secrete many assumptions about human nature, the origins of human personalities, and the general social situations and imperatives of individual and average social behaviour. I believe they should be more clearly understood, more consistently held, and better articulated by historians if the work of explanation is to advance. This involves, among other things, having a theory of mental processes and powers. Some recent work in the philosophy of mind by Davidson, Putnam, Boyd, and others has shown how intentionalism and realism can be combined. This will be discussed in chapters 7 and 8. It also involves having a general theory of how individual and patterned action relates to social structure. This is discussed in chapters 8 and 9.

5

Holist and Conventionalist Philosophies of Science

In the 1950s and 1960s there was also growing disenchantment among philosophers of science with the logical-empiricist-positivist account of scientific explanation. This opposition took many forms and was directed towards several different aspects of the positivist tradition. Underlying this broad process was a feeling that explanation and the striving for progress in science may not be a matter of developing true factual knowledge in a timeless, objective, and steadily incremental manner. Rather, science should be seen as a socially relative process undertaken within certain historically limited contexts and traditions and having an extra-scientific metaphysical basis, and perhaps even being irrational at times. It was the positivistic theses of objectivism, progress, and rationality and the empiricist thesis of a theory/observation distinction that became the centres of contention.[1]

It was also widely felt that in seeing philosophy of science as the formalised reconstruction of the logic of justification of explanations, rather than an account of what it is that scientists actually do (i.e. a metascience/science distinction), the logical empiricists had lost touch with science altogether. In particular, they had lost touch with the *history of science* (see Kuhn, 1971, 1977b). Thus one of the chief influences on anti-positivism was the historical approach to science, greatly improved in the early twentieth century by the French philosopher historians Pierre Duhem, Gaston Bachelard, and Alexandre Koyre, and the British historians Herbert Butterfield and J. D. Bernal. The study of the history of science revealed to its supporters the basic idea that scientific discourse

[1] For general discussions of the reaction against positivism in the 1960s and 1970s, see Achinstein (1969), Hesse (1969), Lakatos and Musgrave (1970), Newton-Smith (1981), Shapere (1969, 1977).

and knowledge had *non-scientific presuppositions,* and that these *changed* over time.

The idea that knowledge is relative to some set of changing presuppositions or world views or conventions about meaning and/or explanation is an old one (and has nearly always been the view in the non-science discourses, especially literature, art, and history). Max Weber had held strongly to such a view, as had Collingwood. There had been an element of such thinking in the early Vienna Circle, owing partly to Wittgenstein's influence; and Karl Popper's first book of 1934 supported the theory ladenness of observation and made explicit use of a conventionalist thesis in rejecting a distinction between the context of discovery and the context of justification. Popper's ideas were a major influence on all philosophers of science in the 1960s and 1970s, especially those of an epistemological holist and conventionalist outlook. His pioneering attack upon empiricist justificationism served as a catalyst for the later anti-empiricism of Feyerabend, Kuhn, and Lakatos among others.

The later work of Ludwig Wittgenstein (1967) has also exercised considerable influence on the anti-positivists in the philosophies of natural science and the humanities in more recent times. The chief reason for this was his view of the task of philosophy: it should be descriptive, rather than analytical, of the way in which language is used in everyday contexts. In his early book – the *Tractatus* – he had attempted to chart the limits of language, but in his later work he came to believe that there were no factual essences or set of definitions of meaning to be discovered, only *usage.* To grasp meanings and understandings is to situate them in their social and linguistic contexts, i.e. within their 'language games'.

THE IMPORTANCE OF W. V. QUINE

This philosophical outlook is a kind of epistemological holism (not to be confused with ontological holism). Perhaps the most influential holist of recent times has been the American W. V. Quine, who has had a strong influence on anti-positivist thinking. He argued in his famous paper on 'Two Dogmas of Empiricism' in 1951 that the commitments by empiricists to the analytic/synthetic distinction and the possibility of a reduction of meaningful statements to empirical experiences were dogmas, and if abandoned would allow a blurring together of speculative metaphysics and science and a move towards a pragmatic approach to explanation (Quine, 1951, p. 20).

Quine has defended the holistic thesis of indeterminacy of translation: that there is no reliable way of translating meanings from one language or world view or general theory to another, and so meaning, explanation, and truth have to be seen as relative to a linguistic/theoretical whole and not above such wholes (Quine, 1960, ch. 2; 1969, ch. 2; see also

Hookway, 1978). This applies also to ontological questions about the reference of words to things in the world. When referring to entities the meaning of such references is always internally relative to some particular background theory or language and not to some *a priori* external principle, such as the Vienna Circle notion of empirical verifiability (Quine, 1969, ch. 2).

When it comes to deciding between theories constructed within different conceptual schemes it is possible in Quine's view to have a situation of under-determination – that is, of there being no factually objective way to decide between them. Because ontology is relative to conceptual schemes there is no decisive fact of the matter. But Quine did wish to emphasise the importance of empirical enquiry to our understanding of the world. Empirical enquiry takes place at the boundaries of holistic networks or structures of theory – where they meet the world – and those boundaries gradually change, so altering the conceptual structure, but not in any sudden or pervasive way (Quine, 1960, p. 4).

A corollary of this position was a radically different conception of epistemology: seeing it not as the reconstruction of first principles of all knowledge, being transcendent of particular discourses, but rather as *psychology*, being the study of particular acts or behavioural patterns of knowing.

This fundamental questioning of the nature of epistemology, associated also with the later work of Wittgenstein and to some extent with the later work of Carnap, had a profound but unfortunate effect. In Quine's words, it 'loosed a wave . . . of epistemological nihilism', reflected partly, as he says, in a tendency 'to belittle the role of evidence and to accentuate cultural relativism' (p. 87).

With this background, then, there began in the 1950s, with the work of writers such as Michael Polanyi, Stephen Toulmin, and N. R. Hanson, a strong current in the philosophy of science directed to closing the gap between the socio-psychological context of science and its logic of justification.

PAUL FEYERABEND: THE ARGUMENT
FOR THEORETICAL PROLIFERATION

Perhaps the most radical opponent of dogmatic objectivism has been the Austrian-American Paul Feyerabend. His early work in the late 1950s and early 1960s was influenced by Popper, by T. S. Kuhn's historical work, and by the defences of holism of Quine and David Bohm (see Bohm, 1980). In a series of articles at that time he defended the importance to empirical explanation of a *proliferation* of *inconsistent* theories rather than the elimination of rivals. What is needed, he believes, is a conception of science which not only does justice to its true history but enables the development, through the rejection of alien methodologies, of a democratic and liberal practice of empirical enquiry (see Feyerabend, 1963).

Feyerabend epitomises the refusal by many thinkers in this anti-positivist tradition to separate the *philosophical* task of logical reconstruction from the task of uncovering, and appropriating for present purposes, the *history* of actual scientific practice and its relationship to socially specific needs, expectations, and ways of understanding. He does not wish to reject science *in toto*, as some critics believe, but to *rescue* it from some of its philosophers and from manipulative politicians.

Empiricist methodology was dogmatic and authoritarian, he rightly pointed out, and moreover it was these very features which prevented it from achieving its self-proclaimed goal of objective empirical enquiry. It asserted two conditions which new theories must meet – *consistency* with existing theories, and *meaning invariance* of terms (Feyerabend, 1963, pp. 16–18). But Feyerabend believed the history of science showed that it did not observe these conditions and that, furthermore, these conditions are unreasonable in that they prevent a full explanation of the facts they wish to explain. This is because empiricism rests on the false dogma of the relative autonomy of facts, whereas in reality all facts are theory dependent and can only be discovered and explained through some theory. Different facts often require different theories to explain them; therefore the empirical content of science and empirical tests requires a set of overlapping but inconsistent theories (pp. 20–30).

Thus any success a theory may have in eliminating rivals, and therefore more successfully passing tests, is illusory and entirely artificial. Agreement with the facts is then only the result of absolute conformism to the two conditions and the neglect of any refuting evidence. These all-embracing principles become a metaphysical system which is not open to rational criticism. Any such method of uniformity, he said, is a 'method of deception' because it enforces an 'unenlightened conformism' that destroys the power of imagination (p. 33). It is imagination that Feyerabend wishes to restore to a central place.

THE RELATIVISM OF T. S. KUHN

Paradigms and revolutions

Unlike Feyerbend, Kuhn has *defended* a conception of science which emphasises the importance to the day-to-day activities of scientists of *closed*, narrow, conservative, holistic frameworks. For him, as for Hanson, conceptual wholes are essential to meaning and explanation. In his book of 1962, *The Structure of Scientific Revolutions*, he built upon the work of earlier holistic thinkers and went far beyond them in presenting a full-blown historicalisation of the problems of philosophy of science (Kuhn, 1970c). Perhaps no other book this century in the philosophy of explanation has had the same impact, perhaps because it seemed to state in a clear and eloquent way the intuitively held cultural belief of many non-philosophers in the 1960s that all explanation is radically relative.

In his book Kuhn labelled the conceptual complex in which normal scientific research and explanation occurs as a 'paradigm'. This is a set of rules, standards, and examples of scientific practice which is shared by a coherent group of scientists, the commitment to which and consensus produced by it being *prerequisites* to the genesis and continuation of a research tradition. Acquisition of such a paradigm, he believed, was a mark of maturity of a science (pp. 10–11). The transition from a pre-paradigm to a paradigm stage is marked by a disappearance of divergences in selection, interpretation, and evaluation of facts; one of the pre-paradigm schools triumphs because of its power in solving problems which have been recognised by a group as acute (pp. 16–17, 23–4).

Normal science, in which the bulk of practitioners are engaged for most of the time, consists of work aimed at actualising the claims of the paradigm, and further articulating it. That enterprise, said Kuhn,

> seems an attempt to force nature into the preformed and relatively inflexible box that the paradigm supplies. No part of the aim of normal science is to call forth new sorts of phenomena; indeed those that will not fit the box are often not seen at all. Nor do scientists normally aim to invent new theories, and they are often intolerant of those invented by others. Instead, normal-scientific research is directed to the articulation of those phenomena and theories that the paradigm already supplies. (Kuhn, 1970c, p. 24)

In his conception, normal science is puzzle solving: it aims to solve puzzles thrown up by the paradigm and for which the paradigm is assumed to have solutions. This accounts for the enthusiasm and devotion of most scientists (pp. 36–7). Puzzles have rules and a limited number of possible solutions. The paradigm rules of normal science include such things as explicit statements about laws, concepts, and theory; commitments to types of instruments and techniques; high-level quasi-metaphysical commitments of method and ontology; and value commitments to the importance of scientific understanding (pp. 40–42). Moreover, like Wittgenstein and Polanyi, Kuhn believed that rules and commitments remain at a subconscious, tacit, intuitive level, and are passed on in a 'cultural' manner through exposure rather than in an explicitly pedagogical way (p. 46).

Normal science unintentionally produces many anomalies because the narrow range of its vision and the great attention to precision of prediction and technique make many results seem anomalous relative to expectations. At the same time these factors and the very success of the paradigm produce great resistance to change (pp. 64–5). A persistent failure to solve puzzles causes great anxiety and eventually results in a search for new rules and theories. A crisis sets in, which can be resolved, in Kuhn's view, by the emergence of a new paradigm; but the old one is never renounced until a new one is available. The mere recognition of anomalies is not enough to cause renunciation, since to reject a paradigm without an alternative is to reject science altogether (pp. 77–9).

In achieving such a switch the most fundamental assumptions of a philosophical and theoretical kind have to be re-examined. The new paradigm represents a fundamental break with the past and its adoption and justification is a matter of a holistic and hermeneutical process of reasoning. 'Like the choice between competing political institutions', wrote Kuhn, 'that between competing paradigms proves to be a choice between incompatible modes of community life' (p. 94)

Paradigms are therefore not only incommensurable with each other, in Kuhn's account, but they constitute the scientific process: they provide the scientist not only with a map of nature but with some of the directions for map-making. The choice between paradigms cannot be resolved by the normal scientific meanings of logic and observation but have to be resolved by recourse to extra-scientific arguments about values and commitments (pp. 109–10). Furthermore, the corollary of this is that paradigms are *constitutive of nature itself* in that, as Hanson, Quine, and others have also argued, what is observed and believed to exist depends, as in a *Gestalt*, partly upon previous visual-conceptual experience (p. 113). Thus scientific revolutions, in this hermeneutical account, are changes of world view which cannot be accounted for by the empiricist-positivist understanding of science which gives priority to factual observation. The entire tradition of observation-based epistemology will have to be discarded, in Kuhn's opinion, in the face of strong psychological and historical evidence that perception is a function of pre-existing understandings rather than sense data (pp. 126–7).

How, then, are scientists persuaded to switch allegiance from their old paradigm, which may be in crisis, to another world view if they are denied the independence of observation criteria? In Kuhn's account, empirical testing is insufficient because there are problems of incommensurability between the general outlooks. Communication between them is only partial. In the beginning there has to be a *conversion*, a step which many scientists refuse to take. Conversion is helped by claims about better problem-solving ability and the aesthetic appeal of a new paradigm, but in the last analysis, and especially at the outset of a paradigm change, *faith* must be had, which may not at first be rationally based (pp. 151–8).

As Kuhn was obviously aware, this account of scientific change throws into doubt the whole orthodox account, including its notion of progress.

Progress would seem to be, to begin with, relative only to periods of normal science. In those times puzzles are solved efficiently, but after revolutions previous solutions are sometimes reassessed. However, he does believe that much of what was achieved before is preserved. Progress in puzzle solving is often improved, but this is not progress towards a more truthful account of nature; rather it is progress only towards what we wish to know. The history of science is therefore conceived as an evolutionary process without either a goal or direction. The question of why some sciences are more advanced than others in achieving paradigm status was left unanswered by him, as was that of the possibility of a more concrete criterion of progress, such as success in manipulating nature for the purpose of engineering. The importance of discovery was downgraded in his account.[2]

Kuhn compared with empiricists and Popper

Positivists have always placed great emphasis upon distinguishing the context of *justification* of a theory and explanation from the context of developing the theory and discovering facts about the world. That is, there is a fundamental difference between reconstructing the ideal logical structure of scientific inference and the psychological and social context in which scientists operate and think: in short, a logical/historical distinction (Feigl, 1974). Kuhn's theory attacks this head-on, since his particular reconstruction of scientific inference is not idealised and formalised but is descriptive of how scientists actually operate and how they arrive at and test paradigms and theories. His is in fact a psycho-sociological account of science, part of which consists in arguing that the rules governing the way scientists think remain tacit rather than in the explicit form of the correspondence rules formalised in the orthodox logical conception of theories.

Even more fundamental to empiricists is the theory/observation distinction. This too is completely rejected by Kuhn and by all holists and conventionalists. While the later empiricists had moved a long way from phenomenalism and most had rejected physicalist reductionism, they did wish to defend a distinction between (in Feigl's words) theories and empirical laws. Although laws were not incorrigible they do form, Feigl believed, a relatively stable testing ground for theories, a ground which in some cases has survived for centuries (Feigl, 1974, pp. 8–9).

Popper's philosophy has important elements in common with the empiricists as well as with Kuhn (see Popper, 1970; and Kuhn, 1970a, 1970b). But on some fundamental questions they are diametrically opposed since Popper wishes, like the empiricists, to distinguish between

---

[2] In later writings Kuhn has considerably modified his position in response to criticisms. See Kuhn (1974, 1977a, 1977c).

theories and conventional 'basic statements' about the nature of the world; to defend a notion of objective progress towards truth about nature, even if it is never reached; and to defend a rational as well as empirical basis for scientific advance. Although he held that scientific enquiry is always conducted within a pre-existing organised structure of assumptions and theories, which constitute a problem situation – i.e. a research programme – he believed that Kuhn had overstated the role of paradigms so that he had become a victim of the 'myth of the framework', i.e. of relativism. Popper's central point is that a critical discussion and comparison of frameworks is always possible. He wrote:

> It is just a dogma – a dangerous dogma – that the different frameworks are like mutually untranslatable languages. The fact is that even totally different languages . . . are not untranslatable . . . .
> The Myth of the Framework is, in our time, the central bulwark of irrationalism. My counter thesis is that it simply exaggerates a difficulty into an impossibility. (Popper, 1970, pp. 56–7)

Science does *advance*, he believed, partly through a continuing critical discussion of theories, frameworks, and former views, so that change is constant, rather than in bursts. Kuhn's position was that the normal activity of scientists was puzzle solving, not theory or framework testing, and so Popper had in effect expanded the revolutionary science episodes into the whole picture. 'Frameworks must be lived with and explored before they can be broken', wrote Kuhn. However, he continued,

> that does not imply that scientists ought not aim at perpetual framework-breaking, however unobtainable that goal. 'Revolutions in permanence' could name an important ideological imperative. If Sir Karl and I disagree at all about normal science, it is over this point. He and his group argue that the scientist should try at all times to be a critic and a proliferator of alternate theories. I urge the desirability of an alternate strategy which reserves such behaviour for special occasions. (Kuhn, 1970b, pp. 242–3)

THE CONVENTIONALISM OF IMRE LAKATOS

Lakatos's important contribution to the philosophy of science has been to defend and to extend significantly Popper's ideas on theory change and demarcation through developing the influential notions of 'research programme' and 'rational reconstruction'. Against Kuhn and Feyerabend he has defended a conception of science as rational and progressive. As I showed in chapter 2, he is important not only for this particular arguments but for the way in which he approached the problem of *meta-*

philosophy of explanation. Surely the task of philosophy is not restricted to understanding the structures of empirical explanation. It must also attempt to compare, criticise, and transcend the ways in which those explanations have been *appraised*, i.e. philosophies and methodologies.

Thus for Lakatos an explanation is *scientific* if it is part of a *progressive* series of theories in empirical terms. Corroborated excess information is the crucial criterion, not confirming instances (as with empiricism) or refuting instances (as with falsificationism). Proliferation of theories is therefore important since only through the development of better theories can existing ones be rejected. (This accords closely with Feyerabend's view, but for different reasons.) Empirical testing remains, for Popperians (including Lakatos), the final arbiter but such testing always takes place against a set of rational decisions about what aspects of background knowledge to hold firm.

The continuity inherent in a progressive series of scientific theories arises in Lakatos's view from the research programme which is outlines at the beginning. The programme is a set of methodological rules about what to avoid in research (the negative heuristic) and what paths to pursue (the positive heuristic). Such rules could be considered as metaphysical principles (p. 132).

The negative heuristic concerns the 'hard core' of a programme – the area which is not subjected to tests or readjusted in the light of tests on hypotheses. It consists of the conventionally agreed upon background knowledge and accepted basic laws (p. 133). The positive heuristic concerns the new hypotheses which are derived from or based upon the hard core and which protect the core from refutation. It contains suggestions on how to develop the refutable variants of the research programme; and although there are always many unexplained anomalies produced, these are ignored. The scientist concentrates on building ever more complicated models of reality, following the instructions of the positive heuristic, and adopting some *ad hoc* strategies, virtually ignoring the data, in Lakatos's account (pp. 135–7).

Lakatos's research programmes are similar to Kuhn's periods of normal science, but the big difference is that Lakatos, like Popper and Feyerabend, advocates pluralism and competition. Science has not been, and should not be, characterised by periods of theoretical monism, with the attendant risk that research programmes become arbitrating world views. This again raises the central question of how programmes are eliminated and replaced. Can there be any objective reason for such elimination, given that anomalies are supposedly often ignored and that even a degenerative programme can be saved by creative innovation? His answer was that such a reason is provided by a rival programme 'which explains the previous success of its rival and supersedes it by a further display of *heuristic power*' (p. 155). This power in turn depends upon how factual novelty is understood and assessed since the ability of a programme to produce new facts may take a long time to become apparent, even if it is able to explain all the existing ones. Therefore a new programme should be sheltered from a powerful rival for a time, until it can be reconstructed as a progressive problem shift. There must be tolerance. But in the end a choice is *gradually* made and this depends upon *crucial experiments*, which are agreed to be genuine tests of the relative strengths of the two programmes. Even then, the seemingly defeated theory may be amended and make a comeback. But if no comeback is made then, with hindsight, it can be seen that the battle is lost and the theory is abandoned (not disproved), in the sense of a decision to cease working on it. Thus no one experiment is really crucial and only time will tell the fate of a defeated programme, which can always produce a new progressive version of its old theories (pp. 154–8).

FEYERABEND'S EPISTEMOLOGICAL ANARCHISM

For empiricists, Popperians, and Lakatosians, *rationality* is the watch-word both for science and for its philosophical methodologies, whether the basis of rationality is seen as the autonomy of facts, or conventions, or progressive research programmes. Theories are adopted or discarded for good, conscious reasons. For Feyerabend, on the other hand (and to a lesser extent for Thomas Kuhn), science is no more rational or pro-gressive than other systems of thought. Like witchcraft, magic, Aristotelian science, and so on, modern science is held to be simply one system of thought which has grown out of a particular world view and has no more validity than any other. But of course it does not recognise this! Feyerabend believes this is because it has become massively dogmatic. Its self-image, and the one shared by most of its historians and philosophers, is that of superiority to non-science – a superiority provided by its supposedly rational and universal methodological foundations. He objects to this basic idea on both historical and normative grounds. For him, science has not been and should not be run according to fixed and universal rules. In *Against Method* (1975a) he advocates, instead, radical methodological libertarianism and epistemological anarchism. Without this science becomes supposedly less adaptable and more dogmatic.

Clearly, Feyerabend's ideas are potentially revolutionary in their implications. Not only has he argued, as many others have done, for the rejection of the theory/observation distinction, but his irrationalist and anti-methodological views mean that there is no place in his account for either a methodological/historical distinction or a descriptive/prescriptive distinction. If universal methodological rules and standards are used to evaluate and criticise contexts of actual discovery then, he believes, science itself would be wiped out. For science has survived and prospered only because the psychological and social conditions of discovery have sometimes been at variance with the prevailing rules. Only because certain scientists have supposedly not followed rational procedures have they made certain basic discoveries. Others, of course, have chosen methodological rules to evaluate theories. For Feyerabend, the contexts of discovery and justification are not distinct, as positivists believe, but constitute one domain of procedures which are all open to the scientist to exploit.

THE STRONG PROGRAMME IN THE SOCIOLOGY OF KNOWLEDGE

In the anthropological and conventionalist spirit of Feyerabend, Kuhn, Hanson, and others, some recent sociologists of science, notably Barry Barnes (1974, 1977, 1981) and David Bloor (1976, 1981; and Barnes and Bloor, 1982) have attempted to construct a sociology of scientific knowledge which denies and replaces the possibility of critical philosophy establishing non-arbitrary rational standards for theory appraisal. Perception, belief, and reason are all culture bound, they say, and this applies to scientific knowledge as much as to witchcraft. Therefore, only a 'scientific' programme of enquiry into the *social origins* of science is warranted. Barnes wrote (1974, p. 154) that they are sceptical about philosophy because they believe all ontologies and epistemologies are equally lacking in arguments for their validity and that no set of beliefs is any more objective than another in terms of its proximity to reality or its rationality. Their work constitutes perhaps the most serious threat to the whole programme of critical philosophy.[3]

In David Bloor's formulation of the strong programme in the sociology of knowledge he outlined the scientific approach to the study of scientific knowledge as consisting of the following four tenets:

1 It would be causal, that is, concerned with the conditions which bring about beliefs or states of knowledge . . . .
2 It would be impartial with respect to truth and falsity, rationality or irrationality, sucess or failure . . . .
3 It would be symmetrical in its style of explanation. The same types of cause would explain, say, true and false beliefs.
4 It would be reflexive. In principle its patterns of explanation would have to be applicable to sociology itself . . . . (Bloor, 1976, pp. 4–5)

Like earlier anti-empiricists, Bloor and Barnes stressed the conventional and socially relative nature of all perception. Even science demands that experience be admissible only if it is repeatable, public, and

[3] For criticisms and discussions of the strong programme in the sociology of knowledge, see Harré (1983b, Postscript), articles in Hollis and Lukes (1982), Laudan (1981b).

impersonal; other activities and forms of knowledge stress other kinds of experience – perhaps inward and individual (p. 26). In Bloor's argument, knowledge (i.e. collectively enclosed beliefs) is a result of the impingement of experience upon a set of prior beliefs, bringing about a change in those beliefs. The result is a new combination of beliefs. Thus

> processes such as education and training must be invoked to explain the enplanting and distribution of the states of prior belief. They are absolutely necessary if experience is to have a determinant effect. These processes are also necessary for an understanding of how the resultant beliefs are sustained and to account for the patterns of relevance that connect experiences to some beliefs rather than others. Although this view incorporates some of the insights of empiricism it entails that no belief falls outside the sociologist's purview. There is a social component of all knowledge. (Bloor, 1976, p. 28)

What place is there then for the critical philosophical notions of truth and correspondence? 'Truth' usually refers to a belief that corresponds correctly to some external reality in the world. But Bloor believed such correspondence was at best vague and, furthermore, that science operates rather with an *internal* notion of correspondence: judging a theory is a matter of coherence and consistency (p. 32). Theories are instrumental in manipulating objects to produce interactions and results. Errors crop up not in external correspondence but within the terms of theories, purposes, interests, problems, and standards. 'There are as many forms of correspondence as there are requirements' (p. 34).

One of the fundamental problems with Bloor's strictures upon critical philosophy is the old one of straw man construction. While it may be possible to demolish such a conception of philosophy, philosophy is not restricted to such a socially relative, non-reflexive mould. Critical philosophy, like sociology, can also be reflexive and non-dogmatic. Furthermore, a realist conception of theories can replace the functionalist and pragmatic idea that truth is relative to social conventions and groups and what seems to work for them, with the idea that successful engineering in open systems reveals something truly *natural* about the world, which in fact transcends particular ways of knowing. This is not to say that there can be a simple correspondence between a fixed uni-dimensional reality and true knowledge of it. Reality is very complicated and our theories hook on to it in various ways and to various degrees and with various effects upon it. But the idea of a material reality is a powerful regulative principle, as Bloor also argued, and in the end there is not much of a gap between the strong causal programme of the sociologist and the critical programme of the realist philosopher, who sees philosophy as empirical and scientific as well as critical. Causation is not restricted to a sociological approach to beliefs. Beliefs can be caused by reasons as well as social and psychological imperatives, and the articulation and *criticism* of reasons are two of the tasks of philosophy.

THE RATIONALITY OF PROBLEM SOLVING
WITHIN RESEARCH TRADITIONS

The old problem of the interrelationship of the history and philosophy of science is central to the whole discussion about good and bad explanation. Is good explanation that which has been deemed to be so by scientists, or are there extra-scientific normative standards to which they should try to conform and which can be used to judge their methods and results? Is explanation rational and progressive only if it meets certain *a priori* standards, or have there been historically specific canons which cannot be generalised? The recent work of Larry Laudan (especially 1977a, 1981b, 1982) has built upon the earlier writings of philosophers such as Carnap, Hempel, Popper, Kuhn, and Lakatos, and gone a significant distance beyond them in suggesting solutions to these problems. He believes that one way of doing justice both to the variety and complexity of explanations and their historical vicissitudes and to changing notions of rationality is to adopt a *comparative problem-solving* criterion of appraisal of theories. That is, theories must be judged in relation to whether they constitute 'adequate solutions to significant problems' and not to whether they are 'true', 'corroborated', 'well confirmed', and so on. He is agnostic about these realist notions, preferring to adopt a pragmatic attitude to appraisal (Laudan, 1977a, p. 14).[4]

In general, then, theories are evaluated by a combination of their empirical and conceptual problem-solving abilities relative to unresolved and newly generated problems, in a context or domain of rival theories. This allows Laudan to say that progress occurs 'if and only if the succession of scientific theories in any domain shows an increasing degree of problem-solving effectiveness' (p. 68). Because of the important element of *conceptual* problems it is thus possible for progress to occur without an accumulation of solved empirical problems and, conversely, for regression to occur even when there has been such an accumulation (p. 69). This clearly runs counter to a great deal of earlier philosophy of science, including those anti-empiricists (such as Popper and Lakatos) who wish to retain an important cumulative-empirical component in conceptions of progress. Laudan believes that the link between accumulation and progress must be broken; there must be some form of

---

[4] For discussions of Laudan's ideas, see Doppelt (1981), Feyerabend (1981b), McMullin (1979).

cost–benefit analysis to set off gains against losses (Laudan, 1981b, p. 149).

The *comparative* aspect of his account of theory appraisal is equally important. In order to make meaningful comparisons of theories it is essential to see them in their context of a *research tradition*. This is a set of guidelines for the development of specific theories. It contains an ontology of fundamental entities and their interactions, and a methodology for enquiry into them (Laudan, 1977a, pp. 79–81). Every intellectual discipline contains them – for example, Darwinism, quantum theory, behaviourism, Freudianism, Marxism, and so on. Each contains a number of specific explanatory theories, contemporaneously and in temporal succession, many of which will conflict. These theories will usually be empirically testable and comparable. But research traditions, because of their generality and their normative elements, are not explanatory, or predictive, or directly testable. They do not entail theories but they do set the domain of empirical and conceptual problems in which their theories operate, and so play a heuristic role in the construction of specific theories and a role in justifying assumptions, questions, and theories as admissible (pp. 81–93).

If research traditions are not directly empirically testable, how are they to be appraised? This is obviously the crucial question for all conventionalist accounts of knowledge. Laudan's view is that there are two criteria for evaluating traditions. Firstly, of course there is the *adequacy at problem solving* of their constituent theories. And secondly, there is the *progressiveness* of a research tradition in its problem-solving ability. Progressiveness is measured both in terms of the *relative* problem-solving adequacy of the latest compared with the earlier set of theories, and in terms of the *rate* of problem-solving progress over a set period. These may diverge sharply: that is, the general overall progress of a tradition may differ from the recent rate of progress (pp. 106–8).

The main value of Laudan's account of scientific change lies in his specification of the importance, but flexibility, of research traditions. Any adequate account of the structure of reasoning in science must give a central place, as for example Lakatos (1970), Shapere (1974d), and Harré (1976, 1980a, 1982b) have also done, to the background context of theory construction. This will be discussed in more detail in chapter 7.

The weakness of Laudan's account is his concentration on problem solving, to the neglect of *engineering* in experimental and open situations, as the sole criterion of progress. The simulation, discovery, and manipulation of *real mechanisms* is the fundamental test of progress. Laudan was opposed to the idea that science is progressively *truthful* (Laudan, 1981a), but this was a mistake because only a convergence theory of truth can do justice to the actual situation in the sciences, or so I shall argue in chapter 7.

6

Currents of Hermeneutics in the Humanities

THE HERMENEUTICAL TRADITION

Part II has so far concentrated on the debate over empiricist positivism within the analytical tradition. This tradition is based on the view that it is the task of philosophy to clarify and criticise the structure and logic of causal explanation in existing empirical discourses, such as physics and history. Epistemology is therefore seen as the fundamental role of philosophy. While various general solutions to the epistemological problem of the social sciences have been offered from within this tradition – such as the empiricist, the conventionalist, and the realist – there is no agreement about the relationship of scientific method to the study of man and society. The anti-determinists, such as Dray, however, adopt the view that while there is an external knowable realm of human history to be empirically investigated, only an interpretive method that uses human expressions as evidence of the subjective causal motivations of action can be adopted, since history is a product of free individual agents.

The chief philosophical defenders of an interpretive approach have come from an alternative tradition in European philosophy. This broad but disparate phenomenological and hermeneutical tradition is united at least on one question: it rejects any possibility of a unification (on empiricist or realist grounds) of natural science and the study of action, history, and society. It sees the task of philosophy not as the arbiter of true empirical causal knowledge but as the actual practice of *interpreting meaning* in social life. It rejects the epistemological problems of the relationship of knower and external social object and of the possible empirical causal connections between given social objects. Philosophy and social life are not divorced.[1]

The hermeneutical tradition's insistence on a radical distinction between natural science and the humanities has very long roots – often traced to Aristotle – but in modern times *The New Science* (1723) of Vico is looked to as a major turning point. His book was based upon a distinction between the separate origins of nature and society. The former was made by God and ultimately knowable only by Him, whereas the latter was the product of people, who were consequently internal to history. Therefore, he believed, humans could come to know history through examining the modifications of the human mind, and so human science was potentially superior to natural science as a form of knowledge since it was an enquiry by a mind into the creations of the human mind in general. But he also drew a distinction between true and certain knowledge:

> Men who do not know what is true of things take care to hold fast to what is certain, so that, if they cannot satisfy their intellects by knowledge (*scienza*) their wills at least may rest on consciousness (*coscienza*).
>
> Philosophy contemplates reason, whence comes knowledge of the true; philology observes that of which human choice is author, whence comes consciousness of the certain. (Vico, 1970, p. 21)

In other words, the distinction was between scientific knowledge (truth) and personal, common-sense knowledge (conscious certainty). As he wrote elsewhere in his book, philosophical or scientific enquiry was into the universal and eternal principles of the general structures of all societies (and nature), whereas philology (or history) studied the particular, and could not alone reveal truth, only certainty. Both depended on each other for the understanding of societies.

Since Vico's time the tradition has been enriched and defended from the various viewpoints of romanticism (e.g. Herder), early hermeneutics (e.g. Schliermacher, Droysen, and Dilthey), neo-Kantianism (e.g. Windelband and Rickert), phenomenology (e.g. Husserl and Heidegger), speculative philosophy of history (e.g. Croce and Collingwood), sociology (e.g. Weber, Mead, and Schutz), psychology (e.g. Freud and Ricoeur), and the philosophy of language (e.g. the later Wittgenstein). In recent decades the tradition has become more widely discussed and adopted than hitherto in places away from its original homeland in

---

[1] See the following for general discussions of hermeneutics: Bauman (1978), Bernstein (1976, 1983), Bleicher (1980, 1982), Gadamer (1975a, 1975b, 1976, 1977, 1981), Outhwaite (1975), R. E. Palmer (1969), Ricoeur (1978, 1981), C. Taylor (1971, 1980, 1981, 1983), J. B. Thompson (1981).

Germany. It now has defenders in all the branches of the human studies, including literature, psychology, sociology, anthropology, linguistics, and history.

In what can be taken to be a recent manifesto of the interpretive approach to society, Rabinow and Sullivan (1979) have reemphasised the view that the failure to establish a naturalistic science of society is a result of the (supposedly) non-objective existence of society itself. They believe, therefore, that any attempt – empiricist, holist, or structuralist – that seeks to organise and explain human phenomena in terms of relations among elements in a formalistic method is doomed to failure. Such approaches leave unresolved, they claim, the problem of the concrete, practical, human and social subject. On the other hand, the interpretive approach

> refocuses attention on the concrete varieties of cultural meaning, in their particularity and complex texture, but without falling into the traps of historicism or cultural relativism in their classical forms. For the human sciences both the object of investigation – the web of language, symbol, and institutions that constitutes significance – and the tools by which investigation is carried out share inescapably the same pervasive context that is the human world. . . . The interpretive approach emphatically refutes the claim that one can somehow reduce the complex world of signification to the products of a self-consciousness in the traditional philosophical sense. Rather, interpretation begins from the postulate that the web of meaning constitutes human existence to such an extent that it cannot ever be meaningfully reduced to constitutively prior speech acts, dyadic relations, or any predefined elements. Intentionality and empathy are rather seen as dependent on the prior existence of the shared world of meaning within which the subjects of human discourse constitute themselves. It is in this literal sense that interpretive social science can be called a return to the objective world, seeing that world as in the first instance the circle of meaning within which we find ourselves and which we can never fully surpass. (Rabinow and Sullivan, 1979, pp. 4–5)

This statement would seem to indicate that hermeneutics is not directly concerned with uncovering the *causes* of human actions or the *origins* of real relational structures but rather concentrates on significance and meaning. Thus, viewed cursorily, it may be thought that the scientific and hermeneutical approaches to society are not necessarily incompatible. However, the hermeneuticists do also claim that theirs is the only viable approach to social understanding since there cannot be an objective scientific study of the human world. This position usually depends crucially on two arguments: (1) that meaningful and intentionally motivated actions (which are distinguished from mere behaviour) are the only objects of enquiry for the human studies, and (2) that 'objective science' necessarily has a positivist methodology, and so it only studies regular causal empirical correlations. Since action is supposedly not caused in this sense it cannot be studied scientifically. (However, in more recent years a quasi-hermeneutical conception of natural scientific explanation has also been developed by Hanson, Kuhn, Feyerabend, and Hesse from the analytical tradition, as we have seen, and also by Gadamer, Habermas, and Apel from the hermeneutical tradition.)

GADAMER'S AND TAYLOR'S DEFENCES OF HERMENEUTICS

No person has done more to trace the lineage of this position and to articulate its modern meaning and significance than the German philosopher Hans-Georg Gadamer. To him the philosophy of the human sciences is not a matter of epistemological elucidation. Rather, the human sciences are a problem *of* philosophy. They are not juxtaposed to it, imperfect realisations of a model science, but contain their own autonomous mode of knowing. Part of that mode of knowing involves having a historical consciousness; i.e. a 'full awareness of the historicity of everything present and the relativity of all opinions' (Gadamer, 1979, p. 110). The Humean tradition, he believed, was unable to grasp historicity, to understand phenomena as unique:

> Historical consciousness is interested in knowing, not how men, people or states develop *in general*, but, quite on the contrary, how *this* man, *this* people, or *this* state became what it is; how each of these particulars could come to pass and end up specifically *there*.
> (Gadamer, 1979, p. 116)

Because historical knowledge has all the characteristics of a historical event itself it cannot be objective.

> Understanding must be comprehended in the sense of an existential act, and is therefore a *'thrown pro-ject'*. Objectivism is an illusion. Even as historians, that is, as representatives of a modern and methodic science, we are members of an unbroken chain through which the past addresses us. . . . Ethical consciousnes is at the same time ethical know-how and ethical being. It is this integration of practical knowledge into the substance of morality, the 'belongingness' of 'education' or 'culture' (in the etymological sense) to ethical consciousness and the concrete knowledge of obligations and ends, that will provide us with the model to analyse the ontological implications of historical consciousness. (pp. 145–6)

The structure of this understanding had to be, for Gadamer, that of the hermeneutical circle: 'the circular relation between the whole and its parts: the anticipated meaning of a whole is understood through the parts, but it is in the light of the whole that the parts take on their illuminating function' (p. 146). In the act of interpretation of a text (or text analogue) the whole formed by the subjectivity of the author is the starting place, and that whole can be understood only by a person who shares the common tradition of the author and who is thus able to mediate between the text and its implications. A circle is then formed between the text and the interpreter who understands it. This understanding takes the form of a 'perfect coherence' which is anticipated by the interpreter and guides the understanding. There can be, then, a unity of immanent meaning between text and understander which is guided by an expectation that the text transmits the *truth* (p. 154). Thus, according to Gadamer, this shows that

> the primordial significance of the idea of understanding is that of 'knowing about something' and that only in a derivative sense does it mean understanding the intentions of another as personal opinions. Thus we come back to the original conditions of every hermeneutics: it must be a shared and comprehensible reference to the 'things in themselves'. It is this condition which determines the possibility that a unified meaning can be aimed at, and thus also the possibility that the anticipation of perfect coherence may actually be applicable. (p. 155)

The possibility of the interpreter understanding things in themselves does depend both upon his having an affinity for them through the shared tradition and upon their being puzzling or 'foreign' in some sense and so requiring interpretation. Therefore hermeneutics is claimed to mediate between a foreign text which nevertheless 'calls out' to the reader, and the goal of a perfect coherence of understanding. Being in the middle, it must be able to distinguish false prejudices from the true prejudices which, being embedded in a tradition, illuminate the 'text' (p. 156). But objectivist history is impossible, in Gadamer's view, because it forgets the historicity of its own position and seeks a non-historical truth outside itself; it postulates a thing in itself, just as hermeneutics does, but then idealises this thing as objective (p. 159).

This surely is the crux of the matter – the *nature of existence* of the thing being examined and hence of how we can have knowledge of it. For the empiricist positivist it is the empirical regularity of recurrent correlations existing between the elements of the phenomenal world. For the hermeneuticists it is the individual human subject acting within a tradition of shared meanings and projecting meaning upon the world. Neither view is able to reconcile itself to the other since they do not share criteria for judgement of the truth of a claim to have made a correct explanation or interpretation of a puzzling situation or problem.

Charles Taylor has argued that the empiricist-positivist approach is sterile because human behaviours and situations do have meanings for persons; those behaviours and situations cannot be characterised and understood apart from those meanings, which in turn are expressed in a language of mutual action and communication. And since human behaviour, in his view, must be seen as 'action done out of a background of desire, feeling, emotion', then 'we are looking at a reality which must be characterised in terms of meaning.' A coherence between the action and its meaning for the actor must be found by the observer in order to make sense of the action. This process is circular:

> Our conviction that the account makes sense is contingent on our reading of action and situation. But these readings cannot be explained or justified except by reference to other such readings, and their relation to the whole. If an interlocutor does not understand this kind of reading, or will not accept it as valid, there is nowhere else the argument can go. Ultimately, a good explanation is one which makes sense of the behaviour, but then to appreciate a good explanation, one has to agree on what makes good sense; what makes good sense is a function of one's readings; and these in turn are based on the kind of sense one understands.
> (C. Taylor, 1971, pp. 35–6)

The empiricist alternative is based on the necessity to verify explanations by reference to empirical data. Social reality is thus empirically identified, and human beliefs, meanings, and so on supposedly have an effect upon that reality and hence can be known empirically through their effects. Thus, although empiricism does allow the investigator to make use of subjective motivations as well as dispositions (and so meanings can be part of an empiricist social science), the problem, from the point of view of Taylor's hermeneutics, is that it cannot allow for intersubjective meanings, only for intersubjective *data* (pp. 42–3). He believes that intersubjective meanings (i.e. 'ways of experiencing action in society which are expressed in the language and descriptions constitutive of institutions and practices': p. 50) cannot be identified or understood empirically but can only be grasped by one who *shares* them through participation in a community of language and meaning which is constituted by those meanings. 'We are aware of the world through a "we" before we are through an "I"', wrote Taylor, 'hence we need the distinction between what is just shared in the sense that each of us has it in our individual worlds, and that which is in the common world.' (p. 53) This distinction, as he points out, is alien to empiricism.

A hermeneutical social enquiry, then, cannot rely upon empirical data, since for it social reality is constituted by intersubjective meanings, which have to be *understood* by the investigator who attempts to make sense of institutions, practices, and actions in a circular, self-reinforcing, interpretive manner. This interpretation is aided by insight, of course, and is open to errors and the illusions produced by a failure to understand consequent upon prior false understandings (pp. 66–8). Naturally it follows that such an enquiry cannot be value free or ideology free and is not open to objective verification or able to make predictions. Predictions are ruled out because, as Taylor concludes, human systems cannot be closed; exact measurement is impossible; and, most importantly, man is not a fixed entity but redefines himself in such a way that he changes himself and his conceptual systems, so making commensurability impossible (p. 69). The social enquirer has to rely upon 'clairvoyance' (as he later put it) for insight into the meanings of conceptual and belief systems (C. Taylor, 1983, p. 85).

ORDINARY-LANGUAGE PHILOSOPHY

For hermeneuticists and phenomenologists the sharing of linguistic meanings is crucial, although such meanings should not be confused with intersubjective cultural meanings. The language community is constitutive of, and the medium of, culture as well as the means of interpreting and understanding culture and action. The analytical philosophical tradition, stemming from the late nineteenth century and embracing the logical empiricists, saw it as a prime task to clarify linguistic meanings, in an *a priori* fashion, in order to aid the precision of empirical enquiry. Growing out of this, partly as a development and partly as a reaction, was the later work of Wittgenstein and those influenced by it, including the ordinary-language philosophers Gilbert Ryle, John Austin, and Peter Winch. These thinkers refused to draw a distinction between the world and language. While philosophy for them was rightly concerned with reality in general, that reality could not be known *a priori* or inductively or independently of linguistic meaning. In Winch's words:

> To ask whether reality is intelligible is to ask about the relation between thought and reality. In considering the nature of thought one is led also to consider the nature of language. Irreparably bound up with the question of how language is connected with reality, is what it is to *say* something. . . . To assume at the outset that one can make a sharp distinction between 'the world' and the 'language in which we try to describe the world', to the extent of saying that the problems of philosophy do not arise at all out of the former but only out of the latter, is to beg the whole question of philosophy. . . . We cannot say . . . that the problems of philosophy

arise out of language *rather than* out of the world, because in discussing language philosophically we are in fact discussing *what counts as belonging to the world.* Our idea of what belongs to the realm of reality is given for us in the language that we use. The concepts we have settle for us the form of experience we have of the world. (Winch, 1958, pp. 11–15)

The effect of such a position is to direct attention to *conceptual* analysis and clarification if the social world is to be better understood. For Winch there are different ways of knowing, not competing methodologies, and it is the task of philosophy to clarify these ways of knowing, to show how their objects can be intelligible, and hence how understanding is possible. The analysis of social understanding cannot be separated from an analysis of the nature of society; indeed, social relations, for Winch, are *expressions of ideas* about reality (p. 23). This brings his position very close to that of the hermeneutical philosophers and to some methodological individualists, such as Hayek, who argue that social reality not only cannot be known apart from individual expressions and actions but in fact does not exist separately. This is also akin to Max Weber's view, and in fact Winch supported Weber's assertion that it was meaningful behaviour that the human studies should be concerned with. This is obviously also close to the position advocated by Collingwood and Dray, who see historical explanation as a matter of understanding the intentional motivations of deliberate acts (see chapter 4).

DIALECTICAL PHILOSOPHY: THE FRANKFURT SCHOOL

A further variation in the broad modern hermeneutical camp has been provided by the work of the inter-war Frankfurt School of dialectical philosophers, who have also manifested a fundamental concern with the place of language in the relationship between philosophy and social understanding. In the 1960s they reacted against what was taken to be the prevalence of 'vulgar empiricism' or 'scientism' in sociology at that time. Adorno held that the nature of society itself precluded the use of a natural science method. Science, he said, 'wished to rid the world of the tension between the general and the particular by means of its consistent system.' (Adorno, 1976, p. 77) The human world, however, he believed, 'gains its unity from inconsistency', and consequently does not possess the required homogeneity that makes science possible. Even though existing empirical social science is able to proceed relatively successfully as though humans were social atoms, which is an adverse reflection upon the composition of modern society, it should not attribute the generalisations made on such a basis to social reality itself. Statistical sociology, in Adorno's view, should become self-critical (p. 78). But if sociology rejects the notion of totality as perhaps 'a crypto-metaphysical prejudice', then it is restricted to the merely phenomenal and hence misses the essential *social* connections (p. 79). The concept of 'totality' and of how it is possible to gain knowledge of such an entity was of central concern to the Frankfurt philosophers.

Adorno drew attention to the fundamental difference in the notions of critical method between Popper and the Frankfurt tradition. Although Popper had advanced what seemed to be a new method it was unable to transcend a rigid subject/empirical object distinction. While, for Adorno, objectivism was ruled out because of the inconsistent and contradictory nature of society – rational yet irrational, systemic yet fragmented, blind yet mediated by consciousness – this external social nature, however, did have to be grasped. It was prior to knowledge and a problem for knowledge (Adorno, 1976, pp. 106–9). But against Popper's empiricist distinction between hypothesis (or theory) and the facts, Adorno wished to defend the crucial role of social *critique* and *understanding*. Popper's critical method of *empirical* falsificationism, he believed, would rob sociology of the moment of *anticipation* of the reality that lies *behind* the appearances of the world. Criticism of the appearances is therefore essential; it must be not only formal but also material. Thus 'facts in society are not the last thing to which knowledge might attach itself, since they themselves are mediated through society. Not all theories are hypotheses; theory is the *telos* not the vehicle of sociology.' (p. 112)

HABERMAS'S CRITICAL THEORY

In his discussion of the Popper/Adorno controversy Jürgen Habermas contrasted two kinds of social science – the empiricist functionalist and the dialectical. He saw the former as drawing analytical distinctions between: (1) theory and its object, (2) theory and experience, (3) theory and history, and (4) theory and practice. Against these distinctions he asserted the importance of a dialectical and hermeneutical *unity* of theory and social reality:

The demand that theory in its construction and in the structure of its concept has to measure up to the object, and the demand that in the method the object has to be treated in accord with its significance can – beyond all representational theory – only be fulfilled dialectically. It is only the scientific apparatus which reveals an object whose structure must nevertheless previously be understood to some degree, if the categories chosen are not to remain external to it. This circle cannot be broken by any *a priori* or empiricist immediacy of approach, but is rather only to be explored dialectically in conjunction with the natural hermeneutics of the social life-world. The hypothetico-deductive system of statements is replaced by the hermeneutic explication of meaning. In place of a reversibly unambiguous co-ordination of symbols and meanings vaguely pre-understood, categories gain their determinacy gradually through their relative position in the context developed. (Habermas, 1976, p. 134)

Since individual persons and phenomena and the social reality are interdependent in the dialectical conception there could not be, for Habermas, empiricist laws or laws of anthropologically enduring structures, or of historical constants. Laws should be, rather teleological, deriving from the 'fundamental dependent relations from which a social life-world, an epochal situation as a whole, is determined as totality and is permeated in all its moments'. Such regularities are permeated through the consciousness of agents and gradually come to prevail over consciousness, and so agents are able then to articulate the 'objective meaning of a historical life-context' (pp. 138–9). Thus a dialectical theory proceeds hermeneutically.

For such a theory, the comprehension of meaning, to which the analytical-empirical theories attach a merely heuristic value, is constitutive. For it gains its categories primarily from the situational consciousness of acting individuals themselves; in the objective spirit of a social life-world, that meaning is articulated which sociological interpretation takes up through identification and critique. Dialectical thought does not simply eliminate the dogmatics of the lived situation through formalisation, in fact it retains the subjectively intended meaning in its examination of the prevailing traditions and breaks this meaning up. (Habermas, 1976, p. 139)

But Habermas's critical dialectics goes further than mere hermeneutics, since it adopts a practical intent: it attempts to confront the real with the possible through making a transcending critique of both positivist and hermeneutical approaches to history. It attempts to unite objectivist procedure with *verstehen*. The former rejects, according to Habermas, the use of theory in the explanation of particular events, while the latter also remains devoid of theory through making only a contemplation of past meanings. If an objective comprehension of meaning rather than its 'philosophical hypostatisation' is to be achieved then the study of history must hold out the possibility of transforming society in the future through first comprehending the laws of development. Objectivity is derived, then, from having a practical transformative intention in studying history. This contrasts, as Habermas pointed out, with Weber's subjectively arbitrary 'value relations' standpoint, and with the technical standpoint of modern science.

The technical orientation of so-called 'functionalist-empiricist' social science has become a major theme in the work of Habermas, as it had been for earlier Frankfurt thinkers. His basic objection to the standpoint of positivist science was its attempt to draw a rigid distinction between facts and values or decisions. It held that history is devoid of meaning, like nature (see Popper), but that it is possible to posit a meaning through making an arbitrary decision and then attempting to enforce it gradually by using 'scientific' techniques. Dialectics, on the other hand, distinguishes sharply between practical emancipatory questions, relating to the whole society, and technical tasks, relating to the manipulation of a reified aspect (p. 142). Habermas was very critical of the positivist dualism of facts and decisions, a dualism which had the effect, he rightly believed, of eliminating questions of life practices from the sciences, since it restricted knowledge to the realm of empirical experience. The thrust of his critique was to show that the positivists and Popper depended in the last instance upon a pragmatic decision made by the community of scientists as to the acceptability of certain basic statements. This decision is enforceable neither logically nor empirically (p. 151). The rules of the research procedure have first to be established. Thus there is an inevitable circle in the application of rules. This is evidence of the research process being embedded in a necessarily *hermeneutical* context.

> The postulates of strict cognition naturally conceal a non-explicated pre-understanding which, in fact, they presuppose; here the detachment of methodology from the real research process and its social functions takes its revenge.
> Research is an institution composed of people who act together and communicate with one another; as such it determines, through the communication of the researchers, that which can theoretically lay claim to validity. . . . The meaning of the research process as a whole must be understood before I can know to what the validity of basic statements is related, just as the judge must always have grasped the meaning of judicature as such. . . . The empirical validity of basic statements is measured against a behavioural expectation governed by social norms. (Habermas, 1976, p. 152)

Thus we return to the starting place of this chapter. The hermeneutical tradition is based upon the view of the inherent unavoidability of interpretive understanding, for natural science as much as social science. (We saw in the previous chapter how this view has become the basis for a radical reinterpretation of the structure of natural science.) To this hermeneutical postulate the Frankfurt philosophers and Habermas added the notions of the necessarily dialectical constitutive wholeness of society and the importance of a critical transformative political orientation to the construction and meaning of social theory.

7

Arguments for Realism

The third phase in recent philosophy of explanation consists of defences of realism as an account of scientific explanation in general and as the possible philosophical basis of social and historical explanation. Realism has been propounded in opposition to empiricism, instrumentalism, relativism, irrationalism, historicalism, and hermeneutics. Having now discussed all these doctrines, my task is to show how realism can overcome the problems they give rise to. In this chapter a realist account of explanation in general is defended, with some reference to social explanation, and in the next chapter its applicability to social explanation is defended in more detail.

Realism *opposes* the interrelated doctrines of:

1 *Nominalism* This is the idea that the universe is only made up of particular entities and that postulated universal or general properties and relations which are shared by particulars do not exist. (Realism claims that there are universals.)

2 *Phenomenalism* That only those entities available to sense perception exist and they do not exist apart from sense data about them.

3 *Instrumentalism* That theories and research techniques are merely instruments for constructing and manipulating data and for prediction rather than for discovering real processes, powers, and causes.

4 *Strict relativism* That theories and explanations cannot be objectively true but at best are potentially 'true' only relative to some philosophical/conceptual framework which determines the entities to be studied and the relationship of reference between words and the world.

Most realists (but not all) hold to the general idea that theories and explanations containing statements about postulated non-observable entities, properties, and relations are, in the last analysis, good or bad, adequate or inadequate, plausible or implausible, true or false, in terms of how they *correspond* to the *actual*, complex, multilayered, partly imperceptible but discoverable world external to us. That is, for them, theoretical terms in physical and social science do *refer* to entities, which are taken to be real and to have definite properties, and which endure through space and time. This means that in the social sciences realists are opposed to all currents of nominalist and phenomenological thinking, since all these deny in some sense that there are real *social* entities with powers and properties that are not reducible to the powers and propensities of individual people. Social realists believe that there are, *in principle*, discoverable real properties of *social structures* which are necessary (but not sufficient) for deciding theoretical and explanatory disputes about both action and social change.

The question of our knowledge of the reality of the natural and social worlds is closely bound up with the question of the rationality of *practices* of research, explanation, and theory choice, and therefore of the rationality of our *beliefs* about our practices and the world. The problem of rationality has come to occupy a central place in philosophical debates about explanation, as we have seen in the earlier chapters of part II, and many realists have been particularly forceful in arguing for the essential rationality of natural and social science, providing it is conducted on realist principles. That is, the aim of science is seen by them as the *discovery* of structural causal mechanisms, and rational scientists should therefore choose theories which move them closer to this general goal.[1]

The question of the aims of science is integral to debates about the meaning of 'scientific explanation'. If we decide that the aim is or should be the discovery of the causal mechanisms of the perceptible world, rather than just the construction of an internally coherent set of ideas or just the solving of problems irrespective of where they come from or what they are about, then the questions concern not only the meaning of discovery and explanation but also how we can know we have made a genuine discovery, and what methodology is appropriate to such a task. These are acute problems for realists because they are opposed to a complete reliance upon common-sense perception or even scientific (and supposedly theory-neutral) observation. They reject both the strict theory/observation distinction and the conflation of theory and observation.

Realists attempt to specify a different, more complicated but more

[1] For debates about the rationality of science, see: Hollis and Lukes (1982), N. Maxwell (1974), Newton-Smith (1981, ch. 1), Nickles (1980).

viable relationship between frameworks, theories, common sense, and reality. They claim that nature and society exist independently of our knowledge and in ways which are not obvious to common sense. The *objective* complexity of the world has to be *discovered* but that is a very difficult process requiring a conceptual/methodological framework which tells us what sorts of connections to make between theory, sensory data, and reality. That is, the crucial questions concern: (1) our mode of *access* (from our two bases of our linguistic/theoretical framework and our perceptual data) to the strange levels of micro entities, structural relations, processes, powers, and causes; and (2) the mode of testing of our claims to have made discoveries at these levels.[2]

COMMON SENSE AND CRITICAL REALISM

In defending a realist account of explanation a good place to begin is with a criticism of the popular idea (shared by some phenomenalist, empiricist, and naïve realist philosophers as well as by many non-philosophers) that uncritical and unmediated sensory observation is the only method that gives us a reliable picture of the reality of the world. (Phenomenalists hold that mind-dependent sense data are the only reality, while naïve realists believe the world to be mind-independent but knowable only through direct observation.) While this view must be criticised by anyone who wishes to give a more plausible account of explanation, at the same time a place must be retained for observations since sensory data are an essential point of access to reality. Showing how observations and descriptions relate to theoretical/conceptual schemes and how common sense relates to scientific views of the world are two aspects of the one general problem of bridging the gulf in our culture between *personal* perception, description, and understanding, and *general scientific* explanations. Three philosophers who have been instrumental in fostering the upsurge of interest over recent decades in critical realist solutions to this problem have been the American philosophers Maurice Mandelbaum, Wilfred Sellars, and Willard van Ormand Quine. Their work helped set the stage for subsequent discussions.

The nature of perception

In his book *Philosophy, Science, and Sense Perception* (1964) Mandelbaum pointed out that direct (or naïve) realists, such as Ryle and Moore, who based their realism upon common-sense perception, failed to make a

---

[2] See the following for general discussions of the varieties of realism: Alston (1978), Boyd (1983), Dummett (1982), Horwich (1982), Merrill (1980), Putnam (1982a), J. J. C. Smart (1982).

crucial distinction between perceptions of objects and objects themselves. There is good reason to believe, even without the findings of modern science, that the *perceived qualities* of an object are not identical with the *real properties* of that object. Our senses are unreliable, or at least give us conflicting information. Objects may appear different in shape, colour, sound, smell, and texture depending upon the location and environment of the perceiver. Moreover, the physical sciences have revealed a great many erstwhile *hidden* properties of objects.[3] For Ryle this was not a problem since he was content to see common sense and science as two quite distinct modes of discourse about the world which are not necessarily incompatible (Ryle, 1954, ch. 5).

But this influential Rylean view is quite implausible. While it is true that in everyday life and in science quite different concepts and knowledge are employed to give descriptions and explanations, those descriptions and explanations concern the very same characteristics of objects. For instance, as Mandelbaum pointed out,

> the boundary between what we mean when we describe a table as hard, and the concepts which scientists use to explain variations in hardness, is not a boundary which it is impossible to cross. In fact it is a boundary which we readily cross as soon as we ask – in either the language of common sense or the language of the sciences – for explanations of what we observe. Once having crossed this boundary, it is imperative that we should know how to speak both the language of science and the language of common sense, regardless of which side of the border we regard as our spiritual home.
> (Mandelbaum, 1964, p. 203)

This does not mean that there is always a perfect translation or that a perfect translation is even possible. But people can and do become bilingual, while not thereby raising radically different questions about the world when switching from one language to another. As Mandelbaum said,

> were there so radical a discontinuity between science and our ordinary experience, one would not only be forced to wonder how the sciences ever took their rise; one would also be forced to wonder by what means their conclusions would ever come to be accepted as confirmed. . . . Ryle seems to have forgotten that it is people who learn to speak languages, and that the problems which

---

[3] The nature of perception – its relationship to the properties and qualities of things, to conceptual frameworks, and to the neurological structure of the brain – is one of the oldest and most central problems in philosophy and psychology. For some recent discussions, see Armstrong (1979), Dummett (1979), Gregory (1974; 1981, ch. 12), G. Maxwell (1968), Strawson (1979), C. Taylor (1979).

interest these people do not necessarily change as they learn to speak new languages. Because so many problems remain the same, people are forced to translate from one language into the other. (p. 204)

Indeed, common-sense thinking (including common-sense epistemology of the Rylean kind) and science are interconnected. For instance, the common-sense and philosophical problem of perception (to do with the meaning of such terms as 'see', 'hear', 'touch', and 'perceive') involves *causal* assumptions about the relationship between objects and our sense organs, the structure of the organs, the nature of the intervening medium, and so on. These are problems which are also of central concern to *science* (pp. 206–7). The sciences have always begun with everyday problems and have refined methods of enquiry which first have been used in that context but later have become a means of going beyond common-sense experience. Science is able to uncover certain properties of objects, and the causal relations and processes that they have, which are not available to the senses. Consequently, if we wish to defend the results of the sciences we must defend a realism which is critical of common-sense understandings.

Our perception is not simply a matter of recording sensory experiences. It is a much more complicated process that employs certain assumptions about the world such as stability and continuity of objects, and interprets the sensory data received in a context of these assumptions and beliefs about the nature of objects in general (pp. 225–7). Indeed, these assumptions and beliefs amount to a *common-sense realism*, which leads us in the first place to be sceptical about our own senses, especially if they produce contradictory evidence. In other words, it is sensory experience which gives us initial access to the real, but this experience is *critically ordered* by hypotheses about the nature of objects and how they impinge upon us and appear to us. Science must then depart from common-sense perceptual experience to uncover the real properties of objects. But historically, of course, science remains rooted in problems which arise in the everyday attempt to defend common-sense realism.

Physicalist and manifest images of man

In the wake of successful physical science has come physicalist philosophy – the attempt to defend the reality of physical structures and to establish their ontological priority owing to the apparently causal relationships they have with our perceptions, and perhaps with our ways of knowing. Against phenomenalism, radical physicalists have claimed that we cannot know that any perceptible objects really exist (Sellars, 1963, pp. 96–7).

This argument is a kind of *super realism* (see Hesse, 1974, pp. 288–90) since it rejects the reality of all ordinary phenomena. But what of the phenomena produced by scientific experiment and observation, e.g. electron micrographs and bubble chamber tracks? Are they, too, unreal? But this argument is not necessary to the maintenance of less radical forms of realism, and, moreover, in the end it is incoherent because its result is a complete inability to know about anything because we could have no access to such a level of reality if we are denied a base in sensory observations. *Criticising* sensory observations is not the same as entirely rejecting the existence of macro entities.

However, Wilfrid Sellars has pointed out that the claim that perceptible objects are unreal is a claim about the epistemological and semantical *framework* of such objects, not about what the framework contains. Once inside it, statements about objects are evaluated by the criteria of the framework. His belief was that science was making available an alternative, more adequate framework, which *in principle* could serve all the functions, including perception, of the other (Sellars, 1963, p. 97). Although he was strongly of the view that all phenomenalism (including common sense) is false, i.e. that *esse* is not *percipi*, this metaphysical ontological doctrine did not lead him to the methodological doctrine that common-sense observation should or could be abandoned. This was indeed the radical view of Paul Feyerabend who attempted, as shown in chapter 5, to develop a pragmatic theory of observation, rejecting completely the notion of the givenness of observations and attempting to replace the common-sense view of the world with conventional theoretical constructions. But, as Sellars said, to abandon completely common sense, despite its ontological falsity, would result in a serious loss, since its rock-bottom concepts and principles remain binding until a *total structure*, which can do the job better, is available. And that will require, at the very least, a great deal more knowledge about how people perceive the world (Sellars, 1965, pp. 189–93).

The implications for social science of the critical realist arguments of Mandelbaum and Sellars are clear. If sensory perception of physical entities is an unreliable (or at best a partial) guide to the true nature of reality then any social science that restricts itself to the level of observable behaviour runs the strong risk of missing a great deal of the non-phenomenal reality of persons and societies. In particular, it would fail to grasp (1) that real but imperceptible structures can exist, and (2) that causation is more than the association of individual perceptible entities. Now obviously, very few serious students of society are so shallow. But the great divide in the social studies over scientific versus hermeneutical approaches is not necessarily bridged by an awareness of the importance of the principles of critical realism. Even if all those espousing a scientific approach adopted critical realism the hermeneuticists would still be able to say that the label 'scientific' is inappropriate to social enquiry because their object can only be approached at the level of the common-sense meanings and reasons given by persons, and persons and society must be seen as wholes and not as micro-physical structures.

The potential or real conflict between the two frameworks of hermeneutics and science lies at the heart of modern thought. We have seen in the previous chapters of part II that debates over this question have occupied much time in the philosophies of history and social science. It certainly seems at first sight that the two frameworks have quite different approaches to the problem of the nature of persons and the causes of their actions. But the thrust of much of Sellars's work is to argue that these frameworks are not incompatible (Sellars, 1962, passim). He believes it should be the task of philosophy to try to reconcile the two idealised images of man in the world – what he called the manifest image and the scientific image. Rather than upholding one or the other or uniting them completely, he sees the task, as with a stereoscope, to fuse them together into a single vision – a coherent synoptic experience (p. 4). He rightly pointed out that the manifest, holistic/common-sense image of man in the world has constituted one of the perennial poles of ancient, medieval, and modern thought, being the core of contemporary ordinary-language and hermeneutical philosophy. It has centred on the notion of man as a holistic person, with certain powers, abilities, and attributes who lives and develops himself in a social group (pp. 8–13). The social group is essential to understanding how persons come to develop a conceptual framework about the world and why that framework enables them to explain the world in some general way. The common-sense conceptual thinking of the group mediates between the individual and the intelligible order. However, as Sellars argued,

> any attempt to *explain* this mediation within the framework of the manifest image was bound to fail, for the manifest image contains the resources for such an attempt only in the sense that it provides the foundation on which scientific theory can build an explanatory framework; and while conceptual structures of this framework are *built* on the manifest image, they are not definable within in. . . .
>
> It is in the *scientific* image of man in the world that we begin to see the main outlines of the way in which man came to have an image of himself as man-in-the-world. For we begin to see this as a matter of evolutionary development which explains the correspondence between the dancing of a worker bee and the location, relative to the sun, of the flower from which he comes. This correspondence, like the relation between man's 'original' image and the world, is incapable of explanation in terms of a direct conditioning impact of the environment on the individual as such.
> (Sellars, 1962, pp. 17–18)

Thus the scientific-physicalist image grows out of the manifest image and attempts to explain it and transcend it. Like the manifest one, it represents itself as a complete framework, containing potentially the whole truth about the world or its particular part of it, and sees itself as a rival to the manifest framework. It theoretically postulates the imperceptible but real states, processes, characteristics, entities, and causes to explain the phenomena of the world, including human behaviour. In the physicalist conception man is thought of as a complex physical system and both behaviour and action are explainable by correlating them with physical processes, so there is claimed to be an *identity* between brain and mind, as many physiologists and some philosophers now argue (see the section on 'Physicalist materialism' later in this chapter).

But the two images are not necessarily incompatible. Human thought, for instance, can be seen in both physical and conscious-rational terms. Any attempt to reconcile them clearly does not establish the primacy of the physical. Humans as *persons* are confronted by moral standards, choices, and obligations which quite often force them to conflict with their physical desires and influences. Attempts to reduce psychological and social explanation to physicalism seem to be unsuccessful because people and societies are more than physical entities, as I shall argue later in this chapter and in the next chapter.

Given this scientific/manifest dichotomy there have been four possibilities open to the human studies, the first three of which accept the dichotomy:

1 *Cartesianism* Postulating dualism of minds and bodies, each requiring a separate explanation.
2 *Physicalism* Rejecting the reality of personality and social relations in favour of exclusively physical explanations.
3 *Hermeneutics and phenomenology* Affirming the primacy of the manifest person and seeing theories about the physical causes of actions as at best auxiliary.
4 *Structurism* Seeing man as both a physical and a social being constrained by nature and society and structuring nature and society through action; i.e. rejecting the dichotomy.

Wilfrid Sellars is not alone in proposing a version of the fourth option. Similar views have been advanced by many others in recent years, notably Jean Piaget, Jürgen Habermas, Mary Hesse, Rom Harré, Hilary Putnam, Roy Bhaskar, Anthony Giddens, and Alain Touraine. These writers attempt to show in effect that structurism is the way forward towards both social science and the unity of all sciences.

The importance of natural kinds

Mandelbaum and Sellars have stressed the idea that common-sense and scientific explanations are contained within linguistic/conceptual frameworks but that there is a development from one to the other such that translation between them is possible. Quine took these ideas further. He was more of a holist about meaning and translation, but nevertheless his work does show that a commitment to ontological realism is not incompatible with such views, as some other holists seem to believe. We saw at the beginning of chapter 5 that he was opposed to the 'epistemological nihilism' of Polanyi, Toulmin, Hanson, Kuhn, and Feyerabend, which had come about partly as a result of his influence (Quine, 1969, pp. 87–8). It is true that his arguments and those of Wittgenstein had been largely responsible for dislodging epistemology from its old status of *a priori* philosophy, in which it had attempted to show that knowledge could only be based on a firm, supposedly objective, foundation of empirical observations. However, he believed that epistemology does still have an important task (pp. 82–4). Its problem is to study the relationship between sensory input and the subject's output of descriptions of the three-dimensional external world so that we can assess how evidence relates to theory and how theory transcends evidence. And crucial to this project is still the notion of *observation* (pp. 88–9).

An independent role for observations in science was repudiated by the relativists. Quine argued that observations are important in two senses: as the repository of evidence for scientific hypotheses, and as the cornerstone of semantics since they provide the basis for the sharing of *meaning* and so of *communication* and *translation* (pp. 88–9). Observations can be 'objective' within linguistic communities because of a sharing of reference which makes assent possible. But this does not solve the problem of the relationship of shared observations to reality. While assent about the meanings of observations may be possible within communities this does not get us any closer to a discovery of non-observable (or non-common-sense) properties and levels of reality *external to all thought*.

In his influential essay on 'Natural Kinds' (Quine, 1969, ch. 5) he approached this fundamental question in an illuminating way by discussing the interrelationship of the notions of 'similarity' and 'kind' and their relationship in turn to logic and science. Our ability to observe similarities or resemblances seems to be innate and our common-sense reasonable expectation is to depend upon resemblance for our understanding of the world. This includes defining similarity in terms of kinds of entities. But when we attempt to formalise this notion we run up against the difficulty of accurately defining the properties or qualities of things in order to see which ones are shared so that kinds can be defined by them. Universal surface qualities such as colour and shape, even if defined, can be shared by entities which are often dissimilar in other ways. The more our definitions of properties and qualities are refined and the more of them we include in our definition of kinds, the more difficult the attempted similarity/kind equation becomes and the further removed is the possibility of formalising the situation in logic or set theory (pp. 116–21).

Quine argued that perception of similarity is basic, and therefore so is inductive reasoning since our expectations are based upon correlations of similarities – i.e. through habits in the first instance, particularly the learning of the meaning of words by ostension (pointing to objects). To the extent that this learning is a socially shared process, communication is possible. But this very sociability creates a fundamental problem. Quine expressed it like this:

> Always induction expresses our hope that similar causes will have similar effects; but when the induction is the ostensive learning of a word, that pious hope blossoms into a foregone conclusion. The uniformity of people's quality spaces virtually assures that similar presentations will elicit similar verdicts.
>
> It makes one wonder the more about other inductions, where what is sought is a generalization not about our neighbour's verbal behaviour but about the harsh impersonal world. It is reasonable that our quality space should match our neighbour's, we being birds of a feather; and so the general trustworthiness of induction in the ostensive learning of words was a put-up job. To trust induction as a way of access to truths of nature, on the other hand, is to suppose more nearly, that our quality space matches that of the cosmos. The true irrationality of our sense of similarity, its irrelevance to anything in logic and mathematics, offers little reason to expect that this sense is somehow in tune with the world – a world which, unlike language, we never made. Why induction should be trusted, apart from special cases such as the ostensive learning of words, is the perennial philosophical problem of induction. (Quine, 1969, pp. 125–6)

Quine's answer to the problem is one which offers cogent support to all realists, and is one whose essence was and has been developed in various guises by several other philosophers in recent years (see later sections). In essence his answer rested upon the proposition that there is an *isomorphism* between human abilities to perceive regularities, on the one hand, and the actual proven regular nature of the world on the other. Why we have this ability as a species is partly an outcome of *evolution*: 'creatures inveterately wrong in their inductions have a pathetic but praiseworthy tendency to die before reproducing their kind.' (p. 126) But the problem with this is that modern science has taught us that the perceivable qualities of things are secondary to more fundamental properties. However, colour, taste, and smell do help us in food gathering, for instance, and this supports the evolutionary hypothesis. Thus man has gradually come to depend upon *both* common-sense perception and science:

Things about his innate similarity sense that are helpful in the one sphere can be a hindrance in the other. Credit is due man's inveterate ingenuity, or human sapience, for having worked around the blinding dazzle of colour vision and found the more significant regularities elsewhere. Evidently natural selection has dealt with the conflict by endowing men doubly: with both a colour-slanted quality space and the ingenuity to rise above it.

He has risen above it by developing modified systems of kinds, hence modified similarity standards for scientific purposes. By the trial-and-error process of theorizing he has regrouped things into new kinds which prove to lend themselves to many inductions better than the old.... In induction nothing succeeds like success. (Quine, 1969, pp. 128–9)[4]

Science has modified intuitive inductions of kinds and uncovered entirely new ones at odds with common sense. *Theoretical* kinds are crucial to science in uncovering the *hidden dispositional* properties of entities and in ascribing causation. Singular causal relationships can also be better understood as examples of *kinds* of connections rather than in the Humean sense of invariable succession.

It was Quine's great merit to have emphasised that the evolution of human perception and consciousness about the external world is a progress *towards knowledge* of the *reality* of the world and so man comes to transcend both his linguistic/conceptual framework and his perceptual common sense by adopting a critical realism. Basic to this progress is the success of mankind in uncovering the *causal* connections between things, events, and processes and expressing this in shared linguistic meanings. The causal theory of reference contained in Quine's semantical theory is crucial to the realist's project of giving a plausible account of the progress of science. This was later built upon by other realist philosophers, notably Kripke, Putnam, Boyd, Harré, and Hesse, as we shall see.

TRANSCENDENTAL ARGUMENTS AND THE PROBLEM OF CONFIRMATION

The common-sense and scientific intuition that the world is real, layered, and structured can be supported in the first place by a transcendental argument. Such arguments can be seen as tacitly underpinning the ideas

---

[4] Quine seemed to be unaware of the powerful ethnographic and theoretical support given to his argument by the writings of Claude Lévi-Strauss, who has developed a similar argument about the relationship of 'primitive' classifications to scientific ones. See especially Lévi-Strauss (1972, ch. 1).

of Mandelbaum, Sellars, and Quine discussed above. Transcendental arguments have their roots in the work of Kant.[5] In Charles Taylor's (1978) formulation, they have a structure which begins with something in our experience which is taken to be indubitable and then moves to a stronger conclusion about the nature of the human subject and the world in which he exists. They do this via a string of apodeictic indispensability claims. That is, *D* is indispensable for *C*, which is indispensable for *B*, which is indispensable for *A*, which is indubitable. The status of *B*, *C*, and *D* depends upon our being certain of the status of *A*.

Such arguments are important to realists because they provide a means of establishing *a priori* the general existence of a *natural necessity* linking observable events and entities. But they should be sharply distinguished from idealist arguments which attempt to establish an *a priori analytical* necessity linking universal mental categories and concepts with our understanding of events and entities. Transcendental realist arguments are anti-sceptical, anti-reductionist, and anti-idealist (Rorty, 1979b, p. 77). They are *synthetic a priori* defences of natural reality. They give a realist and structurist answer to the question: what must the world in general be like for us not only to perceive the world successfully and so live our ives but also to develop and apply truthful explanations of the world?

Synthetic *a priori* arguments are controversial because it has generally been held by philosophers that *a priori* arguments must contain *analytic* (i.e. logical and definitional) truths, and analytic statements must be strictly separated from synthetic ones, which relate to matters of fact. However, there is now an influential school of thought, including Quine, Putnam, and Sellars, which holds that the analytic/synthetic distinction, once so dear to the hearts of logical-empiricist philosophers, might be ill founded, or at least far too sharply drawn. It seems that there can be many statements about the world which don't fit neatly into one or the other category. Indeed, most of the laws of science may not be completely one or the other. In his famous paper 'Two Dogmas of Empiricism' Quine argued that a science contains a complex interlocking network of statements, which cannot be divided into analytic and synthetic. Some theories may be better or worse confirmed than others but no statement is immune from revision in the light of experience, and any statement may be held true come what may (Quine, 1951, pp. 42–3).

Is it possible to develop a convincing synthetic *a priori* argument for the existence of real unobservable structural mechanisms of the phenomena of the world? In order to do so it is essential to claim first that it is an incontrovertible fact that natural science is *successful* and then argue that indispensable to its success must be a world that is ontologically layered,

---

[5] For discussions of transcendental arguments in science, see Buchdahl (1980), Bennett (1979), Bhaskar (1975, pp. 30–6), Rorty (1979b), Taylor (1978).

structured, and independently real. If it is denied that science is progressively truthful and successful then of course such an argument cannot be used. But in order to deny it the seemingly obvious power that we now collectively have to control and manipulate nature would have to be denied. How we develop such knowledge is an important question, but that we do seems incontrovertible.

Such a transcendental realist argument has recently been developed at length by Roy Bhaskar (1975). His argument, and any other like it, presupposes an important role for philosophy – as prior to science and providing contingent hypotheses (1979, p. 7). Indeed, every philosophy of science presupposes (tacitly perhaps) an ontological answer to the question about what the world must be like for science to be possible. If it is to make sense of the practices of science this commitment should be realist. Moreover, as Bhaskar pointed out, a realist ontology is justified by how science actually proceeds. Rather than seeking for constant conjunctions of events in order to assert causal laws the scientist typically constructs (stating it a little oversimply for the moment) a *theory* which states a connection between a sequence of events, on the one hand, and a causal mechanism of that sequence on the other. It is only by assuming such mechanisms to be real, independent of events, and naturally enduring that the scientific practices of experimentation and engineering are rational. That is, it makes no sense for a scientist to attempt to isolate experimentally a causal mechanism unless he believes that mechanisms both exist before his actions and will go on existing afterwards. Science is a process aimed at uncovering the enduring mechanisms of nature. Thus, Bhaskar said, constant conjunction of events cannot be necessary for the efficacy of a law, otherwise there would be no science, and real mechanisms can be out of phase with the actual pattern of events (Bhaskar, 1975, pp. 12–14, 56–7).

This argument about scientific explanation is transcendental in two senses: epistemologically, in that it has a synthetic *a priori* argument for the necessity of science as a critical-experimental and realist practice; and ontologically, in that reality is claimed to be partly an unobservable, relatively enduring structure of generative mechanisms. These two senses support each other in that for science to exist the world must be of this general nature, and if the world is of this general nature then a science of this type is necessary for an enquiry into its peculiar nature. But Bhaskar rightly stressed the importance of grasping the real nature of the relationship between science and reality, and it is this that sets his argument apart from transcendental idealism. That is, the order of analysis is from science to the world but the real dependency (which is contingent) is the reverse. It is the nature of the world that makes science possible but this could only have been discovered after science and engineering had developed (Bhaskar, 1975, pp. 29–30).

There is thus an interconnection between science and philosophy, each reinforcing the other. But such an argument tells us nothing about the actual nature of the world, only that it is layered, persistent, and independent relative to our senses. It leaves open the problem of access to and confirmation of particular theories about reality. Since we are beings with biologically limited sensory abilities we have had to devise ways of circumventing these limitations through inferential reasoning and technology. But sense perception always remains basic to the scientific enterprise.

How to have confirmation of theories about unobserved and unobservable causal mechanisms is thus a big problem for realists, since despite the value of transcendental arguments realism is ultimately a contingent thesis (see G. Maxwell, 1970a and 1970b). That is, realism is true if and only if the unobservable entities referred to by science actually exist and false if they do not. This contrasts with empiricist confirmation of the inductive and hypothetico-deductive kinds which rest upon the ideas that only observations can be used for tests, that statements about unobservables are merely instrumental, and that the confirmatory relationship between hypotheses and observations is purely logical in character.

But logical empiricism has several major problems. Firstly, a purely logical approach leads both to paradoxes and the production of many unacceptable or incompatible, but logically correct, conclusions (G. Maxwell, 1970b, pp. 7–10). Secondly, the instrumentalist specification of unobservables is unable to account satisfactorily for the shift from unobservable to observable (and hence from 'unreal' to 'real') merely as a result of improved techniques. And thirdly, the instrumentalist is unable to explain why his predictions are increasingly powerful and successful. The realist can explain this simply by arguing that good predictions are the consequence of true or nearly true theoretical suppositions about the world.

Thus the problem with relying solely upon observables is, obviously, that some at least of the causal powers and structures of the world are unobservable. They can be known about only by inference. Structure is abstract but shared by all things. It can be characterised not in descriptive terms but only in formal terms about quantities, relations, variables, and their connections in systems. However, what is important for human knowledge, as Mandelbaum, Quine, and Grover Maxwell have emphasised, is that there is clearly an isomorphic relationship between our sense impressions and the structures of the world. This is crucial because, in Maxwell's words,

> not only are there numerous important structural properties common to items in our experience and physical objects; these same structural properties are, in general, also shared by the (nonexistent) naïve realist objects of common sense. This explains why

our common-sense perceptual judgements, though strictly speaking false, nevertheless stand us in such excellent stead. They are close enough to the truth for most purposes because they attribute structural properties to ostensibly external objects that are identical with or very similar to the structural properties of the actual, external physical objects. Moreover, there are structure-preserving causal chains between the parts of these physical objects and the corresponding parts of the patterns in our private experience that are mistakenly identified with the external objects that cause them. (G. Maxwell, 1970b, p. 25)

This isomorphism points to something that many realists have drawn attention to: that we have evolved in such a way as to be 'wired' to perceive the world as naïve realists and that these perceptions are a first approximation to reality. It is then possible for us to move from this base in common sense, using a complex structure of inference, to structures. But in doing so it must not be forgotten that the way in which we *act* in the world is crucial since we are *agents*, making our knowledge as we interact with the world, and transforming the world as well. The interaction between our manmade explanatory frameworks, which are partly social and partly personal, and the world must be a central question for all critical realists. I shall have more to say about it in later sections.

DISPOSITIONS, CAUSAL POWERS, AND NATURAL NECESSITY

Transcendental arguments support an ontology of natural necessity. Those in the Humean empiricist tradition, of course, reject any notion that there is a natural necessity underlying the apparent order and patterns of the world. For them there are only observable regularities between particular things and a logical necessity between concepts, so that explanation of the behaviour of particulars by reference to laws is a matter of deductively inferring the causes of their behaviour. Causation is for them a matter of regular association of events, not internal necessity. Realists on the other hand hold that there must be universal causal mechanisms linking particulars in *necessary* rather than accidental ways. A solution to the resultant problem of how to have epistemic access from the appearances of particulars to their causes can be approached by supporting a *dispositional* rather than a qualitative account of particulars and an *inductive-analogical* account of how we infer from them to general statements about kinds and causation.

Thus the identification of the properties of natural kinds of things is crucial for science, and for everyday life, as Quine showed. The correct identification of particular things is a matter, as Rom Harré and Edward

Madden (1975) have argued, of discovering *a posteriori* their essential dispositional properties and liabilities after first hypothetically conceptualising their natures. Once discovered it is then possible to make general statements about natural necessity since the general structures and processes of the world are a result of the complex interaction of powerful particulars. Thus the conceptual necessity inherent in the classificatory names given to designated kinds of things is wholly dependent on our being able to discover the natural necessity of the world. In this account the references of terms and truth are trans-theoretical and it is the task of science to discover the essential natures of things.

In contrast with this, those in the empiricist tradition, who are tied to correlations of observable events, are unable to give a convincing account of lawful necessity that is able to distinguish genuine laws from merely accidental correlations. In fact, in science law-like statements are of many sorts and there is no formal set of characteristics that separates them from other sorts of universal statements, as Harré and Madden pointed out (1975, pp. 32–3). There are many criteria that could be the basis for the prima facie case of lawfulness, but in order to go further there has to be a discovery that links conceptual necessity to some *real* connections between the properties specified by the law-like statement. That is, underpinning law-like statements there has to be a *natural necessity* in order for it to be possible to distinguish genuine causal explanatory laws from accidental and summative generalisations (pp. 33–8).

From this it can be seen that the basis of Harré's and Madden's realist specification of laws is the notion of *causal power*. This refers to the fundamental dispositional properties of particular things. To say that a thing (X) has power is to assert that:

$$X \text{ or } {\text{will} \atop \text{can}} \text{ do } A, \text{ in the appropriate conditions,}$$

in virtue of its intrinsic nature (Harré and Madden, 1975, p. 86). That is, things have specific abilities which are not just a result of the conditions in which they exist. These powers are associated with agency, activity, and causation. But powers do not have to be activated to exist. They can be *liabilities*, i.e. passive abilities. The expression of a power or liability as some action or form of response depends upon the conditions, internal and external, enabling and stimulus, in which the thing exists (pp. 87–90).

The importance of this concept of causal power lies in the use that can be made of it for explaining the events and processes of the world. Descriptive statements asserting a causal relationship between entities or events rest upon conceptual necessity. That is, a statement such as 'acid turns litmus paper red' involves a relationship of meaning between the two precise terms 'acid' and 'litmus paper' such that we can understand the causal relationship in a way not possible if the description 'colourless fluid' had been used instead of 'acid'. The description 'acid' conceptually necessitates the description 'turns litmus paper red' (see Harré and Madden, 1975, pp. 8–10). This is in effect the same argument as that of Saul Kripke and Hilary Putnam to the effect that natural kind words like 'acid' are 'rigid designators', i.e. they designate natural kinds in such a way that captures their identity in a logically rigid way. (More on this in the next section.)

Conceptual necessity can then be seen to reflect a natural necessity between the powers, states, and natures of the things and systems of the universe. Once the fundamental causal powers of things are known then the necessity of certain effects can be inferred. But the actual effects observed in any particular system or world will depend upon the particular conditions influencing the results of causal power. That is, worlds are contingent, and it is the task of science to discover *a posteriori* the real causal powers of things and to show how they interact in complex ways to produce the effects observed in the world. In order to achieve this there has to be the use of a combination of induction, hypotheses, and analogical inferences. (See 'The structure of scientific explanation' later.) These all follow from the notion of the powerful particular since (stating it very simply for the moment) the 'starting point' for an explanation is the description of a particular entity by reference to its dispositional powers. Then, providing there has been no conceptual mistake and there is evidence for the truth of the description, it is possible to make a general statement about past, present, and future effects of the behaviour of the causally efficacious particular, given also knowledge about its conditions of behaviour (pp. 71–2).

REFERENCE, NATURAL KINDS, AND TRUTH

The problem of meaning variance

We have seen so far that the possibility of explanation involves the identification, in the first place, of the properties and powers of particular things and, secondly, of the universal properties and powers which they share and which thereby constitute them as members of natural kinds. Such identifications open the possibility of uncovering the structural relations which both link things together into systems and processes and help cause changes in their states and the ways in which they appear to us.

Clearly, it is essential to uphold the idea that there are universals. The doctrine of nominalism – that all entities are particular in their nature, there being no universals – if true would not only make science impossible but also prevent life, language, and communication, since descriptive language, pattern recognition, learning, ascription of causation, and consequently survival all depend upon the recognition of similarities and classes in our natural and social environment.

But the question we have to ask is whether science is able to build upon the 'given' appearances of things to make *correct identifications and descriptions* of the true essences of natural kinds such that theories about the causes of the world can be true or false, good or bad, in relation to how they correspond to these correctly (or approximately) described entities. Given the importance of correct identification, the questions concern the invariance and truthfulness of the references of our descriptive terms. Without stable references for classificatory and descriptive terms there cannot be comparison and translation between theories and languages, or the possibility of explanatory progress.

The problem of identity and classification has always been a central one for science, and scientific progress has sometimes occurred through changes in classification and conceptualisation of natural kinds.[6] The problem is even more acute in the social studies where there are almost as many classificatory schemes as there are theorists. Even the beginning of progress there has been thwarted in some places by a lack of widespread agreement about the basic kinds of entities to be studied. If this situation is to be remedied it seems essential that some understanding be gained of the prior *semantical* problems (i.e. about meaning) associated with making designations descriptions, and classifications of entities.[7] Some realist philosophers have recently made important arguments about the causal and social processes of establishing the meaning of terms referring to real entities.

Positivists give an account of meaning in which observations are supposedly theory neutral and the meanings of terms in successive theories are always a matter of empirical verification. Against this, relativists argue (see chapter 5) that descriptions, observations, and meanings are completely theory laden – i.e. relative to a set of theoretical presuppositions (or paradigm) such that translation between paradigms is impossible.

A realist theory of objective meaning

The realist approach to giving an objective account of meaning has been significantly reinforced recently by Saul Kripke, Hilary Putnam, and Richard Boyd. Kripke (1971, 1980) has argued that the usual way of identifying by name a particular entity (such as a person) or kind of entity is not, as is often thought, by making a description of its qualities or

---

[6] The problem of the role of conceptual schemes and categorical frameworks is discussed in illuminating ways by Davidson (1974a), Körner (1974).

[7] For recent debates over the meaning and reference of theoretical terms, see Platts (1979, 1980), Putnam (1975d, chs 1–13), Schwartz (1977), Shapere (1982b), Strawson (1970).

properties. The first 'baptismal' naming of an entity may be either by ostension (i.e. by pointing and labelling) or by description. From then on, once the name is fixed, there is a causal chain of usages stretching away to every other user of the name, each of whom thus relies in the first place upon the previous user to have used the name correctly to refer to the entity. In this way, names become what Kripke called *rigid designators*: i.e. they are names chosen to designate the unique identity of an individual or kind irrespective of the context (or possible world) in which it exists or the constituent elements of which it is made (Kripke, 1980, pp. 48–9).

But how does a name *identify* a thing or kind of entity? Identification must always be of one statement in terms of another; e.g. '*x* is the child of *A* and *B*' or 'gold is a yellow metal' or 'light is a stream of photons'. Kripke, like Harré and Madden, rightly argued that such identities are not *a priori* true, rather they are contingent, but if they turn out *a posteriori* to be in fact true then they are *necessarily* true (pp. 104–5, 108–9). If someone asserts that child *x*, referred to by its ostensively given name, is the offspring of *A* and *B* then this cannot be known *a priori* but it can be investigated for its truthfulness. If it turns out to be true then it is *necessarily* identifiable as such and will be in all possible worlds. It is therefore important for Kripke to distinguish *a priori* truths from necessary truths. In order to understand common-sense or theoretical identities of natural kinds, such as 'gold is a yellow metal' or 'light is a stream of 'photons', we have to know how the references for kind names are arrived at. He argued that it was by a *social* process. A community of speakers 'agrees' upon the use of a word to refer to a group of objects which are thought to be a kind due to their identifying marks. The name is then spread by a causal chain. For example, tigers may be thought of as large, black and yellow striped, quadrupedal, carnivorous animals. These qualities and properties are contingent but they serve to fix an original reference (pp. 116–21).

It is then the task of science to investigate the truthfulness of such common-sense identities. Once the essential nature of a kind is discovered, such as 'gold has atomic number 79', then it is necessarily true that gold is a natural kind with its own defining properties. Essential properties are not known *a priori* but are *a posteriori necessary*. Natural kind names are thus like proper names in being rigid designators, but only *a posteriori* rigid. Theoretical identities such as 'light is a stream of photons' therefore contain two rigid designators (pp. 123–33).

Notice the similarities of Kripke's argument with those of Mandelbaum, Quine, and Harré and Madden. They all argue in effect that an original inductive and social process of naming takes place, using the 'given' data provided by the senses. But a scientific process is then required to test these contingent identifications in order to arrive at necessary truths. Scientific identifications of one rigid designator in terms of another are in Kripke's account necessary identifications. His argument therefore helps to support realism since names refer to real entities, fixed in their nature, whether those entities be observable macro-physical or social ones, or micro-physical ones. The conceptual necessity linking names to particulars and kinds of entities is in effect made possible in the first place by a synthetic *a priori* commitment to the reality of the world in general and then underpinned *a posteriori* (as Harré and Madden showed) by science, which discovers the hiden dispositional and structural necessity that common-sense observation and reasoning point to.

Building upon this argument, Putnam rejected an earlier theory of meaning which held that the *intension* a user had when using the term (i.e. the mental concept associated with it) determined the *extension* of the term (i.e. the set of all things the term is true of) (Putnam, 1975b, pp. 216–19). He argued that the extension of a natural kind term, such as 'water' or 'gold', is always the same, irrespective of language, intension, or context. Like Kripke, he believes that when naming a natural kind such as water an ostensive definition is given. When the nature of water is later investigated it is found to have the molecular structure H_2O. Once discovered, it must have that structure *in all possible worlds*. A statement such as 'water is H_2O' is then epistemically contingent but metaphysically necessary. It is logically impossible for water to be anything but H_2O. The word 'water' thus has an indexical component: all substances called 'water' have to have the same structure as that we call 'water' (pp. 229–34). This is another way of making Kripke's point that natural kind words are *a posteriori* rigid designators.

This argument has obvious implications for an objective realist notion of truth. If 'gold' has always had the same extension but only recently have we known its molecular structure, then it was possible in the past for people to have been mistaken when labelling a piece of metal as gold, even if when they used the label 'gold' they believed and meant the metal had the correct essential structure. We are now able to judge the truth or falsity of their labelling. An alternative relativist argument would say that in the past there was a different operational definition of 'gold', which allowed the piece of metal to be correctly included. This implies sceptism about truth. Truth would then be intra-theoretical. But as Putnam pointed out, the idea of extension is related to truth, and those notions must belong to a realist perspective in order to make sense. As he put it,

> if there is a hidden structure, then generally it determines what it is to be a member of a natural kind, not only in the actual world, but in all possible words. Put another way, it determines what we can and cannot counterfactually suppose about the natural kind ('water would have all been vapour?' yes/'water could have been XYZ?' no). (Putnam, 1975b, p. 241)

Not only is extension rigid and not fixed by a mental concept but Putnam argued, as Kripke and Quine also did, that there is an essential *social* component to the use of words. Once a natural kind term like 'gold' is fixed there arises the possibility (and probably the necessity) for a linguistic division of labour. It is not possible for all members of a linguistic community to know the precise extension of every term. For each term there is a sub-class of speakers who acquire the term and all other speakers then depend upon a structured cooperation with them. Putnam called this his hypothesis of the Universality of Division of Linguistic Labour. It obviously depends upon a prior division of non-linguistic labour (pp. 278–9).

A convergence theory of truth

The importance of the Quine–Harré–Madden–Kripke–Putnam line of argument cannot be doubted. It goes a good deal of the way towards clearing up the philosophical problems of reference, truth, and scientific progress. Putnam's Principle of Reasonable Ignorance (1975c, p. 278) indicates that users of words about their own psychological states or about the actual world do not have to have precise extensions for those terms in order to be able to use them competently. For example, when a person speaks of being in pain, it does not indicate that she uses the term actually to mean a functional state or a body state or whatever. She can communicate the concept 'pain' without meaning any of these precise states. Or when talking about natural kinds such as water it does not follow that a person knows the necessary and sufficient conditions for a substance being water. And to be a competent user of a language in general does not require a person to have a good knowledge of the rules of grammar; nor is it necessary that a person fully understand the rules governing the hidden structure of his society for him to be a competent participant in that society. An acceptance of the linguistic division of labour makes this possible.

The individual's reference of words is thus determined by both society and the world. How does the *world* bring this about? Clearly, there has to be at bottom a *causal* relationship between the world and words, as Mandelbaum, Quine, and Putnam, among others, have argued. Humans as a species first established the primitive references of words to objects through *sensory perception* of the qualities of those objects. In time, of course, reference (and language in general) was greatly extended to include notions of reference, quantification, theoretical properties, proper names, and so on, through a process of deductive and inductive reasoning (cf. Lévi-Strauss, 1972, ch. 1). As language develops, the causal and non-causal relationships between words and the world and between words become very complex, and besides, as Quine and later Mary Hesse have shown (see 'The structure of scientific explanation' below), the original observational and inductive basis is not wholly reliable. But, realists must hold to the view that *in the end* reference and truth are constructed so that in the paradigm case, at least if things are as they should be,

> sentences will tend to be accepted in the long run if and only if they are *true*, and predicates will be applied to things if and only if those things have the properties *corresponding* to those predicates. It makes no sense to say language maps the world unless we have some parametrization of 'the world' in mind; what a reference concept does, at least in the ideal case, is to specify a parametrization of the world and correlate it to a parametrization of a language in such a way that accepted sentences tend in the long run to correlate to states of affairs (in the sense of parametrization) that actually obtain. (Putnam, 1975c, pp. 289–90)

There is, then, an interconnection between the notion of truth as *correspondence* to the world and truth as *coherence* within a set of concepts about the world. There is a gradual *convergence* between them, in the paradigm case, so that accepted sentences do come to mirror the world. The relationship is thus one of a complex, *converging correspondence* between theory and reality, but Putnam's Principle of Benefit of the Doubt (1975c, pp. 274–5) must be applied in every case. The obvious success of science is then made plausible by arguing (as Richard Boyd has done) that the terms of *mature* scientific theories do typically *refer* to real entities and processes and laws are typically approximately *true* (Boyd, 1973, p. 290. See also Putnam, 1978, lecture II). The convergence account is opposed to the strict causal (or physicalist) theory of reference and the relativist theory. The point about convergence is crucial for realism.[8]

Relativists such as Kuhn want to say that there is no warrant for believing that the theoretical entities referred to by scientists in past eras or within different paradigms are more or less the same. There is then apparently no intertheoretic reference and no convergence between theories on the notion of truthful explanation. Diametrically opposed to relativism is the physicalist version of the correspondence theory of truth, defended by Hartry Field, for example. Like other physicalists, he argued that primitive reference and truth have an objective physical relationship with the world and the investigation of neurophysiology is necessary to discovering the mechanisms involved (Field, 1972, p. 105).

But Field also rightly pointed out that we cannot make investigations of the relationship of our language to reality from outside our language and conceptual schemes (pp. 104–5). Similarly, the thrust of the Kripke/

---

[8] The convergence theory of truth is controversial. For further discussion and defences of it, or something like it, see Boyd (1979, 1983), Harré (1982b), Hesse (1973a; 1974, chs 1, 2, 12; 1978a, 1982).

Putnam theory that names are rigid designators is that there is no source external to our linguistic/conceptual/social scheme with which to make references to fundamental things in the world. Thus making statements such as ' "electron" refers to electrons' or ' "gene" refers to genes' is similar to saying as in Tarski's semantical/correspondence theory of truth that ' "snow is white" is true if and only if snow is white' (Putnam, 1978, pp. 31–2). But on the other hand, it does indeed seem that science *converges* upon better and better explanations because the world is more or less the way that mature science says it is. So, truth is an explanatory notion about overall scientific behaviour and success and not just a logical notion. Truth depends upon the notion of warranted assertability within a theory. Putnam has summed up this point by saying that

> realism depends on a way of understanding truth, not just a way of defining the word 'true'. The concept of truth is not philosophically neutral. The catch is that the meaning of 'true' and the logical connectives is not fixed by their *formal logic*; these are terms that very much fit Quine's account of meaning: that is, these are terms for which the distinction between total theory and term meaning is *useless*. But 'total theory' . . . means here just that: *total* theory, not just total *logical* theory, but total theory of knowledge; and this involves our theory of nature and our interactions with nature. (Putnam, 1978, p. 37)

Interest relativity, indeterminism, and underdetermination

The corollary of the Quine/Putnam argument is that truthful explanation is partly (but not wholly) an interest-relative notion. It is relative to what we wish to know as social beings but within a broad framework of ultimate convergence upon explaining the real causes and structure of the world. The relativists of course ignore this realist framework and treat scientific enquiry as constrained only by a personal and social context. If only this latter context is relevant then the problem of indeterminacy of translation between the meanings of terms of different theories is insurmountable. But it is clearly the case that the radical sociologists of science, such as Barnes and Bloor, give little attention to the *content* of scientific knowledge as opposed to its context of development. They are therefore unable to account for the real progress that occurs in natural scientific explanation (cf. Harré, 1983b, postscript). The case of social science may seem to be different. But there too the question of indeterminacy is a red herring (as I argued in chapter 4) because translation is no less essential to communication and scientific explanation than it is for natural scientists.

However, to ask for complete precision of reference and translation is utopian because reference is always, to some extent, context dependent.

And in the social studies, the data to be used for arbitrating referential disputes are either inadequate or too loaded with particular meanings to make unequivocal judgements possible. Theories are thus underdetermined.[9] But this is also sometimes the case in the physical sciences. Putnam goes too far when he claims that there is a fundamental gap between physical and social science because we lack a detailed explanatory model of a person owing to the complexity of humans as a system (Putnam, 1978, pp. 62–3).

We can and do know a great deal about persons and societies. The failure of both positivists and some hermeneuticists was to make the equation: objective knowledge = physicalist science = formalised N–D method. But this is much too restricted a view of knowledge. We know much (but certainly not everything) about our own culture and societies, about how to use our language, about our own psyches, about how to translate between languages, all without having formalised precise models or knowing the laws of structures.

On the other hand, as Amartya Sen (1983) has recently argued, we do need explicit ways of arbitrating factual claims about actions and society. And we do wish to explain objectively large-scale social change, for instance. The example of knowing a language and how to translate is of little use as an example of the sorts of knowledge required in these cases. *Verstehen* as a method is of little use to the explanation of macro social *structural* patterns and causes. While we do not yet have a detailed model of the natural kind 'person' or 'society' or 'institution', social science has made considerable progress in observing patterns, systems, and types of behaviour and social arrangements (such as rituals, forms of exchange, families, institutions, modes of production, and so on) and in hypothesising generative mechanisms of their functioning and evolution. Modelling is now widespread and significant in the social studies and rapid strides, even if from a low level, are now being made towards plausible explanations employing models.

THE STRUCTURE OF SCIENTIFIC EXPLANATION: THE PROBLEMS OF ACCESS, CONFIRMATION, AND PLAUSIBILITY

The complexity of explanatory structures

Given that the task of science is to explain the causes of the phenomena and processes of the world and that a large part of the causal structure of the world is unobserved and unobservable *in principle*, it is crucial that

---

[9] The closely related problems of indeterminacy of translation and underdetermination of theories by data have been much discussed lately by philosophers of science, including Boyd (1973), Harré (1980a), Hesse (1974, ch. 12), Hornstein (1982), Lukes (1978), Newton-Smith (1978), Quine (1970).

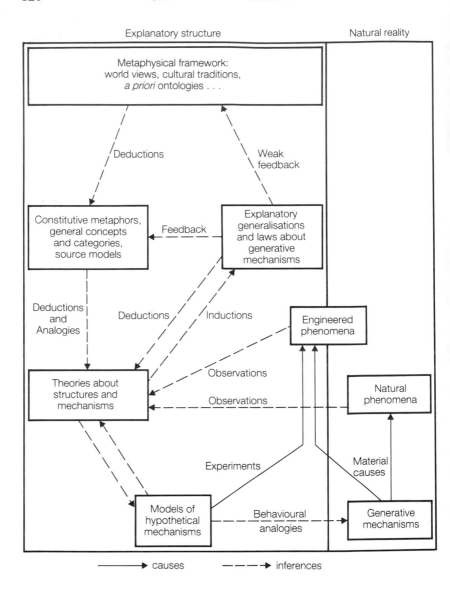

Figure 2   The structure of reasoning in natural science: a realist account

there be a coherent, rich, and adequate account of the explanatory and methodological principles used for the construction and testing of plausible theories. The structure of reasoning in science is a complex matter and one about which there is much dispute, as the foregoing chapters have revealed. Figure 2 summarises a realist account (or rational description), which I shall defend in the following two sections. (The diagram is inspired by but significantly amends that of Rom Harré, 1980a, p. 7.) I shall be arguing that science paradigmatically employs a combination of induction, metaphors, models, analogies, and deduction to construct plausible theories of the deep generative levels of reality and of how they relate to and link together the entities and processes of the observable world. The partly causal relationship between phenomena and our perceptions gives us a point of access for initial references and therefore a way into theory construction. But the problem of acceptance, confirmation, and plausibility of theories remains a large one.

It is essential to realise the importance of the mediation of linguistic conventions, conceptual schemes, general metaphors, and so on – indeed, explanatory frameworks in general. Human beings don't 'simply' mirror the world because the world is not 'simply' available for mirroring in spite of any evolved isomorphic relationship we may have with it. Our explanations are *framework bound*. But there has also been *progress* towards greater and greater knowledge, as shown by success in engineering and replicating nature and also (to a much lesser extent) society.

Against this, the claim by empiricists and naïve realists that some descriptions are indeed immune to revision in the light of further knowledge – that there is a theory/observation distinction – seems to be justified by the actual stability of many observational descriptions, due perhaps to a stability in the way the world is. But this apparent stability can be accounted for in Quinean terms by seeing such descriptions as closer to the established well-confirmed core, rather than the unstable periphery, of a set of laws and theories (Quine, 1980, pp. 42–3). And what constitutes the core itself is also theoretically determined and may in the future be revised (Hesse, 1980, pp. 74–5). If this is the case then it seems essential to replace the old theory/observation distinction with a *network* account of theories, laws, and observations, which is able to do justice to the *interaction* between theory and observation. In this conception, as Mary Hesse put it,

> no fundamental distinction is made between observational and theoretical languages. Both are assumed to have the aim of true description of the world, but the concept of 'true description' is not simply that of correspondence, but involves a more complex account of the application of learned predicates in particular empirical situations, together with the connection of these in scientific classifications and theories, and subsequent prediction, test, and confirmation or correction. Neither theory nor observation language are immune from correction; the distinctions between them concern rather their relative directness of empirical reference and application, and the relative entrenchment of terms in the natural and theoretical languages. (Hesse, 1980, p. xvi; see also pp. 83–108)

It may be objected against such an account that the notions of truth and confirmation that it contains are indeed circular in so far as they depend upon the coherence of the network of laws and empirical observations, so that crucial test situations for theories are themselves determined by those theories. Hesse agreed that the crucial test was provided by the totality of the network and particularly by the points of intersection of well-confirmed laws (pp. 96–7). This obviously depends upon *agreement* about test situations and the meaning of the whole network, as the conventionalists have argued. If the proponents of different explanatory theories are denied the possibility of theory-neutral tests then this agreement is essential. Thus the network approach depends upon a commitment to rational communication at crucial intersections (p. 99). This seems to concede the case to the hermeneuticists and conventionalists, and indeed Hesse has something in common with them, especially Habermas.

However, a network account of the theory/observation interaction does not have to collapse into relativism, providing a central place is retained for the idea of logical support for networks of an inductive analogical kind and empirical support of a probability kind.

> In this model, science retains its empirical basis, because the initial criteria of learning the correct use of descriptive terms in the natural language are empirical, and the self-corrective feedback process depends essentially on recognition of the success or failure of empirical predictions. The account therefore retains also the essentials of the correspondence theory of truth, but without the assumption of a stable observation language unpermeated by theoretical interpretation. The view of truth is, however, also essentially *instrumental*, since it derives from situations of prediction and test, and its relation to theories is indirect. Since the thesis of underdetermination of theory by data is built into the model, the sense in which 'truth' can also be predicated of theoretical frameworks remains undetermined. (Hesse, 1980, pp. xvi–xvii)

Therefore, as Hesse pointed out (1974, pp. 54–60) the epistemological consequences for realism of the network account can be strongly positive, including the following. Firstly, while the account does remove the possibility of a timelessly true and objective observational basis for science, an empirical basis can be retained if it is assumed that *most* initial classifications are correct (as Kripke, Putnam, and Harré also argued), although any particular one might be false and any particular meaning might be changed. This can only be determined relative to the network subsequently systematised. Hesse drew upon Neurath's well-known raft metaphor to express this idea: 'We may remain afloat on the sea of empirical facts by replacing the planks [of the raft] one by one, but not all at once, and there is no particular set of planks that must be retained intact throughout the whole operation.' (pp. 54–5) Furthermore, it must be added that there has never been a time when we were not on the raft. There is in fact no temporal sequence between initial observational classification of the world and theoretical processing – both go on together. We are never innocent of coherence conditions and their applications.

Secondly, the network account does not rely upon exemplary cases of universal terms. The classification of an object is not just a function of its properties or resemblance to an exemplar but a matter of locating it in its complex relationships with other objects and the coherence conditions of the network. Any examples which are used are not timeless. As Hesse said,

> An amoeba passes through the ocean continually changing its shape and changing its internal make-up of molecules, but it remains in some sense the same 'entity'. Similarly, a *P*-class that is continually changing its membership defines in this sense the 'same property' *P*, although what constitutes 'same property' can only be determined by looking at its history and its continuous interaction with its environment. (Hesse, 1974, p. 56)

Thirdly, and most importantly, the network account rests ultimately upon the *correspondence theory of truth*. Although initial classifications take place within a learned language and there is no external check on reference, only internal coherence, nevertheless the basic assumption has to be that most classifications correspond to the world. In short,

> that the truth-*value* of an observation statement is relative to coherence conditions is a matter of epistemology, but the *concept* of truth that is presupposed is a matter of ontology. That is, of a relation between existents. Truth is *a relation between the state of the world that produces empirical stimuli and the observation statements expressed in current descriptive language.* (Hesse, 1974, p. 57)

This is crucial. Without a correspondence theory reference collapses, as Putnam has shown, and there can be no progress. A realist ontology, however hedged about, is essential for a theory that attempts to make sense of science. Against those, such as Bloor and perhaps Habermas, who would adopt a consensus theory of truth, Hesse cogently pointed out that such a theory,

> in suppressing reference to the *world* and emphasising relations between speakers ... conjures up a threat of newspeak in which a consensus with respect to apparently descriptive statements might

be manipulated for purposes other than communication of empirical expectations.... If the consensus model is developed adequately, it needs a conception of the environment to avoid the threat of newspeak, and then what counts as consensus will become identical with what counts as truth in the naturalistic model. The differences between the models are more verbal than substantial, but the model using the notion of truth is less open to the currently dangerous misinterpretation of mistaking brain-washing for objectivity. (Hesse, 1974, p. 61)

Thus the network epistemology allows for and incorporates convergence of the Putnam–Boyd kind and shows the necessity for a sharing of meaning, reference, and the validity of certain test situations in order to move towards that convergence between coherence conditions and correspondence with the world.

Against logicism

One of the elements common to Quine's theory of the naming of natural kinds, Hesse's network account of theories, and Harré's ontology of powerful particulars and natural necessity, is an inductive-analogical account of explanatory inference. The nature and legitimacy of purely inductive inference – i.e. generalisations from known instances to unknown ones – has long been a central question for philosophy, especially since Hume argued strongly against its *logical* legitimacy. Induction is used constantly in common-sense and historical understandings and explanations, but does it have a proper place in science? Karl Popper and Imre Lakatos have been among those who have rejected it, although in later works Popper softened his opposition somewhat when discussing the question of degrees of corroboration (see chapter 3 and Putnam, 1974). His basic contention is that science consists fundamentally of the testing of hypothetical conjectures, which can be falsified but not inductively proven true. Where the conjectures come from is relatively uninteresting to him, but the research programmes in which they are situated are not to be thought of as generalisations from observations and tests. Carl Hempel also argued strongly that deduction is the proper logical form for scientific explanation and that history could become a science if it employed deductive arguments (see chapters 3 and 4).

There is a belief common among many self-styled empiricist and anti-empiricist practitioners alike in the social studies that induction is the empiricist method *par excellence*. Consequently, induction has come to be seen by *anti-empiricists* as illegitimate (e.g. T. Parsons, 1937, Introduction). This is unfortunate because empiricism has not necessarily been wedded to either induction or deduction. This mistaken identification has probably come about as a consequence of the simplistic equating of scientific method with inductivist epistemology, and the 'theory-neutral' counting of individual events by some social scientists who wish to see their procedures as genuinely scientific. The result has been scientism. Good examples are quantitative history and behaviourist psychology, in both of which it was thought that if sufficient atomistic events were carefully counted then 'explanations' consisting simply of a 'generalisation' of those results could be made. This account of science should properly be called 'vulgar empiricism'. It has little resemblance to the actual procedures of practitioners in the advanced sciences since it is based on a simple phenomenalism and nominalism. It cannot lead to the discovery of genuine mechanisms and in effect it does not even aim to do so.

One of the hallmarks of logical empiricism has not been vulgar empiricism as such but an adherence to logicism – the attempt to construe nature and scientific reasoning as conforming to the canons of formal logic – and because only deductive logic has been shown to have full coherence it has become since the 1930s the standard form against which all supposedly correct causal explanations have been judged. (Statistical explanations are also legitimate in the eyes of Hempel and Carnap but they are only explanations of the probability of the occurrence of certain events, not, strictly speaking, causal explanations.) But if logicism as an account of science is rejected then the way is clear for an account of the structure of scientific reasoning which is able to provide a richer understanding of its true complexity. Natural science stubbornly refuses to be fitted into either the purely deductivist or inductivist moulds, so why should history and the social studies (let alone common sense) be thought to do so? (For a critique of logicism and deductivism, see Harré, 1970, ch. 1.)

Modern deductivist positivism is based upon the *a priori* assumptions that logical order reflects natural order and that the task of science is to seek for the atmostic components of complexes. But because of their logicism the deductivists overlook the importance to science of what Harré has described as Gassendi's Principle; that is,

the inference from observables to hypothetical states, objects, or processes is proper, even though it commits the fallacy of affirmation of the consequent. . . . So, if E then P. P is observed, but not E. So to infer E from P we affirm the consequent. (Harré, 1970, p. 23)[10]

---

[10] The logical structure of Gassendi's Principle of Affirmation of the Consequent is similar in form to (1) the transcendental argument outlined by Charles Taylor (1978) and discussed earlier in this chapter, (2) the case of retroduction discussed by Hanson (1958, pp. 85ff), and (3) consequence explanations in the social studies (see Cohen, 1982a; Elster, 1983, ch. 2; and chapter 8). All of these appear to make the crucial step from observables to hypothetical states by affirming the consequents of those states. Clifford Geertz has also argued that the form of inference used in clinical medicine, which does not fit the deductive model, is appropriate to the social and psychological studies. See Geertz (1975, p. 26).

While such an inference conflicts with the canons of deductive logic it is nevertheless widely employed in the natural and social studies. Harré's comments upon its importance bring out its significance:

> In effect this principle allows theory to change without our having to abandon observations, and, at the same time, by pointing out the propriety of the inference, it allows one to pass from known effects to possible causes. How is this principle to be justified? First it is the principle which is used, and hence is required, if what we now think we know is to be preserved. Further, the method of analogy ... supplies us with the required content for the theoretical terms. Any logical system which asserts that this mode of inference is improper must be too narrow. It is a mistake of the first magnitude to abandon a perfectly *proper* principle because of its conflict with whatever logical system one happens currently to possess. (Harré, 1970, p. 23)

Analogical inference is a crucial aspect of realist explanation since it is *unobservable* mechanisms and dispositions that are being explained by reference to observable patterns. And induction is one intuitively employed method for the initial establishment of plausible hypotheses, which eventually give rise to analogies and models about the likely causation of observed regularities. But induction does not exhaustively describe the essential method of science either. To substitute a simple inductive account of scientific inference for the deductive one would be no improvement. Generalising from observed regularities to causes without the mediation of a complex network of concepts, models, hypotheses, theories, and deductions is not the method of science and cannot lead to the uncovering of hidden and unactualised dispositions and mechanisms. In short, science is interested in uncovering *real causes*, not in establishing *logical* relations or truths.

Thus the problem of induction is not one of how the scientist can avoid it, as Hume and Popper thought, but of how to give a satisfactory explication of the way in which such inferences are rationally employed (often intuitively) in science as well as in other systematic discourses and in common sense. A detailed explication would involve, *inter alia*, stating the implicit set of rules underlying inductive behaviour and systematising them into a postulate system based upon probabilistic confirmation theory.[11] The details need not concern us here since the point of interest is not the precision of the logical justification but rather one of practice and plausibility. That induction is used in science cannot be doubted. Its chief roles are to provide hypotheses and to underpin analogical explanation. The hypothetico-deductive model of scientific reasoning is unable

---

[11] Mary Hesse, among others, has attempted to carry this out (1974, chs 3–8).

to give an account of where problems, classifications, and questions come from.

Some positivistic defenders of the H–D model do claim, however, that what they are providing is an account of the logic of justification rather than of discovery. They say that a good scientific explanation must be presented in a deductive way although it may have been arrived at in some other way. Popper did not even concede this much, claiming, rather, that scientists actually begin with hypotheses and conjectures from which testable theories are deduced. The conventionalists and relativists (such as Kuhn and Feyerabend – discussed in chapter 5) refused to make the discovery/justification distinction.[12]

Metaphors, models, and analogies

In order to explain the occurrence of some phenomenal event, process, or pattern, reference must be made to causal mechanisms and their conditions of effectiveness. This will consist, paradigmatically, in referring to:

1 The properties, liabilities, and dispositional powers of things to behave in certain ways,
2 The structural context in which those powers are exercised or not, and
3 The impact on things of external causes.

Thus part of adequate explanation consists crucially of reference to unobserved (and sometimes unobservable) properties, powers, and structures. In order to make such references and to represent such entities the use of metaphors, models, analogies, and similes is indispensable. They make possible hypotheses about the existence and nature of entities in the first place, and sometimes stand in lieu of definite descriptions after their existence has been inferred.[13]

Metaphors, models, analogies, and similes thus serve heuristic purposes in explanation by providing means of access from what is known to what is unknown. They are vehicles for creative thought and penetrative explanation. They are all ways of representing something that is little known or understood in a manner which is less precise than a detailed direct description. They do this in an indirect manner and employ as their source something that is more familiar or better known and understood.

---

[12] On the relationship of the logic of discovery to the logic of justification, see Curd (1980), Laudan (1980), Nickles (1980), Popper (1972a, chs 1, 2, 3, 10), Radnitzky (1979), Wartofsky (1980).

[13] For general discussions of the role of metaphors, models, and analogies in science, see: Achinstein (1968, chs 7, 8), Black (1954, 1960, 1979), Boyd (1979), Davidson (1978b), Harré (1970, ch. 2; 1975, 1976), Hesse (1961, 1965, 1966, 1974, 1975), Kuhn (1979), Lakoff and Johnson (1980), Leplin (1980).

They thus have the power to bring separate objects into an explanatory relation through the device of one of them serving as a lens to see the other (Black, 1960, p. 236). They are devices through which, in Boyd's apt phraseology, the scientific community is able 'to accomplish the task of *accommodation of language to the causal structure of the world*' (Boyd, 1979, p. 358). This is the task of 'arranging our language so that our linguistic categories "cut the world at its joints"' (p. 358). Each accomplishes this in a different way and, indeed, a great variety of metaphoric and modellic forms can be identified (see Harré, 1970, ch. 2, 1975; Achinstein, 1968, ch. 7).

Metaphors and models are closely related. Metaphors are vaguer and less analytical expressions than models. They are sometimes used as a source for more precise analytical models of some entity or process but are usually not themselves refinable into models usable in research and precise explanation. Both gain their power through their relationship of analogy or simile with the entity or process in question. Analogies and similes are inferential relationships, properly speaking, not metaphorical or modellic expressions, although they are sometimes wrongly thought of as being such in their own right. Thus metaphors and models are devices which express putative analogous and comparative relationships.

Analogical inference

As I have said, models and metaphors enable us to infer by analogy from the known phenomena of the world to their unknown or partially known causes. This is a form of inference separate from that of logical deducibility. To see how it works and why it is more applicable to science consider the following discussion, drawn from the work of Mary Hesse (1974, ch. 9).

In order to explain a process or field of phenomena, we need to have knowledge of the natural kinds of entities constituting the domain. In classifying objects according to their properties and behavioural dispositions there are two possible ways to proceed:

1 By arguing by analogy from the properties of one object to another in the same species and from a species to another in the same genus; or
2 By using a classification system to pick out the analogous properties of objects.

The priority of either one depends upon circumstances and the stage of development of a particular science (pp. 208–9). In the earlier stages an analogical relation between objects is first proposed and then applied in other domains to make predictions about behavioural dispositions. Following Hesse's formulation, we can say that the confidence we have in the prediction of a second set of evidence (e_2) about behaviour is due to

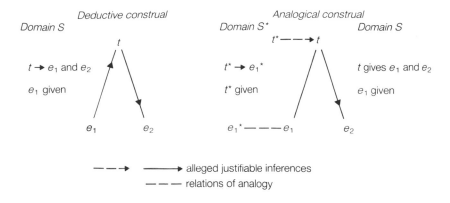

Figure 3 The analogical and deductive forms of construal

the analogy relation between it and an initial set (e_1). A theory (t) only enters the picture after this analogical inference is drawn. Its role is to extract the essence from e_1 and e_2 and show how it is possible to pass from one to the other (pp. 210–12). In making the inference from e_1 to e_2 external models are important in providing a source of truth for theories by analogy.

The analogical and deductive forms of construal between evidence and theories are shown in figure 3 (Hesse, 1974, p. 217).

In *deductive* construal there can be no justifiable inference from e_1 to e_2 (unless there is an analogical relation between them independent of t). But without a model that gives the probable truth of t by analogy with it there can be no external support for it apart from its own entailment. Thus the possible lines of inference in the diagram cannot in fact be justifiably made, according to deductivism.

In *analogical* construal there is a model (shown by *) which provides the basis for an analogy with e_1 and an assertion of the truth of t. Then if t^* states the causes of e_1^* then by analogy it may be justifiable to say that t states the causes of e_1 and of e_2 as a consequence of t. Thus truth in S is fed in from the model S^* and then passed on to e_2. This depends upon t^* and e_1 summarising all the available evidence and therefore having a high degree of plausibility.

Another way of stating this is that in putative deduction the relation of observation to theory cannot just be deductive, otherwise there would be no support other than a purely logical one for believing in the truth of a theory. Induction, analogies, and external models seem to be essential to first establishing support for a theory before any confident inference can be made from it to new situations.

Analogical construal thus fits together with metaphors, models, induction, and deduction to form a methodological framework for giving access to causal mechanisms and thereby plausibility in explanation. This structure of reasoning can be redescribed as shown in figure 2 on p. 120.

Plausibility and truthful discovery

The plausibility of theories – i.e. their power to prompt acceptance by rational people – depends upon five main considerations:

1 The degree of inductive empirical support for the hypothesis.
2 The strength of the behavioural analogy, i.e. the power the hypothetical mechanism has to simulate the real mechanism, as revealed by observations (see figure 2).
3 The strength of the material analogy, i.e. the degree of match between the properties of the hypothetical mechanism and the essential properties of things as dictated by the background framework, including especially the source model.
4 The relationship between the properties of the model and the general ontological principles of the social and intellectual background framework.
5 The relationship between explanation and the prevailing conception of truth.

Thus plausibility is partly an empirical notion, partly a logical notion, and partly a sociologically determined notion. But the notion of *objective truth* defended previously cannot be so considered. There is no simple truth to be had in science, but a convergence-correspondence theory does operate as a regulative notion affecting the behaviour of scientists and provides a *post facto* explanation of the rationality of their behaviour. And it is, at bottom, the only notion of truth that explains the objective long-term success of mature science in uncovering the causal structure of the world. Any attempt to abandon entirely the notion of truth in favour of plausibility alone is unable to do justice to this success. Discoveries do, in the long run, feed back upon the background framework to alter it. To hold otherwise is to slide into relativism.

But it can be argued that so far we have not made any true discoveries but have only moved closer to uncovering the causal structure of the world. Truth may be hypothesised as possible but as yet unattainable. Something like this has long been the view of Karl Popper (see chapter 3) and recently also defended by some others (see the previous section). Popper argued that there is no absolute basis to discoveries and no warrant for believing there is an absolute structure of the universe. Our theories are like piles driven into a swamp (Popper, 1972b, p. 111). Any *critical* realist, in order to be coherent, must support such a view, since realism holds not only that there is a realm of unobserved reality but that the frontier between that realm and the one of the observed has been shifting ever since scientific enquiry began. As discoveries in the realm of the hitherto unobserved have been made, that realm has been found to go on 'existing', as it were, always disappearing out of our grasp like a shadowy ghost of our own world. The frontier is constantly shifting due to technological advancement so that there have been discovered many entities and structures once thought purely hypothetical, or at least (given the benefit of the doubt) analogous ones that play the same causal role in theories. (Some also have not been found, as the famous case of cosmic ether exemplifies.) There is little reason to believe that we are approaching some sort of final discovery of the structure of the universe.

The rejection of the phenomenal as a reliable guide to structural reality must prompt all realists to be cautious about truth. Our sense organs are severaly limited in the type and amount of information they can process. The sciences have discovered, through analogical and comparative inferences from the phenomena of the world, that it is possible to build machines which extend our senses so that we can convert forces and processes, which are in principle beyond our sensory range, into sensory displays. For example, electromagnetic radiation in frequencies on each side of visible light can now be easily detected by machines. In this way we have advanced our knowledge but not thereby provided support for eschatological philosophies. What other forces and processes remain to be discovered? We cannot predict them all in advance.

THE BACKGROUND OF THEORY CONSTRUCTION

We have seen so far that the construction of causal theories is clearly not a simple matter of inductive generalisation. Neither is it just a matter of deduction from general principles, laws, or hypotheses. Theories are related (as figure 2 indicates) both 'forward' and 'backward': forward to models, observations, experiments, analogies, and laws; and backward to a complex of problems, obserational and theoretical categories, concepts, general metaphors and source models, and ultimately to a metaphysical structure of world views, ontologies, and myths. And of course the forward and backward linkages are joined through feedback links at various places. Not all the components in the backward linkage are of equal direct or specific effectivity. Three levels can be distinguished:

1 A domain of problems, concepts, categories, and methods
2 Constitutive metaphors and source models
3 A largely tacit realm of metaphysical world views, ontologies, myths, and so on.

The early logical empiricists argued that metaphysics should have no place in science and that experience is the only legitimate basis for truth and rationality. The relativists have held that the framework or paradigm, roughly corresponding to levels 1 and 2, determines both truth and plausibility, as well as rationality. This chapter has emphasised that many critical realists (such as Mandelbaum, Sellars, Quine, Putnam, Hesse, Bhaskar, Harré, Boyd, and Shapere) share with the relativists (such as Hanson, Kuhn, Lakatos, and Laudan) a central concern to articulate and investigate the influence of frameworks upon observations and explanations. There is thus a good deal of overlap in their arguments. However, realists also want to argue that plausibility and truth are *ultimately* a matter of correspondence with the world, although *provisional* plausibility arises from the relationship of laws to their background framework as well as to the network of observations and theories. Rational scientific practice then consists of the attempt to make *discoveries* about the world.

The positivist account of theories as a deductive structure linking axioms with observations via correspondence rules, and therefore relying on the theory/observation distinction, fails to grasp the actual structure of scientific reasoning and of explicit theories. One way to gain a better understanding of theories and to illuminate the reasoning actually employed lies in Shapere's concept of *domain*. (This concept has a good deal in common with that of 'research programme' developed by Lakatos and 'research tradition' developed by Laudan, discussed in chapter 5.)

Domains of theories

A domain is a body of associated information which in a mature science is characterised in the first place by the following four main features (Shapere, 1974d, p. 525):

1 The association is based on some relationship between the items.
2 There is something problematic about the body so related.
3 That problem is an important one.
4 Science is 'ready' to deal with the problem.

The first question to be asked about a domain is how it came to be considered as such. Obviously, in the first place, as Quine, Hesse, and others have argued, sensory similarities of objects and processes are important. Also important are general world views and ontologies of a metaphysical or quasi-metaphysical kind which influence observations and categories. But as a science matures so, as with language and explanation generally, these become less important. Associations of items are subjected, as Shapere put it, 'to critical review, and are often revised on the basis of considerations that are far from obvious and naïve' (Shapere, 1974a, p. 413). Differences and similarities are altered in their significance from superficial to fundamental and conversely. Items become redescribed in important ways.

Theoretical inadequacies within domains usually arise because a theory is incomplete or inadequate to account for the composition and/or evolution of the domain. But these weaknesses are not in themselves grounds for rejecting a theory. A theory may even be known to be fundamentally incorrect but be retained because of its usefulness, especially if there is no alternative available (Shapere, 1974d, p. 560). Perhaps, as Shapere said, a principle of non-rejection of theories could be proposed: theories should not be rejected until (1) their simplifications have been examined in case they are responsible for discrepancies between predictions and results, (2) repeated attempts have been made to supplement a theory in order to overcome gaps, and (3) another theory is available which *at least* accounts for the gap (Shapere, 1974c, p. 194; 1974d, p. 563).

This argument contrasts significantly with those of the empiricists, of Popper, and of the relativists. The empiricists argue for rationality on the basis of empirical tests to confirm theories. Against them, Popper argued for a combination of conventions about tests and falsifiability. The relativists usually argue that there is no logic of discovery. But Shapere showed that falsification and rejection are ambiguous and that rationality is not simple (Shapere, 1974c, p. 195). The strength of his argument is that it emphasises that the rationale of science cannot strictly be equated with a *logic* of discovery. The rationale is to search for compositional and/or evolutionary theories to explain what are taken to be ordered domains. There is no ideal logical way of proceeding to do that. There are different ways of viewing domains which suggest alternative lines of research and therefore different theories. And there is no guarantee that a line of research will be successful in terms of discovery (Shapere, 1974c, pp. 197–8). Nevertheless, underlying the search for theories is the desire to make *discoveries* and *progress* in explanation. To this extent Shapere's position supports realism for, while he rejects any *a priori* commitment to an external source for truth, he is not arguing for a closed relativism in the way that Kuhn was, for instance. The domain constitutes the problems, but those problems in turn relate to how the world is and how it changes.

Source models and constitutive metaphors

How do emerging, immature sciences construct domains of enquiry? They first require some set of concepts and categories to bring more order to their otherwise intuitively but vaguely delimited, partly ordered and little understood, domain of entities and processes. Those concepts and categories cannot be generated internally; they hve to come from some already existing source of ideas. As M. H. Abrams put it:

Any area for investigation, so long as it lacks prior concepts to give it structure and an expressed terminology with which it can be managed, appears to the enquiring mind inchoate – either a blank, or an elusive and tantalising confusion. Our usual recourse is, more or less deliberately, to cast about for objects which offer parallels to dimly sensed aspects of the new situation, to use the better known to elucidate the less known, to discuss the intangible in terms of the tangible. This analogical procedure seems characteristic of much intellectual enterprise. (quoted in Black, 1960, p. 240)

Perhaps the obvious place to begin in constructing a domain is with direct observations of similarities and processes (i.e. ostension). While that is correct we need to go much further, as we have already seen, because observation is always theory laden and part of a network of ideas. Moreover, the world is always covered by and interpreted to some extent through a network. We never come truly naïvely to any part of it, although there are large areas about which we have only very vague ideas and concepts and for which we have very inadequate explanations. This is certainly true in most of the socio-historical studies.

In attempting to construct new domains the most important direct influences upon observations and conceptualisations are source models and constitutive metaphors.[14] These comprise a realm of largely explicit but partly implicit cognitive materials from which scientists draw to build domains and models. How this realm in turn is developed is mainly a matter of the influence of other more developed sciences, of intellectual/ artistic traditions, and of general world views. These are discussed in the next section.

Source models consist of various sorts of notions about the structure of the world in general and especially of particular parts of it. They are usually general pictures about the constituents of nature which are employed as a source from which to generate theories and more precise models and as a standard against which to compare them. The billiard ball concept of matter, for example, was a source which licensed certain constructions about chemical interactions. In the human studies, two fundamental models of man hold that humans are either plastic or autonomous (cf. Hollis, 1977). And in sociology, society is conceived of variously as an organism, a machine, a beehive, and so on. These models have had powerful effects upon almost all socio-historical explanations, particularly ones dealing with action. But the degree to which they are *explicitly* adopted and employed varies a great deal.

An important form of source model is that of metaphor. We saw above

---

[14] The influence and importance of general source models and constitutive metaphors is examined in Boyd (1979), Harré (1975, 1976, 1980a, 1980b, 1982b), Hollis (1977), Sternberg et al. (1979).

that sustained and systematic metaphors have the power to bring separate domains into (as Max Black put it) 'cognitive and emotional relation' (Black, 1960, p. 236). They do this through a transference of ideas. Richard Boyd has persuasively argued that some metaphors help to *constitute* theories through catechresis – i.e. by introducing terminology where none existed before. But their success does not depend upon conveying specific similarities or analogies, as with ordinary interaction metaphors. Rather, their utility flows from their open-endedness. And in time they are explicated, thus ceasing to be metaphors and becoming scientific terms. He rightly argued that

> the employment of metaphors serves as a non-definitional mode of reference fixing which is especially well suited to the introduction of terms referring to kinds whose real essences consist of complex relational properties, rather than features of internal constitution. . . . [This] provides the basis for a clearer understanding of the (itself metaphorical) notion that reference fixing in the case of theoretical terms in science involves *ostension*. . . . The issue of reference for a general term is the issue of its role in making possible socially coordinated *epistemic access* to a particular sort of thing or natural phenomenon. (Boyd, 1979, p. 258)

Examples of general constitutive metaphors in the sciences are atom as solar system, brain as computer, man as machine, society as organism, or society as building. Such metaphors are more prevalent in the social sciences, which is an indicator of their immaturity, since their chief mode of access remains metaphorical and analogical rather than experimental or mathematical. Such metaphors have the function of drawing attention to relations of similarity or analogy with the secondary subject of the metaphor and thus directing our research and theory constructing in that direction.

Metaphors not only help constitute our theories about the world, they also help constitute our social actions and behaviour. They do this by providing a source of understanding of the social world and thus a motivation to action. Whether or not they also help constitute the social structure is a crucial question for social science. The idealist/hermeneutical/phenomenological tradition has always argued that conceptual/linguistic frameworks do play such a role. They argue that society has no existence apart from our understandings of it. Goffman (1959, 1974), Berger and Luckmann (1966), Harré (1975), and others have recently argued that unlike natural science, which employs models to analyse an independently existing reality, social science must conceive of its object not as independent but as *constituted* by societal icons. I shall be arguing against this view in chapters 8 and 13, but it is important to realise that models of various sorts are essential to social explanation.

Metaphysics and world views

The indispensability of a background framework for scientific research and explanation can no longer be doubted. But the extent to which that background is *metaphysical* in fact and necessarily so is greatly disputed.[15] Hume and the early logical empiricists wished to expunge all metaphysics from science. But in recent decades, under the influence of the history of science, of holistic and relativistic philosophies, and of the sociology of explanation, metaphysics has been re-established as a serious aspect of the philosophy of explanation. Many philosophers and historians now argue that all explanation necessarily takes place within a context of metaphysical ontologies, world views, traditions, myths, and so on.

The notion of metaphysics is much abused and notoriously vague. As the word indicates, it should properly be confined to the study of the fundamental nature of the physical universe – its constituents, structure, and causation. But the word has also tended to take on an additional meaning to do with the supposedly *a priori*, untestable, mystical, and often implicit nature of general views about the world. However, it would be a mistake to try to confine the study of metaphysics to implicit and untestable views. There are in fact four kinds of metaphysical doctrines:

1 *Explicit analytical ontologies* Ideas about such abstract things as properties, objects, events, propositions, dispositions, and existence in general.
2 *Explicit speculative cosmologies* General accounts of the main features of the world such as minds, bodies, space, time, God, and their causal relations.
3 *Implicit cosmological views* Like the former but unarticulated, vaguer, and tacitly subscribed to.
4 *Implicit societal myths* Ideas of a largely tacit kind about the nature of persons and societies.

Each of these has a set of categories of things, processes, and causes. The task of metaphysics as a branch of philosophy and science is to explicate and analyse the content and structure of these doctrines (1) in order to assess their significance for other more precise theories and methodologies, and (2) so that their truth can be assessed. In doing so, it is possible that many metaphysical ideas will be found either to be untestable for their truth value or to have no truth. But not all metaphysical doctrines are bad, as the early logical empiricists tended to

---

[15] For some examples of recent discussions of the place and significance of metaphysics in science, see Agassi (1964), Davidson (1979), Jardine (1980), Sellars (1968).

believe. And it has become apparent that even they had metaphysical foundations for their ideas. The question of the existence and influence of metaphysics must be separated from the question of truth.

In the last three sections, I have been dealing mainly with epistemological and semantical matters – i.e. those relating to problems about if and how we can have knowledge of the unobservable realities of the world. Not much has been said since the section on 'Dispositions, causal powers, and natural necessity' about ontological matters – i.e. about the nature of reality. In the section before that I discussed very briefly the transcendental approach to establishing the reality of underlying generative structures, and in the 'Dispositions' section I outlined a general approach to defending the interrelationship of dispositions, powers, and structures as the fundamental level of reality. But it was then important to establish a realist *epistemology* before proceeding any further to discuss ontology, because there seems little point in making more detailed pronouncements about the nature of the world unless we have some warrant for thinking that we can indeed have access to postulated dispositional and structural realities. Both the existence of science and the arguments I have discussed so far do give us good reason to believe that there is a world of universals and that we have an ability to develop increasingly plausible and truthful accounts of them. However, the ontological problem remains: of what nature is the world? Is it wholly material or is there a plurality of realities? Is the world only micro-physical, all the appearances being merely epiphenomena, or are there real emergent macro systems and things? Most importantly for present purposes, can society be considered real in the way that material entities are?

The most basic divisions between realists on the ontological level are over the questions of (1) whether or not there are non-material forms of reality, and (2) whether or not macro entities and systems possess emergent properties which cannot be described or reductively explained in terms of the properties of their constituent elements. *Materialists* are those realists who hold to the ontological doctrine that there is only a material kind of substance in the universe (i.e. substance monism). This means that they deny the existence of such postulated non-material substances as mind, spirit, entelechies, God, vital forces, and Platonic forms. But they in turn divide on the question of whether there are *emergent properties and powers* of a *non-physical* kind (such as mental and social structures) possessed by material macro entities and systems. Thus there are two basic categories of materialists:

1 *Physical materialists* Substance monism, property monism;
2 *Emergent materialists* Substance monism, property pluralism.

Another way of describing this difference is in terms of *levels* of properties – emergent materialists believing that emergent properties exist on a different level from the material substance of macro entities or systems such as tables, humans, societies, and galaxies. Because physicalists reject emergence they are *ontological reductionists*, believing not only that the phenomena of the world are misleading but also that there are no real macro properties and powers. They are usually also *explanatory reductionists*, attempting to explain the macro appearances of the world by reference to micro-physical constituents. However, it is possible for physicalists to adopt, along with emergentists, the notion of *explanatory emergence*. In this case they would argue that it is unavoidable, for the time being, theoretically to postulate properties of apparent macro entities in order to explain human behaviour, for instance. This is a kind of instrumentalism in reverse, as advocated by a long list of writers and including Sellars for the physical sciences and Hayek and Brodbeck for the social sciences (see chapter 8), in which concepts about *wholly theoretical* macro entities are used to explain micro entities in the absence of knowledge about the laws of micro entities.

A key issue for materialists and their opponents is the mind/body problem; or, to put it another way, is there a realm of the mental which is not wholly reducible to the physical structure of brains? The importance of this perennial problem lies in its direct relevance to the central questions of the explanation of human action and expression. If it could be established beyond doubt that mental attributes can be studied completely through neurophysiology then this would be a step towards resolving many age-old philosophical, psychological, and sociological problems. However, so far the physicalist reductionists have not succeeded. And I shall now try to show why I believe their attempts are necessarily in vain.

PHYSICALIST MATERIALISM

Since the 1950s an influential physicalist current of thought has developed under the influence of the rapidly developing sciences of neurophysiology and artificial intelligence. Before that time the dominant conception of humans was dualist – i.e. brains and minds are separate entities with their own structures, processes, and powers. But for many of those who thought about this problem there was an obvious connection between minds and brains, since it seemed minds were dependent for their existence in some way upon brains. For some others, however, there was little or no connection, since they believed in the possibility of disembodied minds and souls and the power of minds to effect things at a distance.

A turning point in the debate came with Herbert Feigl's important essay on *The Mental and the Physical* (1958). He rejected dualism (as well as the empiricist epistemology which tended to go with it) and defended physicalism as a solution to the mind/body problem and hence of the explanation of human action and behaviour. He believed it to be possible *in principle* to make a reduction of psychological terms about human behaviour to terms about micro-physiology, although this was not yet possible in actual practice. He advocated an explanatory reduction of the observable behavioural data to the theoretically inferred, unobservable, physical mechanisms of the brain. This implied a realist epistemology resting on the idea that observable data are only the conceptual 'anchors' for real unobservable entities, and are not ontological equivalents (pp. 75–7).

Feigl's theory did not deny the existence of the mind as such but claimed that there was an *identity* of mental and physical properties, which were linked through making explanations on both levels. That is,

the states of direct experience which conscious human beings 'live through', and those which we confidently ascribe to some of the higher animals, are identical with certain ... aspects of the neural processes in these organisms.... [That is] we may say, what is *had-in-experience*, and (in the case of human beings) *knowable by acquaintance*, is identical with the object of *knowledge by description* provided first by molar behaviour theory, and this is in turn identical with what the science of neurophysiology *describes* (or, rather, will describe when sufficient progress has been achieved) as processes in the central nervous system, perhaps especially in the cerebral cortex. (Feigl, 1958, p. 79)

The identity theory, then, is the claim that there is an isomorphism between the mental and the physical such that there is a 'one-to-one correspondence of elements and relations among the phenomenal data with the elements and relations among the referents of certain neurophysiological terms' (p. 103).

One of the central questions prompted by this account concerns the *causal* powers of mental events. The related doctrine of materialistic parallelism holds that mental events are somehow epiphenomenal appendages of brains – dangling at the end of physiological chains and having no causal powers. Against this Feigl claimed that the identity theory avoided epiphenomenalism because it is monistic:

Mental states experienced and/or knowable by acquaintance are interpreted as the very realities which are also denoted by a (very small) subset of physical concepts. The efficacy of pleasure, pain, emotion, deliberation, volitions, etc., is therefore quite definitely affirmed. (Feigl, 1958, p. 107)

How complete can the physicalist-identity theory of mind or the world be? Can it give an account of all causal powers and structures such that, in principle, there is nothing left over – no 'nomological danglers' left to explain? Wilfrid Sellars rightly argued, as we saw in the 'Common sense and critical realism' section above, that even a strict physicalist must concede that there is an alternative 'manifest' image or framework in which to study man (and perhaps the world in general). The physicalist framework is certainly not yet capable in practice of giving a complete account.

Feigl believed his identity theory of mind and brain to be a metaphysical hypothesis, capable of being tested only in the future when neurophysiology is further advanced. Some advances were made in the 1960s, and in the closely related field of artificial intelligence, one outcome of which was a boost to physicalist philosophers. The doctrine of central-state materialism of the Australian school of materialist philosophers, notably J. J. C. Smart and David Armstrong, built upon these developments and the ideas of Feigl.

In his influential book on *Philosophy and Scientific Realism* (1963), Smart argued that all sense data about the world should be understood purely in physical terms, i.e. as light rays, sound waves, and so on, stimulating the brain (Smart, 1963, pp. 26–7). Experiences, or reports of our experiences, do not depend, he believed, upon 'inner experiences', or mind, or a ghost in the human machine. On the contrary, for him humans are very complex, physical, self-regulating 'machines'; no more, no less. Humans are like computers, but of a degree of complexity not yet artificially replicable, although in principle it may be feasible and perhaps will be in the future (pp. 114–15). The 'human computer' has intelligence and originality, the ability to learn from experience, to make choices, and so on (pp. 124–5).

If it is possible that a computer could be constructed with the same material complexity of a brain, this would then constitute a good test for the existence of brain/mind identity. Indeed, it is encumbent upon dualists to show that mental abilities are not dependent *in some sense* upon neuronal complexity and the precise physical structure of human brains. Does the postulation of mental *independence* (i.e. dualism) explain anything about human expressions and behaviour which cannot be explained by materialism? Materialists are surely right to believe not. But it is important to see that both monism and dualism are, as Feigl pointed out, partly metaphysical doctrines, and will remain so until physiology and psychology are further advanced.

Central-state materialism has reached its apogee with the work of David Armstrong. Mental concepts, such as desires and beliefs, he took to be causally linked to our behaviour and to the world. Some (e.g. purposes) are the causes of actions and some (e.g. perception and beliefs) are the effects of the physical world, i.e. mappings within us created by the world's impingements upon us. There is a complex interdependency of the concepts of purpose, perception, and belief (Armstrong, 1977, pp. 20–4). But for Armstrong mental concepts do not have irreducible powers, i.e. the brain has no emergent properties: the presence of concepts must be explained by physical causes. His argument was summarised this way (Armstrong, 1978a, p. 271):

1 The cause of all human (and animal) movements lies solely in physical processes working solely according to the laws of physics.
2 Purposes and beliefs, in their character as purposes and beliefs, cause human and animal movements.
3 Purposes and beliefs are nothing but physical processes working solely according to the laws of physics.

This is a clear statement of an identity theory. But notice that, firstly, such a theory does not say anything precise about the nature of the physical processes which mental processes are. That is, it does not specify that those processes have to take place in complex neuronal structures of live human cells. Secondly, in the theory of Feigl, Smart, and Armstrong there is the claim that each mental property and process is precisely identical with a particular physical property and process such that neurophysiological detection will in principle reveal the precise electro-chemical process of each thought. But this may never be possible, since it may be the case that although materialism is committed to mental events being *necessarily* also physical states, it does not follow that there must be a simple identity of events. These two points indicate the need for more sophisticated versions of materialism, such as were provided by other thinkers, to be discussed in a moment.

Strict physicalism does seem to run counter to plausibility because of its denial of the possibility of studying amergent properties of systems. It confuses *physical dependence*, which relations and minds have to their organic 'containers', with *identity*. Materialist explanations do not need to postulate identity, and it is in fact a hindrance to explanations of mental and social structures.[16]

EMERGENT MATERIALISM

Thus the hallmark of strict physicalism is reductionism. Mental events and powers are explained by uncovering their causal identity with physical processes. But it is possible to be a materialist without subscribing to brain/mind identity. To be such involves arguing for a concept of

[16] For general discussions of identity theory, see Armstrong (1968), Børst (1970), Bunge (1980), Meehl (1970), Rorty (1980), Taylor (1970).

the mental as an *emergent* set of properties and powers of the brain which, while being dependent upon the brain for its *physical* existence (i.e. it cannot exist independently as a disembodied entity), is nevertheless not completely explainable by physical processes. Several versions of such a materialism have been argued for in the 1970s as reactions against what has been taken to be the false move of reductionism. It is important to stress that these arguments are not dualist in the old sense. They are all attempts to go beyond the old monistic/dualistic dichotomy by defending the very plausible view that minds have powers and dispositions which are beyond the reach of neurophysiology.[17]

The first to be considered is that of the American philosopher Hilary Putnam, who abandoned in the late 1960s an earlier commitment to the identity theory and developed in the 1970s his *functionalist* argument. He argued (1973) that discussions about the *substances* out of which systems (such as minds, machines, organisms, economies) are made is beside the point when attempting to explain their *functioning*. His reasoning about this involved two sets of ideas:

1 The notion of *functional isomorphism* between different systems, and
2 The possibility of *non-reductive structural explanations* of the functioning of macro systems.

To take functional isomorphism first. Two systems are said to be functionally isomorphic if there is a correspondence between the states of one and the states of the other that preserves the functional relations within each system. That is, if there is a correct theory of the functioning of system 1 at the functional or psychological level, then an isomorphism between system 1 and system 2 would show that each property and relation of system 2 would come out true in the theory when references to system 1 are replaced by references to system 2 (Putnam, 1973, pp. 291–2). Functional isomorphism does not require that the two systems have the same material constitution, e.g. a computer made of electrical components can be isomorphic to one made of cogs and wheels, or even to a group of human clerks using paper and pencils. (Some philosophers nowadays argue (e.g. Boden, 1977, 1979a; cf. Dreyfus and Haugeland, 1974) that computers are isomorphic to humans, but this seems to be a mistake since the psychological states of humans have no corresponding states in a machine.)

Furthermore, Putnam argued that the mind/brain identity theory could not be correct. Even if we are no more than physical organisms, our mental states are not necessarily identical with physical or chemical states of the brain in that the same organic structure can contain quite different

---

[17] On emergentist materialism in general, see Block (1982), Boyd (1980), Bunge (1981), Fodor (1983, ch. 1), Healey (1978), McGinn (1982a, ch. 2).

psychological compositions. And from computers we know that the same program can be produced by machines with quite different physical structures. 'It is as if', he wrote, 'we met Martians and discovered that they were in all functional respects isomorphic to us, but we refused to admit that they could feel pain because their C fibers (i.e. brain neurones) were different.' (p. 293) What matters to Putnam is the *structure* of the system, not its substance.

This brings us to the point about explanation. If substance is not important to function, then the point of making a physical-reductionist explanation of function is lost. It depends upon our *aims* in making explanations. Explaining a macro system by referring only to its macro structure makes good sense if a reductive explanation obscures certain important macro relationships and laws and if it enables us to generalise to other systems. The lesson from this for behavioural and sociological explanation is clear: there is *relative autonomy* of the mental, so behaviour cannot be explained by neurophysiology; and there is relative autonomy of the social, so structural change and social behaviour cannot be explained by psychology alone.

Thus Putnam is an emergentist about macro systems and the explanation of behaviour, while being a defender of the materiality of mind. A similar position, and one which gives considerable support to the intentionalist methodology in historical explanation as proposed by, for example, Dray and Scriven, has been argued for in a series of essays by the American philosopher Donald Davidson. He described his position in 1970 as *anomalous monism*. It

> resembles materialism in its claim that all events are physical, but rejects the thesis, usually considered essential to materialism, that mental phenomena can be given purely physical explanations. Anomalous monism shows an ontological bias only in that it allows the possibility that not all events are mental, while insisting that all events are physical. (Davidson, 1970b, p. 214)

This allows him to argue that while there are no psychological laws of the sort that Smart, Armstrong, and other reductionists hope will be discovered, there is still a *causal dependence* of the mental upon the physical.

For Davidson the fundamental aspect of the realm of mind is *intentionality*. This is a property which makes the strictly lawful explanation of mental events impossible and legitimises *rational* explanation instead, but always on a basis of nomic generalisations (cf. discussion of Dray and Scriven in chapter 3). The possibility of correctly translating mental concepts such as 'belief' and 'desire' into physical concepts is impossible because appeals to actors' reasons and beliefs are the constitutive evidence for our theories about mental events, and so those theories constantly evolve. But people think, believe, and behave relatively consistently, which is part of being a person, so rough generalisations about mental processes are possible (Davidson, 1970b, pp. 221–3). Thus Davidson's innovation was to try to combine three principles: the causal dependence of the mental upon the physical; the nomological character of causality (i.e. the idea that ascriptions of causation can only be made on the basis of laws; see chapter 4); and the anomalism of the mental (i.e. there are no strict deterministic laws for explaining it). Mental events cannot be explained by universal laws because the mind is not a closed system and because only rough generalisations about reasons are available as our source of information. Although mental events are physically caused we cannot know accurately about those causes. This then allows a place for the efficacy of thought and purpose in a material world through the autonomy of intentional action. Humans are at once wholly physical beings *and* free agents (pp. 223–5).

These arguments of Putnam and Davidson are examples of ones which have become increasingly attractive in recent years as the hoped-for neurophysiological support for physicalism has not materialised (*sic*). The implications of their emergentist materialism for social science are obvious, since if the precision of physical science is the goal then it will never be reached. Social science is dependent upon (among other things) uncovering agents' *reasons* for action rather than just physical mechanisms. But even if physicalist scientific precision is not the goal there is still the possibility, at least, of an objective approach to explaining behaviour.

The idea of emergent properties and powers should be contrasted with the non-materialist doctrines of vitalism, animism, and spiritualism, all of which hold that the group powers of certain organisms or social systems not only do not emerge from the combination of their elements but are not explainable by reference to the elements or their combination. They are ontologically and explanatorily distinct. Emergence does not imply (as some may suppose) such dualist or pluralist ontologies. It is thus important to distinguish ontology from epistemology. An epistemology which supports or requires explanatory emergence, such that the functioning and history of systems cannot be explained without postulating and investigating emergent levels of properties and powers, does not thereby imply that those properties and powers are not material. To paraphrase Donald Davidson, all events and processes are material but some events are also emergent. However, some emergentist philosophers (notably Karl Popper) are indeed ontologically ambivalent, and they constitute the alternative metaphysical current to materialism within realism. That is, Popper, has a metaphysical theory which postulates the reality of *three* levels of entities in the world rather than just the one of matter. For him the emergent levels lose, to some extent, their dependency upon their generative levels.

It is sufficient, to begin with, to argue (as Meehl and Sellars, 1956, Putnam, Kim, and others have done) that emergence is possible *in principle* and then leave it as a matter for empirical investigation as to its existence and character in particular cases. Support for the idea of the possibility of emergence is given by Putnam's concept of functional properties and Kim's concept of supervenient properties (see Kim, 1979), both of which show how it is possible to explain macro structure and causation without resorting to reduction. The strict physicalist, such as Smart, rejects *a priori* the possibility of genuine emergence, seeing supposedly emergent properties (e.g. the property possessed by a radio receiver to translate radio waves into sound) not as constituting a separate level of properties but as being perhaps epiphenomenal. But clearly there is nomological incommensurability (to use Kim's phrase) between certain macro events and processes and any supposedly corresponding microphysical process or state. What matters for emergence is that systems with it are governed by different causal laws than those without it. Thus if two macro entities have identical physical constituents and at least one has emergent properties and powers, then it must have a different causal structure. Alternatively, if two emergent systems have the same properties and powers it is possible for them to have different physical constituents. Putnam's example of the same computer functions being possible in differently constituted machines bears this out.

Clearly, biology and sociology in general and evolutionary theory in particular require a concept of emergence because evolving systems of organisms or species or societies acquire new characteristics, structures, and processes which have proven to be not explainable by reduction to previous stages or lower levels in their hierarchies. That is, as Brodbeck (1958, pp. 309–11) argued, *explanatory emergence*, at least, is indispensable in the biological and social sciences (see chapter 8). Given this, the problems are to delineate the boundaries of organisms, species, and societies; and to gauge their degree of integration so that the level and specificity of causal relationships can be isolated.[18]

The most developed and influential version of an emergentist and evolutionary theory of knowledge is that of the Swiss philosopher, biologist, and psychologist Jean Piaget. He attempted to develop what he called 'genetic epistemology' by combining a structural conception of the human person with a systemic-evolutionary theory of learning, knowledge, and mental development. Contrary to widespread belief, it is primarily as epistemology rather than as psychology that Piaget sees his work. Psychology and biology were for him mainly a means to understanding how humans perceive and explain the world.[19]

His genetic epistemology stressed the notion that knowledge is not *a*

---

[18] For recent discussions of evolutionary theory and philosophy and its relevance to social explanation, see D. T. Campbell (1974, 1975), Elster (1983, ch. 2), Ghiselin (1981), Hooker (1978), Toulmin (1972, ch. 5), Van Parijs (1981), Wilden (1972, chs 8, 12). There is, of course, now a vast literature on sociobiology. But this is not an epistemological doctrine but a theory of human behaviour and is not of interest for the moment.

[19] For discussions of Piaget see Boden (1979b), Gruber (1982).

priori or innate but must be considered as a novel *emergent* structure, with its own necessary relationships and objective connections with reality. Knowledge is a continuous *construction* and *transformation* growing ever richer in a dialectical process of synthesis, revolutions, and extensions (Piaget, 1972a, pp. 14–17).

The central problem for Piaget (as for most epistemologists) is to account for the genesis of both *new* knowledge and for the *truthfulness* of knowledge of the external world. Innatism stresses the role of predetermination; empiricism stresses the role of direct experience. He was opposed to both of these. Should cognitive structures be viewed either as the outcome of a totality of structural presuppositions for knowledge, or as the constitutive conditions for knowledge of pre-existing structures in the world? In the former case, it makes little sense to speak of the details of creative human thought as predetermined (p. 85). In opposition to the notion of preformed structures he proposed his *psychogenetic* view of knowledge, which sees it as the result of a constant interaction between the human subject and the external object in a complex of biological and intellectual transformations that constantly throw up novel emergent structures. 'Objects certainly exist', he wrote, 'and they involve structures which also exist independently of us.'

> But objects and their regularities are known to us only in virtue of operational structures which are applied to them and form the framework of the process of assimilation which enables us to attain them. They are therefore only arrived at by successive approximations, that is, they represent a limit never itself attained. On the other hand, every causal explanation also presupposes the attribution of our operations to objects, and consequently is evidence of an isomorphism between their structures and ours. But this makes so much more difficult any assessment of the nature of these objective structures independently of ours, their independent nature becoming in its turn a limit never attained though one in whose existence we are compelled to believe. (Piaget, 1972a, pp. 90–1)

Piagetian epistemology is obviously opposed to any form of apriorism or reductionism. And it supports the general idea of an emergent realism, or what he called 'constructivism' or 'structurationism', but one which contains a central notion of the human subject and objective reality being in a dialectical relationship (Piaget, 1971b, pp. 8–13). This prompts the obvious question of how these cognitive constructions are to be validated. That is, how are we to know that the construction of new systems of concepts about new irreducible macro structures in the world are justified? His answer is simply to say that such constructivism is both constitutive of new knowledge and also enriching of existing knowledge. Many sciences have been better able to explain existing levels of systems by positing higher, irreducible levels rather than attempting to make causal reductions. There can often be a demonstration of reciprocal assimilation between two levels of a system, and hence a more complete explanation of structure, if the desire to make a causal reduction is removed (1972a, pp. 92–3).

Piaget's developmental psychology is the keystone to his epistemological conclusion that our knowledge of the world is neither innately nor externally determined and so there is no *a priori* limit to human cognitive development. Transformations and the emergence of novel structures in the evolutionary processes of biological, psychological, and intellectual development must be accounted for, not avoided. The partial affinity that such a view has with the hermeneutical conception of knowledge is clear but the differences, centring upon Piaget's realism, are also clear. While cognitive structures, for him, are constitutive of knowledge, those structures are in turn constituted by the action of the subject both in the objective world and through attempting to explain the causality of the world. Man does not make the world in any idealist sense but he does construct cognitive structures about it which are constrained by both his own biological nature and his psychological/intellectual development, as well as by the nature of the external world itself. And it makes no difference whether the subject is conceptualising and explaining the structure of society or nature or mind. All sciences are alike in their genetic, dialectical, and evolutionary character. Or at least they should be. In this respect Piaget is far removed from most hermeneutical and holistic philosophers, while having a close affinity with some realist philosophers such as Putnam and Hesse, who employ a convergence theory of truth.

Piaget has also significantly influenced agency theories of structural change. His epistemology rests upon a well-developed agency conception of man as subject: structuring and transforming the world and his mind as he acts in the world. Many sociologists from the dialectical tradition have drawn upon his ideas in developing their theories of action and social history, as will be discussed in chapter 14.

8

Social Explanation: a Defence of Realism and Structurism

Having defended realism as an account of scientific explanation and showed in general how it is relevant to social and historical explantion, my task now is to argue in more detail why it should be the proper philosophical foundation for social science. I propose to do this mainly through contrasting it with its rivals. If we examine what passes as social and historical explanation we find a great variety of philosophical and methodological doctrines being tacitly or explicitly employed. And, similarly, in the current discussions about the human studies among philosophers, there is also a wide variety of doctrines being defended.

Eighty years ago Max Weber attempted to transcend the German *Methodenstreit* debate about the appropriate foundations for social explanation by trying to combine interpretation of intentions and meanings with law-like generalisations about society. But the problem is still with us, as I have demonstrated at length. Essentially it boils down to whether the explanation of human action, events, and social structures can be causal and, if so, whether the mode of causal explanation is to be similar to that of natural science. There is no doubt that it cannot be the same in terms of the actual causes referred to and discovered because humans are conscious purposive beings in a way that no other entity is. But how much difference should this make to the structure of causal arguments? And what other types of causes are important?

In order to defend the realist/structurist methodology of social explanation against its rivals I shall attempt to argue to the effect that:

1 Social explanations must involve reference to the *causes* of actions, events, and processes, whatever else they may refer to.

2 Causal social arguments cannot use empiricist laws but must use *generalisations* about the *dispositions, powers,* and *processes* of persons and social structures.

3 Social and mental structures and processes are *real* and have *causal power and so causal explanations are not reductionist.*

Jon Elster (1983) has recently claimed that there are three general modes of explanation – causal, functional, and intentional – and that social science can legitimately employ only the first and third while actually trying to employ all three. I believe this to be partly correct but wish to go further and claim that there are in fact five distinct pure modes or epistemologies of explanation extant in the social and historical studies. These are interpretism (or intentionalism), functionalism, and three modes of explicitly causal explanation: statistical probabilism, and behaviourism (which are both empiricist), and realism. They are distinguished mainly by their ontologies and the form of the inferences they draw between particulars and universals. They in turn give rise to three different methodologies, as shown in figure 4. However, when these

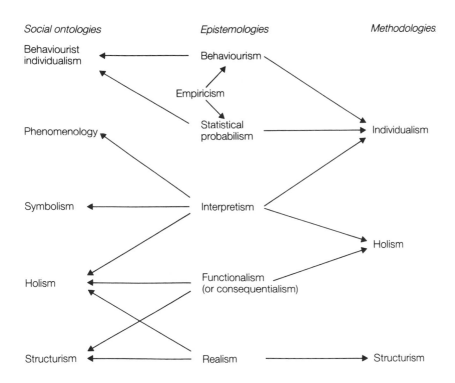

Figure 4   Social ontologies, epistemologies, and methodologies

epistemologies are examined more closely I believe it will be seen that they are all causal in some sense except for one version of interpretism.

In order to grasp the differences between these epistemologies and methodologies and to begin to criticise them we must first briefly examine their ontologies. But this order of treatment does not indicate the priority of ontologies in general. As I have argued in the previous chapter, ontologies should be seen as subordinate to epistemologies.[1]

SOCIAL ONTOLOGIES

Firstly, *behaviourist individualism* asserts in its simplest form that we can have no knowledge of entities other than those that can, in principle, be observed. Thus the postulation of non-phenomenal entities, such as social relations, rules, norms, classes, mental processes, and so on, is warranted only for heuristic purposes in explaining behaviour. Society is a theoretically postulated observable aggregation of discrete individuals and their patterns of behaviour. Behaviour is explicable only by reference to the environmental stimuli and brain processes of individuals. 'Society' is then a purely taxonomic categorisation of atomistic individuals who may form meaningful, but always loose and actually unstructured, patterns and arrangements to further their individual purposes.

Secondly, the *phenomenological* theory holds that society 'exists' but in no objective fixed form. It is not real in the sense that physicalists accord reality to the external objects of sense data, nor is it just an emanation from the minds of social observers or some omnipient Mind. Rather, a phenomenological concept of society sees it as always observed and understood from some particular viewpoint and mode of understanding and it does not exist independently of all understandings of it. This is not to say that it is purely ideal or wholly theoretical. The general perspective of phenomenology, in Thomas Luckmann's words, is

> 'egological' (i.e. taking the individual human being as the centre of a system of co-ordinates on which the experience of the world is mapped) and 'reflexive': it reinstates human experience in its place as the primary datum about the world and it describes this experience by turning and returning to the intentional features of experience. . . .
> Phenomenology places between brackets the ontological claims which are an intrinsic trait of our everyday experience and at the same time describes the sources of these claims. . . . The goal of

---

[1] There is a vast literature on the philosophy of social explanation. Some helpful overviews are provided by the following: Benton (1977), Elster (1983), Keat and Urry (1975), Polkinghorne (1983), Ryan (1973).

phenomenology is to *describe* the *universal* structures of *subjective* orientation of the world, not to explain the *general* features of the *objective* world. (Luckmann, 1978, pp. 8–9)

Thirdly, *symbolic* social ontologies usually have a foundation similar to phenomenology in that they too believe that understandings of society are always mediated by some historically specific cultural framework or symbol system. For symbolists, society does not exist independently of small group interactions undertaken on the basis of shared cultural understandings and meanings. People act and their action and interaction are patterned according to their understanding of group rules, roles, and relations. It is the shared belief or symbol system that constitutes social collectives, institutions, situations, and which controls action; and so society must be studied not as an objective structure but as a web of beliefs about society.

All of the foregoing social ontologies have either reductionist, epiphenomenalist, or relativisit ways of conceptualising structure. They do not support the idea of society as an objective entity with properties and powers of its own. Nevertheless, they usually do accept that there is something sociological to be explained – social order conceived in some way – whether it is the product of subjective consciousness or merely an epiphenomenal pattern of events. Opposed to them are the following two kinds of objectivist ontologies.

Fourthly, a *holistic* ontology of any sort of entity takes it to be an irreducible, tightly integrated, individual with properties and powers of its own which are not emergent from or reducible to the properties and powers of its parts. There are two types of social holism: systemic and idealist. A *systemic holist* conception sees society as a macro set of deep and/or institutionalised rules, roles, and relations that tightly bind together and determine the behaviour of individuals, groups, and practices within it such that these have to serve the needs and roles of the system in a way analogous to the parts of the machine or the cells of an organism. That is, the system is a supra-individual organisation with powers, needs, and goals of its own, although it does not have consciousness.

It is the notion of organisation that sets systemic holism apart from *idealist holism*. This latter idea is that society is a cultural entity existing in the form of an integrated set of possible ideas and symbols, which are available for thinking but do not have to be thought in order to exist, although it is only after they have been thought and given a recorded form that we can know of them. Cultural wholes are taken to have the power to constitute and integrate forms of social behaviour but are not reducible to the behaviour of groups.

Fifthly, a *structurist* ontology also sees society as a set of institutionalised rules, roles, and relations that together organise behaviour. But unlike holism society is here conceptualised as a loosely integrated structure whose properties and powers are the historically emergent product of collective action and understanding by individuals, groups, and classes *through time*. There is a historically changing and causal interaction between society and individual action. There has never been a time when society did not exist: it is not created by individuals but reproduced and transformed by them. Society and action should not be theorised completely independently, according to structurism, although there may be relative autonomy of structures from particular actions.

It is important to realise that these ontologies, like the following epistemologies and methodologies, are pure types and not descriptions of actual doctrines that theorists adhere to completely. There is in reality a good deal of synthesising of these ideas.

SOCIAL EPISTEMOLOGIES

One of the basic problems to be encountered when considering social epistemologies is what is to be considered as an *explanation* of some social object, event, situation, or process? Does it have to offer an account of its *causation* and if so, what counts as a cause? If not, what other sorts of statements and arguments could be considered explanatory? Perhaps compositional, functional, and interpretive statements are also explanatory? Are these necessarily incompatible with each other or with causal statements? And what sorts of logical structure of arguments and generalisations does social explanation have to have? The philosophers of natural science, whether empiricist, instrumentalist, conventionalist, relativist, or realist, do not have to face the problem of deciding whether natural explanation should be causal, as we have seen. It always is, so the main question for them concerns the structure and type of causal arguments. But as we have also seen, many influential philosophers of history and the social studies have held that these discourses must be different because they deal with human freedom and intentionality.[2]

But there does seem to be a consensus that explanation to be such must involve the answering of a *why* question about an explanandum – i.e. about a designated object, event, process, or state of affairs regarded as problematical. To explain, i.e. to provide an explanans, therefore means to give an account of why it is or occurs in terms of its constituents, structure, and powers, and interrelationships with other things. As shown in chapter 3, the empiricists, notably Popper, Hempel, and Braithwaite, argued that the proper logical form of a causal explanation

---

[2] On the problem of causation, see the thorough discussions in Beauchamp and Rosenberg (1981), Mackie (1974).

should be a deduction of the explanans from statements about universal laws and the initial conditions of the thing in question. According to them explanation can also employ statistical laws, in which case explanation expresses only a probability about the likely occurrence of an event. Furthermore, empiricist explanation usually aims at a reduction of macro phenomena to the laws governing the micro-physical constituents of each level, so that, in principle, all explanation will eventually be atomistic; and it draws a sharp distinction between theories and empirical observations.

However, this received view of explanation, of which the N–D model is the heart, has been widely criticised, notably by realists and relativists who oppose the Humean concept of causation and the logicist reconstruction of causal arguments. All of this has been argued in detail in chapters 4 to 7. Here the question is to see how the existing modes of social explanation approach this problem. How they do so is closely related to how they sepcify ontologically their objects of enquiry.

Empiricism

In a strict empiricist social epistemology there can be no reference in causal laws to entities such as essences, Platonic forms, entelechies, minds, social relations, social rules, or norms. There are two versions of empiricism in the social studies: statistical probabilism and behaviourism. *Statistical probabilism* is based on the idea that there are no universal laws of behaviour, only statistical averages and correlations, so it attempts to explain behaviour by reference to average propensities and probabilities. The laws are thus inductive generalisations of many theory-neutral observations and are not taken to refer to individuals as such. *Behaviourism* holds that there can be universal laws of behaviour of a psychological or physicalist kind which refer to the mental or brain states behind fixed dispositions. These laws provide the premises for deductions about individual behaviour in the context of knowledge of environmental stimuli that trigger these dispositions.

Interpretism

The interpretist epistemology denies (as we saw in chapters 4 and 6) that there can be an empiricist causal science of action and society because there are no physical laws of behaviour and society. Society does not have an objective existence – it is holistic, symbolic, or phenomenological – and persons are more than physical beings. The task of the social investigator is to understand the intentions of actors in order to interpret social phenomena in terms of the motives and the meanings that social 'structures' have for them.

There are two kinds of interpretist strategists depending on whether they see the task of interpretation as to seek for mental antecedents of motivations for action or for the social meanings of actions and cultures. The *mentalists*, such as Dray, Scriven, and Davidson, consider reasons to be indicators of the causes of action. In this case to explain an action is to interpret the stated reasons for action in terms of what agents say, and whatever else may be known, about the mental (or psychological) antecedents of action, especially intentions, beliefs, and desires. Mental events, which are not epiphenomena of physical brain processes but real processes emergent from (or supervenient upon) neurophysical processes (see the section on 'Methodological individualism' below), are the causes of action. But they cannot be expressed in universal laws of the Humean type since they are not reducible to physical regularities although, in the view of these thinkers, there can be normic generalisations of a less precise kind about these mental antecedents. The generalisations are expressions of the tendencies and propensities of normal social action derived from historical observations and from some theoretical ideas about human nature and the conditions under which types of acts occur.

In the other strategy, the *hermeneutical interpretists* (see chapter 6) maintain that it is sufficient for 'explanation' to *understand* in an empathetic, circular, 'clairvoyant' manner the meanings that actions have for the actor. They try to rethink, in Collingwood's formulation, the subjective thought processes of the actor. Questions about the general social and psychological antecedents of motives are not of much interest. Action is studied only in so far as it is meaningful for the actor; and the historian, sociologist, or anthropologist is necessarily restricted to interpreting action by reference to stated reasons for acting within a context of the interpreter's understanding of the linguistic/cultural context of the actor. Actors' understandings are supposedly constitutive of their actions and their social relations. Accordingly, the theories of observers are similarly constitutive of their own understandings of other actors and their situations.

Functionalism

Functionalist epistemologies try to explain social events, states, and processes by showing their functional consequences (whether intended or not) for the benefit of the system of which they are a part. There are various versions of functionalism, all of which assert some explanatory relationship between the ends or goals of a system and the phenomena within it. The existence of an integrated system is vital. Elster's recent discussions (1982b, 1983) have clarified such arguments by showing that there are in fact weak, main, and strong versions of sociological functionalism:

Weak Functional Paradigm: an institution or behavioral pattern often has consequences that are (a) beneficial for some dominant economic or political structure; (b) unintended by the actors; and (c) not recognized by the beneficiaries as owing to that behavior. . . . If we use 'function' for consequences that satisfy condition (a) and 'latent function' for consequences that satisfy all three conditions, we can go on to state the Main Functional Paradigm: the latent functions (if any) of an institution or behaviour explain the presence of that institution or behavior. Finally, there is the Strong Functional Paradigm: all institutions or behavioral patterns have a function that explains their presence. (Elster, 1982b, p. 454)

As Elster went on to point out, the weak version explains nothing, although it is widespread in the social sciences, because it shows no causal connections. For the main and strong versions to be valid explanations they would have to show that there is a causal feedback step at the end. The full argument would have this structure:

An institution or a behavioral pattern X is explained by its function Y for group Z if and only if:

1 Y is an effect of X;
2 Y is beneficial for Z;
3 Y is unintended by the actors producing X;
4 Y – or at least the causal relation between X and Y – is unrecognized by the actors in Z;
5 Y maintains X by a causal feedback loop passing through Z.
(Elster, 1983, p. 57)

This structure can be shown by figure 5.

Thus functionalism is explanatory in so far as it can show causal feedback but, as Elster pointed out (1983, pp. 58–61), many sociological functionalist arguments are unable to do so. They content themselves with tacitly asserting either that if the unintended consequences are apparently beneficial for the system or apparently reinforce some process then they have meaning, or that there is some unknown but objective teleology within the system. But without a causal mechanism the explanation fails. (In biology the general theory of evolution does provide a causal mechanism.) That is, the social system is asserted to be either purposive without containing a purposive actor (objective teleology – a process without a subject, analogous to a 'dedicated' machine) or purposive with an intentional subject (subjective teleology). These contrast with teleonomy, in which there is some mechanism analogous to natural selection, such as market competition (cf. Elster, 1982b, pp. 454–5). I believe that both versions of systemic teleology are false because they unjustifiably impute agency powers to collective entities. Teleonomy is contingently true.

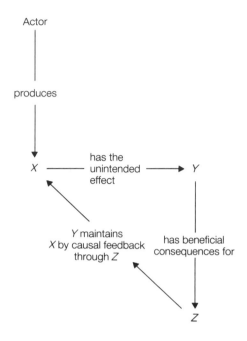

Figure 5 The structure of functionalist explanation

Realism

A realist epistemology attempts to uncover the causal powers and propensities which are the necessary ways of behaving inherent within kinds of entities. In the social sciences this involves, at its most general, discovering the structures, powers, propensities, and liabilities of both persons and social structures so that general law-like statements about both of them can be made. These statements thus do not refer to event–event observable regularities and so universal laws about such regularities are not required. The structure of reasoning is more complex than the logical empiricists allow. To make causal explanations of phenomena by referring to the essential but unobservable powers and tendencies of natural kinds involves, as I showed in chapter 7, a combination of theories, observations of regularities, induction, models, analogies, and deductions in the way that figure 6 indicates. (The similarities and differences between figures 6 and 2 will be readily apparent.) In order to explain actions and social processes there have to be, then, (1) general models and theories of humans, societies, social processes, and the interaction of society and action; (2) knowledge about

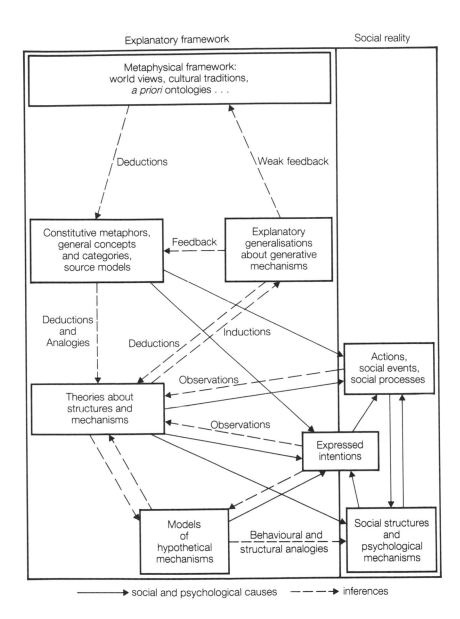

Figure 6 The structure of reasoning in social sciences: a realist account

the particular conditions under which actions, events, and processes occurred; (3) knowledge of actors' intentions. That is, unlike natural science, a crucial part of the observational evidence for social scientists is actors' stated reasons for acting and their statements about their understandings of their social situations. But these must not be treated in an epistemologically privileged way. Society exists relatively independently of understandings with its own causal powers and actors' understandings can be misleading, both of themselves and of social scientists. Models of society as a macro entity do not in any direct sense constitute society but there is an indirect causal relationship in the sense that society is a social product and so the ideas that actors have about society do influence their actions and social relations. However, society preexists individuals and confronts them as an objective force.

It can be seen from this brief survey that all but the hermeneutical mode of explanation are causal and thus explanatory in some sense. The realist mode can be understood as incorporating and transcending the functionalist and mentalist modes and denying the claims of the empiricist and hermeneutical modes because of their impoverished ontologies and concepts of causation. These latter two modes drive a wedge between action and society by insisting on seeing both in either individualistic or holistic terms and thereby, in effect and paradoxically, removing the possibility of social explanation.

IN DEFENCE OF OBJECTIVITY

The nature and structure of causal arguments is only one of the major problems of social epistemology. Another basic problem, or cluster of problems, concerns the objectivity or otherwise of the social scientific explanations of structural processes and behavioural patterns. A strong and long-lived relativist current in social thought[3] holds to all or some of four related ideas about this problem. The first is that truth is always conventional: that is, it is relative to some conceptual framework which is in turn relative to some wider and deeper social and linguistic/cultural structure. The second is irrationalism: theories are adopted on intuitive, pre-rational grounds and not because of any supposed power they have to explain 'independent' reality. The third idea is the underdetermination of theories: it is claimed that there are theories whose truth cannot in principle be decided by reference to evidence either because we will always lack sufficient evidence to decide the fact of the matter or the evidence cannot be considered independent of a theory, and so the

[3] For recent discussions of the objectivism/relativism problem, see Bernstein (1983), Davidson (1974a), Hollis and Lukes (1982: all essays are relevant), Lukes (1973b, 1978), J. Margolis (1984), Newton-Smith (1981), Quine (1969, 1970).

relative plausibility of theories *vis-à-vis* each other cannot be decided by reference to evidence. The fourth is the indeterminacy of translation between conceptual/cultural frameworks, so that even if it were asserted that there is an objectively real world we could never communicate our knowledge of it, if we had any, to those in other cultures.

We have seen in chapters 4, 5 and 6 how influential this set of relativist theses is among philosophers of historical, scientific, and sociological explanation. It is also very influential among practitioners of those enquiries, and not just those who are trying to research the cultural and social structures of very alien societies.[4]

I believe that sociological objectivism can be defended against the relativists. I shall try to state my reasons as briefly as possible, presupposing the arguments made in earlier chapters (especially chapter 7) against relativism and in favour of realism. Firstly, as ordinary social actors we know sufficient about ourselves, our culture, and our social structure to more or less successfully live our lives, avoiding serious mistakes about meaning, identification, power, processes, and institutions. The social world is therefore sufficiently like what we think it is to make this possible.

Secondly, we more or less successfully communicate with each other, otherwise we could not survive because survival depends upon cooperation and cooperation depends upon communication.

Thirdly, successful communication implies sharing meanings and identifications and so successfully translating the statements made by others into our own understandings. Of course, this is not easy for communication between languages, but that we are able to become bilingual is affirmed by those who do so. Nevertheless, the relativist can still claim that we cannot be certain we have successfully translated. But this would apply to any translation, even between speakers of the same langue, because every person's understanding of the meanings of words may be different. Radical indeterminism easily becomes absurd because it quickly reduces to the thesis of the impossibility of understanding because there cannot be an independent test of understanding. We could not even understand ourselves. The existence of social cooperation and therefore human life has to be based upon shared understanding.

Fourthly, it seems that there are some basic universal principles and capacities of humans, irrespective of their cultures. These are to do with such things as: the ability to perceive secondary qualities so as not only to avoid making serious mistakes about the phenomenal world but to move about in such a way as to survive physically and emotionally and to reproduce; the ability to pass on to others (particularly children) the knowledge gained about the natural and social worlds (which presupposes a sharing of meaning); the capacity to classify the things of the

---

[4] For an example of relativism, see Wallerstein (1983, pp. 81–93).

world, i.e. to make identifications of similarity; and so on. Now, this is not to say that these capacities necessarily produce reliable knowledge of the world or that our classifications and knowledge do not change. What is important is the universality of such attitudes. It is a basis on which to build, by a slow process and partly through negotiation and also criticism, more and more reliable knowledge so that progress is made.

Fifthly, while many theories are underdetermined many others are not. The natural sciences have been very successful in corroborating theories *in open systems*. The social sciences are conspicuously less successful because of society's complexity, but there is nothing inherent in the social world that makes determination of theories impossible in principle. Intentionality, for instance, does not imply that there are no objective structures.

Sixthly, truth and rationality do operate as regulative principles of the practice of scientists, and not even the relativists can show that there has been no progress within domains or that scientists are not motivated by a search for truth.

Seventhly, moving closer to the truth is a matter of a complex convergence between coherence conditions for truth and correspondence between our theories and the world. The value of a theory is a matter not simply of truth or falsity but of plausibility/implausibility, goodness/badness, progression/regression, and so on.

Eighthly, while all observations and explanations take place within a network of values and presuppositions, there is a gradual improvement in our ability to explain the world as revealed by the relative independence of empirical test conditions for theories.

In sum, relativism cannot make sense of social life or scientific practice; but a simple objectivism is not very helpful either. Scientific reasoning has a complex structure, as I argued in detail in chapter 7 and tried to show in figures 2 and 6, and our theories do not simply mirror the world. The world can only be known through conceptual frameworks but we can and do gradually improve our frameworks. The 'dividing line' between what we know and what we do not know has a strong long-term tendency to move in one direction.

Having established, I hope, the case for realism and objectivism, my task now is to defend the methodology of structurism, which in effect employs these philosophical presuppositions.

EXPLAINING SOCIAL ORDER AND CHANGE: THE MICRO/MACRO METHODOLOGICAL PROBLEM

The core problem for all social theorists today is, as it has always been (and as many theorists have recently recognised), to try to reconcile the opposition between understandings of the social world as either *action centred* or *social centred*.[5] In other words, the problem is one of trying jointly to comprehend and establish a general relationship between, on the one hand, subjective interpretations, understandings, intentionality, agency, and individual action and, on the other, the macro social totality that transcends the lives of individuals and their common-sense understandings. The problem is particularly acute for social historians because being empirically oriented it is their professed aim to try to explain historical changes in particular *societies*, changes which can be known only by studying the patterns in which persons *act* and express themselves collectively. Holistic and individualistic methodologies, whatever their ontologies, are of no practical use to social historians because they reinforce rather than reconcile this opposition, as I shall try to show, and the hermeneutical epistemology is unable to give genuine explanations, as I have shown.

Social structures and patterns of social phenomena and their histories are rarely the result of rational planning and probably never the result of unknowable supra-human forces. But neither are they random, formless, or meaningless. This may prompt us to ask at the outset, as Norbert Elias recently put it: 'How does it happen at all that formations arise in the human world that no single human being has intended and which yet are anything but cloud formations without stability of structure?' (Elias, 1982, p. 230) But while this general question about the existence of social order as such is important it is not a problem for social historical enquiry as such. Social order in general must be assumed to be a normal part of the world and mode of existence of humans.

This Hobbesian problem to which Elias obliquely refers, and of which Talcott Parsons and others have made much,[6] is in a sense not a problem for social science at all. Hobbes's concept of the atomistic society is not even a heuristically useful theoretical limit case because social disintegration is impossible. Only when an organic or mechanical analogy for society is adopted does the problem of social disintegration arise, because then society is thought of as a holistic entity which has either an equilibrium (live) state or a disintegrated (dead) state. If society is thought of as a looser, more fluid, more fractured entity which is neither 'alive' nor 'dead' – neither a holistic entity nor a mere heap – then the problem of disintegration and transformation takes on a different character. It becomes one of searching for the mechanisms of the reproduction and transformation of structures.

While some societies have undoubtedly disintegrated at the national or state level, order has apparently always remained or very quickly

[5] The action/society relationship has received a lot of attention lately, including by Abrams (1982, Introduction), Coleman (1972a), Collins (1981b), Dawe (1970, 1979), Giddens (1979, ch. 2), Knorr-Cetina (1981).

[6] On the 'Hobbesian problem' of social order, see Coleman (1972a), Ellis (1971), O'Neill (1972, ch. 13), Parsons (1970a, p. 869).

reappeared at the local level. States and political systems are often unstable but this says nothing of a general kind about *social order* as such. The modern histories of Germany, Lebanon, Northern Ireland, and Iran, for example, all seem to indicate that community social order is very strong, even when state order is not. Even when a society does alter it does not therefore lose order but merely changes into a new order. Order can be dynamic and loose but it is still order and very rarely (if ever) gives way to anarchy or war of all against all. Transformations occur but order in general remains.

Therefore, social order must be understood as not accidental or unusual or problematical. Given the basic *social nature* of humans, it is *natural*. They do not live except in ordered social formations: i.e. in more or less *integrated structures* of more or less conscious relations, rules, roles, and interaction, and institutionalised cooperation and exchange. And this can be taken as a rare universal principle about humans. Humans, it seems, are consciously social beings. Social *disorder* is a highly unnatural, unstable, and transitory state, and hence is problematical.

It must be emphasised that by 'social being' is meant something distinct from the merely determined, unconscious drive to behave in a socially cooperative manner which motivates many other species, such as insects. It implies consciousness and communication in a cultural and reflective sense and hence some freedom of choice and action. Few species, if any apart from humans, have such resources or abilities.

The general problem of human nature is thus prior to social explanation – to be dealt with by biology, psychology, and philosophical anthropology. Nevertheless, I do not wish to argue that these discourses can be dispensed with by social science. On the contrary they have crucial effects upon our social explanations since the models of humans that sociologists and historians tacitly or deliberately adopt strongly influence the general nature of their explanations. The influence of the Hobbesian model upon Parsons and others, for instance, is very obvious. What is needed is a better model of man (in which social order is *not* seen as a problem), to underpin social enquiry and direct it towards more fruitful lines of research.

Given this basis of natural social order, the problems for social theory and social history pertain to explaining the very wide *variety* of *actual* structures, institutions, and practices that social order has had and does have, the *causes* of their changes, and the *processes* of their history. The particular relationships between the structures of order and the forces of change in each social formation, which historically have always resulted in change, do need explaining. Part of that involves, as Elias, Boudon, Giddens, Elster, and many others have rightly emphasised,[7] grasping the

---

[7] On the problem of the unintended social consequences of action, see the following: Boudon (1981b), Elster (1978), Giddens (1979), Hayek (1967), Vernon (1979).

unintended outcomes of individual and collective thought and action. Biology, theoretical psychology, and philosophical anthropology are of little help in this since they deal with unchanging aspects of humans.

It is therefore not enough for social science to concentrate only on knowing either about the structures of societies or about action. It is not enough for three reasons. Firstly, society should be seen as a structured macroscopic totality that is determinate on *both* the micro and the macro levels. That is, the actions of persons are caused both individually and socially and a society is an entity which is determined in its structure (at any particular time) by its own compositional laws and by the dispositions, powers, and behaviour of its individual constituents. Society must be continually *reproduced* through individual and collective action but it always pre-exists individuals. Any approach to explaining its structure and dynamics, or the actions of individuals within it, which concentrates only on micro or macro determination, would miss half the picture. Social history thus cannot be reduced to the psychological or hermeneutical study of action, just as it cannot be subsumed by macro structuralism. Studies of action and structure must have a symbiotic and dialectical relationship. Neither methodological individualism nor methodological holism is able to accommodate this symbiosis.

Secondly, society can only exist if collectively mediated by the *minds* of most of the persons that comprise it. If they were all (or even a significant proportion of them) simultaneously to suffer amnesia or cease acting the society would cease to exist. Skilled social action on the basis of shared understandings and beliefs about a society's structure, rules, roles, and processes (i.e. culture in a general sense) is necessary to social production and reproduction. Society has a physical existence in collective behaviour and its products, including the geographical pattern and constraints of behaviour, and a mental existence in collective consciousness and understanding, as well as a social existence in structures of social relations, rules, and roles. It is important to point out that actors' cultural understandings of societies can be false and so action can be 'distorted'. The forms of human culture are very varied and complexly patterned. Social science must be intimately concerned with grasping the contents and power that specific cultures have for influencing action. Therefore, personality, consciousness, action, culture, and social structure can be explained only by explaining all of them. However, this is obviously an impossible task for one person and so some abstraction and division of labour are necessary. But this general context should be kept somewhere in mind when explanations are being made of any of these moments. The more moments that are incorporated into any particular explanation the better, and the best social scientists do see clearly this general context of their abstractions.

Thirdly, a *historical* perspective on society, in both the senses of *actuality* and *change* that the term implies, is essential because the specific consciousness, modes of action, cultures, and social structures are different in every situation and every society is in a state of constant, if gradual and uneven, change. But general theory is required for historical explanation since consciousness, action, culture, and structure do have universal features and powers which can be given general concepts and explanations. If they did not, then no explanation would be possible. Any sharp distinction between structural and historical perspectives is potentially misleading if it is adopted for any purpose other than a heuristic one. Since structures are always changing they should always be studied in a historical mode and they can only be studied using a theory of social history. And conversely, theories should always be revised in the light of the historical enquiries which employ them. Ideally, a situation analogous to that in particle physics, say, or geomorphology, should develop whereby general theories and particular enquiries are continually interacting.

METHODOLOGICAL HOLISM

The holist methodology, as the foregoing indicates, approaches the problem of social explanation from the perspective of the social whole, whether the whole is conceived as an integrated system of relations and roles à la Parsons, or a deep structure of cultural elements à la Lévi-Strauss, or a symbolic cultural form à la Berlin.

Systemic holism attempts to study society as if it were an integrated organic-like system. Its functioning and the behaviour of individuals and groups within it are explained by reference only or primarily to systemic laws of a functional kind. The parts of the system are seen as functionally necessary to the operation and maintenance of equilibrium of the system. This doctrine will be examined in more detail in chapters 10 and 12.

Structural holism attempts to uncover scientifically the deep structures of elements that form logico-mathematical systems which set the limits to thought and social phenomena. The cultural, social, and economic behaviour of individuals and groups is made possible and determined by these structures. The structures exist within the deep unconscious minds of individuals who are predisposed, as humans, to act in structured ways and to be socialised in such a way as to absorb and carry structures. (More on this in chapter 12.)

Hermeneutical holism, as we saw in chapter 5, attempts to interpret the meanings that postulated symbolic cultural wholes have for the actors within them. Action is seen as always motivated out of a context of cultural meanings, and in order to explanatorily understand action these cultural meanings must be fully understood in a hermeneutical manner.

I believe that methodological holism in all its forms is incoherent and inappropriate for social explanation because it cannot account for social *history*. That is, it is unable to give an account of the mechanisms of social change because it postulates a social entity without either a convincing objective teleology or teleonomy of its own or an external causal force to act upon it. In so far as holists postulate society as having 'structural causality' they are unable to demonstrate the source or mechanism of this supposed power, and in so far as they deny human agency they have nowhere to turn for an alternative. Thus Parsonians fall back on a form of evolutionary theory, but one which has no genetic mechanism; and structuralists (e.g. Althusser) postulate that the deep structures of economics somehow causally determine their own history by ensuring that humans act in certain ways to further their teleological development.

METHODOLOGICAL INDIVIDUALISM

The general problem

Methodological individualism developed in opposition to the prevailing holism of Germanic social thought in the nineteenth century. Max Weber defended an early version of it and later the Vienna empiricists took it up as a corollary of their ontological physicalism and nominalism. Methodological individualism, in the words of J. W. N. Watkins, is the belief that 'social processes and events should be explained by being deduced from (a) principles governing the behaviour of participating individuals and (b) descriptions of their situations.' (Watkins, 1953, p. 149) It is important to distinguish this methodological doctrine from ontological individualism. The latter implies the former, but the converse is not necessary.[8]

The grounds of Watkins's defence of individualism were that social objects are formed by individual attitudes, and that social scientists have no access to social systems, only to the dispositions and situations of individuals. After discussing in detail the use of ideal typical theory in social explanation, he concluded:

An individual's personality is a system of unobservable dispositions which, together with his factual beliefs, determine his observable behaviour. Society is a system of unobservable relationships between individuals whose interaction produces certain measurable sociological phenomena. We can apprehend an unobservable social system only by reconstructing it theoretically from what is known

---

[8] There has been a lively debate over methodological individualism among philosophers and sociologists, of which see the following recent works: Elster (1982b), Lukes (1968, 1973a), Mayhew (1980), Miller (1978), Wisdom (1970).

of individual dispositions, beliefs and relationships. Hence holistic ideal types, which would abstract essential traits from a social whole while ignoring individuals, are impossible: they always turn into individualistic ideal types. Individualistic ideal types of explanatory power are constructed by first discerning the form of typical, socially significant, dispositions, and then by demonstrating how, in various typical situations, these lead to certain principles of social behaviour. (Watkins, 1953, p. 167)

It can be seen from this statement that what is at stake for Watkins is primarily methodological rather than ontological. Unfortunately this distinction has not always been clearly drawn, with the result that the recent debate has been rather confused. This confusion really began with the 1940s writings of F. A. Hayek and Karl Popper.

The individualism of Hayek and Popper

Hayek defended (unlike Popper) an essential division of the sciences on ontological grounds. Social science (i.e. *Geisteswissenschaft*) was necessarily subjective, he said, because it dealt with the 'phenomena of individual minds' and not with objective material phenomena (Hayek, 1942–3, p. 35).

His idea of methodological individualism was, therefore, that social science should begin with the ideas and actions of individuals and not with collectivities or general concepts about societies or wholes. But social science, Hayek believed (using Carl Menger's term), should be 'compositive': it constructs so-called wholes by fitting together the known observable properties of the elements of society. Thus while social science does have to explain 'social order' – the unintended regularities of individual behaviour – this order does not have a physical existence and hence, he believed, a natural scientific, 'objectivist' approach can have no relevance to it. Closely associated with this objectivism, said Hayek, is methodological collectivism, or holism – the treating of these 'wholes', such as society, economy, capitalism, industry, class, even country, 'as definitely given objects about which we can discover laws by observing their behaviour as wholes' (p. 44).

Popper's defence of methodological individualism in *The Poverty of Historicism* was in the context of a more realist philosophy than Hayek's. Both were opposed to holism and historicism. Popper defined 'historicism' as the attempt to arrive at social predictions based upon discovering the 'rhythms', the 'patterns', the 'laws', or the 'trends' that underlie the evolution of history. His rejection of it was in turn based upon his rejection of holism. 'Holism' he took to be the attempt to study 'the totality of all the properties or aspects of a thing, and especially of all the relations holding between its constituent parts' (Popper, 1961, p. 76).

This contrasted with the study of a different sort of whole; that where 'certain special properties or aspects of the thing in question, namely those which make it appear an organised structure rather than a "mere heap"', are studied. The second can be studied scientifically, the first cannot. This is because wholes cannot be fully described; all descriptions are necessarily selective. 'Wholes cannot be the object of any activity, scientific or otherwise.' (Popper, 1961, p. 77). Hence, he believed, any attempt to grasp the 'concrete sructure of social reality', or the whole social process, is impossible. This means that historicists, who are supposedly holists in this sense, are engaged in an impossible task because, as he quite rightly said, history like any other kind of empirical enquiry

> can only deal with selected aspects of the object in which it is interested. It is a mistake to believe that there can be a history in the holistic sense, a history of 'states of society' which represent 'the whole of the social organism' or 'all the social and historical events of an epoch'. This idea derives from an intuitive view of *a history of mankind* as a vast and comprehensive stream of development. But such a history cannot be written. Every written history is a history of a certain narrow aspect of this 'total' development, and is anyhow a very incomplete history even of the particular incomplete aspect chosen. (Popper, 1961, p. 23)

However, Popper made the mistake of moving from this correct critique of holism to the defence of methodological individualism: the doctrine that, echoing Hayek, it is the task of social theory to construct and analyse sociological models in descriptive and nominalist terms, i.e. '*in terms of individuals*, of their attitudes, expectations, relations, etc.' (Popper's emphasis, p. 149). By this he does not mean that collective entities cannot be studied, only that they must be studied as collections of individuals, since it is only individuals which are real. But, like Durkheim and many others, he also believes the social situation has a 'logic' of its own and exerts coercive force on human action.

Popper seems to have overstated his case in *The Poverty of Historicism*, for in later writings he presented a more realist position about social entities, saying that he did not deny that wholes exist, only that most theories about them are superficial. Both he and Hayek could have helped their case by making better use of the differences between two sets of distinctions: firstly, ontological differences between individuals, structures, and wholes; and secondly, differences between methodologies corresponding to these ontologies. If *structures* are real (as Popper believes) and characterised by *emergent* rather than holistic powers, which are not reducible to individuals, then it makes no sense to study them simply in terms of their individual elements. The question must therefore be resolved on the ontological level so that a methodology can be constructed that is able to take account of *social causality* as well as agent causality.

Homans's individualism

The sociologist George Homans has continually defended methodological individualism on the basis of behaviourist psychology. His defence is instructive because it is a good example of an attempted application of this methodology to actual social explanation. Like Hempel, he claims that the social sciences are in fact nomological deductive in the logical structure of their causal arguments and that they employ covering laws about individual behaviour, although often in an underdeveloped form. This means that in order to explain the origins, maintenance, and effects of social structures (which he defined as 'relatively enduring . . . relations between individuals and groups': 1982, p. 297; cf. also 1967b, ch. 3), the structures have to be seen as always the dependent variable. And by this he seems to mean that structures are the *creations* of individuals coming together in various ways. In short, structures are the epiphenomenal product of behaviour (1982, pp. 297–8). We will see in chapter 11 how such an approach provides a very impoverished theory of structural change.

Elster's individualism

Jon Elster's argument for individualism, unlike that of Homans, presupposes an ontological structurism. He claims (1982b) that methodological individualism, by which he means game theory and rational choice social psychology, is indispensable to macro structural explanation because it provides a necessary alternative to functionalist and intentionalist explanations which are usually flawed for the sorts of reasons I have discussed earlier in the chapter. Specifically, sociological functionalism has failed to uncover objective teleological social mechanisms analogous to natural selection, and intentionalist explanation cannot provide a full explanation of social interaction. However, in Elster's opinion, individuals interact intentionally and game theory has been devised to study intentional action between individuals whso regard each other not as constraints on their actions but as other intentional beings. In this case individuals have strategic rationality in choosing courses of action and game theory models such interaction (1982b, p. 463).

The social psychological theory underlying the assumption of strategic rationality is rational choice theory. Its basic premises, in Elster's account, are:

1 that structural constraints do not completely determine the actions taken by individuals in a society, and

2 that within the feasible set of actions compatible with all the constraints, individuals choose those they believe will bring the best results. (Elster, 1982b, pp. 463–4)

This theory enables the avoidance of deterministic holisms which in effect deny the existence of human intentionality and rational decision-making (cf. p. 464).

Rational choice theory and game theory are closely related because the latter theory stresses the *interdependence* of decisions, as Elster points out. Specifically, it shows that

the reward of each depends on the choice of all. . . . The reward of each depends on the reward of all ... [and] the choice of each depends on the choice of all. (Elster, 1982b, pp. 464–5)

Therefore game theory does not portray the individual as an egoistic atom.

However, what Elster is arguing for here is not really a methodology for *structural* explanation but one for the explanation of action and interaction – i.e. a micro theory only, which has to be supplemented with or added to a structural theory. In his case it supplements Marxism. Methodological individualism in the form defended by Hayek, Watkins, and Homans rejects the possibility of structural explanation because it rejects the existence of structures. Elster's argument is a useful addition to the defence of *methodological structurism* – which must indeed incorporate, I shall argue, a theory of personality and action of the sort that he advocates – but to stop at methodological individualism is inadequate.

The holistic/macroscopic distinction

Against the methodological individualists it is essential to defend the legitimacy of using macroscopic concepts to refer to collective entities of *every* sort. The universe is in fact full of entities constituted out of smaller elements. 'Planets may be conglomerations of atoms but no one would deny reality to planets', wrote May Brodbeck.

Likewise, crowds may be groups of individuals, but there are also crowds. Universities exist just as much as professors, students, and administrators, although the university is not a separable fourth thing but a name for relations among the other three. Only one who makes such a separation hypostatizes the concept. . . . Since a group concept refers to a complex pattern of descriptive, empirical relations among individuals, there is no reason why the behaviour of this complex should not itself be studied. (Brodbeck, 1954, pp. 106–7)

Thus it is important to emphasise the importance of a distinction between macroscopic concepts and holistic concepts: the former refers to a *relational collectivity* of smaller entities, the latter to an *organic, indivisible* type of entity. Macroscopic entities, such as society, are not organic, but nor are they heaps. Their laws are very different from individualistic laws and holistic laws.

For individualists such as Hayek, Watkins, and Homans, there can only be two possible methodologies – individualistic and holistic – and they usually fail even to consider the existence of non-holistic macroscopic entities. However, while individualists do usually reject the possible existence of extra-personal real social *entities* they do also retain notions of 'social phenomena', 'social order', and 'social situations'. But surely these objects, if they are not simply instrumental aggregations of individual actions lumped together by an observer and having no inherent cohesive relationship, are macroscopic.

Thus the ontological claim that society is not reducible to individuals can be either holist or structurist. Wholes and structures are entities with some general features in common but having decisive differences. Social *wholes* are supposedly *organic*-like entities such that they exist in a manner greater than their parts and in such a way that their parts have their being as constituents of the whole and could not exist independently of the whole or in some other combination. The parts are totally (or organically) integrated. Social *structures* (not to be confused with the deep structures of the mind, à la Lévi-Strauss), on the other hand, are not organically integrated and do not depend crucially upon every particular element in the combination. They may be strongly bonded in certain parts but not in others. However, if the relational arrangement of the elements is altered, which is always possible, the structure is altered but not necessarily destroyed. A structure cannot have an intrinsic intelligence with aims and purposes, although a whole may have these. Both could be called 'systems' in a loose sense and often are, but this term is probably too vague to make the important foregoing distinction.

The important ontological questions for social and human explanation concern the degree of integration of society, the manner of its origin, and its relationship to individual and group behaviour. A holist should argue that society is not only not reducible to individuals but that individuals can only exist and behave as completely integrated, determined elements of the totality. That whole in turn has a life and being of its own. On the other hand, a structure exists as a particular set of relations, rules, and roles linking more or less discrete individuals, and that set may change as an individual changes his relationship with the totality. Thus a structurist should hold that human behaviour is only *partially* explicable as part of a totality and that individuals may move in and out of an arrangement which continues to exist. Behaviour is only partly structural and partly individualistic. While individuals must be seen as structuring *agents* they do not individually create the structure because it always pre-exists them.

It is therefore important to avoid a confusion between the two aspects of what has been described by Piaget (1971b, p. 10) and Giddens (1979, pp. 69–70) as the duality of structure – i.e. structure as both the *condition* for action and the *consequence* of action. The methodological individualist view would seem to ignore the first aspect since it argues that structure is explainable by reference to individual action but not that action is explainable by reference to structure. This seems to support a creationist or phenomenological attitude to structure rather than a realist one – i.e. that structure is not only the creation of each individual but depends upon each individual to maintain its existence. This perhaps commits the genetic fallacy of confusing structure with knowledge of it. If social structure is conceived in relational terms then surely relations between persons exist whether they are conscious face-to-face inter-actions or more distant social, economic, political, or familial connec-tions.

EMERGENCE AND CAUSAL POWERS

Social emergence

Thus in defending the reality of structures (as opposed to wholes) an essential concept is 'social emergence'. If societies are seen as a result of social interactive behaviour and yet in turn have *sui generis* laws and exert a causal influence on behaviour, then it is necessary to argue in the first place that social organisation, relations, rules, and power emerge from interaction over time and are then not epistemologically reducible to it. In sociology the notion of emergence is an old one, first given a prominent place by Durkheim. In analysing the concept, it is important to distinguish first, in the way that Brodbeck (1958) did, between explana-tory emergence and descriptive emergence. Any resolution of this debate must take account of this fundamentally important distinction and its ramifications.

Descriptive emergence is the ontological concept referring to those possible properties of groups which are not definable in terms either of the behaviour of individuals composing a group or of descriptive relations between them. That is, do groups have attributes and powers which *emerge* from and are in adition to the descriptive, or observable, level of their constituents? Since methodological individualism is usually based upon empiricism, it often has as its fundamental metaphysical assumption the denial of descriptive emergence, i.e. of the meaningful-ness of concepts of extra-individual unobservable but real social proper-ties. But it also wishes to deny that there can be laws and theories about such groups as groups, i.e. that there can be *explanatory emergence*.

This problem involves the related matters of deduction and reduction.[9]

[9] On the possibility of sociological reductive explanations see the recent discussions by: Blau (1983), Mayhew (1980), Manicas (1983), Porpora (1983), Turner (1983).

Explanation is always of statements by means of other statements, sometimes by deductive premises. Reduction is a form of deduction whereby the phenomena of one field are explained by means of statements about another supposedly more basic field (e.g. psychology in terms of physiology or sociology in terms of psychology). In natural science it has proven possible to construct group concepts about complex patterns of descriptive empirical phenomena, and to construct macroscopic laws about them which are different from laws about the behaviour of individuals. Social groups are clearly also cohesive and the behaviour of individuals as members of them is not directly or completely accounted for by laws about individuals, i.e. by psychology. In order to eliminate social emergence it is essential for the individualist to show that there can be explanation by means of reduction, involving the relationship between group concepts and psychology.

Brodbeck's account of the logic of reduction goes like this: in order to achieve reduction in principle it is essential to know the laws of composition of social groups, i.e. to know how individuals interact, and to have definitions of group concepts and a statistical description of the composition of the group. Then it may be seen that the reducing area (psychology) is microscopic relative to the reduced macroscopic area (sociology). The composition laws state what happens when several elementary situations are combined in specified ways. These combined situations are the macroscopic complexes referred to by the group terms of the reduced area. The definitions of the group terms provide the common language necessary for the derivation of macroscopic statements from microscopic ones. The composition laws then supply the empirical premises from which the deduction is made. The reduction of group laws to those about individuals thus supplies an explanation of group behaviour in terms of the behaviour of individuals in groups (Brodbeck, 1958, p. 307).

However, even if this is correct the macroscopic social sciences will survive because of the virtual impossibility of developing precise composition laws, the openness and complexity of social systems, and the incompleteness of the variables. If the composition laws, which are empirical generalisations, do not hold, for whatever reason, then the social scientist is forced to admit the existence of at least *explanatory emergence*, i.e. that there are 'laws of group behaviour, which *even though their terms are defined as they should be*, are still not derivable from the laws, including whatever composition laws there are, about individual behaviour.' (pp. 308–9) This is the case in the social and psychological sciences at present. While the individualist denies emergence in principle, the emergentist denies the possibility of reduction both in principle and in practice. Descriptive (i.e. ontological) emergence rules out reduction since it holds that society not only has laws but that those laws are *sui generis*. The methodological individualist, however, cannot rule out *explanatory* emergence since it is a fact! And without that possibility he cannot thereby definitely rule out descriptive emergence. The onus is on the individualist to show that reduction is possible (which he cannot yet do) and on the structurist or holist to show that there are *sui generis* social laws. Therefore explanatory emergence is sufficient to permit methodological structurism in social and historical explanation.

In fact the structurist can go further and argue tht descriptive socio-logical emergence is possible *in principle*. *Proof* of sociological emer-gence then requires the establishment of the necessity of macro causal laws within societies in order to explain both their operation and the behaviour of their constituent parts.

Causal powers of social structures

The defence of structural emergence and methodological structurism requires the demonstration of causal power as an index of social structural existence. Some individualists claim both that macroscopic 'entities' have no causal powers and that those 'entities' are merely abstractions, or theoretical instruments, reified by persons. But, as Ernest Gellner has pointed out, this precludes *a priori* the possibility of human dispositions being the *dependent* variable in any historical explanation, and the possibility of causal initial conditions being a complex macro-scopic fact irreducible to its constituents (Gellner, 1956, p. 254). Of course, individualists do not have to deny that causal statements of a macroscopic kind can be meaningfully uttered, only to deny that they refer to real entities. However, Gellner's rebuttal of this is telling for, as he wrote,

> when we speak of societies we mean partly (a) generalisations about classes of human individuals which indeed are true only in virtue of propositions about those individuals, and can be 'reduced' to them, but also (b) groups, complexes, constellations of facts. These latter can exist only if their parts exist . . . but their fates *qua* fates of complexes can nevertheless be the initial conditions or indeed final conditions of a causal sequence.
>
> The powerful disinclination to allow social or general causes arises from the confusion of (a) and (b). . . . It should be clear that the following three propositions are not incompatible:
>
> A generalisation is true only in virtue of the truth of singular propositions.
>
> A whole is made up of its parts.
>
> No *a priori* legislation is possible concerning the complexity of links in causal chains.

The error of the individualist, Gellner continued,

> is to conclude from the first two propositions, which are analytic,
> the falsity of the third, through the confused identification of the
> hierarchy of propositions in terms of generality with the hierarchy
> of things in terms of complexity and inclusiveness. (Gellner, 1956,
> pp. 257–8)

Watkins replied to the charge that individualists could not account for
the socio-cultural origins of human dispositions by stating that, on the
contrary, individualism explained dispositions as a result of widespread
'human' cultural conditioning, rather than by 'inhuman' historicist
forces. He was worried that to abandon the idea that humans are the
only 'moving agents' in history was to introduce the idea that there are
superhuman or subhuman agencies working in history (Watkins, 1958,
p. 624). But this is to misconstrue completely the structurist position
since no structurist maintains that structures have superhuman powers or
are the result of superhuman forces. Nor does structurism imply that
structures are agents. While holists may mistakenly argue that society has
purposes and hence agency, social structures are in fact the *result* of past
human structuring agency, and are dynamic due only to contemporary
reproductive and transforming human action. Structures have the power
to *causally condition* action but humans also have intentionality and can
choose to act in ways relatively independent of socialisation. Therefore,
as Elster showed, a micro social psychological theory must complement a
macro structural theory.

This means that, for an ideal social structural explanation, knowledge
is required of all the observable actions and events of the individuals who
form a system, which can then be investigated for their powers and
structural organisational relations to see how the emergent properties of
the system relate to the totality of observables. The emergent level is
neither independent of the totality of micro observable constituents nor
reducible to or explainable by any particular subset of them or by all of
them. Furthermore, the emergent social level is a very large historical
organisation that pre-exists any particular constituent element. In other
words, the significance of most elements for the nature of the emergent
level is very small. But *combinations* of particular elements, such as
groups, social classes, corporations, mass behaviour, and so on, are much
more effective at the macro level.

Because this ideal explanation is impossible in practice, selection and
abstraction are necessary. Moreover general theories of both the model-
building and causal kind are required. The powers of persons and their
relationships in organisations and groups have to be modelled in abstract
in order to hypothesise their causal interrelationships and emergent
powers.

GENERAL MODELS OF SOCIAL STRUCTURE

Those who share the general idea that society is a real entity of some sort, i.e. holists and structurists, differ, however, over ways of modelling and conceptualising the properties of society. I shall point to five main abstract types of model.

Firstly, there is the *dramaturgical* model in which society is seen as analogous to a drama, with a theatre, stage, dressing rooms, script, roles, actors, spectators, and even critics. Furthermore, the actors have the power to alter the script, as do the critics. In a sense the actors are also the critics, and this applies to social scientists as much as to those who are thought to be in the play. The play is often enigmatic. As Rom Harré has put it:

> in social matters above all, the patterns that are experienced depend upon the interpretive schemata one brings to bear on a generally enigmatic scene. We enter what is plainly a theatre, but we have to guess what play is being performed. Sociology and social psychology as interpretive activities are parts of the very processes they purport to describe. (Harré, 1979, p. 139)

Erving Goffman, Clifford Geertz, and Rom Harré have richly demonstrated the heuristic power of this analogy in certain small group situations, but its applicability to macro structural explanation is doubtful, as I shall show in chapter 13.

Secondly, there are *nomological* models of society, in which it is seen as a structure of rules and laws of conduct to which people more or less conform. These rules can be of many sorts and operate at many different levels. For example, some social theorists and philosophers, such as Wittgenstein, Lévi-Strauss, and Chomsky, have constructed or influenced models of society as analogous to a language with a grammar, a syntax, and a dictionary of practices. The socio-biologists have tried to see society as conforming to some deep biological genetic or culturgenetic structure. Psychoanalysis has influenced conceptions of social order as arising from deep rule-governed structures of the unconscious human mind. Neo-classical economic theory is based on a general conception of the rationality of man which enables theorists to construct models of economic action and institutions using the analogy of games with fixed and known rules.

The third general model is a *relational-organisation* one. Society is seen as a structure of interpersonal relations of various sorts, or a network of individuals tied together by webs of exchange. Examples of this conception, which is now probably the most influential general approach, include kinship theories, where society is seen as bound together by elaborate ties of blood and marriage. There is the Marxian conception of social class where social action and consciousness are largely a product of class relations which are in turn bound up with the juridical relationship of individuals to property. Institutionalist economics has also emphasised the importance of the institutions of property and political power. Norbert Elias has developed an interesting concept of society as a figuration formed by individuals as nodal points attaching to others via 'valencies'. The chemical molecular analogy suggests itself here. Recently the network and exchange approaches have been elaborated, defended, and applied in impressive detail. They conceive of society somewhat as Elias does, i.e. as nodes with radiating pathways attaching to other nodes with the ties weakening with distance and perhaps occurring in bands or shells, or clusters, and along which exchanges of information, goods, and so on, pass.

The fourth general model is the *systemic-organic-cybernetic* one. As the name indicates, society is seen as a tightly integrated system in which the parts are functional to the maintenance of the equilibrium of the whole through feedback. Different parts play different roles in this integration so there is a complex differentiated and hierarchical structure of units. Some parts have a control function, some information, some reproductive, some feeding, and so on. The units or cells are conceived in different ways, some theorists believing them to be individual persons, others as acts, others as groups, others as social roles, and so on. Talcott Parsons and his followers are the leading exponents of this conception, which they have developed to a very sophisticated level.

Fifthly, and overlapping with the fourth, there is the *ecological* model in which society is seen as a 'natural' open physical system of balanced exchanges of energy. Tendencies for growth, decay, and disequilibrium are usually balanced by tendencies for equilibrium. All parts of the system are essential to its stability or growth and there is a complex division of functions. Humans are seen as part of nature, embedded in and interacting with the landscape, moulding it and being moulded by it. Some of the French Annales historians have employed this model and now it is being widely used in the study of primitive economic systems and even by some economic theorists of capitalist society such as Boulding.

None of these models is ever (or very rarely) employed in pure form. And it is possible to construct different ones using elements drawn from them or to introduce new elements. But it seems that any model is restricted to employing some or all of the following (tentatively defined) set of elements.

> social rules
> social roles
> social relations and institutions

social classes
occupations
spatial distributions
cultural understandings
sources of power or energy
geographic environmental relations.

In concluding this chapter, it is important to say that social explanation is not restricted to employing just one of these or any other model of society. Each is compatible with elements from others and, indeed, some social scientists, such as Geertz, Harré, Ladurie, Gellner, and Elias have employed combinations of them. Furthermore, different societies have to be modelled in different ways. One of the great errors of much modern Western social theory has been to dogmatically generalise a model developed to explain capitalist society and modernist culture to all forms of society. But this is not to say that human society in general does not have certain universal structural features. What they are is a largely contingent question, although I believe that the abstract 'moments' I have identified in this chapter are universal.

PART III

Action, Structure, and History: Approaches to Structural Change

Introduction to Part III

Having now discussed in part II the philosophical problems of explaining social entities and processes, my tasks in part III are (1) to discuss the methodological problems of explaining social change, and (2) to make some evaluation of the existing methodological resources (and to a lesser extent the theoretical resources) available to social historians. My exegesis and criticism of these resources employs the concepts and arguments of the last two chapters.

In chapter 9 I approach the general problem of how to explain social structural change from two perspectives. Firstly, I discuss the concepts that I believe are necessary for developing a viable approach to explanation and for criticising existing ones. Secondly, I briefly survey the existing discourse of social change theorising to show how the various schools and theories relate both to each other and to the philosophical/methodological concepts discussed in the first part of the chapter and in the previous chapter.

In chapters 10 to 14 I summarise and criticise the five main existing methodological traditions of social history theorising, drawing out the general concepts and giving examples of particular approaches and theories that have been developed within them.

These chapters do not, therefore, contain an analysis of the existing institutionalised discipline of social history as such, but only a subsection of it. This is because, firstly, part of that discipline is not, despite its name, actually about social history. It deals, rather, with action history. I argued in chapter 1 that any social history worthy of the name must deal with social structures because society is a structure. And I believe that in chapter 8 I have given good grounds for holding that social structures do exist and so can be objects of knowledge. Secondly, many practitioners of 'social history' (whether action historians or structural historians) do not consciously or consistently employ models of structure and theories of structural change, and so it cannot be said that they have coherent methodologies which can be abstracted, systematised, and clarified. Many empiricist historians fail in both these respects, and so fall through the methodological/conceptual net that I have begun to construct in the previous chapter and will further develop in the next chapter.

9

Towards the Explanation of Structural Change

Society is a macro structure that endures, has powerful effects, and is partly opaque to common-sense knowledge. But it also changes due to social actions and their mental/cultural antecedents. It cannot change spontaneously. To say it can is to commit the holistic fallacy. In order to construct a viable approach to social change, therefore, it is essential to have a general theory of the dialectical interrelationships of the micro and macro 'moments' of the social totality (personality, consciousness, action, culture, and social structure) and the 'levels' of macro structure (economy, politics, state, culture, geography). But such a theory does have to be very general. Some balance has to be sought between its heuristic power as an explanatory model and the risk of theoretical overdetermination of the evidence about the causal power of any particular moment or level in a particular society. All the moments and levels are interdependent and the disciplines that deal with them separately in fact deal with abstractions. Some social scientists, such as Emmanuel Le Roy Ladurie, Eric Hobsbawm, Barrington Moore, Clifford Geertz, Ernest Gellner, and Alain Touraine, do attempt to integrate all the levels and their work stands out for its richness accordingly. They are in effect true methodological structurists, combining micro, macro, and multistructural perspectives.

It is my aim in this chapter not to present a new general theory to underpin structurism but simply to examine briefly some of the concepts and models that seem important to an explication, appreciation, and criticism of the methodologies and theories examined in the following chapters.

ACTION, AGENCY, AND STRUCTURAL CHANGE

The explanation of action

In order to explain social structural change a subtheory of action must be presupposed or incorporated into a more general theory. Conscious human behaviour is purposively motivated (or goal directed) and meaningful, and is rightly called action. Its explanation therefore requires reference to mental concepts, among other things. The relationships that particular actions have with prior conscious intentions is one of the key problems.

Against both the orthodox intentionalist and behaviourist views of action Donald Davidson has argued[1] that actions have mental *causes* and that this is not inconsistent with the notion of freedom to act. Explanation and causal explanation should indeed be seen as synonymous. But, contrary to the positivistic behaviourist view, nomological explanation is only a subclass of causal explanations and, contrary to the interpretists, reasons explanations, and causal explanations are not necessarily opposed. Indeed, in Davidson's account, reasons *are* causes of action and so provide explanations of action. But what is the relationship between reasons and mental events and processes? The main access we have to mental events is via the utterances and actions of persons. Utterances include statements about reasons why acts were performed. Can these reasons be considered as the causes of action?[2]

Statements of reasons for action are statements about various sorts of motivations and purposes the actor thinks he had for acting. But of course actors can be deluded, can deliberately lie, or even can be genuinely unconscious of certain mental antecedents of action. The psycho-analytic tradition has developed a range of concepts to deal with antecedents that remain almost wholly unknown to the actor. Moreover, actors always give selective, context-dependent, accounts of their motives. It is therefore important to see that stated reasons are rationalisations or very partial, or even deluded, descriptions of motives for action; while they may state what the agent believes were his or her motives, they may be misleading as to the real situation. But rationalisations are still *post hoc* (and perhaps *ad hoc*) 'explanations' of a causal kind given by the actor, since they take the form of 'I performed such-and-such an act because of so-and-so motives and purposes to achieve this or that goal.'

---

[1] See Davidson (1963, 1967a, 1970b, 1978a), and chapter 7. A similar argument has recently been developed by John Searle (1983).

[2] For recent helpful discussions of action theory, see Alston (1974, 1976), Davidson (1974b), L. H. Davis (1979), Goldman (1970), Pettit (1979), Searle (1983), von Cranach (1982).

Reasons can thus *justify* actions, as Davidson pointed out, by redescribing them as part of a pattern of events and so also putatively explaining them.[3]

Nevertheless, we need to know much more in order to have a better or more complete explanation about the mental antecedents of action. Furthermore a better explanation would tell us something about the *origins* of the mental antecedents of action. What is it about persons in general that leads them to act in certain consistently patterned and rule-following ways, as we know they do, and to react to certain environmental influences in certain ordered ways? In short, as well as knowledge of reasons, which refer to mental processes, we also need a general model of the powers and propensities of humans and of how they relate to their social and physical environments before we can explain individual and social action. While people do seem to be able to choose to act according to their personal motives, their acts are nevertheless causally conditioned. The freedom/determinism and intentional/causal dichotomies fail to capture the essence of the problem because they are not exclusive alternatives. 'Freedom to choose' does not necessarily imply 'uncaused' because causation does not imply universal empiricist laws. Human action is determinate because humans make choices which cause them to act; they do not have unbounded abilities; and they always live in bounded social and physical situations which condition their choices.

Before turning to the questions of the nature of humans and their social situations, it is important to consider the significance of *purposes* in the explanation of action. The hermeneutical philosophers have argued that because action is irreducible to bodily movement (however conscious and intentional it is) it is not caused in the same way that physical events are. It thus requires a different sort of explanation, one which concentrates on the significance or meaning of purposes for the actor. Charles Taylor, for example, has argued that action requires *teleological* explanation – i.e. a form which argues from the goals of action to its structural origin. In his formulation, action is explicable teleologically because it occurs for the sake of its goal:

> This means that the condition of the event's occurring is that a state of affairs obtain such that it will bring about the end in question, or such that this event is required to bring about that end. To offer a teleological explanation of some event or class of events, e.g. the behaviour of some being, is, then, to account for it by laws in terms of which an event's occurring is held to be dependent on that event's being required for some end.
>
> To say that the behaviour of a given system should be explained in terms of purpose, then, is in part, to make an assertion about the

---

[3] See Davidson (1963, pp. 9–10). See also Pettit (1979).

form of the laws, or the type of laws which hold of the system. But *qua* teleological those laws will not be of the kind which makes behaviour a function of the state of some unobservable entity; rather the behaviour is a function of the state of the system and (in the case of animate organisms) its environment; but the relevant feature of system and environment on which behaviour depends will be what the condition of both makes necessary if the end concerned is to be realised. (Taylor, 1964, p. 9)

Taylor pointed out in a later paper that this was not a claim that reference to antecedents could be dispensed with. Rather, it was about the *form* of the antecedents – i.e. 'a form in which the occurrence of the event to be explained is made contingent on the situation's being such that this event would bring about the end in question' (Taylor, 1970, p. 55).

I believe this form of explanation can be seen as congruent with the realist model discussed in chapters 7 and 8, where it was argued that explanation of events of various sorts consists in discovering the powers and tendencies that kinds of things have to act in certain regular, knowable ways in virtue of their real nature as kinds of entities. Thus we postulate that humans are of a certain character which predisposes them to act in socially rule-governed but purposive ways and that the task for biologists, psychologists, and philosophical anthropologists is to discover this precise character. And since it seems fairly obvious because of the patterned, purposive ways in which they act that humans both follow social rules and construct social structures, it is encumbent on action theorists to adopt a sociological perspective. (This has been fully realised by Davidson and Taylor.)

Taylor's teleological explanation is a form of functionalist argument which explains the antecedents of events by reference to their consequences. As I also pointed out in chapters 7 and 8, this form of argument is widespread in the sciences that deal with systems and seems to be genuinely explanatory in so far as the nature of the systems is such that they incorporate mechanisms of a causal feedback kind. That is, in the human case the desire for an end state dictates the action processes that lead towards it. But the problem for social explanation, rather than action explanation, is whether *society* has such mechanisms, as the functionalists sometimes claim. This will be discussed in chapter 10.

Agency, rationality, and sociality

A person's desires, intentions, and reasons are always formed in a socially influenced context. People are able to choose to act in certain ways but always within a restraining (and enabling) social situation of which they may be partly unaware. Furthermore, it is theoretically possible that they may believe and say that there is no restraint on their actions because their perceptions of the world, their language, and their self-understandings may all be completely determined by their cultural (or ideological) situations. There is perhaps a dialectical relationship between actions, consciousness, stated reasons, and culture. However, such a simplified dialectical conception is ultimately unsatisfactory because these apparently reciprocal relationships are really not so simple. Many kinds of problems arise in explaining these interrelationships of personality, consciousness, action, culture, and social structure.

The explanation of action, social structure, and social change cannot do without concepts which refer, firstly, to the complex *mental structures* of persons as a kind of entity. (Concepts of beliefs, intentions, desires, knowledge, understandings, and so on refer to the particular *content* of minds, not their structures.) Among the mental structural attributes of persons are the abilities to be aware of themselves, to consciously monitor their own thoughts and actions, and to consciously control themselves for much of the time. Moreover, they also have second-order levels of these abilities – i.e. they can monitor their monitorings, and control their controls, and so on. They are objects of their own curiosity and understandings. They are selves for themselves. Concepts of self-identity, self-minitoring, self-motivation, self-control, and such like imply the notion of human agency.[4]

Human *agency* is the power to effect changes in the world. It depends on an ability to evaluate and intentionally control our motivations and actions and thus make choices and act according to them. This implies that persons have sufficient self-knowledge, situational knowledge, and practical reason, i.e. the ability to evaluate options, situations, and possible outcomes. They are characterised by *agent causality*, which is to say that they are not determined by external causality. When 'pure agents' act they do so due to their power and ability to act. There is no separate force involved. But of course there are no pure agents. Consciousness, choice, and action are all situationally conditioned and constrained.

The exercise of agency powers is obviously dependent on the ability to reason in a coherent, consistent, and practical manner. Psychological and social explanation are therefore significantly aided by postulating human *rationality*, as Elster and many others argue.[5] Humans are able to choose reflectively to act for their own good reasons (within certain restraints), whatever those reasons are and however they are influenced. (The influences include false consciousness.) Some economistic theories of

[4] On the problems of selfhood and human agency, see the following: Chisholm (1980), Davidson (1971), Frankfurt (1971), Harré (1979, ch. 11), Hollis (1977), C. Taylor (1977), Thalberg (1980), Vesey (1968).

[5] The rationality of action is a very contentious issue. It is similar to but not the same as the problem of the rationality of belief. See the helpful discussions in Benn and Mortimore (1976), Elster (1979b), Hollis and Lukes (1982).

rational behaviour are seriously flawed, however, because they adopt a behaviourist-dispositional account of motivation.[6] That is, humans are assumed to have a universally fixed disposition to behave rationally to maximise personal utility, and this disposition is supposedly constantly evidenced by their behaviour. The psychological disposition is thought to be wholly present in the observable behaviour, as Ryle and other philosophical behaviourists have claimed must be the case. Without behaviour there can be no psychological disposition.

However, rationality is a culturally relative notion. What are good reasons in one culture may not be in another. But neither this fact, nor the fact that humans sometimes act irrationally or unselfishly or unreflectively, rules out the usefulness of the rationality postulate. A realist account can reconcile the universality of the concept with the variability of the phenomena because it claims that rationality is a *capacity* that persons have which is not necessarily constantly activated. It is not an invariably determining disposition which comes into force automatically upon receiving the right stimuli. It is merely a tendency, a power, which makes certain rational acts possible.

Thus we can see the difference between a realist-agential theory and a behaviourist theory of rationality. To postulate humans as agents does not mean that they have no fixed natural capacities, tendencies, and liabilities, only that there is freedom of choice to act and to alter the world, within certain bounds. The 'voluntaristic' theory of Talcott Parsons and some neo-classical economists is a bit like the idea of 'volunteering' that applies in armies: i.e. 'volunteers are required for a mission, which means you, you, and you!' Action is voluntary but always predispositional. Neo-classical economic actors apparently cannot choose to be irrational. If they were, then predicting their behaviour would be much more difficult and positivist economics wishes to make precise predictions. Economic rationality helps the construction of neat mathematical models of action. But so far it has not met with much success in actually predicting large-scale collective behaviour.

A realist approach to the mental antecedents of action does not seek to predict action, only to explain it. The postulation of rationality as one of the capacities of persons helps in this because empirically it can be shown that humans do often act for good reasons but also that their reasoning process is much more complicated and culturally relative than egoistic utilitarianism believes. Rationality has to be seen against the background of the whole ensemble of powers, liabilities, and needs that persons have, including sociality and the strong desire to maintain the integrity of both their selfhood (i.e. their self-respect) and their social situations. So, acting

---

[6] On economistic theories of rationality, see Barry and Hardin (1982), Elster (1979a, 1979b, 1982c), Latsis (1983), Sen (1976), Simon (1976, 1983).

for good reasons means that these reasons are good for the actor and may not always be readily apparent to the observer.

Besides personal powers and liabilities, humans also have powers to form relationships with and influence the actions of other persons, and in turn they have liabilities to be influenced by others. These are of course *social* powers and liabilities. *Communication* is the essence of sociality and social power, as many social theorists now argue, such as Parsons, Homans, Lévi-Strauss, Blau, and Habermas. Communication makes organisation possible. But what is communicated, how it is communicated, and how the communication is distorted, deflected, and perverted are not agreed. The role of culture in general, and ideologically false understandings in particular, in structuring social interaction, influencing structural reproduction and transformation, and permitting and maintaining relations of domination and subordination, is clearly crucial. We will see in later chapters that culturalist-communication theories of structural change are now widespread in the social sciences.

Categories of social action

In theorising the general relationship between action and society we have to first make distinctions between various categories of social action since not all action is equally significant from the social structural point of view. Firstly, there is *face-to-face interaction* in small groups or social situations. Here individuals communicate directly, and form a temporary micro structure of relations. The ethnomethodologists and some other similar micro sociologists and social psychologists want to argue that concepts of any other form of social structure or power are not permitted. But this would have the effect of reducing sociology to social psychology and so remove any possibility of studying such macro social processes as industrialisation, modernisation, or urbanisation. Face-to-face interaction always takes place within a pre-existing social structure and is partly determined by that structure.

Secondly, there is *collective or group action* in which individuals participate in more or less knowing concert with each other to achieve their goals and perhaps also the collective goals of the group. Such action is of great importance for the structuring and reproduction of institutions and sometimes the transformation of them. Through concerted action groups take on social power and give rise to new social arrangements of rules, roles, relations, and power. The members of a group do not necessarily have to be in physical contact with each other, but ease of communication between them and a shared framework of culture, meanings, and intentions is essential. Communication and exchange make group structure possible. Groups can be structured in various hierarchical or fluid ways and the forms of communication tie them together. Individuals in groups can be oppressed or liberated by them, use them or be used by them, become more powerful through them or lose their power.

Thirdly, there is *patterned social action* in which individuals act in more or less unknowing concert with others to achieve individual goals. They act in patterns because the society is socially and geographically structured in such a way as to channel action. A good example is the traffic pattern, where individuals or small groups move from place to place acting on a wide range of motivations to achieve a wide range of goals, but forced to conform to a set number of pathways. These pathways are an important element of the social structure, one which is very rigid, slow to change, and exerts a powerful influence upon action and consciousness. Speech is also a patterned activity because it must employ the grammar and vocabulary available. The general economic structure of the economy also imposes patterns of many sorts on people's activities. But the fact that many activities are patterned does not prevent some freedom of action within the pattern. The degree of freedom depends upon the rigidity of the economic, cultural, linguistic, and geographical system existing, which depends in turn partly upon the stage of economic and social development that a society has reached.

There is a fourth, more difficult to define, form of social action which I shall call *political (or structural) action*. Such action is that which is more or less consciously aimed at maintaining or transforming the patterns and structures of a culture and society. The intention to achieve this is what is crucial, not the effect, because the actual outcomes of the activity may be unintended. Such activity is usually called political, and it is political in the widest and true sense because its object is the polis, the community, the society itself. It is often also patterned in its manifestation because the society has a structure for channelling and legitimating such action, but sometimes it attempts to break out of and break down its channels. It can be local or global in its significance, occur in face-to-face situations or in impersonal mass communications, be collective or individual.

The structural consequences of social action

All social action, not just political action, is oriented towards either maintaining or transforming pre-existing small- or large-scale structures. It often achieves its effects in largely unintended ways. The intended consequences of such action, including political action, are often less important than the unintended. Ordinary actors cannot usually see, and are not very interested in, goals other than their individual ones or structures other than their small group ones. The macro society itself and the more widespread possible consequences of individual and group actions are usually not well understood by ordinary actors pursuing their daily routined lives. Yet those structures are partly the historical result of routined lives. Common-sense understanding is inadequate to conceptualise and understand all the complexities of society's deep structure of rules, relations, classes, and so on. Understanding goes only so far as is necessary to live one's life. And understandings can be false. But of course this is not to deny that actors must and do have a good deal of insight into their own local social milieu and institutions. 'Local knowledge' is important (as Geertz argues: cf. chapter 13) and is one of the mainsprings of action, but its social origin and its consequences for action go well beyond local action.

Political actors are sometimes not very knowledgeable about their societies. This is for two main reasons. Firstly, they are often themselves 'ordinary' actors embedded in their own societies. Secondly, the social scientific knowledge available to them is not only of limited validity but often expressed in a manner that makes ti difficult for them to 'use'. The unintended consequences of political action are therefore very significant for this reason.

The realisation that there are unintended social consequences of action was one of the original impetuses for the development of social science in the eighteenth century. It remains one of the most important, and puzzling, areas to be dealt with.[7] Central among the unintended consequences are the macro structuring of society itself, and social contradictions, including the production of perverse effects — the opposite of what was intended. And how these consequences relate to social understandings (or culture and ideology) is also a central problem.

The most important type of contradiction in society is the structural (or systemic) — those contradictions that lead to social transformation. Marx insisted that the process of attempted reproduction of society leads gradually and inexorably towards transformation. The mechanisms of this gradual transformation are complex and vary a good deal from society to society. There are also sudden revolutionary transformations which have always occurred in ways largely unintended even by conscious revolutionaries.

THE DISCOURSE OF SOCIAL CHANGE THEORISING

Social change theorising has taken place as a sub-branch of the general traditions of sociological theorising. Figure 7 attempts to show how the contemporary traditions of social change theorising relate to the philosophical foundations discussed previously and to modern schools of social theory.[8] It can be seen that there are five such traditions. The first,

---

[7] On the problem of unintended consequences of social action, see footnote 7 for chapter 8.

[8] Some helpful overviews of modern social theory are to be found in Craib (1984), Wallace (1969).

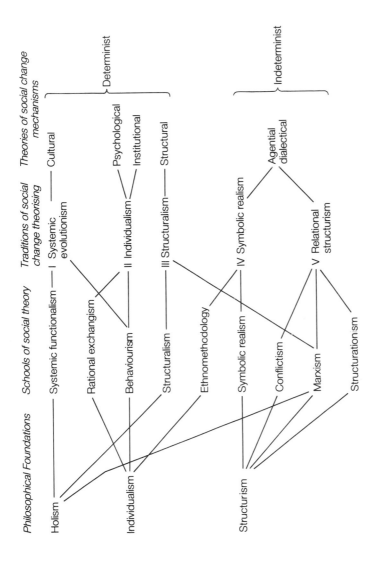

Figure 7 The discourse of social change

systemic evolutionism, is distinguished by its conception that the process of social change occurs in relatively autonomous 'organic' systems and evolves through several distinct stages from lower to higher levels of cultural complexity, technological development, and geographical scope. Secondly, the *individualist* tradition sees change as occurring in networks of interpersonal power relations, which essentially rise out of individual rational exchange in a framework of personality differences. (Both these traditions have an empiricist-positivist epistemological foundation for their attempts to construct knowledge of their objects.) Thirdly, the *structuralist* tradition borders on being ahistorical in its conception of structural change since it concentrates on the continuity of cultures and economic structures beneath superficial changes in society. Certain visible aspects of society do change but the structures of the cultural, social, economic, and ecological determinants change very slowly if at all. The fourth and fifth traditions – *symbolic realism* and *relational structurism* – have a general conception of social change as radically *transformational*, and they usually conceptualise only a basic dichotomy of social structure, i.e. before and after the transformation. Both see action as structuring and transformational but they do differ quite markedly in other respects. The fourth conceives of society in *symbolic* terms, while the fifth conceives of it in *relational-structural* terms. Action in the fourth is symbolic and dramaturgical, while in the fifth it has a dialectical interrelationship with objectified structure.

Thus traditions of social change theorising are first differentiated in terms of their conceptions of structure and stages and the degree of autonomy of the process from conscious human action. The systemic, individualist, and structuralist traditions are broadly determinist, while the symbolic-realist and relational-structurist traditions are broadly indeterminist. This dichotomy is reflected in the division of approaches in the following five chapters.

Determinist versus agency approaches

Approaches within the first three traditions (discussed in chapters 10, 11, and 12) locate the fundamental determining sources of structural change *outside* the conscious agency of human subjects, i.e. in such determining and relatively unchanging locations as the preformed psychological dispositions of humans, or their preformed cultural and institutional structures, or their general socio-geographic environmental situations, or even in their biological composition. Chapters 13 and 14 will deal with approaches developed within the last two traditions, all of which locate the fundamental source of change *within* the conscious human agent, albeit an agent who always acts within a structured social, cultural, and geographical environment.

While all the approaches to be discussed are more or less realist in their general social ontologies, in that they hold that society is a structure or system, they do differ a good deal over their methodologies, their concepts of structure, and their theories of the general causal inter-relationships of structure with action, consciousness, and culture. These last two differences are crucial. Some 'schools' of theorists who apparently share a good many concepts and theories, such as the Marxists and the modernisation theorists, do in fact differ internally on their basic concepts of structure and therefore on the relationship of social structure to action, culture, and consciousness. This basic conceptual difference therefore has the effect, school labels notwithstanding, of making them into quite distinct methodological approaches needing separate analysis. On the other hand, some theorists who share a relational conception of structure – e.g. various networkist, individualist, and Marxist theorists – differ on the causal roles of agency and structural determinism in the interrelationship of action, structure, and consciousness and thus they too have different methodologies. In short, concepts of structure and structural change mechanisms are fundamental and *both* must be shared for writers to be considered as belonging to the same methodological approach.

Another contrast between determinist and agential approaches is in terms of the universality of the concepts and categories of society and change that are employed. The determinists are much more universalistic and ahistorical in their concepts and so much more liable to attempt to categorise all actions, societies, and processes as exemplifying a limited number of structural variables. The agentialists are more historically attuned, alive to the subtle differences and the greater complexities in and between societies.

Determinist approaches to action, society, and change find the basic force for social change in some unchanging, uncontrolled disposition or force existing in humans or society, or the environment. The agential approach finds the force also, in a sense, in the nature of humans but humans conceived of as the agents of their own action and experience, developing themselves in the world and structuring it through their actions. They have this ability, but how it manifests itself is greatly variable and constrained by general parameters of a biological, social, cultural, and environmental kind. The limits of human social structuring power have not yet been found, and probably never will be. The only constant, unchanging aspects of humans, according to this view, are the necessity for social relations and changeability itself. The history of society would seem to bear this out. It always exists but it always changes. Only an agential approach to history and structure can reconcile this because only it can do justice to, among other things, the striking facts of structuration and the unintended (and largely unpredictable) consequences of intentional action.

All the approaches that I discuss in the following five chapters are

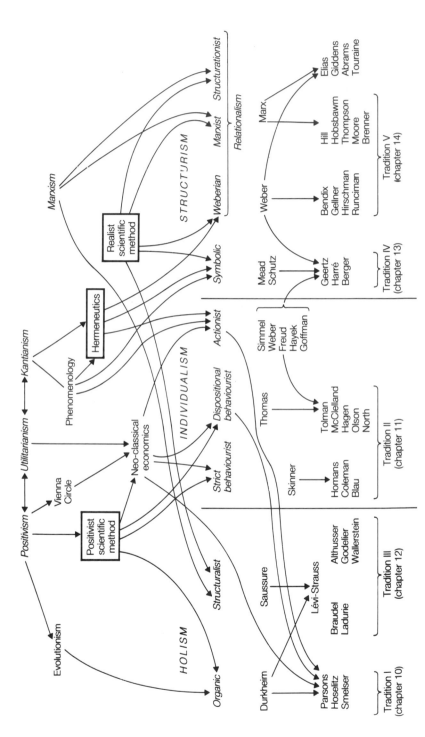

Figure 8 Philosophies, methodologies, and traditions of structural history:
the main lines of influence

actual, explicitly articulated methodologies for studying social change. That is, they are not abstract, formalised models of such approaches. However, my method of exegesis and criticism of these approaches contains two strategies. I try to follow closely the actual writings of particular authors and to construct general outlines of the main concepts and methodologies of each tradition. It is essential that both strategies be pursued. If the latter method were pursued alone it would run the risk of making caricatures or straw men to which no one would lay claim. Such constructs may be easy to capture and destroy but the real quarry often escapes.

Figure 8 attempts to map the interrelationships of philosophical/ methodological presuppositions, individual thinkers, and traditions of structural history theorising. Chapters 10 to 14 follow this map closely.

10

Systemic Evolutionism

POSITIVIST THEORIES

The systemic-evolutionary approach is one of the main forms of positivist social theory. Positivism, as I have shown in chapter 3, is a broad philosophical movement, united by the central ideas of a sharp distinction between science and non-science in terms of method; the potential epistemological unity of all empirical explanations (including sociology and history) on the basis of laws; and the objectivity of scientific explanation, irrespective of the subject matter, on the basis of empiricism. Empiricism is in turn based on the theory/observation distinction and the designation of all non-empirical entities as unreal.

A central component of positivist sociological thought in the nineteenth century was the concept of law-governed evolutionary development, and this idea, with certain vicissitudes, has ever since dominated discussion in the history of social change theorising. Thus any survey of approaches to explaining structural change has first to come to terms with its significance. From a position of pre-eminence in the late nineteenth century the idea of 'evolutionism' declined in importance in the early twentieth century. It was revived in the 1950s, then vociferously rejected again for a time in the late 1960s and early 1970s, until finally it has become once more a central component of social thought, not just of positivist social change theory. This chequered history reflects its own evolution as a concept. The idea of 'development', however, has also been subscribed to by non-evolutionists, particularly Marxists and neo-classical economists.

Evolution has often been mistakenly equated with development (e.g. Lenski, 1976a). But 'development' is an older and more general notion referring to processes of change which operate in the direction of growth in complexity, size, and number of units. It refers to the phenomenal aspects of a process and not to a cause. Society can also be envisaged as changing in non-developmental ways but virtually all theorists dealt with in the following chapters are developmentalists.[1] 'Evolution', on the other hand, has been used to refer both to a particular form of the development process (as unidirectional, progressive, and proceeding through stages) and, especially in recent times, to a particular (Darwinian) theory of its mechanisms. Much of the modern debate over social evolutionary theory fails to make these distinctions.

Similarly, modern evolutionary theorists are wont to hold that all theories of structure are systemic-equilibrium theories. This is false because, as we shall see, other traditions of social change theory have different conceptions. It is a common failing of positivists to see all their rivals as weaker versions of themselves or else not even worthy of consideration as scientific.[2]

THE BEGINNINGS OF SOCIAL EVOLUTIONARY THEORY

In the late nineteenth and early twentieth centuries, 'evolution' was one of the three central concepts, in addition to 'structure' and 'function', of positivist social thought, as exemplified by Comte, Buckle, Spencer, Durkheim, Maine, Morgan, Hobhouse, and Tylor.[3] Evolutionism was not originally derived from Darwin but based on a much older and vaguer organic/holistic developmentalist tradition, traceable as far back as Aristotle, as Robert Nisbet and Kenneth Bock have shown.[4] This older tradition conceptualised society as analogous to an organism with a tendency to grow and decay.

Positivist social theory saw the task of social science as searching for the laws of history by 'generalising' from historical events. But it did this within a largely unexamined *a priori* evolutionary framework, or speculative philosophy of history. Bock (1964, pp. 23–4) has conveniently stated this *a priori* philosophy in eight points, which can be summarised thus:

1 Human society and culture are characterised by change, so laws of history are laws of change.
2 Social change is inevitable.

---

[1] There are discussions of the history of the concept of development in Bendix (1977, ch. 8), Elias (1978b, pp. 145–52), Nisbet (1969, 1970 passim), Wallerstein (1984, ch. 17).
[2] For example, Smelser (1968b, p. 265) falsely construes Marx as an equilibrium theorist.
[3] For overviews and general discussions of nineteenth and early twentieth century social evolutionism, see Bock (1964, 1979), Burrow (1966), Chodak (1973), Hirst (1976b), Nisbet (1969, 1970), Smelser (1967a), A. Smith (1973, ch. 2).
[4] Bock (1964, 1979), Nisbet (1969, 1970).

3 Social change results from endogenous forces – particularly the unfolding of potentials in humans, society, and culture.

4 Basic change is continuous, slow, and gradual; events are the manifestation of change. The pace of change is altered only by external forces.

5 Change is directed towards a goal, which is determined by the nature of the society, culture, or man.

6 The direction of change is from homogeneous to heterogeneous, simple to complex, undifferentiated to differentiated in form and function, and small to large.

7 The laws of change operate uniformly through time and space, so all societies follow the same path, and the whole of human society and culture develops in a particular direction.

8 Social change is thus analogous to the growth of an organism.

Therefore it is important to stress that eighteenth and nineteenth century evolutionism added the Enlightenment idea of *progress* to the older organic tradition (see Bury, 1932).

An early form of evolutionism was first applied to the history of economic and social structures in the mid eighteenth century in the work of Turgot and Montesquieu in France and Adam Smith, Adam Ferguson, John Millar, William Robertson, and other members of the Scottish school of historical sociologists, who saw structural change as conforming to a set of five universal stages of development from primitive to industrial. Saint-Simon and Comte, in the early nineteenth century, were also strongly influenced by such thinking. They added to it the positivist concepts of laws and organic holism, in their attempts to create a science of society like that of nature. But later positivists such as Mill and Buckle were utilitarian individualists and rigid inductivists.

Perhaps it could be argued that Marx too was an evolutionist of the early sort, although he was clearly not a positivist. He saw society in general terms as passing through a set of three universal, dialectically related stages (primitive communal, capitalist, and communist) and having largely internal dialectical mechanisms of change (technological and ecological at the economic level, class struggle and revolution at the political level). But he had a structural rather than organic conception of society, with a corresponding greater place for human agency; a more discontinuous, less deterministic conception of stages and the rate of change; a conception of stages as abstract concepts of internal structure, not descriptive categories, thus allowing for great empirical variety within each stage; and an open-ended rather than goal-directed concept of development. He also allowed very much for exogenous forces such as war and imperialism, as well as social decay. In short, he was more historical than philosophical in his orientation, was more structural than organic in his theory of society, had a realist rather than empiricist theory of mechanisms and laws, and was not a teleologist. Thus although he was a developmentalist, he should not be considered as part of the positivist evolutionary tradition.

Evolution did have a central place in the thinking of the German historical school of economists (which developed contemporaneously with Marxism), i.e. in the thought of Roscher, Knies, Schmoller, Bücher, Sombart, and others. They developed various theories of the stages through which economies must pass from primitive to advanced. These people in turn had some influence on German macro sociology in the late nineteenth century, notably Weber and Toennies. Weber advanced a sociological theory of the economy, partly influenced by them, but he was not an evolutionist as defined above. Toennies did develop a quasi-evolutionary theory of the dichotomy between two basic kinds of society – *Gemeinschaft* and *Gesellschaft*.

Durkheim was also a quasi-evolutionist in that he had a dichotomous theory of social stages and a well-developed theory of differentiation, but this did not imply the thesis of progress that was the central component of much British positivist sociology and anthropology in the late nineteenth century. Positivist evolutionism reached its apogee in the work of Herbert Spencer. He was strongly influenced by pre-Darwinian evolutionary theory, particularly that of Lamarck, Malthus, and Lyell, but rejected utilitarian individualism. He combined the idea of gradual, deterministic development towards greater complexity (the law of evolution) and the organic model of society. Even after the publication of Darwin's *On the Origin of Species*, which Spencer hailed, he nevertheless retained his Lamarckian and fundamentally ahistorical idea that organic social evolution moulds human nature, individuality, and action. The law of evolution is inherent in all things, according to Spencer (cf. Burrow, 1966).

There have been three significant breaks in the history of positivist social evolutionary theory. The first occurred in the 1930s when the original concern with establishing the linear evolutionary laws of history, on supposedly inductive grounds, was abandoned in favour of investigating the functional relationships of stable social structures and employing a hypothetico-deductive method of theory construction and empirical confirmation. The second occurred within the structural-functional paradigm around the late 1950s. This break was due to three developments in the history of ideas coming together to have an effect on social theory at that time: (1) the growth in sophistication (due to Darwin and genetics) of biological theory, (2) the related development of general systems theory and cybernetics in the 1940s and 1950s, and (3) the logical-positivist movement in philosophy of explanation. All these helped to bring about the neo-evolutionist revival. Thirdly, there was a major change within the wider positivist tradition in the mid 1960s due to disenchantment with the 'organic' conception (or model) of society. The main result of this disenchantment was the adoption of an individualist conception of action, society, and change, which revived some aspects of the older nineteenth-century utilitarian positivism deriving particularly from Malthus and Mill.

THE CONTEMPORARY IDEA OF SOCIAL EVOLUTION

The general concept of 'evolution' in contemporary social thought has three related but distinct meanings:[5]

1 The idea that societies and cultures are *organic* holistic systems which steadily or discontinuously change and develop in the direction of greater differentiation and complexity. This contrasts firstly with the idea that societies are not organic, and secondly with the theory that they basically do not change, or that they change in cyclical, fluctuational, or random, non-linear ways.
2 The *Darwinian* and *Lamarckian* types of theories of the supposed mechanisms of growth and development in social systems. That is, the ideas that society evolves either by endogenous mutations allowing adaptation to changing environments or by the inheritance of exogenously acquired systemic abilities to adapt to environments. Neither of these is necessarily teleological.

It is possible for each of the ideas in (1) and (2) to be held without necessarily subscribing to the other. That is, societies can be thought to evolve as in (1) but to have some mechanism of doing so other than Darwinian or Lamarckian evolution. Conversely, societies can be thought to evolve in a Darwinian or Lamarckian sense but not to have an organic-systemic structure; i.e. evolution does not necessarily imply organicism. This is the view of some recent individualist theorists (to be discussed as part of the second tradition in the next chapter) and some symbolic-realist and relational-structural theorists (to be discussed in chapters 13 and 14).

It is therefore important to draw a distinction between organic evolution, which concerns the evolution of a single organism from birth to maturity to death; and population evolution, which concerns the evolution of a large population of individuals through the selection and spreading of mutational changes.

3 The *epistemological* theory of the development and evolution of human knowledge about the world. I showed in chapter 7 that

---

[5] General discussions of modern social evolutionism are contained in: Campbell (1965), Feinman (1980), Feldman (1965), Ginsburg (1961), A. Smith (1973), Utz (1973), Van Parijs (1981).

this position usually argues that human knowledge evolves along with human capacities for knowledge acquisition, and those capacities evolve through the interaction of humans and the environment. Knowledge is thus both an outcome from and has an evolutionary effect upon human development. Furthermore, it is argued that human ontogeny mirrors phylogeny so that an individual's knowledge is also gained partly through environmental interaction.

In this chapter I shall be discussing the tradition that incorporates both 1 and 2 so that its central idea is a theory of social evolution that in fact consists of four component ideas:

1 Society is a tightly bounded and integrated system with a cybernetic hierarchy of self-controls which maintain it in equilibrium.
2 Societies evolve by adapting to their environments.
3 The mechanisms of evolution are endogenous mutations, which may be responses to environmental stimuli (i.e. a Darwinian theory with a Lamarckian element).
4 Societies evolve through stages of ever-greater differentiation and systemic complexity.

So, the basis of the systemic-evolutionary tradition of social change theorising is an organic-systemic model of social structure, to which I turn first.

THE SYSTEMIC-FUNCTIONALIST THEORY OF SOCIETY

All the main European schools of sociology in the late nineteenth and early twentieth centuries (positivist, Marxian, Durkheimian, Weberian) were profoundly concerned with questions of history and social change. They were also, but to a lesser extent, concerned with questions of social order and the structure and workings of society as a totality. However, when A. R. Radcliffe-Brown, Bronislaw Malinowski, Talcott Parsons, and Robert Merton began constructing their general theories in the 1920s and 1930s, the problem of history and change was relegated in favour of a concentration on the problem of how order and structure are possible. The role of cultural norms, continuity, consensus, stability, and equilibrium became more important for them than class structure and conflict, coercion, deviance, alienation, anomie, history, and transformation.[6]

The work of Parsons and his collaborators is perhaps the most

---

[6] The work of Walter Buckley (1957, 1967), Alvin Gouldner (1959), Marion Levy (1968), and Robert Merton (1968, ch. 3) contains helpful general discussions of structural-functional sociology.

influential approach to social explanation developed in the twentieth century.[7] The use of the concept of 'system' is basic to the Parsonian paradigm. The adoption of this concept entailed a certain orientation towards action – one that saw it as occurring within organic systems and not some other less integrated form of structure. In *Toward a General Theory of Action* Parsons and Shils (1951) distinguished between theoretical and empirical systems, the former being a body of logically connected concepts of which their work was an example. The most fundamental property of an *empirical system* is the *interdependence* of parts or variables.

> Interdependence consists in the existence of determinant relationships among the parts or variables as contrasted with randomness or variability. In other words, interdependence is *order* in the relationships among the components which enter into a system. This order must have a tendency to self-maintenance, which is very generally expressed in the concept of equilibrium. It would not, however, be a static self-maintenance or a stable equilibrium. It may be an ordered process of change. (Parsons and Shils, 1951, p. 107)

The importance of this central feature of systems – that there is an internal *determinate* relationship among the parts – is such that if a new relationship or element is introduced to the system it has either to be rejected or to bring about an adjustment to the whole system. Thus for human action systems the ability to maintain *equilibrium* within definite internally self-maintained boundaries is significant. Two fundamental processes – allocation and integration – are necessary for the maintenance of the distribution of parts, and integration is the process of mediation with the environment through which boundaries and internal stability are maintained against external variability. The system is a unity relative to its environment, and has an internal control of tendencies to change (pp. 107–8).

In making conscious choices the actor is, according to their framework, confronted with a series of dilemmas of orientation towards his (or its) situation requiring decisions before the situation becomes meaningful and action is possible. This idea gave rise to the pattern variable scheme of categories for choices and explaining action. According to Parsons and Shils, all actors must make five dochotomous choices. The first three arise from the absence of any biologically given primacy of orientation towards a situation. They are: firstly, choosing between accepting

[7] Parsonian sociology is discussed in general terms by, among many others, Bershady (1973), Burger (1977), Gould (1976), Gouldner (1971), Rocher (1974), Savage (1981). See also the collection of articles and pieces in Demerath and Peterson (1967) and Parsons's own retrospective overviews in Parsons (1970a, 1970b, 1975).

gratification from an object with or without regard to the consequences of doing so; secondly, acting with regard either only to personal significance or to social and moral significance; thirdly, evaluating an object in terms of a universal or a particular personal frame of reference. The other two arise from indeterminacies intrinsic to the object situation. So, fourthly, a choice has to be made between seeing a social object either as a composite of ascribed qualities or as a composite of performances; and fifthly, the actor has to see social objects either as functionally diffuse without a defined set of rights, or as functionally specific with a defined set of rights (pp. 56–60). Thus in summary, the pattern variables are:

1 Affectivity – affective neutrality
2 Self-orientation – collective orientation
3 Universalism – particularism
4 Ascription – achievement
5 Specificity – diffuseness.

In *Economy and Society*, Parsons and Smelser (1956) further developed the concepts of the basic functional problems or imperatives of all action systems which must be met if the system is to have equilibrium and/or a continuing existence. The four functional imperatives are shown in figure 9 (Parsons and Smelser, 1956, p. 19).

A Adaptation	G Goal gratification
L Latent pattern maintenance and tension management	I Integration

Figure 9   The functional imperatives of action systems

They saw the economy as a subsystem of society which served the adaptive function of the whole system. As such, it was one of four such subsystems, the others being the polity, which served to regulate goal gratification; the cultural motivational subsystem, which served the function of pattern maintenance and tension management; and the integrative subsystem, which served to hold the society together. Each of these subsystems has boundary interchanges with the other three, thus giving six sets of internal mutual exchange relations.

In later writings (see, for example, 1960, 1963, 1970b, 1975) Parsons developed a general paradigm of how all the subsystems of society were

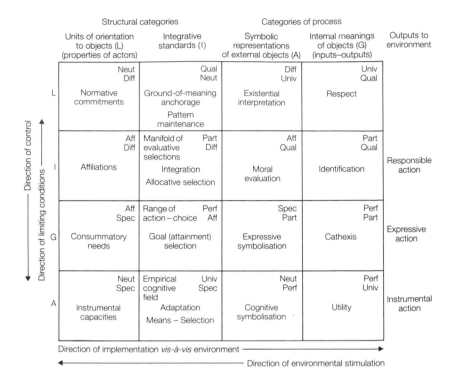

Figure 10   The Parsonian action system in relation to its environment

supposedly organised into a stable cybernetic hierarchy with processes of equilibration and exchange mediating them. Employing the five pattern variables and four subsystems he presented the 16 possible combinations as in figure 10 (Parsons, 1960, p. 208). In this diagram the cells are arranged firstly in vertical columns as a cybernetic hierarchy of control in the integrative order L I G A. That is, each cell categorises the necessary but not sufficient conditions for operation of the next one above it and, conversely, the categories of each cell control the processes categorised in the one below. Secondly, the arrangement horizontally is L I A G. The order here shows the adaptive relationship of structural elements, through processes, to the environment.

Another way of presenting the hierarchy of control between all systems of action is as in figure 11 (Parsons, 1977, p. 10). This shows more clearly that Parsons was in a sense a 'cultural determinist', but the sense is a weak one.

The Parsonian paradigm as thus articulated, especially its 1951

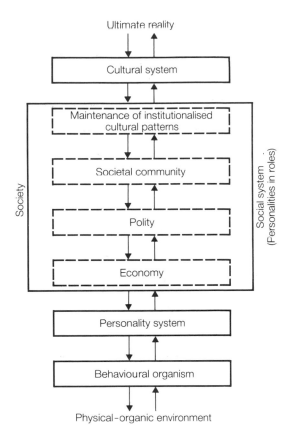

Figure 11   The Parsonian cybernetic hierarchy

version, became the most important influence on the development of functionalist social change theory in the 1950s. This was despite the paradigm's ahistorical nature because the social change theorists employed it as a theory of structure only, trying to marry it with a theory of evolution drawn from other sources.

THE BEGINNINGS OF THE FUNCTIONALIST MODERNISATION SCHOOL

The Modernisation School (and a well-integrated school it was) originated, in effect, at a conference in Chicago in 1951 and was institutionalised by the foundation in the following year of the journal *Economic*

Development and Cultural Change.[8] One of their main intellectual impetuses was a disenchantment with the power of strictly economic theories to explain economic development. Accordingly, drawing upon existing sociological and anthropological approaches, they began to construct a new approach. 'It was found', wrote Bert Hoselitz in the preface of the book that resulted from that conference,

> that the study of economic development not only extends into the field of history but also embraces areas of anthropology, sociology, and politics. Since the social institutions of populations in the process of development are closely related to those customarily designated as 'primitive', a relevant aspect of the study of economic advancement consists in the determination of those culture traits which are hospitable and those which are inhospitable to innovation in the economic and technological fields. This observation comes close to an admission that, in the study of economic and technological development, the ultimate determinants of growth processes cannot fully be understood without crossing the line which separates economics from social anthropology. (Hoselitz, 1952c, p. vi)

However, while these influences were important in providing intellectual tools, the real impetus came from an essentially ideological concern with the uneven state of world modernisation/industrialisation. The American desire to intervene in Third World development, partly for altruistic motives, partly to thwart communism, and partly to maintain a market for American goods and a supply of materials, meant a great need for a theory of social change of a (non-Marxist) technicist kind which could not only offer itself for policy implementation but, in effect, justify intervention to make underdeveloped countries become more like capitalist America.[9]

In the early 1950s the founders of the School (notably Hoselitz, Marion Levy, Wilbert Moore, Everett E. Hagen, and Joseph Spengler; see bibliography for writings) were concerned mainly with laying conceptual, methodological, and theoretical foundations. In doing this they consciously drew upon existing intellectual resources. From Max Weber they took, firstly, a concern with the concepts of 'tradition' and 'rationality', especially as expressed in *Economy and Society* (the first part of which had recently been translated by Parsons and Henderson) and in his work on the sociology of religion; and, secondly, the methodology of ideal types. Traditional and modern societies were conceived as ideal

---

[8] On the origins of the school, see Chirot (1981).
[9] Jacob Viner (1952) was quite open about these ideological and political purposes of the new theory.

types, the problem being to theorise their structures and cultures and the process that leads from one to the other. In theorising structure and culture, they drew upon Weber's concept of rationality and the concepts of structural-functional sociology, as articulated primarily by Parsons, Shils, and Levy in the late 1940s and early 1950s. But because at that time the Parsonian paradigm lacked a theory of change, some of their critics were later to accuse them of failing to develop one.

From the beginning they were also consciously in the older evolutionary/developmental stream and drew upon earlier thinkers such as the German historical economists, Durkheim, and Sorokin. Later they were also to incorporate the neo-evolutionary ideas of Parsons. Of more direct importance in theorising the actual process of change were the ideas of Schumpeter on entrepreneurship, Weber on rationality, Parsons on deviance, Rostow on investment, and behaviourist psychology. These were married together into a putative general theory. Thus the only original aspect about the framework that the early modernisation theorists constructed was its relatively systematic nature. All its components came from elsehwere.[10]

The key ideal-type concepts of the Modernisation School were 'tradition' and 'modernity'. The elaboration of these concepts was seen by Levy, Hoselitz, and Spengler as the first task, since without a notion of the stages before and after the development process there could not be a theory of the process. They needed, therefore, a set of universal concepts with which to categorise the stages if they were to be compared. This meant having a small number of conceptual elements which could be rearranged to characterise different stages. It was natural, given their intellectual milieu, that they should turn to Parsons's scheme of pattern variables. Using these variables, said Hoselitz,

> we obtain a result in which the relationship between what, on the surface, appears as purely economic action to general behavioral typologies is exhibited. The contrast between economically advanced and underdeveloped societies is reduced to its basic sociological foundation if the purely economic magnitudes are stated in terms of these pattern variables. These variables, in other words, come to be regarded as the determinants, on the most generalised level of socially relevant behavior, of average real output of a society. (Hoselitz, 1953c, pp. 29–30)

The five pattern variables, or dilemmas, of choice for action (achievement versus ascription, universal versus particular values, specific versus diffuse scope of interest in an object, gratification versus discipline, and

---

[10] For general discussions of the foundations of modernisation, see Eisenstadt (1974), Tipps (1973), A. Smith (1973), Chirot (1981).

self-orientation versus collective orientation) were employed by Hoselitz, Levy, Spengler, and others to define underdeveloped, traditional, and backward societies as being ones in which action was unachieving (i.e. ascriptive), particularist in its distribution of economic tasks, diffuse in performance of economically relevant tasks (i.e. little division of labour or precision in tasks), and self-oriented. Only the fourth pattern variable was not thought to be relevant (see Hoselitz, 1953c; Levy, 1953; Spengler, 1955, 1961). (This is strange because postponement of gratification is surely one of the characteristics of modern market rationality.) Modern societies were characterised by each of the other four alternatives. Another way of stating the differences between advanced and underdeveloped was put by Hoselitz thus:

> We would expect the former to exhibit predominantly universal-istic norms in determining the selection process for the attainment of economically relevant roles; that the roles themselves are functionally highly specific; that the predominant norms by which the selection process for those roles is regulated are based on the principle of achievement, or 'performance', and that the holders of positions in the power elite, and even in other elites are expected to maintain collectivity oriented relations to social objects of economic significance. In an underdeveloped society, on the contrary, particularism, functional diffusion, and the principle of ascription predominate as regulators of social-structural relations especially in its economic dimension, and the orientation of actors in economically or politically influential roles is determined predominantly by considerations of their ego. (Hoselitz, 1953c, pp. 41–2)

What, then, are the *mechanisms of the process* of passing from one type to the other, i.e. of the process of modernisation and socio-economic development? It is important, in dealing with this question, not to confuse a description of the economic process with an analysis of its human and social causes. Some of the modernisation theorists were aware of this distinction but most macro economic development theorists were not and are not even now, notably Rostow (1971). Sociological approaches to economic development, including those of the Marxists and functionalists, were articulated in the first place because of dissatisfaction with economistic descriptions and analyses of the process, which tend to see both the process and its causes simply in terms of a growth in factor inputs and productivity without asking about the processes of human thought and action that make these possible, or the nature of the social, ideological, and cultural context and how it changes.

All the most important sociological theorists of the economy – Marx, Weber, Sombart, Schumpeter, and Parsons – influenced the modernisation theory of change, although Marx's influence was negative in that they consciously rejected much of what he said because of what they mistakenly thought was economic reductionism (see Hoselitz, 1955b, pp. 57–8). From Weber and Parsons came the theory of social control and deviance and from Weber, Sombart, and Schumpeter came the theory of entrepreneurship. It was a simple matter then of combining them to give the idea of entrepreneurs as deviant, marginal, but creatively innovative individuals or groups. The capitalist entrepreneur of early modern Europe was regarded as the prototypical deviant. He was 'an innovator, a finder and supplier of new combinations' in a situation where innovation was disapproved (Hoselitz, 1955b, p. 62). But entrepreneurship of this sort can arise only under certain social and cultural conditions and not all deviant behaviour or marginalised individuals are entrepreneurial. The mechanisms of entrepreneurship need to be understood in turn. Hoselitz pointed out that the theory of social deviance and the pattern variables have to be supplemented by variables to do with the availability of natural resources (i.e. the man–land ratio) and the constraints exercised by government if we are to have a viable theory of change (Hoselitz, 1955b, p. 68). Later writers such as Hagen and McClelland (see chapter 11) turned to child psychology for a theory of the origins of the entrepreneurial personality.

THE NEO-EVOLUTIONARY/MODERNISATION PARADIGM

The early modernisation theorists were evolutionary in only a general sense in that they subscribed to the notions of stages and developmental progress and to the early Parsonian 'organic' concepts of system, functions, equilibrium, and deviance. Their notion of evolution was not particularly Darwinian or cybernetic, in the neo-evolutionary sense outlined earlier in this chapter. This was mainly because at that time the functionalist paradigm lacked a theory of change and they had to draw upon other sources for it, as we have just seen. But they were centrally concerned with social change, which Parsons and Smelser had not been hitherto.

However, partly due to the influence of the early modernisation theorists, partly also as a result of criticisms of functionalism as being too ahistorical and static, and partly as a result of the developments in biological evolutionary theory and general systems theory, Parsons and Smelser apparently felt the need in the late 1950s and early 1960s to turn to the question of social change. It seems they had an increased confidence in the power of their paradigm to explain long-run historical aspects of society rather than just the structural ones. In then developing a neo-evolutionary approach to social change they in a sense completed the functionalist paradigm (cf. A. Smith, 1973, ch. I).

For Parsons and Smelser the question of social change was predicated upon their conception of society as an open, stable, equilibrating, organic-like system of action consisting of integrated patterns of roles. It has an environment made up of other action systems (personalities, cultures, and other societies), human biological nature, and the external natural situation. All social systems are supposedly cybernetically ordered in a hierarchy in which culture is dominant and society has subsystems which serve the functional needs of adaptation and integration. Endogenous variation is kept within limits by integrative mechanisms, and adaptive mechanisms control fluctuations in relations with the environment. Stable equilibrium is not inert but a dynamic state which oscillates around a strong structural continuity. Given this conception it is a major problem to account for structural change and development and, as it turned out, Parsons in particular was ultimately unwilling, or unable, to present a general theory of evolutionary mechanisms. The closest he came to one was to talk vaguely about cultural 'mutations' and 'cultural determinism' but he ultimately stepped back from a clear-cut position. (On the other hand, Smelser was both more precise and more empirical, as we shall see in a moment.) This leads of course to the question of the potential explanatory power of his argument relative to the more specific theories of historical materialism, say, or other versions of culturalist causal explanations, such as those of Harré, Geertz, and Berger (see chapter 13) or Thompson and Williams (see chapter 14). As a causal explanation it is clearly inferior to these.

Parsons believed that the sources of evolutionary change could be both endogenous and exogenous innovations. The latter would include changes originating in personalities, or the biological nature of humans, or culture as well as the physical environment or other organisms and societies (Parsons, 1961, p. 103). And given the organic conception of system any endogenous source of change would have to be analogous to a genetic mutation. The evolutionary significance of any innovation, whatever its source, depends upon its functional power to promote adaptation. That is, Parsons and all evolutionists characterise the process of structural evolution not as 'progress' (a culturally relative notion) but as one of systemic *differentiation* allowing a growth in the ability to control environments. (Societies can also change in the directions of disintegration or simple segmentation.) Differentiation involves the addition of new kinds of units (e.g. collectivities or roles) such that these units will serve the adaptive needs of the system. They will be a 'higher order' of function than the units out of which they differentiated. If differentiation and not some other outcome is to result from systemic change then concomitantly there has to be a process of reorganisation of the system and particularly of its cultural subsystem, which is cybernetically dominant in the total system (Parsons, 1961, p. 108). Thus when any innovation occurs in a society or its environment its survival depends upon whether it promotes in some way the adaptive capacity of the society and hence the society's survival capacity relative to other societies. Parsons put it like this:

> When somewhere in a variegated population of societies there emerges a developmental 'breakthrough', the ensuing process of innovation will, I suggest, always approximate our paradigm of evolutionary change. Such a breakthrough endows its society with a new level of adaptive capacity in some vital respect, thereby changing the terms of its competitive relations with other societies in the system. Broadly, this kind of situation opens four possibilities for the societies not immediately sharing the innovation. The innovation can simply be destroyed by more powerful, even if less advanced, rivals. If the innovation is cultural, though, it is difficult to destroy completely, and may assume great importance even after its society of origin has been destroyed. Second, the terms of competition may be evened through adoption of the innovations. The present drive to 'modernization' among underdeveloped societies is an obvious and important case in point. A third alternative is the establishment of an insulated niche in which the society can continue to maintain its old structure, relatively undisturbed. The final possibility is the loss of societal identity through disintegration or absorption by some larger societal system. These possibilities are type concepts, and many complex combinations and shadings of them may occur. (Parsons, 1966, pp. 23–4)

What are the possible sources of innovation and the mechanisms of social differentiation? Parsons's answer to this is bound up with his idea of evolutionary universals. He believed that all societies at all stages exhibit certain universals which have significance for evolution, viz. religion, communication through language, social organisation through kinship, and technology. These are all closely related in the evolutionary process in the following way. Humans have an ability to create and transmit culture. Cultural innovations are akin to genetic mutations. But they do not implement themselves. Cultures have to articulate with the environment to make effective adaptation possible. This comes about through technology. Cultures are always shared, so mechanisms of communication are necessary – i.e. language. Language is predicated on social organisation, which arises originally out of kinship (Parsons, 1964, pp. 494–5). Therefore, because society is such an integrated totality, innovations can occur in any one of the subsystems, depending upon the stage of development and particular historical circumstances. In primitive societies stratification is an evolutionary universal. In intermediate, hierarchical societies administrative bureaucracy and money and markets are evolutionary universals. Then, democratic associations become universally significant, making for the modernisation of society.

In this very general and abstract way, then, Parsons married neo-evolutionism with functionalism. The two were naturally complementary and in retrospect it can be seen that neo-evolutionism was implicit in the systemic-functionalist theory of structure. However, Parsons was never a historian and the supposed strengths of the paradigm had to be shown by others, most notably Hoselitz and Smelser.[11]

Smelser's (1959) book on the Industrial Revolution analysed the process of development of the cotton industry, the concomitant changes in the structure of the working class family, and the relationship these processes had with working class political protest. It was thus an attempt to provide an explanatory account of a whole social historical process. For Smelser the process of modernisation was historically too various to be encompassed by an empirical generalisation, so only an ideal-typical model could be employed to theorise in a universal way about it. That model was used to analyse three supposedly closely related phases of the process − structural differentiation, integration, and socio-political disturbances. Differentiation is 'the evolution from a multifunctional role structure to several more specialised structures' or, more precisely, is the process whereby

> *one* social role or organisation ... differentiates into *two or more* roles or organisations which function more effectively in the new historical circumstances. The new social units are structurally distinct from each other, but taken together are functionally equivalent to the original unit. (Smelser, 1963, p. 35)

He argued that differentiation manifests itself in economies, family structures, religions, and social stratification systems, and it requires people either to adjust to it or to revolt against it. The adjustment process he called integration. It is necessary because differentiation breaks down the established relationships between production and consumption and within the family. Problems arise to do with such things as information about employment opportunities, with a clash of interests between families and firms, and with the effects of market fluctuations on families. In pre-modern society the kinship, community, and patriarchal structures provided integration. Modernisation 'creates', in Smelser's view, new institutions and organisations for providing integration such as labour exchanges, unions, government regulation of labour allocation, welfare and relief agencies, cooperatives, and saving institutions.

Differentiation thus disrupts the social order, creating new activities norms, and sanctions. It is uneven and promotes anomie. Responses to these disruptions, according to Smelser, are anxiety, hostility, and

---

[11] For sympathetic but critical discussions and applications of evolutionism, see also the work of Eisenstadt (especially 1964, 1966, 1973, 1974).

fantasy. These can in turn often crystallise into social movements of various sorts.

Smelser's account (1967b) of the origins of structural differentiation and social conflict during the Industrial Revolution is clearly not a descriptive model of the historical process but an ideal-typical construction for interpreting actual processes. Moreover, it is not really a causal theory, although some causation is implied when he says that one of the assumptions behind it is that people are psychologically disturbed by inadequate performance in roles. Nowhere was there a discussion by him of the structural causes of the process or how they relate to the motivations of individuals in entering into new structures of roles. That is, questions about why new kinds of economic activity arise in the first place or why people are attracted to them, thus loosening their kinship ties, or why they are attracted to new religions or ideologies, or why new status systems are developed and become accepted, were not analysed. The theory is one simply of stages in a process with a beginning and an end. Differentiation is both the process and (apparently) its own cause. This is an (incoherent) version of structural causality.

Smelser's approach, then, like all others in the neo-evolutionary/ modernisation tradition, contains an equilibrium model of society. By this he meant the general principle that a society is a system constituted by definite and identifiable relations which persist in a definite structure over time and which change by certain processes of adjustment towards new equilibrium structures (1968b, p. 211). The sorts of structural dependent variables that he believed social change theorists typically wish to explain by finding independent variables that disturb equilibrium, include aggregated attributes of the population of a social unit, changes in rates of behaviour in a population, changes in social structure, and changes in cultural patterns. The independent variables (or causal determining factors) he saw as falling into four classes (1968b, pp. 269–80). The first is the social structural setting of change, which provides opportunities and obstacles for change. The second is the impetus for change, which involves some kind of 'pressure' (also called strain, tension, imbalance, or disequilibrium) pushing towards change. When briefly discussing the origins of these pressures Smelser came the closest he ever did to developing a genuine causal theory (as opposed to an incoherent structuralist causal theory). He mentioned such forces as the overloading of transport systems as an unintended consequence of mass uniformly patterned behaviour bringing about a change in that system; or external events such as war or natural catastrophes; or the uneven development of a social system causing demands for changes in particular sectors to compensate as, for example, when universal suffrage creates a demand for universal education to create a responsible electorate. Thirdly, the effects of a conducive social setting and pressures for change have to be mobilised in certain ways to bring about change. And fourthly, the strength of social controls influences the mobilisation and the outcome.

Finally we come to the question of the relationship that Smelser saw between his theory (or model) and the actual historical process. He drew a rather sharp distinction between them, as one would expect of a positivist. But he pointed out that all historical explanation requires a model to formalise the selection of data and went some way towards conceding that the data are theory laden (Smelser, 1967b, p. 25). However, he stopped short of this, preferring to see the historical data as relatively objective and providing an independent test of the model. He was rightly critical of those social historians who think they can do without explicit models. It is important to endorse his argument, which consisted of the following. Firstly, atheoretical social historians usually offer inadequate explanations because they miss important causal connections which only a model can help uncover. Secondly, a formal model imposes discipline upon explanation, preventing *ad hoc* interpretations. Thirdly, a model makes systematic comparison possible; and fourthly, a general model makes it possible to incorporte various types of common-sense social knowledge about, say, structural differentiation, institutional change, personality change, and so on, into a larger framework (Smelser, 1967b, pp. 34–7). The crucial question then concerns the nature of the actual model employed. Too narrow a model, or too rigid an application of it, runs the risk of theoreticism, the counterpart of empiricism – i.e. a theoretical overdetermination of the historical evidence. This was a failing of Smelser's model.

CRITICAL SUMMARY

I shall now try to give a critical and very brief summary of the essential points of the systemic-functionalist neo-evolutionary approach to social change as it existed in the mid 1960s.[12] To construct this summary is not to imply that all theorists in the tradition adopted all or any particular one of these points.

Firstly, it has an incomplete scientific method borrowed from positivist epistemology. The hallmarks of its particular version of this are the claim of objectivity and scientific unity, a theory/observation distinction, nomological deductivism, instrumentalism, and a phenomenalist conception of social relations. A sociological positivist typically sees his task as the construction of 'models' which are then tested against the available independent evidence. The models are developed, in the view of Parsons

[12] For extended critical examinations of neo-evolutionism, see Bendix (1977, ch. 8), Eisenstadt (1964, 1974), Feinman (1980), Gellner (1964), W. Moore (1970), Shiner (1975), A. Smith (1973), Tipps (1973), Utz (1973).

and Smelser for instance, by making deductions from hypotheses or more general theories about the processes being studied. These models are considered to be convenient instrumental fictions – ideal types – about structural processes and not causal theories about the real structural mechanisms of observable phenomena, or empirical generalisations.

Secondly, human action is explained by a behaviourist-dispositional theory which relies upon observations of environmentally presented choices and an *a priori* model of humans as rational decision-makers, choosing between the dichotomous variables presented by the social situation. But human action is voluntaristic only in a manner analogous to the way 'volunteering' occurs in the army – i.e. 'volunteers are required for a mission: you, you, and you are volunteers'. People are not seen as agential actors. Rather, structural processes always occur as if autonomous – presenting actors with very limited opportunities to choose but rarely if ever the possibility individually or collectively consciously to alter the structural situation. In fact society does not appear to depend on their action for its reproduction either. It just *is* and persists as a reified abstraction. Furthermore, the pattern-variable choices that Parsons believes society presents seem to have little relationship to the sorts of actual choices that real actors have to make in real situations.

Thirdly, the theory of structure is also related to positivism in that it has a concept of structure as a set of observable roles and patterns of behaviour. However, the addition of the concept of 'organic' system linking these structural units into a holistic entity, which has a strong equilibrium stability due to the role of cultural *meanings* and *norms*, takes the theory beyond positivism and into a form of idealism. The autonomous and *determining* role given to these elements, which are essentially unobservable and introduced in an *a priori* fashion, indicates the half-baked nature of Parsonian positivism. It is possible to develop a non-positivist and non-idealist culturalist account of structure and change, providing that a dialectical, rather than hierarchical, relationship between culture, politics, and the economy is argued for and there is a theory of the interrelationship between consciousness and action (see chapters 13 and 14).

Fourthly, this theory of structure determines the concept of the process of structural change because the notion of stable equilibrium forced on its adherents the idea of stages of natural equilibrium states punctuated by phases of unnatural, unstable disequilibrium; the whole process being one of a series of progressive stages of differentiated complexity.

Fifthly, the tradition lacked a well-developed concept of structural mechanisms of change apart from vague intimations about either cultural mutations or change originating anywhere in the system and then ramifying through it. (This lack was not in fact a result of their systemic-functionalist theory of structure. It is possible to develop coherent (but false) theories within a neo-evolutionary approach to society, as the sociobiologists have done.) In so far as they had a causal theory it was an incoherent structuralist one; i.e. the process of structural change is somehow its own cause, but it is never clearly specified how that could be so except by the metaphysical notion that the process must take the form of differentiation. Then the process is one of disequilibrium, caused by a 'mutation', necessarily leading to a new equilibrium stage, which in turn becomes destabilised, etc. This process is predicated by the reified idea of structure.

Finally, we come to the question of objectivity and scientific unity. As supposed positivists, Parsons, Smelser, Davis, Hoselitz, and others saw their approach as constituting a scientific sociology which not only transcended other approaches but incorporated them. This required them to reconstruct those other approaches in their own terminology. A good example was Smelser's (1968b, p. 265) claim that Marxism was yet another equilibrium-evolutionary theory as were also supposedly the theories of Spengler, Spencer, Durkheim, and Malinowski. In other words, there is no alternative to their own approach because it is the only legitimate and coherent one. Thus Davis (1959) argued that functionalism and science are the same thing.

BEYOND SYSTEMIC EVOLUTIONISM

With the breakdown of the paradigmatic status of the functionalist neo-evolutionary approach to structural change in the late 1960s three main lines of theoretical development were possible within the broad positivist and evolutionary tradition. These were:

1 Rejection of the systemic-functionalist theory of structure in favour of some form of individualist theory while retaining some theory of evolutionary mechanisms.
2 Retention of some form of systemic functionalism but marrying it with some other theory of change, such as a 'dialectical' theory of conflict.
3 Rejection of both systemic functionalism and evolutionism while retaining a general positivist approach to objective knowledge of social change. This implies the retention of some form of individualism.

All of these possibilities in fact retained a commitment to positivism. This set them apart from some similar theorists (such as Habermas and Luhmann) who converged on theories of systemics and evolutionism in the late 1970s and early 1980s from non-positivist perspectives, particularly hermeneutics and Marxism, and from some other theorists who shared many of the internally produced criticisms but went further in rejecting evolutionism altogether from standpoints in other traditions.

11

Individualism

INDIVIDUALIST PHILOSOPHIES

The defence of an individualist basis for social and historical explanation has come from several widely differing sources in philosophy and social theory. There is, firstly, the influence of empiricism which has been taken to indicate that only observable individuals can be studied, all so-called structures being metaphysical. Secondly, there is the intentionalist tradition in analytical philosophy, springing mainly from Wittgenstein and to some extent from Collingwood, which teaches that all action is intentional and is to be explained by reference to subjective meanings and actors' understandings. The third influence, phenomenology and hermeneutics, also tries to explain action by reference to subjective meanings and actors' understandings. Fourthly, behaviourism tries to explain action by reference either (in its strict form) to external stimuli or (in its dispositional form) to internal dispositions.

Because all of these are essentially individualist philosophies they have on the whole not given rise to well-articulated approaches to the explanation of social structural change. But they have been very influential in the human and social studies that deal with action and collective behaviour. In chapter 4 I discussed positivist and intentionalist methodologies for history and showed that they have been flawed by their failure to develop a theory of the role of structures. In chapter 6 I argued that a hermeneutics that concentrates on subjective meanings and understandings cannot give an adequate account of the social structural origins of those meanings and understandings or of the history of structures themselves. In chapter 8 I argued that individualism as a methodology is flawed because it is ontologically reductionist and fails to take account of social power. In chapter 13 I shall discuss the influence of phenomenology on approaches to social change.

217

That leaves this chapter to concentrate on the positivist-individualist behaviourist tradition in economics and sociology which has sometimes tried (half-heartedly perhaps) to develop a theory of structure and structural change. The roots of this tradition go back to nineteenth-century utilitarian positivism (not to be confused with Comtean or Spencerian organic positivism) as exemplified by the historian H. T. Buckle and the classical economists Thomas Malthus and J. S. Mill.[1] The latter was especially important for establishing the canons of so-called inductive scientific method.

MAIN COMPONENTS OF THE POSITIVIST INDIVIDUALIST TRADITION

This tradition is institutionally located primarily in neo-classical economics and economic history and in economistic sociology. It contains the following elements, which conceptually reinforce each other in the way shown:[2]

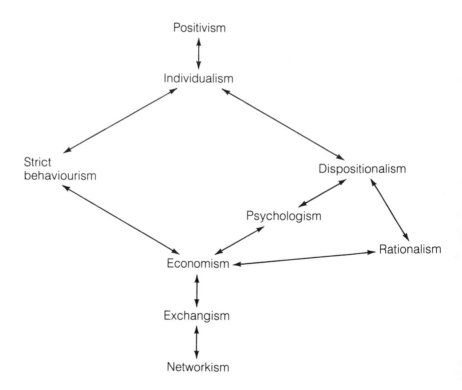

[1] There is a helpful discussion of Buckle and other positivists in Semmel (1976).

[2] For discussions of the tradition, seen from the various viewpoints that these concepts indicate, see Barry (1970), Becker (1976b, 1979), Berkhofer (1969), Bredemeier (1979), Coleman (1976), Ekeh (1974), Heath (1976), Kunkel (1970, 1977), Mitchell (1978).

The first component is a self-conscious *positivism*. Following fairly closely the teachings of the logical positivists, by 'positivist social science' they seem to mean that the task is to establish the general causal laws of individual and collective behaviour. The method for this is to be hypothetico-deductive and 'experimental' testing, employing abstract instrumental models of firms and economies. The test of a theory is successful prediction. Prediction and explanation are synonymous. No value judgements are to be employed in constructing empirical theories or in observing and organising data.[3]

Most importantly, the tradition is *individualist* in its methodology, attempting to explain action and collective behaviour by reference to the wants, desires, preferences, dispositions, drives, and so on of individual actors. Individualists are also usually (but not necessarily) *ontological reductionists*. Many individualist social theorists would like to construct a theory of society which employed concepts not of structure but only of individual motivation and behaviour. But they have been unable to achieve that and in fact cannot do without structural concepts in one way or another, as some of them have recognised. There is a major source of tension, then, between the inherent logic of the approach – towards reductionism – and the obvious (to some) necessity of retaining irreducibly social concepts. (See the discussion of methodological individualism in chapter 8.)

Whereas Parsonian systemic functionalism sees humans as a combination of rational actor, cultural norm follower and social role filler (i.e. 'oversocialised' in Wrong's 1961 term), the individualist tradition sees them in simplified Hobbesian and behaviourist, psychological, or rational terms (see Coleman, 1971a, p. 273). The aim of the individualists, in Homans's words, was to 'bring men back in' (Homans, 1964a). There are in fact four main ways that individualists have conceived of the actor and his motivations and different emphases are placed on each by different currents in the tradition: that is, strict behaviourism, loose behaviourism (or dispositionalism), psychologism, and rationalism.

Strict *behaviourism* is a theory of the causes of action and a closely related methodology for studying them. Behaviourism was developed by J. B. Watson and Ivan Pavlov, working separately in the early decades of this century, and further developed by B. F. Skinner (see 1953), as a deliberate attempt to create a scientific psychology on positivist principles and opposed to introspection and dualism. Their fundamental principle was that in explaining human behaviour it is permissible to postulate in the causal process only observable behaviour, environmental stimuli, and brain states. For them the human is a physiological organism interacting with a physical environment, and no supposed mental variable intervenes.

---

[3] The positivist foundations of individualist economics and sociology are analysed in Friedman (1953), Hollis and Nell (1975), von Mises (1960).

Dispositional behaviourism, which is an alternative form of behaviourism to Skinner's radical stimulus–response (S→R) model, has been developed by those, such as Edward Tolman, who have placed much greater weight upon the concept of intervening variables, which broadly refer to *internal* states of behaving organisms. (Thus it is an S→O→R theory.) These are sometimes referred to as 'black-box' explanations because the internal state of the organism is unavailable to our inspection and so we can have no direct knowledge of it. But, although we lack precise knowledge of 'mental' states, they can be modelled as consisting of certain relatively fixed dispositions or traits which, when combined with knowledge of situational stimuli and employing the received view of scientific theories à la Carnap or Feigl (see chapter 2), are used to try to explain behaviour by linking *observables* at each end of the postulated causal sequence.[4]

One of the immediately obvious questions about this concerns the ontological status of the social and cultural influences on action.[5] Behaviourists have a strong tendency to see the social situation as consisting of groups constituted by individuals and having no emergent powers of their own. The relationship between groups and structures is not dealt with in a systematic way because of their desire to avoid what they mistakenly take to be the fallacy of composition.[6] Social structures, in so far as they do appear in the theory, are often seen as epiphenomenal – at the end of causal chains that begin with the internal states or rational actions of individuals – and not playing a significant causal feedback role. For individualists society is not an emergent structure.

There have been two main theories of the internal mental states of actors and thus for explaining action: psychologism and rationalism. These differ according to whether personality dispositions are learned or innate and thus differ as to the fixed and universal nature of persons, and the hidden versus actualised traits of personality.

Psychologism stresses the developmental learning of personality through childhood influences and that these psychological influences are not necessarily rational but are much more complex and difficult to uncover. Depth psychological theories such as those of Freud and Piaget have been influential on their thinking. Once developed, personality is

---

[4] On dispositional psychology, see Alston (1974, 1976), M. Rosenberg (1979), Tolman (1951).

[5] Behavioural situational analysis is extensively discussed by Berkhofer (1969). See his diagram on p. 34.

[6] See Barry and Hardin (1982, p. 40). There is a discussion of the fallacy of composition in Mackie (1967, p. 173). The fallacy is the imputation to groups and collectivities of properties which are simply the aggregate of those of their individual members. For example, if people are seen as rational utilitarians, then nations or institutions are said to be such. This fallacy must not be confused, as Barry and Hardin do, with the idea of *emergence*. See the discussion of emergence in chapters 7 and 8.

taken to be the chief cause of behaviour. (See next section.)

Rationalism stresses the innate and supposedly universal disposition to behave rationally in the actor's self-interest. But how the rationality disposition causes specific behaviour is in turn a consequence of specific environmental conditions, so that in this model behaviour is actually more flexible and purposive than in the psychological model because the actor can learn new strategies and make genuine choices. Psychologism is more deterministic because action is more the result of powerful, pre-rational, subconscious motives.

The micro *economistic* approach to social explanation, which now enjoys widespread popularity, employs the innate conception of personality dispositions – particularly economic rationality – to explain behaviour. A dispositional theory employs the idea of preferences as *revealed* through action to explain the inner state of the organism. That inner state is assumed (as a first principle) to be in general one of rationality and egoistic self-interestedness. What an actor decides are his true interests and what is the best strategy to achieve them are to be known by social scientists through the actor's behaviour, which in the pure theory is always taken to be directed towards satisfying his wants and so maximising his utility. The theory is thus one about actors' conscious decisions about choices as revealed through actions. The rationality postulate serves to link actions to decisions and so helps explain actions. The egoistic utility principle helps explain decisions. The question of the freedom of choice (and agency in general) then arises. If humans are completely rational and egoistic utilitarians then their actions in a given situation could be construed as *determined* by these internal dispositions. However, some form of rationality principle may indeed be indispensable to the psychological and social studies, as I showed in chapter 9.[7] But such a postulate does not have to be based on the behaviourist and empiricist idea that intentions and decisions can only be known by observing their supposedly resultant consequences. As Albert Hirschman has cogently pointed out,

> the intended but unrealised effects of social decisions stand in need of being discovered even more than those effects that were un-intended but turn out to be all too real: the latter are at least *there*, whereas the intended but unrealised effects are only to be found in the expressed expectations of social actors at a certain, often fleeting, moment of time. (Hirschman, 1977, p. 131)

---

[7] For discussions of the 'rational economic man' postulate, see Elster (1979a, 1979b, 1982c), Harsanyi (1977a, 1977b), Hollis and Nell (1975), Latsis (1972, 1983), Pettit (1978), Sen (1976), Simon (1976, 1983), Watkins (1970), and the articles in Barry and Hardin (1982), Benn and Mortimore (1976).

The rational man model is thus one of the central pillars of the micro economistic approach to social explanation. This treats behaviour as always oriented towards *rational exchange* within markets. The market coordinates actions so that collective behaviour can theoretically reach a stable equilibrium of gratification in terms of costs and benefits. This is not to say that the market is formal or that exchange is only of goods. There are many media of exchange and many types of 'goods' traded, including emotional gratification. Exchange theory has influenced much recent sociological theorising. What economistic theory lends to exchange theory are the concept of social structure as analogous to a market and the assumptions of stable preferences and rationality of behaviour towards maximising utility from exchange. This is a micro theory of society and social action, examples being the work of George Homans, Gary Becker, and James Coleman.[8]

There is also a psychological-economic approach to social explanation which, while employing the model of society as a market, emphasises the pre-rational psychological motivations of actors which lead them to act in ways not predictable simply by postulating rational utilitarian motivation. Classical and Marxian economics employed these ideas to some extent.

Finally, the exchange theory is also related to a concept of society as a *network* of 'trading' relations, along which flow the 'goods' and media of exchange. This approach has given rise to an alternative macro theory of structure and action, such as in the work of Peter Blau and John Kunkel.[9]

THE PSYCHODYNAMICS OF MODERNISATION

Many of the early modernisation theorists recognised that attention to the psychological motivation of action is an important aspect of explaining the 'deviant' entrepreneurial behaviour that they believed in turn helped explain social change. There was soon developed a sub-branch of the modernisation school which sought to explain economic development by reference primarily to the psychology of innovators. These writers were dissatisfied with the orthodox approach to economic change which stressed rationality and factor inputs and ignored psychological and sociological constraints.

The main influences on these psychological modernisation theorists were the pattern variables of Parsons; the theories of personality of

[8] See Homas (1958, 1961, 1964b, 1967a, 1976), G. Becker (1974, 1976a, 1976b, 1979), Coleman (1966, 1971a, 1971b, 1972a, 1972b, 1974, 1976, 1979b, 1979c). On rational exchange theory, see also P. Birnbaum (1976), Blau (1964, 1968, 1970, 1971), Bredemeier (1979), T. Clark (1972), Ekeh (1974), Gergen (1977), Heath (1976), Lively (1976).

[9] Network theory is discussed in a general way by Blau (1982), Boissevain (1974), Kunkel (1970, 1977), Wellman (1983).

developmental psychologists such as Gordon Murray, Piaget, and Freud; the Schumpeterian theory of entrepreneurship; and Weber's work on the relationship between religion and entrepreneurship. But by concentrating on the social psychology of motivation and the behaviour of important individuals for affecting social change, these psychodynamic theorists, in effect, rejected the systemic-functionalist paradigm in favour of the individualist one.[10]

Two of the most prominent psychodynamic theorists are David C. McClelland and Everett E. Hagen. Both have stressed the necessity of investigating the unobservable personality traits of innovative entrepreneurs rather than the rationality of their behaviour. And both also strongly stressed the familial rather than the inherited influences on personality development.

McClelland studied in impressive detail (see 1961a) the influence of a psychological trait that he called 'need for Achievement' (nAch) as a prime determinant of entrepreneurial behaviour and hence of economic development, and, in turn the possible cultural origins of this trait in modernised and modernising peoples. His key hypothesis linked these three aspects: i.e. that there is a link between certain sorts of cultures, a high need for achievement, and economic development. More specifically, the so-called Protestant ethic was a good candidate for the right cultural background when linked with the idea that certain Protestant child-rearing practices were strongly correlated with high nAch in boys (McClelland, 1961a, p. 47). Indeed, McClelland argued that there was some correlation (in 1950 at least) between Protestant countries and their level of economic development compared with Catholic countries (1961a, p. 100; 1961b, p. 112). But even if this is so, the key questions concern the *causal* relationships between (1) Protestantism and nAch, and (2) nAch and economic development. Clearly, as McClelland recognised, things could not be as simple as a straightforward Protestantism → economic development link because capitalist Japan and communist Soviet Union, for example, have both experienced rapid development without Protestantism. This led McClelland to concentrate on the role of child-rearing practices as the key causal mechanism for promoting nAch and on nAch itself, rather than rational profit seeking, as the causal mechanism of entrepreneurial and modernising behaviour. Thus the hypothesised causal relationships were in the following sequence:

$$\text{cultural values} \longrightarrow \text{child-rearing practices} \longrightarrow \text{nAch} \longrightarrow \text{innovating and modernising entrepreneurship} \longrightarrow \text{economic development}$$

[10] On the general theory of the psychodynamics of social change, see Argyle (1967), Gerth and Mills (1954), Inkeles and Smith (1974), Lerner (1963).

If there is a correlation between Protestantism and high nAch, what is it about Protestantism that promotes it? He argued that for boys with high nAch their parents set higher standards of aspiration in tasks and are much warmer towards them, showing positive emotion towards their performances. The mothers are relatively more domineering and the fathers less than for boys with low nAch. In other words, fathers set high standards but do not interfere with their sons' performances, so giving their sons the opportunity to develop initiative and self-reliance (McClelland, 1961b, p. 92).

Why do parents behave like this? He believed the most important reasons to be a religious value structure which emphasises individual (rather than ritual) contact with God, and the extent to which the father is away from home – long absences meaning the father does not interfere with the son's development (1961a, ch. 9; 1961b, p. 92).

A similar but more Freudian argument was presented by Hagen, in his book *On the Theory of Social Change* (1962). His explanation of social change boils down to the influences of two different personality types – authoritarian and creative – and of how they come to develop. The elites of traditional societies, he argued, are typified by the authoritarian personality. This is characterised by low need for achievement, low need for autonomy, high need for dependence, high need for submission/ dominance, and a sense that the world consists of arbitrary and fearful forces. Such a person has a low capacity to analyse problems, a low anxiety threshold, finds comfort in relying on authority, and likes to exercise arbitrary authority (Hagen, 1963, p. 129). Hagen cited evidence that this personality type is prevalent in traditional societies and that it is in turn reinforced by their child-rearing practices which repress any natural adventurousness and problem-solving capacity (Hagen, 1962, ch. 8; 1963, pp. 130–3).

The creative personality, on the other hand, is characterised by high need for achievement, high need for autonomy, high need for order, and a sense of the world as systemic and comprehensible. This personality likes to solve problems, seeks new ideas, has a capacity to be surprised and is open to new experiences. The child-rearing practices that lead to the development of such a personality include the encourgement of exploration, problem solving, and self-reliance (1963, pp. 28–30).

If traditional societies supposedly reinforce authoritarian personalities and vice versa, then Hagen's problem is how a change ever occurs. That is, how do creative, innovative personalities develop and come to have social influence in such a closed situation? Hagen's argument was that in erstwhile traditional but subsequently modernised societies one import- ant cause of change was some major historical event or shift,

> which caused some group or groups of the lesser elite, who
> previously had had a respected and valued place in the social

hierarchy, to feel that they were no longer respected and valued. This derogation in some societies consisted of explicit indication of contempt for the functions or position of the lesser elite, in others of behaviour by a new higher elite which seemed immoral, unmanly, or irreligious to the groups below them, and thus indicated contempt for the moral standards of the lesser elite. (Hagen, 1963, p. 134)

Hagen believed that this withdrawal of status respect could have produced anger and anxiety in those directly affected. Their children find their parents' role model unsatisfactory and retreat into negativism. The process is cumulative across generations, so that after several generations there appears what he called 'normlessness, shiftlessness, anomie, or . . . retreatism'. He claimed that retreatism could be observed among, for example, Negroes of the southern United States, American Indians, first and second generation immigrants, and colonial peoples. Historically, he thought it also characterised the Antiqueños of Columbia, the Samurai of Japan, and the Old Believers of Russia (1963, p. 135). But the result of retreatism, which affects men more than women, is that after several generations women are less retreatist and have stronger personalities than men, which then leads them to raise their sons to be more effective than their husbands. The combination of intense maternal attitudes and weak paternal models supposedly provides an environment for the formation of the anxious, driving, creative personality. Thus there gradually emerges a group of creative, alienated individuals, 'driven by a gnawing burning drive to prove themselves'; turning against the (traditional) values of the group disparaging them, they therefore become innovators (1963, p. 136).

The basic problems with such psychodynamic theories are that they are (1) psychologically reductionist, (2) individualist, (3) monocausal, and (4) unable to account, in their own terms, for many individual cases of entrepreneurial activity. There seems to be no scope in their approach for the *emergence* of personality differences or the role of groups and classes in bringing about innovations. However, their emphasis upon the role of culture and historical experience was important; these were aspects that the rationalists tend to disregard.

RATIONAL EXCHANGE THEORIES OF STRUCTURE AND CHANGE

One of the main alternatives to the psychodynamic approaches stresses the role of a purposive market *rationality* rather than psychological drives for explaining behavioural patterns and change. The nature of market exchange has long been a core problem for classical and neo-classical economists. In recent decades, under the influence of such writers as von Neuman, Arrow, Simon, Becker, Downs, Harsanyi, Sen, and Olson, the purposive utilitarian aspects of the decisions and behaviour of economic individuals, more than their structural situations (i.e. the micro more than the macro), has been the area of focus for the rational exchange approach. In particular, the problems of the rationality of collective decisions and the resulting patterns of (often unintended) macro phenomena have been analysed using game theory. This in turn has had a strong influence on some sociological theorists. It is the latter writers who are of interest here because it is they who have tried to develop a theory of social structure and change. But as we shall see their interest in structural change is underdeveloped and largely peripheral to their concern with behaviour.

At the centre of the social exchange paradigm lies the work of George C. Homans. His theory of social structure, in accordance with his methodological individualism, is nominalist and instrumentalist in that he believes society to be institutonalised (i.e. persistent) patterns of behaviour rather than something with real properties and powers (Homans, 1976). But as yet, for him, complete explanatory reduction of these patterns to psychology is not possible so structural concepts are still explanatorily necessary, although explanation should be as far as possible by reference to psychological dispositions and external stimuli in the Skinnerian mode (see Homans, 1964a, 1964b, 1967b, 1970). The paradigm of elementary social behaviour he saw as a simple exchange of values between two people. Each emits behaviour towards the other and incurs a cost in such a way that the exchange is profitable, rewarding, and hence psychologically reinforcing for each other. A practical equilibrium of behavioural exchanges may develop within small groups due to social control, a balance between profits and costs, and some form of distributive justice (Homans, 1958).

In his key book *Social Behaviour: Its Elementary Forms* (1961) he systematically developed a general social theory on these foundations in which society was conceived as consisting of nothing but individual actions, and so social explanation was in principle the same as the explanation of behaviour. In short, human choices continually create social institutions. Behaviour was theorised as a social learning or reinforcement process in which the basic princile is that activities are repeated if rewarded, and so the stimulus that led to a rewarded activity will elicit the same activity next time because it has been reinforced. There is then an exchange between the activity and its reward (Homans, 1967a, pp. 33–9).

Homans's exchangist postulates apply to sub-institutional (i.e. small-group) behaviour which is a realm of face-to-face interaction. But what about macro social phenomena at the institutional level? Here behaviour is more complex and other stimulus/reward relations of exchange come into play, such as money and social approval (Homans, 1961, p. 380).

But in his theory, institutions (i.e. explicit social rules of mass behaviour) are created by primary, small-group exchange and have to be continually maintained by social sanctions and rewards.

His very underdeveloped theory of social change (i.e. of institutional development) is premised on the idea that institutional innovation is an investment which must, sooner or later, pay off for individuals. That is, macro institutions are dependent upon micro choices and needs (1961, p. 389). Elementary social behaviour in small groups always persists beneth the institutional appearances and reasserts itself fully when institutional breakdowns occur. Micro interactions and the macro institutions always exist separately. Sometimes the micro reinforces the macro, sometimes it is in opposition to it, but always only it has socially constituting ower. Individual needs and micro social interactions must be served by institutional developments or those institutions will perish, according to Homans (1961, pp. 390–8). For Homans the psychological imperatives of behaviour are the moving force of history and so he remains a reductionist and individualist.

Homans's work has been very influential on social exchange theorists of recent years such as James S. Coleman and Peter Blau. They have attempted to derive a theory of structure from a theory of individual rational action, although they do differ in their recent writings as to the significance and value of macro sociological explanations. But their theories of structural change, like that of Homans, are impoverished largely because of the explicit or residual individualism in their writings.

Coleman advocated the economistic approach to action (1972a, p. 209), i.e. to conceive of the actor as a free, purposive being: 'unsocialised, entirely self-interested, not constrained by norms of a system, but only rationally calculating to further his own self-interests' (Coleman, 1971a, p. 273). With such individuals existing in a free market (i.e. supposedly without norms) it is then postulated that each person will attempt to exchange the resources over which he has power for others in such a way as to maximise his utility. Society was thus seen as analogous to a game which the individual enters and leaves voluntarily according to his interests. If the rules cause him to act against his interest he will change the rules or leave (Coleman, 1971a, p. 286)!

Coleman sees social groups, organisations, and systems as built up out of individual persons and not having *sui generis* laws (1979c, pp. 75–6). The laws of opertion of his social entities are therefore derived from the actions of persons so that a theory of action will mirror a theory of society. It does this by starting with persons, then shifting to the higher levels of organisation that they constitute (1976, pp. 85–6). Organisations are systems of social exchange, consisting of a definite set of events and persons. 'The system is defined by the actors, the events, the structure of control of actors over events, and the structure of interest of actors in events.' (1976, p. 86) If the system of exchange is seen in turn as an integrated corporate actor its interests are given by the events taking place at the lower level, i.e. among the persons within it. In turn it partly controls those events and its own actions are controlled by the relative power of the persons in it (1976, pp. 86–7). Thus the shift in levels is brought about by conceiving of corporations as 'actors' and of humans as (apparently) a kind of homuncule within them!

The origins, nature and growth of corporate actors have been central concerns of the rational exchange theorists and their work derives partly from Weber's concern with the baleful effects of bureaucracy. In so far as these theorists have an approach to structural change, then, it is in terms of the history of organisations, since society for them, as we have seen with Homans and Coleman, is constituted by both natural and corporate purposive actors. The emergence of corporations in late medieval Europe was traced by Coleman (1974, 1979a, 1982a) to legal disputes involving the rights and powers of churches, towns, and kings to engage in and profit from the new opportunities for trade then developing. Men began to assert their individuality and to gain rights as persons before the king's law to engage in certain activities; and a different kind of intermediate organisation arose – the chartered corporate actor licensed by the king. This new actor became the instrument through which men could collectively exercise their new rights and powers. In turn two political doctrines arose to justify the new structure – the theory of the absolute power of the state and the theory of the natural rights of the individual (1974, pp. 24–9).

Once arise, the corporate actor underwent a history of its own but all the while retaining the essential principle of legal individuality. In recent years it has grown in power relative to natural persons. And no longer are persons its component parts. Those parts are now 'positions' which can be filled by almost any person (1974, pp. 36–7).

Thus Coleman's rational exchange theory of society obliges him to see social change as a result of purposive action by individuals using the resources available to them, including natural, economic, and legal resources (1973, p. 73). But crucially for his theory modern corporations are now also seen as purposive individuals with powers and resources, so the growing powerlessness of natural persons to achieve their goals is accounted for by the opposed interests of corporate actors.

A similar approach has been developed by Peter Blau, especially in his early work (see 1964), but he is now less of an ontological reductionist than Homans and Coleman (see Blau, 1970). He has recently argued (see especially 1974, 1977, 1978) that social structure should be conceived in more *objective* terms – as consisting of groups or classes of people occupying certain interrelated positions which reflect their roles, relations, and social associations. Thus

to speak of social structure is to speak of social differentiation among people, for social structure, as conceptualised, is rooted in the social distinctions people make in their role relations and associations with one another. These social distinctions give rise to differences in roles and positions, which in turn influence subsequent social intercourse. What is meant here by social structures is simply the population distributions among these differentiated positions. (Blau, 1977, p. 3)

A structure of positions is in turn delineated according to certain nominal and graduated parameters, which are the attributes of people that influence their role relations and thereby differentiate their social positions. Nominal parameters divide people into distinct groups, e.g. sex, race, religion, occupation, and so on, and graduated parameters according to rank orderings, such as education, wealth, income, power, prestige, age, intelligence, and so on. These parameters provide the framework for the differentiation of people in terms of heterogeneity and inequality. Heterogeneity is the horizontal differentiation of a popultion among groups in terms of a nominal parameter. Inequality is the vertical differentiation of status in terms of a graduated parameter (Blau, 1977, pp. 6–9).

Social structures conceived in this way contain two basic kinds of process, in Blau's theory: mobility and association. These are essential for social integration because they connect social positions by providing conduits of transmission among them and thus facilitate the exchange of messages of information, approval, advice, respect, disagreement, and so on, and also the transfers of persons from one group or stratum to another. Therefore

extensive social mobility as well as extensive social associations strengthen inter-group relations and equivalent transfers of either kind do so particularly. Mutual exchanges in social associations cement inter-group relations and so does exchange mobility, that is, the exchange of persons in both directions between two groups, whether through marriage, migration, or other kinds of moves. (Blau, 1977, pp. 5–6)

The degrees of differentiation are crucial because, paradoxically, the greater the differentiation the greater the integration and the more rapid, orderly, and less violent the process of social change. This is because multiform (i.e. unconsolidated) differentiation weakens in-group loyalties and strengthens inter-group ties, and these foster tolerance and flexibility in adjusting to new situations. It stimulates interaction and communication among diverse groups and also social mobility. Strong in-group bonds have the opposite effects. Social mobility is important because it is the process through which social structures adjust by redistributing people among their positions, such as happened during the Industrial Revolution and the recent technological revolution. Multiform differentiation also tends to prevent political violence and extremism because individuals belong to many groups and hence have many loyalties (Blau, 1974, pp. 248–9).

But in addition Blau believed it is essential for the avoidance of social cleavages and disruptive strife that social parameters be not consolidated. Consolidation occurs where parameters are substantially correlated and social differences in one respect are markedly related to differences in other respects, e.g. differences in resources, training, skill, prestige, economic and political power being closely related to differences in race, sex, and religion. Consolidation counteracts multiform differentiation and thus impedes integration by making the social structure more rigid and resistant to change. By impeding gradual change, rigidity fosters an explosive revolutionary situation (Blau, 1974, p. 251).

Thus, unlike Homans and Coleman, Blau does have a more developed theory of social change derived from the rational exchange approach to structural explanation. His great merit has been to go beyond the psychological and individualist basis of many others in the tradition and to give more weight to the structural conditions and constraints on action. But his theory does still depend to some extent on the economistic rationality postulate and it seems to have no place for the roles of culture, ideology, and consciousness in social action.

From this discussion I believe it can be seen that all these versions of the rational exchange approach contain variations of the basic conception that institutions and social structure are the *epiphenomenal* products of behavioural patterns and exchange. This is shown most markedly in the work of Homans and Coleman, which have various reductionist concepts of structure. Blau attempted to go beyond this and develop a more emergentist concept of structure. The degree to which he did so is an indicator of the failure of the individualist approach. Therefore, as we would expect, very little of value to social historians emerges from this approach.

RATIONAL-INSTITUTIONALIST THEORIES OF ECONOMIC HISTORY

The third main approach within the individualist tradition also draws upon the neo-classical rational exchange paradigm to explain long-run economic change. But in this case more emphasis is placed on the role and history of organisations, institutions, and groups as *collective* entities, on how they make decisions on choices of action, and the consequences of those decisions and actions for structural change.

One of the main influences on these recent institutionalists has been the older American institutionalist approach to economics, propounded in various forms in the early twentieth century by Thorstein Veblen, John R. Commons, Robert F. Hoxie, John Maurice Clark, Wesley C. Mitchell,

Clarence Ayers, and others. They stressed the importance of institutionalised organisations (such as business cartels and trade unions) rather than just factors of production and entrepreneurs, for economic behaviour and growth (on institutionalism, see B. Seligman, 1971, vol. I). Another influence has been Marxism, which is also a kind of institutionalist theory but certainly not a neo-classical one.

The work of Kenneth Arrow, Harold Simon, and Anthony Downs (see bibliography) on collective decision-making and action has also been very influential on the theories of historical institutional change developed recently by Douglass C. North and Mancur Olson. And Olson's early work on collective action has been an important ingredient in both North's recent theories and Olson's own recent work.

In *The Logic of Collective Action* (1965) Olson argued that even if individuals are seen as acting largely for rational self-interest it does not therefore follow that large groups will also act in their own self-interest. That is,

> even if all the individuals in a large group are rational and self-interested, and would gain if, as a group, they acted to achieve their common interest or objective, they will still not voluntarily act to achieve that common or group interest. The notion that groups of individuals will act to achieve their common or group interests, far from being a logical implication of the assumption that the individuals in a group will rationally further their individual interests, is in fact inconsistent with that assumption. (Olson, 1965, p. 2)

His conclusion is that in so far as individuals support and take part in large groups and collective actions (such as cartels, trade unions, paying taxes, and voting) and they do so in large numbers, it must be that there are incentives to do so other than the rational expectation of material benefits – such as coercion, or perhaps a feeling of moral well-being from participation. The possibility of false consciousness, ideological understandings and motivations, or irrationality, was not considered and the problem of false or imperfect information was downgraded. Perhaps this has something to do with the positivism inherent in neo-classical economics, which prevents such theorists from asking questions about the cultural specificity of definitions and understandings of social reality and actors' ideological self-understandings of their own true interests. For Olson, all action is intentionally rational whether for public or private ends. Therefore, rationalism is able to explain very little about the real motivations of individual actors.

Olson applied his theory of the logic of collective action to problems of explaining long-run economic growth and social change in *The Rise and Decline of Nations* (1982). He said that the theory has the following general significance in this connection:

The growth of coalitions with an incentive to try to capture a larger share of the national income, the increase in regulatory complexity and governmental action that lobbying coalitions encourage, and the increasing bargaining and complexity of understanding that cartels create alter the pattern of incentives and the direction of evolution in a society. The incentive to produce is diminished; the incentive to seek a larger share of what is produced increases. The reward for pleasing those to whom we sell our goods or labor declines, while the reward for evading or exploiting regulations, politics, bureaucracy and for asserting our rights through bargaining or the complex understandings becomes greater.

These changes in the patterns of incentives in turn deflect the direction of a society's evolution. (Olson, 1982, p. 72)

In short, the growth of collective action in the form of distributional coalitions has an effect opposite to that intended by the actors who act in consort, and hence, in Olson's account, such collective actions turn out to be irrational.[11]

As far as growth in the industrialised countries is concerned, Olson argued from this that (1) in those countries where distributional coalitions have been emasculated or abolished by totalitarianism or foreign occupation and a free and stable economic order has also been established, the economy will grow rapidly; and (2) those countries with the longest history of stable democracy will have developed the most growth-repressing organisations and combinations, other things being equal. These two tendencies seem to be contradictory in that it is precisely under conditions of free democracy that restrictive practices by organised interest groups develop. Indeed, Olson saw clearly that this is a theory of internal social contradictions leading to long-run decline because there is 'an inherent conflict between the colossal economic and political advantages of peace and stability and the longer-term losses that come from the accumulating networks of distributional coalitions that can survive only in stable environments' (Olson, 1982, p. 145).

Olson believed that underlying this contradictory process was a form of Lamarckian evolution which results from a struggle for survival. Society supposedly always rewards the fittest, however it defines fitness. Therefore

if a society mainly rewards production or the capacity to satisfy those with whom one engages in free exchange, it stimulates the development of productive traits. It does this particularly through

---

[11] For discussions of Olson's work and related problems of explaining collective action from a rationalist perspective, see Barry (1970), Barry and Hardin (1982), Elster (1984), Mueller (1983), Offe and Wiesenthal (1980).

cultural or Lamarckian evolution, whereby learned or acquired behavior can be passed on to descendants. If the accumulation of distributional coalitions increases the incentive for distributional struggle, augments regulatory complexity, encourages the dominance of politics, stimulates bargaining, and increases the complexity of understandings, this encourages the development of different attitudes and attributes. What we loosely call intelligence, or aptitude for education, will probably be favored as much as or more than before because the articulte and educated have a comparative advantage in regulation, politics, and complex understandings. This, in turn, probably limits the extent to which intellectuals oppose their elaboration. (Olson, 1982, pp. 72–3)

Hence Lamarckian evolutionary mechanisms are allied to rational individual action to produce an irrational collective historical result. Unfortunately, Olson's theory does not well fit the evidence of recent growth performance by industrialised countries (see the articles in Mueller, 1983) and, moreover, without a theory of culture, ideology, class consciousness, and political institutions it is unable to explain the many differences between countries.[12]

---

[12] The main political lesson that Olson's work apparently points to is that societies wanting more economic growth should try to weaken the power of distributional coalitions that restrain innovation and the freedom of the market, i.e. a *laissez-faire* lesson. But this lesson would ignore the contradictory tendencies that he rightly pointed to of democracy allowing such coalitions *inevitably* to develop. In this case the lesson would be one of right-wing repression in order to supposedly permit what would be the nightmare of *laissez-faire* – the Chilean 'solution'. Clearly this is abhorrent. But there is another lesson from Olson's theory which is that a democratic, corporate, *cooperative* society is more successful in providing *encompassing* institutions which can promote *consensus* around the need for innovation, modernisation, full employment, and economic growth with redistribution. Growth then provides more public and private goods because the total economic cake is bigger at the same time as redistribution takes place. This is the Swedish, Austrian, and Norwegian solution and to some extent also the Japanese, and now also being attempted in a limited way in Australia. It seems to be no accident that it is precisely these countries, with the addition of the USA, that are growing most rapidly in the 1980s, thus confounding Olson's theory in regard to some of them. In other words, it may not be distributional coalitions that are the problem, given that they are inevitable, but a lack of encompassing organisations and ideological consensus around the need and benefits of growth with redistribution. (This last point underlines the necessity for a theory of ideology in any institutional analysis.) And in the case of the USA it points to two things: that that society contains in fact many different regional subeconomies, some of which are growing fast and some not, and the fact that indeed there are less distributional coalitions in those newly developing subeconomies of the South because they have a much shorter history of democracy. Trade unions and the welfare state in particular are virtually non-existent there. While they may have economic growth they are not good societies in terms of equality, integration, welfare, and fairness. But, as Olson has recognised (see 1983), given that they too are now democratic they will certainly develop their own distributional coalitions in time.

Although the pure neo-classical model, in which people always act as rational utility-maximising individuals in a free market with perfect information and no transaction costs, was modified by Olson to include the free rider, his theory still begs all the interesting questions when it comes to explaining actual economic history. While it can apparently explain self-interested action, including free rider action, it cannot easily explain non-selfish, altruistic action or socially conformist action or, in general, any culturally motivated action. In short, the pure neo-classical model, as Douglass North has accurately observed, has a basic asymmetrical dilemma because it assumes both wealth-maximising individual behaviour and the Hobbesian model of a state which will constrain behaviour to produce a viable political system. But these are contradictory, as Olson and others have shown, because if the first is rational the second cannot be. North pointed out that

> it is certainly in the interests of a neoclassical actor to agree to constrain behavior by setting up a group of rules to govern individual actions: hence the view that the Hobesian state is a logical extension of the neoclassical model applied to a theory of the state. But it is also in the interests of the neoclassical actor to disobey those rules whenever an individualistic calculus of benefits and costs dictates such action. That action would, however, result in the non-viability of any state, since enforcement costs of the rules would be, if not infinite, at least so large as to make the system unworkable. Yet everyday observations provide abundant evidence that individuals obey rules when an individualistic calculus should have them act otherwise. Casual observation also provides evidence that an enormous amount of change occurs because of large group action which should not occur in the face of the logic of the free rider problem. (North, 1981, pp. 45–6)

Consequently, the neo-classical model cannot account for much group behaviour; people do vote, donate blood, and contribute to charitable causes, indicating that their 'utility functions' are more complicated and their behaviour is constrained and motivated in more complicated ways. Thus the task, as North sees it from his modified neo-classical perspective, is to broaden the theory in order to be able to explain the large investment that societies make in legitimacy, for example, or education, which go well beyond what is required for human capital or consumption.

Therefore North's approach to explaining change and stability in history requires more than a rationalist behavioural assumption and a theory of the role of groups. There must be: (1) a theory of ideology and morality to help explain behaviour; (2) a theory of property rights to help explain incentives for economic behaviour; (3) a theory of the state as the enforcer of property rights and the setter of the rules of exchange and cooperation; (4) a theory of the structure of the economy in terms of these constitutional rules; (5) a theory of the population/resource relationship (North, 1981, pp. 46–7).[13]

All these are predicated, however, on the assumption that individual economic rational action is supposedly the fundamental cause of structural change. But – and North was adamant on this – the individual always acts within institutional, moral, and ideological constraints and is never completely free (pp. 17–18). Institutions are the framework in which interaction occurs and it is they that change when the structure changes. Institutions are the 'rules, compliance procedures, moral and ethical behavioral norms designed to constrain the behavior of individuals in the interests of maximising the wealth or utility of principals' (pp. 201–2). This is achieved by exploiting the gains from trade which result from specialisation of all kinds, including specialising in violence. The constitutional rules specify the property rights and the control of the state. The moral rules are derived from ideological constructions of reality. Constitutional rules and consensus ideologies in combination give stability to institutions and make them slow to change and then only incrementally (p. 205). But how does the system change? The two basic sources of change for North are the mortality of owners of capital and the incremental changes of capital stock. New inheritors are often in a different bargaining position with other owners and their agents than previously, so contractual relationships tend to alter. The capital stock changes due to population and knowledge changing. Changes in capital affect institutions in many ways (pp. 208–9).

While North's theory is an advance on Olson's, the fundamental problem for him is the micro/macro relationship. Olson saw much more clearly that the two levels of the theory have to be in accord, particularly in the behavioural aspect. On the one hand, North wishes to retain a rationalist, perhaps even an agential model of man, but, on the other, he also rightly wishes to limit the rationality and gency of persons when accounting for structural change by emphasising the *causal* powers of institutions, ideologies, and technological and demographic change. But unfortunately these changes are apparently seen as exogenous to the system of action in his theory, and therefore greatly overconstrain the decision-making capacity of (theoretically) rational actors. In fact, North has gone so far in the institutionalist/technological/demographic direction that he has been carried almost out of the individualist tradition into the structuralist one. That is a measure of the inherent logic of an institutionalist approach. His theory would have been improved if he had

---

[13] For other similar rational-institutionalist accounts of economic action and change that give an important place to ideology and culture, see Ellis and Kumar (1983), Hirsch (1976), Hirschman (1970), Wiener (1981).

abandoned the neo-classical individualist remnants left within it and developed the structurationist elements that are implicit there (i.e. the interrelationship of personality, action, consciousness, culture, and structure) which he seems to have been groping towards.

12

Structuralism

COMPONENTS OF THE STRUCTURALIST TRADITION

The structuralist tradition is diametrically opposed in almost all respects to the individualist tradition but does have a good deal in common with the systemic-functionalist tradition. One of its major differences from both traditions concerns the concept of 'structure'. While, as I have pointed out several times, all the approaches to explaining social change do employ concepts of 'structure' and see themselves as 'structuralist' theories to some extent they do employ these terms very differently. I have argued before that it helps to avoid confusion if all such theories are called 'structurist' and the term 'structuralist' is reserved for those in the (largely) Francophone tradition centring on the work of Lévi-Strauss and the Annales School. For this tradition, as opposed to the two previously discussed (positivist) traditions, structures are not surface phenomena but are the deep *unobservable* levels of languages, cultures, minds, economies, and societies.[1]

I think it can be fairly claimed that the four chief intellectual sources for structuralism were the writings of Ferdinand Saussure on linguistics, Emile Durkheim on sociology, Marx on political economy and history, and Freud on the unconscious mind. These thinkers share to various degrees the ideas of the *abstract* nature of structures, the *causal power* of structures to influence the observable world, and the necessity of a *penetrating science* that goes beneath the appearances of the world to *analyse formally* the elements and levels of systems and to separate the

---

[1] The concept of 'structure' is employed in a very wide variety of ways in the social sciences. General discussions of the concept are contained in Alexander (1984), Blau (1976a), Blau and Merton (1981), Boudon (1971), Craib (1984), Mayhew (1980, 1982).

synchronic from the diachronic features of systems. The differing roles given to information theory and to abstraction were crucial differences between Francophone structuralist and Parsonian structural-functionalist approaches to social history. The latter, being also influenced strongly by empiricism, and not by Saussurian linguistics, was concerned with the *observable* relations of systems and the processes of maintenance of equilibrium (rather than transformation) through functional relationships. Functionalism was largely alien to the Francophone tradition, in spite of Durkheim.

Building upon these background ideas and employing the statements of Piaget it is possible to construct a working list of the basic components that make up the core of the structuralist movement. But it must be emphasised that not all structuralists emphasise them equally, or agree about the relative significance of each. The point of constructing this list is to provide the concepts necessary for grasping the thought of the writers discussed below.[2]

Structure

The fundamental concept is that of structure. Piaget wrote in *Structuralism* (1971b) that structures are considered to have three fundamental properties: wholeness, transformation, and self-regulation. The idea of wholeness serves first to distinguish structures from aggregates of independent elements. Structures also have elements but are subordinated to the laws of the whole which confer on the whole its overall irreducible systemic properties. But, as Piaget pointed out (see chapter 7) and as I emphasised in chapter 8, there is a third alternative between atomism and holism, i.e. structurism, or what Piaget called 'operational structuralism', in which the processes by which the whole is formed and not the whole itself are primary. Piaget's structures are genetically formed and transformed and are not ungenerated or immutable wholes.

The idea of transformation is thus essential. The character of structures depends upon their laws of composition and for Piaget these laws must be *structuring*:

> It is the constant duality, or bipolarity, of always being simultaneously structuring and structured that accounts for the success of the notion of law or rule employed by structuralists. Like Cournot's 'order' (a special case of the structures treated in modern algebra), a structure's laws of composition are defined 'implicitly',

---

[2] There is a very large literature on French structuralism. For good overviews and discussions, see Bottomore and Nisbet (1979), S. Clarke (1981), Giddens (1979, ch. 1), M. Glucksmann (1974), Kurzweil (1980), Piaget (1971b), Rossi (1974), Runciman (1969), Sturrock (1979).

i.e. as governing the transformations of the system which they structure.... Indeed, all known structures – from mathematical groups to kinship systems – are, without exception, systems of transformation. (Piaget, 1971b, pp. 10–11)

Structures are thus constituted by elements and laws. The laws apply to the arrangement of the elements. Some structuralists, such as Chomsky and perhaps Lévi-Strauss, believe the laws to be immutable and so capable of being given a formal, non-temporal foundation. But, as Piaget rightly pointed out (pp. 12–13), this tries to avoid the unavoidable question of genesis – of *construction* – and of the relationship between constructivism and structuralism, which was discussed in chapter 7. There is therefore an important internal division between holistic and genetic structuralists.

Piaget's third property of structures is self-regulation (or self-maintenance and closure); this proceeds by explicit rules, and those rules define the structure itself. For atemporal, mathematical systems the rules are perfect operations. For the temporal structures of language, mind, and society the regulative principles are not perfect and depend upon feedback. But in fact none of the structuralists discussed below adopts this idea, which is drawn from systems theory.

Reality

The second aspect of the tradition is to do with the specification of the reality of structures and how they relate to observable phenomena and relations. As I have mentioned several times, the systemic functionalists discussed in chapter 10 above envisaged social structure (under the influence of Durkheim and Radcliffe-Brown) as a real observable totality requiring an empiricist method of enquiry. Against this, some Francophone structuralists, especially Saussure, Piaget, and Lévi-Strauss, envisage structuralism more as an analytical method that attempts to uncover and systematise the deep *abstract* logico-mathematical principles underlying observable social relations and cultures. There is, however, another current in the tradition, represented by many of the Annales School historians, who consider structure to be a *real* macro, geographic, economic, and political arrangement, independent of the action and usually also of the consciousness of individuals and groups.

Relationship between individual and structure

The third aspect – the individual/structure relationship – is perhaps the most contentious among the structuralists themselves. Their natural orientation is to downgrade the role of individuality and agency, especially under the influences of Freud's theory of the Id, Saussure's emphasis upon a synchronic analysis of language rather than the individual use of speech, and Marx's emphasis upon class consciousness, ideology, collective action, structural levels, and structural contradictions. The human subject has tended to disappear, to be replaced by the abstract order (cf. Sturrock, 1979, pp. 13–15). But Piaget, as we saw in chapter 8, and Lévi-Strauss, as we shall see in a moment, emphasise the epistemic subject: 'the cognitive nucleus which is common to all subjects at the same level' (Piaget, 1971b, p. 139). Furthermore, as Piaget put it,

> the always fragmentary and frequently distorting grasp of consciousness must be set apart from the achievements of the subject; what he knows is the *outcome* of his intellectual activity, not its mechanisms. . . . The subject's activity calls for a continual 'decentring' without which he cannot become free from his spontaneous intellectual egocentricity. This 'de-centring' makes the subject enter upon, not so much an already available and therefore external universality, as an uninterrupted process of coordinating and setting in reciprocal relations. It is the latter process which is the true 'generator' of structures as constantly under construction and reconstruction. The subject exists because, to put it very briefly, the being of structures consists in their coming to be, that is, their being 'under construction'. . . .
>
> *There is no structure apart from construction*, either abstract or genetic. (Piaget, 1971b, pp. 139–40)

Unfortunately, not all structuralists agree that 'construction' is fundamental; Althusser, for instance, has no place for it, and Braudel very little. As I shall argue, this is their fundamental weakness.

Relationship between structure and history

Piaget's idea gives us one way of approaching the fourth aspect – the relationship of structure to history. But since this is our central problem it will be discussed in more detail in a moment by examining the work of some of the main exponents of the tradition, particularly to see how these writers approach the explanation of social change and history from a structuralist point of view.

In general, then, when the structuralist movement is observed as a quasi-institutionalised entity, it can be seen that there are three parallel currents within it. Firstly, there is the cultural current, which concentrates on examining and formalising the structures of the cultural products of the human mind in their various forms and in societies of all sorts, whether capitalist or non-capitalist, past or present. Some anthropologists, historians of ideas, psychologists, and literary analysts fall into this stream. Secondly, there is the geographical, economic, and social current which examines the long run structural processes and continuities underlying the observable events of history. This current is broadly synonymous with the Annales School of historians and includes some recent Marxists. The third current is one which concentrates on epistemological and methodological problems of explanation, and of how structuralism relates to other modes of explanation. Some Marxist structuralists fall more or less into this group, but most structuralists at some time or other engage in methodological reflection. Indeed, most of those in the movement engage in all of these facets at various times, which is an indication of the sophistication of their work. The three central figures in the structuralist movement are therefore Claude Lévi-Strauss, who represents the first and third currents, Fernand Braudel, who represents the second, and Jean Piaget, who represents the third. Piaget's work has already been examined in chapter 7 and so will not be discussed here. Lying outside at a critical distance and recently strongly influencing erstwhile structuralists is Michel Foucault – the central figure of post-structuralism.

LÉVI-STRAUSS'S STRUCTURALISM

Lévi-Strauss's work has had a great influence on the social sciences, and not just in France.[3] In one of his first methodological articles (1945), he argued that structural linguistics will have a revolutionary effect on the social sciences because it is able to formulate *necessary* relationships. It does this because of its four basic aspects:

> First, structual linguistics shifts from the study of *conscious* linguistic phenomena to study of their *unconscious* infrastructure; second, it does not treat *terms* as independent entities, taking instead as its basis of analysis the *relations* between terms; third, it introduces the concept of *system*.... Finally, structural linguistics aims at discovering *general laws*, either by induction 'or ... by logical deduction, which would give them an absolute character'. (Lévi-Strauss, 1945, p. 33)

Extrapolating from this, the anthropologist could use the same method in the study of kinship because the basic kinship terms are *elements* like phonemes, which are integrated into *systems* of meaning and which are in turn *universal* for all societies. Thus observable kinship phenomena result, like speech, from implicit but general laws (p. 34). Kinship

---

[3] There are helpful discussions of Lévi-Strauss's struturalism in S. Clarke (1981), M. Glucksmann (1974), Kurzweil (1980), E. Leach (1973, 1974, 1981), Rossi (1974, 1981), Sperber (1979).

systems, like myths, primitive classifications, totemism, and social structures are all abstract universal systems of symbols existing at the
unconscious, or deep, levels of the human mind and capable of being
given a form logical presentation by the social scientist. It is then a matter
of grasping the unconscious, systemic, unchanging structure underlying
each type of institution and custom in order to understand all such
institutions and customs (1949, p. 21). Structures are therefore not
entities in the world in some observable sense but are the products of
analytical human thought in all the sciences. The degree to which a
science is structuralist is the degree to which it is indeed a science, in his
account.

Lévi-Strauss's social *structures* are not to be confused with social
relations. Social relations, rather, are the 'raw materials' of models of
structure and these models cannot be reduced to them. He said that a
model in any science is truly a *structure* if it is an integrated *system* of
elements such that: if one element changes it affects all the others; the
model can go through a series of transformations which result in a series
of models of the same type; predictions of the model's changes can be
made if one element is changed; and all the observed facts are made
intelligible by the model (Lévi-Strauss, 1953, pp. 279–80). This distinction between the raw material of sociological data and models is the basis
for his division of the social sciences into empirical-statistical discourses
such as history, and the model-building sciences, such as sociology and
anthropology. They need each other. Models are constructed to explain
social relations but social relations are always situated in time and space.
Therefore the temporal and historico-geographical parameters are also
essential to social studies (1953, pp. 281–90). These dimensions have
been of crucial importance to the Annales historians.

How do the various orders or levels of social totalities relate to each
other? This is the key theoretical question for social explanation in
general. Historical materialism asserts some form of a determination
between the economic infrasructure or level and the levels of the
superstructure. Some culturalist theories of social change, such as those
of Parsons and others to be discussed in the next chapters, hold that
culture is more important for explanation. Where does Lévi-Strauss
stand on this? Does his kind of structuralism presuppose a culturalist
theory of action and social change? From the following passage we can
get an idea of his position:

> I do not postulate a kind of pre-existent harmony between the
> different levels of structure. They may be – and often are –
> completely contradictory, but the modes of contradiction all belong
> to the same type. Indeed, according to dialectic materialism it
> should always be possible to proceed, by transformation, from
> economic or social structure to the structure of law, art, or religion.

But Marx never claimed that there was only one type of transformation – for example, that ideology was simply a 'mirror image' of social relations. In his view, these transformations were dialectic, and in some cases he went to great lengths to discover the crucial transformation which at first sight seemed to defy analysis.

If we grant, following Marxian thought, that infrastructures and superstructures are made up of multiple levels and that there are various types of transformations from one level to another, it becomes possible – in the final analysis, and on the condition that we disregard content – to characterise different types of societies in terms of the types of transformations which occur within them. These types of transformations amount to formulas showing the number, magnitude, direction, and order of the convolutions that must be unravelled, so to speak, in order to uncover (logically, not normatively) an ideal homologous relationship between the different structural levels.

Now, this reduction to an ideal homologous relationship is at the same time a critique. By replacing a complex model with a simple model that has greater logical value, the anthropologist reveals the detours and manoeuvres, conscious and unconscious, that each society uses in an effort to resolve its inherent contradictions – or at any rate to conceal them. (Lévi-Strauss, 1958, pp. 333–4)

This passage and others like it reveal Lévi-Strauss's debt to the concepts of Marx's historical materialism. He clearly saw his work as a sort of completion or fulfilment of Marx's work by developing the concepts of the cultural level. His structuralist analyses were almost exclusively confined to the cultural products of the human mind and he had little to say about the structures or relations of society, or about how they change.

STRUCTURES, MENTALITIES, AND THE LONG DURATION

The social and historical current in the structuralist tradition concentrates on the long-run continuities in the history of the large-scale geographic, economic, social, and cultural structures that lie beneath the surface of the short-run social phenomena of politics, wars, and day-to-day personal activities. These structures are postulated as *external* to thought, setting the conditions for human mental and physical life and having a large degree of autonomy. Such an object of enquiry has been one of the main concerns (but certainly not the sole one) of the Annales School, which originated in the work of Lucien Fèbvre and Marc Bloch in the 1920s and was quasi-institutionalised when they founded *Annales d'Histoire Économique et Sociale* in 1929. But like all such 'beginnings' it was not a complete rupture with the past, only a significant turning point in a process which looked back to or was contemporaneous with the work of other economic and social historians, such as Michelet, Fustel, and Mantoux in France, Pirenne in Belgium, Schmoller, Weber, and Sombart in Germany, and Tawney in England; of French sociologists such as Durkheim, Simiand, and Mauss; and the historical geography of Vidal de la Blache. But on the whole they were opposed to the abstracting and comparative methods of sociology and defended a historical approach to society instead. Society and its history were not to be 'forced' into the mould of an *a priori* sociological theory (Fèbvre, 1932, ch. II).

Fèbvre and Bloch saw the proper task of history as the study of the interrelationship of the individual and society. It was not a question of choosing between them. The historian has to locate his work in a social environment, said Fèbvre. this is because society is a *necessity* for the individual and

> the forces that determine the individual emanate from that society; they are a necessary complement to the individual. . . . If, in the case of the individual, what we first have to do is distinguish personality characterised to varying degrees by a number of features that are his very own, put together according to an individual formula and mixed together in a very special way; if, in addition, we have to see that same individual both as a representative of the human species with distinctive features common to the members of a certain group of the species, and as a member of a very distinct society existing at a precise moment in time, then two things are plain. Firstly, the opposition between the individual and society is seen to weaken considerably, and secondly, the correct method of investigation, where the individual is concerned, begins to become clear. (Fèbvre, 1973, p. 4; see also Bloch, 1954, pp. 25–6)

The method was psychological. The individual and the mentality of past epochs were to be investigated in a historical (rather than comparative) psychological manner. In doing this it was therefore crucial that no attempt be made to project into the past ideas about the mentality of persons gained from a study of people and society in the present (Fèbvre, 1973, chs I and II, especially pp. 5–6). Psychological concepts were necessary but not psychological universals. The task was to uncover 'the whole physical, intellectual and moral universe' of a generation and to grasp the technical and conceptual shortcomings which distorted their image of the world, life, religion, and politics (Fèbvre, 1973, pp. 9–10). That is, as we would now say, the task was to grasp their ideological world view (see Fèbvre, 1982, for an example). Furthermore, each mental universe is constantly being transformed through practical activity which must also be studied. And mental universes and practical activity always exist within geopolitical structural contexts, to the study of which Fèbvre and Bloch devoted much energy (see Fèbvre, 1932; Bloch, 1962, 1966).

In summary, the new kind of historical methodology that Fèbvre and Bloch advocated for studying the past life of individuals and groups in their geographical, social, and cultural environments had several features which were radical for that time and which were later to be influential in the structuralist (and post-structuralist) movement. First, in Bloch's opinion at least, it was to be a *science*, but not a positivist one à la Comte. By this he seems to have meant that it was concerned neither with universal evolutionary laws nor with just providing an interpretive narrative of obvious events. Rather, the idea of science, in the wake of the kinetic theory of gases, Einstein's mechanics, and quantum theory, was now more flexible and less precise. Now at last, he said, 'history struggles to penetrate beneath the mere surface of actions, rejecting not only the temptations of legend and rhetoric, but the still more dangerous modern poisons of routine learning and empiricism parading as common sense.' (Bloch, 1954, pp. 13–14)

Secondly, being a science meant, as this indicates, attempting to uncover the deep, hidden structural conditions and mechanisms of history – the geographical, economic, demographic, and cultural structures.

Thirdly, and following from this idea, Fèbvre conceived of history as analogous to archaeology (1973, p. 10). By this he seems to have meant that it is a *totalising* attempt to gather, by a great team effort employing all the social sciences, as much data as possible by digging and sifting the 'deposits' of past societies (p. 10, pp. 32–3). (Bloch's work on agrarian history (1962, 1966) exemplified this.) However, Fèbvre was completely opposed to the idea of fact grubbing for fact's sake (1973, pp. 36–7). What was needed was 'organisation' of facts. This was crucial in two senses: in terms of explanation (or making sense of facts) and in terms of the social function that history writing serves. Without organisation (would we now say 'theory'?) the past becomes a burdensome but infatuating weight, crushing the living, flattening the present (p. 40). But

> history is a way of organising the past so that it does not weigh too heavily on the shoulders of men. Of course . . . it does not resign itself to disregarding the heap of 'historical' facts available to our civilisation for the writing of history; indeed it takes pains to add to it. There is no contradiction here. For history does not present men with a collection of isolated facts. It organises those facts. It explains them and so, in order to explain them, it arranges them in series to which it does not attach equal importance. For history has no choice in the matter, it systematically gathers in, classifies and assembles past facts in accordance with its present needs. It consults death in accordance with the needs of life. (Fèbvre, 1973, p. 41)

Thus the fourth aspect of Annales historiography was the study of the past to serve a social function in the present.

Towards the end of his career Fèbvre commended the massive book of Fernand Braudel on *The Mediterranean and the Mediterranean World in the Age of Philip II* (originally 1949) as an exemplar of how history should be written in the new archaeological, structural, and scientific manner. the themes that Fèbvre and Bloch enunciated in the inter-war period were carried forward with vigour after the war by men such as Braudel and institutionalised by their control of the VI Section of the École Pratique des Hautes Études.[4] But the differing emphases upon the two sides of the individual/structure relationship made for significant differences in methodologies. And the role given to theorising the causes of structural change varies with this difference.

Braudel is strongly opposed to individualist/narrative history of the traditional kind. As one of the five themes of this volume I quoted a passage from his inaugural lecture at the Collège de France in 1950 in which he situated himself against the Rankian approach to history as a narrative of events. He saw that as being merely the first stage of history. History should then go on to study *social* realities *in themselves and for themselves* (1980, p. 11).

The unification of the historical and social studies is a central project for Braudel, one about which he has written often. His argument is that the core of their unification should be a concern with the different levels and aspects of time and structure. The historian, he said, is concerned fundamentally with time: 'time sticks to his thinking like soil to a gardener's spade.' (1980, p. 47) Braudel identified, and employed as the fundamental organising structure of his work, three levels or speeds of time: the event, the conjuncture (or cyclical phases), and the very long time span, the *longue durée* (1980, p. 27).

It is structure that Braudel sees as dominating the problems of the *longue durée*. His two great books attempt to integrate all levels of time on a basis of structural change. By 'structure' he means 'an organisation, a coherent and fairly fixed set of relationships between realities and social masses' (1980, p. 31). Structures have different durations but they all, he said, provide both support and hindrance to action – 'as hindrances they stand as limits ("envelopes" in the mathematical sense) beyond which man and his experiences cannot go' (p. 31). Structures are therefore independently real.

The most basic level of structure is the geographical environment – the ecology of society. Like Fèbvre and Bloch, Braudel spent a great deal of effort on examining the ecological basis of history; and geography was to

[4] The significance of the Annales School is discussed and analysed by Burke (1973, Introduction; 1978), Forster (1978), Harsgor (1978), Hexter (1972), Hutton (1981), Perrott (1976), Revel (1978), Ricoeur (1980), Stoianovich (1976, 1978), C. Tilly (1978), Trevor-Roper (1972).

remain a central concern of the Annales School in general. Another aspect of structure is the economy with its cycles and secular trends. The *longue durée*, which he studied in such exhaustive and penetrating detail in *Civilization and Capitalism*, is the

> endless, inexhaustible history of structures and groups of structures. For the historian a structure is not just a thing built, put together; it also means permanence, sometimes for more than centuries (time too is a structure). This great structure travels through vast tracts of time without changing; if it deteriorates during the long journey, it simply restores itself as it goes along and regains its health, and in the final analysis its characteristics alter only very slowly. (Braudel, 1980, p. 75)

How are we to study such deep unconscious, almost ahistorical, structural processes according to Braudel? In doing so, models of various sorts are obviously essential: they are 'hypotheses, systems of explanation tied solidly together in the form of an equation, or a function' (1980, p. 40). They are of a generality such that they can be applied to more than one society. The models that he seems to have had in mind are often of a simple, rough-and-ready kind, stating not very precise relationships but rather vague generalisations about stages of development such as those of Marx, or game-theoretic models drawn from economics, or even models of the type employed by Lévi-Strauss which attempt to reduce structures of culture to their atomistic elements in order to rearrange them into logico-mathematical patterns (1980, pp. 41–5).

Allied to model building is a wide-ranging, exhaustive search for empirical evidence – 'a whole vast body of documentation must be brought to light so as to be able to answer the new questions.' (1980, p. 13) And this implies a team effort to prospect methodically for sources in all places and pertaining to all levels of time and structure. His books on *The Mediterranean* and *Civilization and Capitalism* exemplify this dictum, containing vast amounts of archival data.

In short, Braudel's history is claimed to be the *total* of all possible histories. Such a totalising historian, he said,

> is led to bringing together different levels, time spans, different kinds of time, structures, conjunctures, events. These taken all together go to make up for him a fairly precarious global balance which can be maintained only through a constant series of adjustments, clashes, and slight alterations. In its totality, social reality in flux is ideally, at every instant, *synchronous* with its history, a constantly changing image, although it might repeat a thousand previous details of a thousand previous realities. Who would deny it? That is why the idea of a global structure for society disturbs and

embarrasses the historian, even though there must be, of course, a considerable gap between a global structure and a global reality. What the historian would like to rescue from the debate is the uncertainty of the mass movement, its various possibilities for alteration, its freedoms, its particular 'functional' explanations, offspring of the moment and the particular. (Braudel, 1980, p. 76)

So Braudel's total history is a *structural* history. It is not totalising in the sense of including the interaction of all the *moments* of social reality. Nor is it theoretical history. But what is the role of theory in such structural historical explanation? Although Braudel is enamoured of model building, on the one hand, and sceptical about sociology as presently practised, on the other, he is relatively silent about the part that theories of the *causes* of change play in his writings. However, theoretical concepts of an *organisational* kind – i.e. categories, abstractions, models, analogies, statistical generalisations – do play a central part in his work, as can readily be seen from the general organisation of his two books. *The Mediterranean* is organised primarily around concepts of differential time – geographic, economic, and event durations were examined for the era of the second half of the sixteenth century. *Civilization and Capitalism* is organised around the history of the four 'sets' of the social totality (economy, social hierarchy, politics, and culture) and, more importantly, the three levels of the economy over the *longue durée* from the fifteenth to the eighteenth centuries (i.e. from the ending of feudalism to the Industrial Revolution). The later book is in fact based on a half-articulated version of historical materialism.

In what sense is Braudel's book historical materialist? First, his model of the *levels* of the civilisation of that time is a necessary theoretical construct for such a framework. All versions of historical materialism must see the social totality as consisting (in theoretical abstraction) of at least two levels – a base and a superstructure – and perhaps of more than two levels. (This is further discussed in chapter 14.) Braudel saw the social totality as consisting of four 'sets' or 'orders': economy, social hierarchy, politics, and culture. Total history implies (although probably not achievable) the study of their complex interrelationships (1981, p. 46). On the face of it these are not levels but subsystems akin to those of Parsons. But they are best seen as levels when the causal relationships between them is revealed, as I shall show in a moment.

The economic or productive 'set' in turn consists of three genuine levels. At the bottom, forming the barely visible base, is what he called 'material life', the informal economy – the realm of small-scale self-sufficient production, of barter, and of local market exchange. On the second level is the market economy – the visible realm of production and exchange, small shops, workshops, banks, exchanges, fairs, and markets. At the top level is the real capitalism of international trade and financial transactions, and of big monopolies (1981, pp. 23–4). Now, this tripartite model is obviously not meant to be a description of real life since the world does not divide quite so easily, but this division is the fundamental set of abstract categories of his huge book.

The second aspect of historical materialist explanation concerns the relationships between these levels and between the economy and the other three orders of society. On this he wrote the following pregnant passage, which is worth quoting at length:

> An economy never exists in isolation. Its territory and expanse are also occupied by other spheres of activity – culture, society, politics – which are constantly reacting with the economy, either to help or as often to hinder its development. It is all the more difficult to distinguish these orders one from the other since what is visible to the naked eye – the reality of experience or the 'really real' as François Perroux calls it – is a *totality* which we have already described as society *par excellence,* 'the set of sets'. . . . One could formulate the following equations in any order: the economy equals politics, culture and society; culture equals the economy, politics, and society; etc. Or one could say that in a given society, politics governs the economy and vice versa; that the economy benefits or discourages culture and vice versa; or even as Pierre Brunel has said, that 'everything human is political, therefore all literature (even the hermetic poetry of Mallarmé) is political.' For if one of the specific characters of the economy is that it extends beyond its own area, can the same not equally be said of the other social 'sets'? They all nibble at frontiers, seek to extend their territory and create their own Von Thünen circles. (Braudel, 1984, p. 54)

But this is not his last word. If it were then we could not justifiably call his framework 'historical materialism' because in this statement there is no actual or explanatory primacy given to the economic. He went on to say that the primacy of the economy became increasingly more overwhelming with modern times – 'it directed, disturbed and influenced the other orders. Exaggerating inequalities, it imprisoned the various partners in the world economy either in poverty or in wealth . . . .' (1984, p. 47) And the state was not as powerful relative to the economy as it is now (p. 51). Social arrangements, too, became dominated by the economy, always with local aberrations and departures (pp. 62–6). It was possible for many forms of social hierarchy and social exploitation to coexist simultaneously in the world economy (pp. 63–4). On the other hand, he thought cultures had a life of relative independence from the developing world economy (pp. 65–7).

Thirdly, the most important aspect of his historical materialism is that of capitalism itself. It is capitalism that dominates his analysis of the developing world of early modern times, and capitalism grows to pervade all the other sets of society, not just the economic. The worst error of all, said Braudel, is

> to suppose that capitalism is simply an 'economic system', whereas in fact it lives off the social order, standing almost on a footing with the state, whether as adversary or accomplice: it is and always has been a massive force, filling the horizon. Capitalism also benefits from all the support that culture provides for the solidity of the social edifice, for culture – though unequally distributed and shot through with contradictory currents – does in the end contribute the best of itself to propping up the existing order. And lastly capitalism can count on the dominant classes who, when they defend it, are defending themselves. (Braudel, 1984, p. 623)

Therefore, it can be seen that Braudel's 'historical materialist' analysis is not a theoretical history; not a history dominated by an *a priori* construct of the primacy of the base or any other level. The concepts of levels are used as organising models only, heuristic devices, and any attempt to force history into the mould of the theory is rejected. It is historical materialist only in so far as the basic working idea of the mechanisms of change is the ubiquitous power of capitalism and the capitalist class to control developments to favour their shifting, developing interests in the long run and at all levels. This means that capital adapts, insinuating itself here, retreating there, always seeking for opportunities and legitimising itself in new ways. It stamps and moulds, in turn, all those areas and levels that it touches.[5]

This brings us to the final question about Braudel's approach, which

[5] Braudel's historical materialism can be compared with similar approaches to the history of capitalism developed by Marx and Weber. Marx would have agreed with Braudel that the economy in general, and capitalist production in particular, may not always appear to be predominant but there is nevertheless a *general* determination by the economy at all times and by capitalist production, in particular, from early modern times onward, although other modes of production may also exist with it (cf. Marx, 1857–8, pp. 106–7; 1867, p. 176). Therefore for Marx the superstructure is not a mere reflection of the base, and Braudel would agree.

However, the major differences are due to Marx's much greater theoretical sophistication and precision. His historical work was not a theoretical history either but it is much more closely informed by his definition of 'capitalism' and his theory of the forces and relations of production and of the mechanisms of structural change. (Braudel wrongly believes that Marx did not use the term 'capitalism' until sometime after 1867 (1982, p. 237).) In Braudel's definition, 'capital' is a thing, a means of production, whether fixed or circulating (1982, pp. 239–41). 'Capitalism' is a system of large-scale investment, trade, exchange, and production for profit, not equatable simply with money-making or the market but with the *scale* of such things. As such it existed in a limited sphere in early modern Europe and the ancient world. Marx would have strongly disagreed with both definitions. For him 'capital' concerns the human agency/structure relationship. For Marxist historical materialism, class struggle is the fundamental agent of historical change – i.e. groups of people acting in their class interests. Braudel hints in places that he has something similar in mind, especially with regard to capitalists, but in others he is much more structurally determinist (or holistic) in his 'explanations' of structural change, especially in the *longue durée*. Even though he said at one point that the long term is made up of cycles of 'structuration, destructuration, and restructuration' (1984, p. 621), these processes seem to be overly structurally determined in his work and he did not offer an account of the role of groups, classes, and individuals and their forms of consciousness, in changing history. Indeed, as he wrote on the last page of *The Mediterranean*:

> When I think of the individual, I am always inclined to see him imprisoned within a destiny in which he himself has little hand, fixed in a landscape in which the infinite perspectives of the long term stretch into the distance both behind him and before. In historical analysis as I see it, rightly or wrongly, the long run always wins in the end. Annihilating innumerable events – all those which cannot be accommodated in the main ongoing current and which are therefore ruthlessly swept to one side – it undubitably limits both the freedom of the individual and even the role of chance. I am by temperament a 'structuralist', little tempted by the event, or even by the short-term conjuncture which is after all merely grouping of events in the same area. (Braudel, 1973, vol. II, p. 1244)

Structural necessity asserts itself in the long run, apparently, and is not deflected by mere humans! The organisational category of 'structure' wins out over the question of the causes of structural change. The three

---

and 'capitalism' were not primarily things or systems, but *relations of production* between things and people and between people, specifically between owners of means of production and free wage labourers (see Marx, *Grundrisse*, pp. 512–14). For Braudel, capital, as investible funds, essentially grows out of exchange and is then reinvested, perhaps in manufacturing. For Marx, capitalist production as such can only come about on the prior basis of a dissolution of non-capitalist modes of production so that workers and investible funds can be rearranged into a capitalist production relationship. And that can only occur essentially as a result of a violent class struggle in the countryside (see 1857–8, pp. 493–515; 1867, section VIII).

On the other hand, Braudel is much closer to the spirit and the letter of Weber's analyses (in 1909, 1923). While Weber's account had many elements in common with Marx's, one of the decisive differences was over the specification of 'capitalism'. Weber saw it in rational exchange terms, as external to the productive process and hence existing in many forms of society, such as ancient Rome. For further discussion of recent Marxist and Weberian approaches, see chapter 14. There is an interesting comparison of Weber and Braudel in Roth (1979). Braudel's work is also discussed by Day (1980), Kellner (1979), Santamaria and Bailey (1984), Stoianovich (1976, 1978), Trevor-Roper (1972).

levels of time are not tied together as a causal theory but are ways of merely *describing* the structure. But the idea of structural causality was not articulated by Braudel. That was achieved by the philosopher Althusser (see below).

Individuals and groups are not denied a role in transforming social structures in the work of the leading member of the third generation of Annales historians, Emmanuel Le Roy Ladurie. In one sense his work, taken as a whole, forms a bridge between and a synthesis of the two broad streams of the structuralist movement: the Lévi-Straussian concern with deep structures of the human mind which have to be constructed out of the cultural products of societies; and the Annaliste concern with the geographic, economic, and social structures of the environment of historical events. He has undertaken both kinds of analyses and, more-over, sometimes attempted to combine them with narrative history of individual and small-group actions in such a way as to show the dialectical relationships of action, consciousness, and structure. The human actors in his writings are much more agential than in Braudel's work. In fact Ladurie straddles the deep structuralist, symbolic-realist, and relational-structurist traditions. He is an exemplar of how to do social history.

Ladurie began his career with an attempt at total structural history – *The Peasants of Languedoc* (1974) – which studied the geography, demography, economy, sociology, and collective mentalities of peasant society in Languedoc from the fourteenth to the eighteenth centuries. In a sense this book established the framework for most of his subsequent writings, which have been largely concerned with the same broad area and era. Just as with *The Mediterranean* Braudel made the sixteenth-century Mediterranean his own province, or Pierre Chaunu made sixteenth- and seventeenth-century Seville his, or Lucien Fèbvre made sixteenth-century Franche-Comte his, so Ladurie has become the social historian *par excellence* of medieval and early modern Occitania – the south-west part of France where was spoken the Romance language of Oc. (For an overview of the region's history and problems of its historiography, see Ladurie, 1977.)

In addition to his total history book on the peasant economy and society he has written, among other works, a study in the social-anthropological history of one Pyreneen village in the early fourteenth century (*Montaillou*, 1980), a detailed study of one social event in one town in 1579–80 (*Carnival in Romans*, 1981a), and a large structuralist study (in the Lévi-Straussian sense) of the subconscious levels of the 'infraculture' of Occitan literature and folklore and its relationship to changing social structures (*Love, Death, and Money in the Pays d'Oc*, 1984).

In all these works he attempted to combine analyses of economic processes, social structural change, and the deep structure of cultural forms to show how they interrelated with the conjunctures and events of the short term. His methodology for structural analysis of culture, particularly in the last-mentioned book, was inspired by Lévi-Strauss; however, unlike him, Ladurie showed how cultural expression was related to economic and social conditions and processes (see especially 1984, Conclusion). His methodology for economic and social history was inspired by Fèbvre, Bloch, and Braudel, but unlike them he analysed the deep *logico-mathematical* structures of the unconscious level of mentalities. In addition to these works of total history he has also done extensive research on the ecological environment of human affairs, particularly the history of climate and land use (see 1959, 1972b, 1981b).

Like Braudel and other Annalistes Ladurie has also written at length about his methodological and theoretical frameworks. He is one of the most sophisticated Annalistes in these respects, self-consciously employing methods and models drawn from the social sciences, particularly anthropology, sociology, and demography, in the way that Braudel taught was necessary providing it was done cautiously. Moreover, unlike Braudel or other leading Annalistes such as Labrousse, Goubert, or Vilar, he wished to restore to importance the events, the accidents, the sudden ruptures and turning points of history. He believed that total structural history was a great advance but 'a trend or a structure can quite easily be unmasked'; only patience, a lot of work, and imagination are required. However,

> the aleatory transition from one structure to another, the *mutation*, often remains, in history as in biology, the most perplexing zone, where chance appears to play a large part. Once one has reached this zone, factors which are often mysterious delineate the poles of necessity within the field of possibilities: once they have surfaced, their existence is obvious – but a moment before their appearance, they were as unpredictable as they were unprecedented. (Ladurie, 1979, p. 114)

But this does not imply a return to traditional narrative history which neglects structures altogether. The two must be combined. The study of actions and events must be located in their structural contexts (see Ladurie 1981b, ch. 1) and in *Montaillou* and *Carnival* we have two supreme examples of such work. Both deal with a small set of small-scale but significant events – a rupture in the processes of their places and times. These events are then not only narrated from several points of view but investigated for their own deep structures. They are then placed in the complex structural situations and processes – ecological, economic, political, cultural – and shown why they are significant. Consequently these books are at one and the same time narrative stories, historical geographies, anthropological and sociological analyses, and economic and political histories. They are great achievements, exemplars of social history.

But we must also ask of Ladurie what we asked about Braudel: what is the role of theory? In this case, the answer is: an ever-present, powerful, but *eclectic* one. His writings are continually informed, enriched, and structured by theories, particularly those of Marx, Freud, Weber, Lévi-Strauss, and population biology and ecodynamics (see Ladurie 1981b, ch. 1). His eloquent statement (quoted in my five themes) at the conclusion of his inaugural lecture at the Collège de France on the relationship between natural science, social science, and history is a fitting summary of the ambitions (but not all the achievements) of the Annales School.

MARXIST STRUCTURALISM

The relationship of structuralism to Marxism is a question that has come up in several places in the discussion of this tradition. Lévi-Strauss was obviously very indebted to Marx and even saw his own work as completing Marx's historical materialism on the level of the super-structure. The early Annales historians knew little of Marxism and it wasn't until well into the post-war period that Marxism became influential for their work. Braudel's *Civilization and Capitalism* is heavily indebted to Marx both explicitly and in spirit. Some other French structuralists have attempted to bring about a complete union of structuralist method and Marxist social theory, most notably the philosopher Louis Althusser and the anthropologist Maurice Godelier. And the American historian Immanuel Wallerstein has attempted to combine the Annaliste approach with Marxist theory to construct a massive history of the 'modern world system', as a system. It is important to bear in mind that there are several kinds of Marxism extant in the social and human studies – i.e. not all Marxists are structuralists. The influence of and interpretations of Marx have been various and ambiguous and there is now an extensive debate about the explanatory significance of historical materialism, to be discussed in chapter 14.

In what sense can Marx be said to be a structuralist? When we compare the generality of his work with the outline of the main components of this tradition given above, some similarity becomes apparent.[6] However, there are three important questions about this

---

[6] The question of the relationship of structuralism to Marxism has been extensively discussed by Althusser, Balibar, and Godelier (see later in this chapter). There have also been helpful discussions by Benton (1984), M. Glucksmann (1974), Heydebrand (1981), Krader (1974), Lecourt (1975), Topolski (1973), Veltmeyer (1974), Walton and Gamble (1972). See also the discussion in chapter 14 and the references given there.

similarity. Firstly, to what extent is Marx's structure a *holistic system* of elements characterised by self-regulation? Secondly, to what extent is his structure universal and logico-mathematical? And thirdly, what part do human agency, conflict, exogenous influences, and even historical 'accidents' play in his theory of structural transformation? Let us see how some of the structuralist Marxists deal with these questions. That is, how and why do they interpret Marx as being a structuralist?

Louis Althusser has argued that Marx's mature works contain a *scientific* breakthrough. For Althusser a science is characterised by being structuralist in the way that Lévi-Strauss taught. Each science is underpinned by a theory which in turn is a 'system of basic scientific concepts' (Althusser, 1971, p. 75). Such concepts are abstract in the sense of being non-empirical yet they designate 'concrete' objective realities which cannot be sensed. Althusser uses the concept 'system' deliberately. A scientific theory and a social totality are for him both systems in the sense of being hierarchical, integrated, ordered, holistic totalities of elements with internal control and transformation mechanisms.

As is well known, Marxism claims that class struggle at the political level is 'the locomotive of history' but it also claims that the economy is determinant 'in the last instance'. Althusser believed that these ideas can be reconciled by a holistic/structuralist conception of the social totality and of social causation.

This conception implies, wrote Althusser, that the

> structure is immanent in its effects, a cause immanent in its effects in the Spinozist sense of the term, that *the whole existence of the structure consists of its effects*, in short that the structure, which is merely a specific combination of its peculiar elements, is nothing outside its effects. (Althusser and Balibar, 1970, p. 189)

How then does structural causality determine structural transformations? Althusser was adamant in rejecting 'humanism', i.e. the idea of people consciously and deliberately deciding to change society – that 'man makes history'. Rather, he believed that

> history is an immense *natural-human* system in movement, and the motor of history is class struggle. History is a process, and a *process without a subject*. The question about how '*man* makes history' disappears altogether. Marxist theory rejects it once and for all; it sends it back to its birthplace: bourgeois ideology.
>
> And with it disappears the 'necessity' of the concept of 'transcendence' and of its subject, man.
>
> That does not mean that Marxist-Leninism *loses sight* for one moment of real men. Quite the contrary! It is precisely in order to *see* them as they are and to free them from class exploitation that

Marxism-Leninism brings about this revolution, getting rid of the bourgeois ideology of 'man' as the subject of history, *getting rid of the fetishism of 'man'*.... Have the warnings of Marx been heeded? 'My analytical method *does not start from man*, but from the economically given social period (*Notes on Adolph Wagner's 'Textbook'*). 'Society *is not composed of individuals' (Grundrisse).* (Althusser, 1976, pp. 51–2)

Structural causality is inescapable because, for Althusser as with Lévi-Strauss, Braudel, and all holists, the social totality is a *systemic whole* with a definite internal hierarchical structure which dtermines what is possible for each of the elements.

In its ontological essentials there is little difference between this conception of the totality and that of Talcott Parsons, although the specification of the internal structure and its mechanisms are different. For Parsons culture is the more or less determining level, whereas for Althusser it is the material conditions of production that are determining. For Parsons the systemic mechanisms are phenomenal processes of observable (or Humean) relations of supposedly functional causality, directly linking the levels up and down into a cybernetic hierarchy (see chapter 10). However, for Althusser, Lévi-Strauss, and Braudel the causality is essentialist in the sense that the structure's supposedly essential organisation acts to limit and condition the actual causal relations within the structure (which can be of many different sorts) and the essential nature of each of the elements.[7]

Therefore, the fundamental problem with Althusser's account both of Marx and of history is holism. Marx is interpreted as a holist and Althusser's theory of history is thoroughly holist – ascribing complete agency powers to social entities and seeing the elements as subordinate to the whole.[8] However, there is an alternative reading of Marx's mature

---

[7] Althusser and Balibar seem to be little aware of the large literature on systemic/ structural determination produced by game theorists, communication theorists, cyberneticians, and so on. Both Lévi-Strauss and Piaget, of the French structuralists, were well aware of the concordances between their own work and this other tradition of largely Anglophone thought.

[8] Althusser's work has been discussed and criticised by Benton (1984), Callinicos (1976), Geras (1977), A. Glucksmann (1972), M. Glucksmann (1974), Kurzweil (1980), Lecourt (1975), Mepham (1973), Vilar (1973), Walton and Gamble (1972). See also my discussion and the references given in chapter 14.

The Althusserian project of reconstructing the system of concepts of historical materialism in their correct relationships, pursued especially by Etienne Balibar in *Reading Capital* (Althusser and Balibar, 1970), was taken to its logical extremity by Barry Hindess and Paul Hirst. Their original project was to construct the concepts of various modes of production in complete abstraction. They saw scientific 'theoretical practice' as taking place entirely abstractly, completely independently of any empirical research: its task is to construct general concepts and investigate 'real conditions'. But the real conditions are never 'given'

writings which is not holistic, and so retains a place for the dialectical interaction of structure and human conscious agency. To say that society is not composed of individuals is not necessarily to say that there are no individuals or that society is characterised by only holistic powers. The problem of the relationship of individual to society cannot be resolved by simply denying agency. The problem is to explain *structuration*, as Piaget emphasised: *'there is no structure apart from construction*, either abstract or genetic' (see the first section of this chapter).

The French anthropologist Maurice Godelier has attempted, in a much more explicit and theoretically informed manner than Althusser, to unite Marxism with Lévi-Straussian structuralism and to situate this project in relation to systems theory, empiricist political economy, and functionalist anthropological theory. His aim in doing so is to explore the possibilities of a general historical materialist theory of social transformations (Godelier, 1972a). The problem is to explain history scientifically, he said. History is not itself an explanation (Godelier, 1977, p. 6), which is what Braudel has a tendency to believe. Such a science should be based, Godelier believed, on a structuralist reading of Marx, and particularly the idea of a systemic-structural causality.

The Althusserian conception of the social totality sees it as a system of instances unevenly structured by the dominance of the forces of production and in which this essential unevenness and domination is present within each instance (i.e. in the economy, politics, culture, ideology, religion, and so on). For Godelier, the distinction between infrastructure, superstructure, and ideology is one between *functions* rather than institutions, or levels, or instances (Godelier, 1978, p. 763). The 'infrastructure' includes all of the physical means of production which bring the physical and intellectual forces together in various ways. The 'superstructure' includes politics, religious ideas and practices, but these

---

to knowledge – they are always constructed by general concepts (Hindess and Hirst, 1975, p. 4). Their 'mode of proof' for the validity of these concepts was entirely axiomatic deductive (p. 18), having no claims to empirical validity. This idea thus takes Lévi-Straussian logico-mathematical structuralism to its extreme by concentrating entirely on constructing a logically coherent set of concepts. They quite wrongly believed that all attempts to see any correspondence between concepts and the social world were forms of empiricism. Their basic epistemological description of scientific discourses is therefore completely relativist; their concepts and their objects were constructed entirely theoretically and could only be evaluated theoretically (p. 3). Therefore they rejected the notion of history as a coherent and worthwhile object of study (p. 321). Their concepts were not applicable to some 'empiricist' idea of the past. But we are left wondering what the point is of constructing concepts at all? Is it just a game, a purely self-gratifying exercise? It seems not, because they concluded their first book by saying that the use of the concepts is for constructing a political practice for intervening in the (entirely theoretically constructed) 'current situation' (pp. 322–3). This is then a form of absoslute idealism; the current situation is constructed within theory and then political practice intervenes in that current situation! 'Reality' is irrelevant. Only the theorist is real.

in turn, he claimed, are also relations of production (1978, pp. 764–5).

In some societies, especially pre-capitalist ones, the superstructure is clearly dominant over the infrastructure. Therefore, as Godelier put it, Marxists have a problem to reconcile this with the idea of the infrastructure being determinant in the last analysis (1978, p. 765). His solution was the functionalist one – the superstructure can be dominant when it *functions* as a relation of production within the infrastructure. This depends upon the idea that a social totality necessarily contains a hierarchy of functions in order for it to exist and carry on reproducing. Thus the economy does not 'select' the level of the totality which is to be dominant at any particular time, as Althusser believed. That dominance comes about because it is functional for the system as a whole (1978, pp. 765–6. See also 1982a, 1982b).

Immanuel Wallerstein has made one of the most notable and impressive recent attempts to construct both a theory and a history of what he has called 'the modern world system'. His achievement ranks with that of Braudel but, unlike Braudel, Wallerstein has argued for the *priority* of theory and of a present-oriented political commitment. Objectivity for Wallerstein is desirable but it is always an 'objectivity' that is relative to present problems of the whole social system and the present distribution of power and knowledge within the system (Wallerstein, 1974, Introduction; 1979, Preface and ch. 9).

In developing his theory and history of the modern world system Wallerstein has drawn heavily on the ideas of Marx but, in a sense, has transcended orthodox Marxism by allying Marx's concept of 'mode of production' to his own concept of 'world system'. He argued that modes of production do not exist as states in a linear development but coexist in the peripheral areas of a world system dominated by capitalist production and exchange in the core areas. That is, the capitalist system is characterised by a necessary unevenness of development and capitalism is the determinant of both the unevenness and the existence of different modes of production with the system. (For a general overview of his theory, see 1979, chs 1 and 9.)

The almost inevitable corollary of his 'relativistic objectivism' and systematism was a type of teleological theory of history, despite his forceful rejection of the evolutionary school of theory. But his teleological argument was not fully developed and it remained in an uneasy association with what we could call his structuratioist theory of history, which centred on the role of class struggle.

In *Historical Capitalism* (1983, pp. 40–3) his (half-hearted) use of teleological functionalism took the following form:

1 The fact is, feudal Europe was going through a severe crisis in the fourteenth and fifteenth centuries that might have resulted in the destruction of the ruling elites, the strengthening of the great

mass of the population, and a much more egalitarian society of small-scale producers.

2 This must have appalled and frightened the upper strata.

3 Without verbalising the intent, the upper strata must have created historical capitalism as the system that served their interests so that by 1650 the same elite was firmly in control again.

Now Wallerstein does not actually spell out this last point in so many words in *Historical Capitalism*, but it is the clear thrust of his argument to assert that capitalism as a new system was a more or less deliberate creation by the controlling strata of the old system to maintain their own power. In an earlier essay (1979, ch. 9) he said that there was in the sixteenth century 'a sort of creative leap of imagination on the part of the ruling strata' which involved 'trying' the market as a mechanism of surplus appropriation in order to restore its real income. This involved geographic expansion, spatial economic specialisation, and the rise of the absolutist state (p. 161). And the bulk of his work shows that he believes that this elite went on maintaining the system against anti-systemic tendencies until the final crisis of the system began in the later twentieth century.

How else could we characterise this argument but as a subjective teleology? The structure of such an argument was summarised and criticised in chapter 8. The fundamental fault with it is that it must be able to demonstrate the continuous *identity* of the class, the *intentionality* of the controlling class, and the *effectivity* of the class, *as a class*, within an integrated systemic situation, or it fails. It is not enough to assert retrospectively that it was in the 'interests' of the class to act in this way. Of course it was. But for history to be *explained* by the rational pursuit of class interests there has to be shown the existence of class solidarity, class consciousness, class power, and a clear concordance between class aims and actual historical outcomes. Otherwise the argument slips into an expedient and *post hoc* holistic reification. In order to explain the origins of capitalism it is not necessary to show that it was the almost inevitable outcome of a subjective systemic mechanism. The distinction between class as an economic taxonomic category and conscious class action is crucial, as Hobsbawm and many other non-structuralist Marxists have fully understood. (See chapter 14.) In fact, when Wallerstein writes social history this distinction is not glossed over so that there is something of an (inevitable?) gap between his sytemic methodology and his actual practice.[9]

---

[9] There is already a large literature on Wallerstein's approach – criticisms as well as applications. The journal *Review* is devoted to doing socio-historical research within his world-system framework. The following works contain critical discussions: Bendix (1984, ch. 1), Bonnell (1980), Brenner (1977), Chirot (1981), Holton (1981), Skocpol (1977).

Wallerstein represents one attemptd way out of the holistic problem that structuralists (and systemic evolutionists) place themselves in. That problem is to account for *change*. Wallerstein's 'solution' is to posit a reified collective agent – a carrier of history (the bourgeoisie) – within the structure. Althusser's and Godelier's 'solution' is to postulate the struc- ture as its own cause. Braudel's 'solution' is a tendency to ignore change in favour of describing continuity and cycles. On the other hand, Ladurie populates his social structures with real agential people – making their history within structural conditions and constraints.

POST-STRUCTURALISM: FOUCAULT'S ARCHAEOLOGY OF DISCOURSES

Another proposed way out of the structuralist problem is represented by Foucault. His early work had elements of a Lévi-Straussian concern with deep structures of thought. In *the Order of Things* (1970) he wrote that his aim was not to write the history of science, which would be to describe the processes and products of the scientific consciousness. Rather, he said, what he aimed to do was reveal a 'positive unconscious' of knowledge by use of an archaeological method (1970, p. xi). But this method was not structuralist and he rejected such a label (see 1970, p. xiv; 1972, p. 15). He was also opposed to the historical causal method and to speculative philosophies of history.

The metaphor of archaeology was not invented by Foucault but goes back to Fèbvre at least, and it was also employed, in a slightly different sense, by Braudel and later by Ladurie under Foucault's influence. What Fèbvre, Foucault, and Ladurie seem to have had in mind is the totalising attempt to reconstruct the intrinsic (even unique) context, structures, meanings, significance, and so on of an epoch, collective mentality, or discourse – independently of *a priori* theories about how that epoch or discourse relates to the past or present. Each discourse is to be seen as self-contained and discontinuous with ones before and since – a 'civiliz- ation' (in the archaeological metaphor) or a totality with its own time, place, unity, relations, and significance. It has to be reconstructed in its own terms.

The first step, then, is to question all preconceptions about the continuities and unities within and between supposedly established discourses and synthetic understandings of them; even such things as the 'book' and the 'oeuvre' are questioned. Once these are suspended a vast 'raw', 'neutral', field consisting of 'the totality of all effective statements (whether spoken or written), in their dispersion as events and in the occurrences that is proper to them' is opened up. The project then becomes to make a '*pure description of discursive events* as the horizon for the search for the unities that form within it' (1972, pp. 26–7).

Archaeology tries to establish the discourse as a set of practices which 'articulate' to particular political practices in 'direct' rather than simply causal ways (1972, p. 163). Therefore it was a question not of how the political practice of a society constituted or modified objects but of how particular objects and practices became articulated to other practices through the hands of particular individuals. The discourse is not the surface projection of deep social structural processes (1972, p. 164). Thus the aim of an archaeological approach is

> to discover the domain of existence and functioning of a discursive practice. In other words, the archaeological description of discourses is deployed in the dimension of a general history; it seeks to discover that whole domain of institutions, economic processes, and social relations on which a discursive formation can be articulated; it tries to show how the autonomy of discourse and its specificity nevertheless do not give it the status of pure ideality and total historical independence; what it wishes to uncover is the particular level in which history can give place to definite types of discourse, which have their own type of historicity, and which are related to a whole set of various historicities. (Foucault, 1972, pp. 164–5)

This project of apparently theoretically neutral 'rewriting' had been previously employed by Foucault to study several discourses and their institutionalisations, such as clinical medicine (*The Birth of the Clinic*, 1976) and psychiatry (*Madness and Civilization*, 1971), and later for criminal punishment (*Discipline and Punish*, 1979a), and sexuality (*The History of Sexuality*, 1979b).

Viewed from the perspective of narrative, descriptive, or structural history this archaeology of discourses and systems of ideas is not history at all (cf. Henretta, 1979, p. 1299; Megill, 1979, pp. 451–503) because it does not concern itself with causes, continuities of processes and structures, or colligations of events. Foucault is concerned not only with discontinuities, with drawing a sharp line between world views or scientific theories and between present and past, but also with articulations rather than causal relations. Discontinuities are marked by revolutionary transformations which change our very way of understanding the universe, society, and humankind. Thus past systems of thought cannot be understood, let alone evaluated, on the basis of present knowledge and understandings. They have to be grasped in their own terms. Discourses are complex *systems* of practices, concepts, ideas, objects, a bit like Platonic forms, which are available for thinking. They are not the products of particular people or embodied in particular events or texts. Here he differs markedly, in both respects, from Kuhn and Feyerabend, who played up the role of powerful individuals and dealt at length with the process of transformation.

Therefore the major related problems with his approach from the point of view of the explanation of social change are his almost total lack of a theory of change, of transition from one discourse or mentality to another; his almost complete rejection of the role of the individual and his creativity of production in discourses; and his subjectivist theory of truth.

Foucault squarely confronted the problem of transformation in chapter 5 of *The Archaeology of Knowledge* – only, in effect, to reject it. He did not reject the idea of discontinuous change; indeed, he sought to map it. Rather, he rejected the idea of succession as an absolute principle of enquiry.

The problem of human agency and subjectivity is bound up with the problem of power. Foucault increasingly came to see discourses – systems of knowledge – as institutionalised power structures, and truth as something not independent of power. However, as with discourses and transformations he refused to develop a general theory of power or the human subject. Rather, he always studied, as he said in one of his last works, the actual modes in which human beings are made 'subjects' in our culture (1982, p. 208). His archaeological proposal for transcending this subjectiity, by somehow bracketing all existing objectivist and causal theories about the past and employing only a theory-neutral approach, is impossible in his own terms, unless he wants to see himself as (heroically) external to his own culture and to all cultures. To say that we are all subject to some form of domination is to say very little unless the possibility of escaping domination exists but escaping into a realm of discourse freedom is impossible. The solution to this problem that I proposed in chapter 7 is applicable here – i.e. to see truth as a *convergence* between coherence conditions and *correspondence* with the world so that there is, in the long run, objective progress.[10]

---

[10] There is also now a large literature on Foucault. The following contain interesting and helpful analyses: Dreyfus and Rabinow (1982), Hacking (1979b), Poster (1982), Sheridan (1980), B. Smart (1982), C. Taylor (1984), Weeks (1982), H. White (1973, 1979).

13

Symbolic Realism

THE INTERPRETIVE ALTERNATIVE

Partly under the influence of the broad phenomenological and hermeneutical tradition in philosophy there has developed an interpretive approach to understanding culture and society. As shown in chapter 6, what tends to unite such writers is a concentration upon interpretive understanding of their chosen objects rather than objective causal explanation of them. And the objects they attempt to understand are not independently existing external entities but systems of symbols and ideas, forms of consciousness, and the social action that grows out of actors' symbolic understandings. The interpretive understanding of understandings (artistic, literary, ideological, religious, scientific commonsense, and so on) is the prime task.

However, there are some sociologists and historians who, while undoubtedly influenced by phenomenology and hermeneutics, have attempted to go beyond them to combine such a methodology with a more realist conception of society. In this way hermeneutics is allied to criticism and structurism in order to transcend the inadequacies of cultural (or ideological) subjective understandings as related to *objectively* existing social structures and power relations. In philosophy, the work of Hesse, Habermas, and Apel epitomises such a conception of the aims of social science. But their work has not yet been very influential on the actual approaches to structural change that I will discuss in this chapter. Among sociologists and social historians, Rom Harré, Clifford Geertz, and Peter Berger have combined these perspectives in various ways and to various degrees and their work will be the main focus of this chapter. Some of the work of Emmanuel Le Roy Ladurie is also relevant here, but he was discussed in the previous chapter. The recent work of

263

these writers together with that of Thomas Luckmann, Paul Ricoeur, and Erving Goffman (see bibliography) can be seen as collectively forming the nucleus of a symbolic tradition of social theory which is constituted by four main strands of thought.

MAIN INFLUENCES ON THE SYMBOLIC-REALIST TRADITION

Phenomenological/symbolic ontology of society

Firstly, and as these comments indicate, there was some influence from the phenomenological/symbolic ontology of society. One of its sources is the symbolic interactionist psychology and sociology of George Herbert Mead, whose *Mind, Self and Society* (1934) is one of the key texts of twentieth-century social thought. He described his approach as behaviourism but a behaviourism that concentrated on the socially formed selfhood of individuals. Individual behaviour for him could only be understood in the context of a whole social group because the acts of individuals are part of larger social acts. The mental processes antecedent to individual action are formed in the context of social interaction and communication, which are in turn dependent upon shared symbolic meanings. Meaning is therefore crucial to the emergence and operation of mind, and meaning is dependent upon the existence of language: 'out of language emerges the field of mind', and out of social interaction emerges language (Mead, 1934, p. 133). It is the sharing of meaning that enables individuals to interact with each other and the natural world, and meanings are embodied in symbols. Thus for Mead all human behaviour is social behaviour – it takes place as a process of symbolically mediated action between an individual self and a social group, or what he called 'the generalised other'. The self and the group are formed together and depend upon the universality of language.[1]

American symbolic interactionism was influenced by and bears a strong similarity to the Germanic phenomenological tradition in philosophy, which has its roots in Kant, and which has also strongly influenced modern hermeneutical philosophy. Phenomenological philosophy is concerned with the frameworks of understanding rather than with some supposedly independent real object of understanding.[2] These traditions – symbolic interactionsim, phenomenology, hermeneutics – are all interested primarily in how individuals come to experience, understand, give meaning to, and symbolise the world. Action, expression, and social reality should always be approached from the point of view of the actor's understandings, according to these theorists.

[1] For discussions of symbolic interactionism, see Blumer (1969), Craib (1984, ch. 5), Fisher and Strauss (1979), Mitchell (1978).

[2] On phenomenological sociology, see Luckmann (1973, 1978, 1982), Schutz (1940, 1945, 1960, 1967).

Symbolic realism

However, some symbolic and phenomenological theorists wish to try to go beyond what they see as the subjectivism of symbolic interactionsim and phenomenological-individualist approaches to explaining social behaviour, in order to try to explain the social structural situations and constraints of individual and collective action and understanding. Therefore the second strand in this tradition is social realism, or more accurately symbolic realism, since their qualified form of realism should be distinguished from those of the thinkers in the other four traditions being discussed in these chapters.[3] Harré, Ladurie, Geertz, and Berger are not 'orthodox' phenomenologists. Social structure, for them, does have a more or less real existence and its history is an important problem for science. Symbolic realism conceives of society as an *umwelt* – a symbolically constructed order of meanings, rules, conventions, and so on, about behaviour, which forms the structrural setting for action, power, morality, and beliefs. But it is forever being reconstructed by persons through their agential powers. This conception can be compared with Durkheim's concept of the 'milieu' (Durkheim, 1938, p. 113) which refers to a powerful 'social fact' that causally structures action. Unlike Durkheim and other structuralists, some symbolic realists, such as Harré, want to bestow this social fact with little power. For them, persons are much more powerful than structures. For others, such as Geertz, cultural structures are more powerful and exist as the macro contexts of individual and collective action.

Hermeneutical theory of knowledge

A necessary corollary of a phenomenological ontology and a symbolic model of action is the hermeneutical theory of knowledge. There is little need to elaborate here what was said in general terms about hermeneutics in chapters 6 and 8 except to recall the essential points of the *circularity* of such understanding, and the claim by its proponents that *all* understanding, including science, necessarily has a central hermeneutical element. The necessity of hermeneutic interpretation for social and cultural explanation has been defended in several different ways, as we saw in chapter 6, and I shall discuss in the following sections some examples of this variability in the work of Harré, Geertz, and Berger.

It is important to bear in mind that for symbolic interactionists and phenomenologists, explanation always begins at the *micro* level of the action, culture, and consciousnss of individuals and small groups. But it does not have to stay at that level. What distinguishes the writers

---

[3] Symbolic realism is defined and discussed by Brown (1978), Brown and Lyman (1978), and Harré (1978).

discussed below is their desire also to explain social change. They have therefore been among the foremost thinkers about the general problem of linking micro and macro explanations from a phenomenological and hermeneutical perspective.

Dramaturgical model

One of the main devices (or analogies) used, to varying degrees and effects, to try to link micro and macro levels is the dramaturgical model of action and social reality. This model is in fact a very old one, having originated with the ancient Greeks. The Renaissance saw further developments of the idea in, for example, the work of Cervantes and English drama: recall Shakespeare's passage in *As You Like It* that begins with 'All the world's a stage . . . .' In recent times the psychologists Freud and Harré, some sociologically minded literary critics such as Kenneth Burke, hermeneutical theorists such as Paul Ricoeur, and sociologists and anthropologists such as Goffman, Berger, and Geertz, have all fruitfully employed this conception.[4]

In the dramaturgical conception the individual is performing a part, for which there is a 'script', and which has the purpose of managing the impression that others have of him. Social action and interaction are thus like a drama and social reality is always something that is constructed within the social-cognitive framework of the 'play' in which actors are performing. As Kenneth Burke has pointed out, the dramaturgical approach is implicit in the word 'act':

> For there to be an act, there must be an agent. Similarly, there must be a scene in which the agent acts. To act in a scene, the agent must employ some means, or agency. And it can be called an act in the full sense of the term only if it involves a purpose. . . . These five terms (act, scene, agent, agency, purpose) have been labelled the dramatistic pentad; the aim of calling attention to them in this way is to show how the functions which they designate operate in the imputing of motives. (K. Burke, 1968, p. 446)

The dramaturgical perspective on action is thus a source model or analogue which can be usefully employed to construct a set of concepts and to begin to uncover mechanisms of action. Goffman has employed this approach primarily for the analysis of action within social establishments, especially closed or total institutions, such as hospitals. He professed to find underlying all social interaction a fundamental dialectic

---

[4] Dramatism is discussed and analysed by Berger (1963, ch. 5), K. Burke (1968, 1973), Harré (1979, ch. 10), Harré and Secord (1972, ch. 10), Lyman and Scott (1975), Mitchell (1978), Strong (1978).

between the individual self and the others in a situation such that each individual self is divided into two parts – a performer and a character. The performance is an attempt to control the impressions that others have of one's character (see Goffman, 1959, pp. 241–7).

The most radical version of the model is the Pirandello one where plays are not just spectacles but predicaments for the audience, who are intimately involved in the situations and conflicts of the actors so that the actor/audience distinction dissolves (see Gellner, 1979a, p. 6).

The major problem encountered by all those in the symbolic-realist tradition, then, is to try to give an account of what they see as the problematic relationship between subjective understandings and the objectivity of society. Harré's solution is to emphasise the structuring power of persons as clever, creative beings; Geertz's is to emphasise the power and necessity of cultural structures to enable persons to navigate their way successfully through the world. But first let us look at the attempt to grapple with this general problem that has been made by Peter Berger and Thomas Luckmann, who have also attempted to show how their solution can help account for social change.

DIALECTICAL INTERACTIONISM

In *The Social Construction of Reality* (1966) Berger and Luckmann attempted to comprehend the dual character of society as subjective meaning and objective facticity and so to answer the question: 'How is it possible that subjective meanings *become* objective facticities?' In other words, they believed that an adequate understanding of the 'reality *sui generis*' of society requires an enquiry into the manner in which this reality is constructed by intentional social actors (p. 30).

For Berger and Luckmann social reality is a human product – the result of *face-to-face subjective interaction* and the externalisation of the power that humans have to *objectify* their expressivity. These products then become *intersubjective*, the enduring indices of the subjective processes of production (p. 49). These products include signs and sign systems, i.e. languages and especially symbolic language. Language 'bridges different zones within the reality of everyday life and integrates them into a meaningful whole.' (p. 54) It enables realities to be transcended, a detachment from the here and now of everyday life, and the accumulation of a social stock of knowledge (pp. 54–6).

Out of this necessary social interaction, which is habitual, grows institutionalisation (p. 70). Institutions are typified, repeated, reciprocal, actions. Once arisen they play a crucial role because they are historical and controlling of action. Society as a set of institutions confronts the individual as a given objective reality and each person is socialised into perceiving it as a social fact, whether he or she reflectively thinks about it or not. But Berger and Luckmann rightly remind us that in spite of its appearance we should always remember that society is a human product. Humanity and society are in a dialectical relationship. In fact, the heart of their account is the idea of social reality as consisting of three moments of a dialectical process: '*Society is a human product. Society is an objective reality. Man is a social product.*' (p. 79) Furthermore the process is inherently historical because only with the transmission of the social world to a new generation is it fulfilled. And it can only be transmitted through socialisation and legitimation.

If society is the product of action over time, action which is motivated by a structure of thought or by what they called a 'symbolic universe', which in turn serves to legitimise society as an objective structure, then the process of emergence and crystallisation of a symbolic universe is crucial for the history of society. The possibility of structural change arises, then, basically as a result of the failure of a symbolic universe to be externalised or reproduced fully. And this implies a failure of the universe to be maintained fully. Moreover, Berger and Luckmann were adamant that all symbolic universes change as a result of human action. While reality is socially defined, definitions of it are embodied in concrete individuals and groups who do the defining. There is, therefore, always the possibility of conflict between rival groups of definers (pp. 134–7). Hence,

> definitions of reality have self-fulfilling potency. Theories can be realised in history . . . . Consequently, social change must always be understood as standing in a dialectical relationship to the 'history of ideas'. Both 'idealistic' and 'materialistic' understandings of the relationship overlook this dialectic, and thus distort history. The same dialectic prevails in the overall transformations of symbolic universes that we have had occasion to look at. What remains sociologically essential is the recognition that all symbolic universes and all legitimations are human products; their existence has its base in the lives of concrete individuals, and has no empirical status apart from these lives. (Berger and Luckmann, 1966, pp. 145–6)[5]

ETHOGENIC DRAMATISM

Rom Harré (and various collaborators) has attempted to construct a general approach to explaining social action and social change on the basis of an ethogenic-realist social psychology. The real mechanisms of

---

[5] Peter Berger (and various colleagues) has extended the dialectical interactionist approach to the study of the role of culture in the modernisation process and in modern society generally. See the essays in Berger (1977), and the books by Berger, Berger and Kellner (1973), and Berger and Kellner (1981).

action he takes to be the *meanings* that actors give to their social situations. The discovery of these meanings – ethogeny – involves ascertaining actors' accounts of why actions are performed and analysing them for the social rules that underlie them (Harré and Secord, 1972, pp. 9–10). This is obviously based upon a presumed close relationship between actors' self-understandings and social rules. For Harré, the causes of action are therefore found not in the social situation but in *people*. His starting place, then, is not social action, or social structures, or biological drives, but the real powers and propensities of *individual persons* (Harré, 1979, p. 140) and persons conceived of in a special way.

His model of the person is the Renaissance *architectonic* image, according to which

> the unrestricted and unreformed activity of men is to conceive and try to realise a variety of structural forms, a variety controlled only by the demands of mathematical harmony and order.... The imagination is central to human functioning, since it is there that we generate icons, sensual representations of structures which we try to realise in the public world.... The creation and maintenance and reinvention from time to time of the social order is ... just such a process, the realisation in public and collective form of privately conceived and individually registered representations of structures.
> (Harré, 1979, pp. 5–6; see also 1978)

Architectonic man is therefore a true social *agent*. The root ideas of the concept of agency Harré took to be 'autonomy' and 'reflexivity'. The existence of human autonomy is dependent upon the conditions of (1) being able to represent to oneself a wider range of possible futures than can be realised; and (2) after a decision has been made, being able to realise a choice or goal from among the feasible ones or being able to abort an action process aimed at realising a choice or goal. Reflexivity implies a hierarchy of rational principles for making choices (1979, pp. 246–7). The crucial point is that agents can make 'shifts of hegemony', i.e. they can be detached from their immediate environment and from the principles under which they have been acting hitherto and move to new situations and new principles. Human actions are not the result of simple linear causes but spring from the complex hierarchic and systemic structure of principles of the mind which are allied to physiological mechanisms and conditions of possibility (1979, pp. 245–7).

Two further associated sets of concepts underpin Harré's social psychological approach. Firstly, there is the practical/expressive dichotomy which distinguishes between (1) activities directed towards material and biological ends (theorised mainly by Marx) and (2) those directed towards the presentation of self as a rational and respectable person and the expression of opinions (theorised mainly by Veblen) (1979, p. 19). Secondly, this distinction is in turn based on the idea that the ritual marking and earning of respect and contempt are the basic activities towards which the expressive level of social life is directed. Respect and contempt are reciprocal social relations which have become largely ritualised in all societies but the forms they have vary enormously (1979, pp. 24–5). Harré conceives of social structure in a combination of phenomenological and realist terms. Architectonic humans structure the world according to their thought forms (or icons or templates), and in turn the way in which the world has been structured srongly influences thought and action. But the more important question for us is: how does the ethogenic theory and methodology approach the explanation of large-scale *macro-social* entities such as nations, economies, social classes, social movements, and so on? For the ethogenist, the reality of such entities is in doubt because ethogenics relies upon a negotiation between socially constitutive common-sense understandings and an ethnographic theory. Hence

> the folk neither have, nor could have, beliefs about the *conduct* which would be constitutive of macro-collectives of any scale, since it is a central doctrine of the macro-collective approach that there be ramifying systems of unintended consequences, and that it is those that, as systems, are constitutive of the non-taxonomic aspects of a large-scale collective. So any route from people's declared norms of interpretation, maxims and so on is blocked by this consideration. (Harré, 1981, p. 153)

But obviously macro-social concepts are constantly employed in both common sense and social science. According to Harré, their status is primarily conceptual and rhetorical rather than ontological. The role of concepts like 'France', 'working class', or 'economic depression' is as a device for making points, taking a stand, expressing deference and contempt, and so on, i.e. they are part of the expressive order (1981, p. 150). But interestingly, Harré argued that though it may be impossible in principle to have true empirical knowledge about macro-social entities there is still an important place for hypotheses about them providing that an important distinction is made between the agential focused *power* of persons and the diffuse causal *influence* of macro structures. Macro structures provide necessary but not sufficient conditions or opportunities for the exercise of personal structuring power (1981, pp. 156–8).

If only persons have power and structures provide the influences on and opportunities for the exercise of their power, we must look to micro-sociology and personality for the mutational sources of change and to structures for the selection conditions of those mutations.[6] That is,

---

[6] For other discussions of the micro-symbolic approach to explaining social structure, see the articles in Knorr-Cetina and Cicourel (1981), especially those of Cicourel, Collins, and Callon and Latour.

mutations occur in micro-social practices and these spread or fail to spread through the society by virtue of some diffuse influence exerted by the macro-social order, whatever that might be. We can admit some measure of Lamarckism in the relation between selection environment and mutant practice, mediated by growing but imperfect social knowledge, without being tempted into any extravagant claims about social causation. The Lamarckian relationships are likely to change, becoming stronger as more anthropological and historical knowledge becomes part of the culture. (Harré, 1981, p. 158)

Harré's theory is therefore an evolutionary one, but not a teleological one. It hinges on a tension between the practical and the expressive orders. These orders, being only analytically distinct, can, if in disequilibrium, generate a psychological tension within an individual or group which prompts a motivation to act in some new way in order to resolve the tension. But whether and how this mutant form of action survives and affects the structure is a problem of environmental selection and of how that environment itself is changed by the mutation. Therefore the theory incorporates Darwinian and Lamarckian mechanisms.

In the Darwinian scheme mutation and selection conditions are causally independent. In the Lamarckian scheme they are interdependent. This means that social innovations either can be random production of new rules, habits, practices, and customs or can come about by deliberate design. Moreover, in literate, record-keeping societies, there is a collective memory of past innovations and their fates so that in these societies change becomes increasingly Lamarckian. Studies of anthropology, psychology, sociology, and history have powerful social effects because they provide material for the imagining of new social practices and information about the conditions for the propagating of these practices (Harré, 1979, pp. 364–7).

However, Harré was opposed to a completely Lamarckian theory. There must be a Darwinian element. For there to be a Darwinian theory of social change there needs to be an analogue of genes which are the mechanisms of replication or innovations between generations of organisms. Harré proposed that the analogue is given by the rules governing social practices. When rules are not passed on in unchanged ways then mutations arise leading to the possibility of new practices, depending upon the selection conditions (1979, pp. 370–3; see also 1980c).

The difference between Harré's evolutionary theory and that of Parsons is very important. For Parsons, society is seen as a cybernetically regulated system with an objective teleological structure. It has a powerful tendency to maintain itself in equilibrium in order to satisfy its own needs. That is, the analogue is an organic one and the theory is derived from organic biology. For Harré, macro society is a demographic

structure of relatively independent elements which serves as the population in which mutations either spread or do not spread according to a
combination of the external and internal relations among the elements.
That is, there have to be mechanisms of replication and selection and
these can vary a good deal. Small groups are the units of the population
and the source of mutations. Here the analogue is with population
biology.

The problem, then, with Harré's approach to structural change is his
conceptualisation of macro structure as being taxonomic and the corresponding overestimation of the power of persons as individuals. While
undoubtedly a few individuals are the powerful architectonic creators
that he models – i.e. cultural heroes – they are exceptional. Most people
find themselves as role players in already existing and fairly rigidly
established plays, the scripts of which are largely beyond their control to
alter when acting as individuals. That is, their thought is dominated by
ideologies, cultures – 'discourses' in Foucault's terminology.

CULTURAL REALISM

Attempting carefully to steer a course between cultural creation and
cultural domination has been Clifford Geertz. Drawing upon and
transcending the influences mentioned in the first section of this chapter,
Geertz has developed a distinctive cultural hermeneutics which views
culture and society both as a 'text' or 'drama' to be deciphered,
described, and interpreted for its meaning as an artefact, and as a real
structure of action which is formed by symbol systems. Therefore for him
culture is not just a symbol system, existing in the mind. It is a shared
structure of events and practices – a public 'acted document' that has
significance and meaning (Geertz, 1975, p. 10). Consciousness, culture,
action, and society are inextricably bound together. Any understanding
of them has to be a 'thick' one. The idea of 'thick description' was
developed by Gilbert Ryle and given a central place by Geertz. To give a
thick description is to place an event, artefact, or text in its particular
micro local web of meaning as understood, as far as possible, from the
point of view of the actor or culture that produced it – i.e. to give a
complete, semiotic description. This is tantamount to saying that thick
description is hermeneutic understanding.

But Geertz was very aware of the fundamental problem of such an
approach – its relativistic, untestable, self-validating nature. His criticism
of its failings is all the more telling because of his affinity with it.

The besetting sin of interpretive approaches to anything – literature, dreams, symptoms, culture – is that they tend to resist, or to
be permitted to resist, conceptual articulation and thus to escape
systematic modes of assessment. You either grasp an interpretation

or you do not, see the point of it or you do not, accept it or you do not. Imprisoned in the immediacy of its own detail, it is presented as self-validating, or, worse, as validated by the supposedly developed sensitivities of the person who presents it; any attempt to cast what it says in terms other than its own is regarded as a travesty – as the anthropologist's severest term of moral abuse, ethnocentric. (Geertz, 1975, p. 24)

To avoid these failings interpretation has to be grounded in theory, i.e. general concepts, models, hypotheses, and methodologies about social reality. But clearly interpretive theories are very difficult to construct, as Geertz knew, and they must remain vague and essentially contested.

The core of his approach to cultural and social explanation, therefore, is his concentration on the socially determining role of human *thought*, or, more particularly, on a conception of *humans as symbol users and rule followers – cultural beings*, with a particular consciousness of the world through which they discover and structure the world. It is culture in general which sets the context for and gives meaning to social action. The various cultural systems all play the role, he believed (in a manner somewhat similar to Karl Popper and Talcott Parsons) of mental maps of the world, enabling us to find our way about. Moreover, because humans are the agents of their own realisation, in Geertz's view, they construct as symbolic models the particular capacities that characterise themselves. They complete themselves through these constructions of cultures, ideologics, symbol systems in general, which in turn act as feedback controls over their behaviour. And these systems are most crucial where other kinds of institutionalised guides and information are lacking: 'It is in country unfamiliar emotionally or topographically that one needs poems and road maps.' (1975, p. 218) Therefore the interpretation of actual instances of human culture must be his starting place. This is required for any attempt to move from the symbolic systems and cultural maps of individuals and groups to explaining social action and the history of economic, social, and political structures. This is a kind of sociology of knowledge in reverse. But how are we in fact to get from micro individual consciousness to understanding and explaining macro culture and then explaining social structure? What is the role of general theory in his approach? Must we be restricted to building only an *aggregate* understanding through interpretation of forms of local knowledge? And does social structure have an existence independent of cultural understandings of it?

The best way to appreciate the relevance to social historians of his approach is to see how he actually proceeds in describing and explaining particular cases because his work lacks extended theoretical articulations.[7] In the 1950s and early 1960s, under the influence of his training

---

[7] Geertz's work and its significance for historians is analysed by Henretta (1979), Rabinow (1983), Roseberry (1982), Walters (1980).

in the Harvard Department of Social Relations (which included Talcott Parsons) he employed in sociological analyses a more 'orthodox' macro-systemic approach, including the concepts of functionalism and ecologism, which were then prevalent in sociology. But at the same time he was developing his micro interpretive ethnographic approach to cultural analyses. While the former concepts never disappeared entirely from his work they have become overshadowed by his anthropological perspective. However, he has also retained a strong interest in explaining macro social and economic history and to do so has attempted to marry the two approaches – macro socio-economic and micro anthropological. It is in these attempts that the chief interest and value of his work to social historians lies.

He first attempted to combine the two approaches in his books on Indonesia of the mid 1960s: *Pedlars and Princes: Social Change and Economic Modernisation in Two Indonesian Towns* (1963b) and *The Social History of an Indonesian Town* (1965). The former contained an examination of both the micro cultural/ideological milieu of individuals and groups at a village level and the macro changes in employment, investment, production, transport, and so on, which formed the economic context for their activities. His belief was that only when such analyses were brought together would economic growth be effectively explained. The result in the book was a set of conclusions regarding the social and cultural conditions for the emergence of capitalist entrepreneurs and the sorts of activities and scale of operations they were likely to engage in according to their differing cultural backgrounds.

The second book is especially important as an exemplification of the importance to the methodology of social history of Geertz's two-pronged approach. In analysing social history it was his intention, he said, in a manner very similar to the Annales historians,

> to present a picture of the interaction of ecological, economic, social-structural, and cultural factors over a reasonably extended period of time and to come to some conclusions as to the relative importance of these factors in shaping human life. It is a history not of particular men and specific occurrences but of the changing forms of a particular sort of human community. It represents an attempt not so much to recreate the past as to discover its sociological character. As such, it is not a story and so need have neither moral nor plot. It is a theoretically controlled analysis of certain processes of social change and contains instead an argument. (Geertz, 1965, p. 2)

The theory that controlled this social history, thus conceived, of an Indonesian town had two aspects:

(1) that ordered social change involves the attainment by the members of the population concerned of novel conceptions of the sorts of individuals and the sorts of groups (and the nature of the relations among such individuals and groups) that comprise their immediate social world; and (2) that such an attainment of conceptual form depends in turn upon the emergence of institutions through whose very operation the necessary categorizations and judgements can be developed and stabilized. [This] ... comes down to an investigation of the reciprocal interplay between the evolving forms of human association (social structures) and the no less changing vehicles of human thought (cultural symbols). (Geertz, 1965, p. 5)

In order to carry out this social analysis, structure is analysed from the point of view of the natives' cultural understanding of their own society. A model of the society is constructed which approximates to that of the inhabitants, which in turn takes the form of a symbolic structure – i.e. 'a system of public ideas and attitudes embodied in words, things, and conventional behaviour' (p. 8). Social action is then understood by both native and sociologist in terms of this symbolic structure. At that point, a *circle* of understanding, which begins and ends with the symbolically mediated ideology of the group or society, is established, at least ideally.

An illuminating way to show how common sense, culture, and social structure are linked is through the dramaturgical analogy, of which Geertz has made particularly striking use. Furthermore, he has shown very vividly that drama is not always just an anthropological or sociological concept – a way of ordering social practices by an observer – but that social life *is* a drama in a real sense and, sometimes, directly perceived as such by ordinary actors not theoretically tutored. This is similar to Harré's point that in some societies, such as Renaissance Europe, where the expressive order dominates the practical, social dramas are the real structures of social interaction and are perceived as such by the actors. Geertz has shown how the Balinese social custom of cock-fighting is a real-life drama:

What sets the cockfight apart from the ordinary course of life, lifts it from the realm of the everyday practical affairs, and surrounds it with an aura of enlarged importance is not, as functionalist sociology would have it, that it reinforces status discriminations (such reinforcement is hardly necessary in a society where every act proclaims them), but that it provides a metasocial commentary upon the whole matter of assorting human beings into fixed hierarchical ranks and then organizing the major part of collective existence around that assortment. Its function, if you want to call it that, is interpretive: it is a Balinese reading of Balinese experience, a story they tell themselves about themselves. (Geertz, 1972, pp. 217–18)

The cock-fight for Geertz is a kind of text which contains a metaphorically expressed education into certain universals of human nature and social relations in the way that *Macbeth* and *David Copperfield* also do. Texts, works of art, complex cultural expressions in general, act as a focus for everyday experiences by being 'paradigmatic events' – they enable us to see a dimension of our own subjectivity.

The dramaturgical analogy was the fundamental methodological concept of what is probably his most important book – *Negara: the Theatre State in Nineteenth Century Bali* (1980). This is a work of total history that ranks with Ladurie's *Carnival in Romans* for comprehensiveness. Geertz studied the history of Balinese states on two levels: that of major events and that of socio-cultural processes. The first sees history as a series of clusters of events and bounded periods, while the second sees it as a structurally continuous process of development. Time is crucial to both: 'In the first it is the thread along which specific happenings are strung; in the second it is a medium through which certain abstract processes move.' (1980, p. 5) To interpret socio-cultural history there has to be, he said, a 'conceptually precise and empirically based model' of the process. This was constructed from three sources: by generalising from existing knowledge of comparable processes elsewhere in the world, existing Weberian ideal-type concepts about historical sociology, and ethnographic data about a current (or recent) case which is taken to have a resemblance to the past object of enquiry (p. 6).

The second kind of model that he constructed and employed was a conceptual one rather than a historical one – i.e. a model of the negara as a distinct political order – which could be applied experimentally to other empirical data about similar state forms in the South-East Asian area. This model is a sort of 'sociological blueprint' for the 'construction of representations' of similar institutions (pp. 9–10).

The third model employed was that of the state as a drama and, more particularly, the version of this known as the doctrine of the exemplary centre (developed by Weber and Shils) in which the court and capital is seen as an ideal material embodiment or paragon of the political order so that it 'shapes the world around it into at least a rough approximation of its own excellence' (p. 13). Exemplary centres played an analogous role in many pre-modern societies and, as Geertz has argued, in modern societies as well (see Geertz, 1977).

THE PROBLEM OF SOCIAL REALITY

The discussion in this chapter shows, I believe, that the relationship of subjective understandings, human agency, and objective social reality is a complex and perplexing one. If humans are seen as truly agential then the social world is seen as their product and dependent in some way upon their actions and understandings. But it is easy to go too far in the direction of agency, as I believe Harré and many other microsociologists have done, because it carries the possibility of the necessary rejection of the independent reality of society; then the only option left is a methodological individualism on the basis of phenomenology. How to save both methodological *structurism* and *agency* is the problem. Clifford Geertz's more developed concept of culture *as* action is one fruitful way. For him a structure of action *is* a structure of thought – a constellation of enshrined ideas. Thought (or culture) and patterns of action are inseparable. Moreover, as he said, it should be unnecessary to say that such an assertion contains no committment to idealism. This is because ideas

> are not, and have not been for some time, unobservable mental stuff. They are envehicled meanings, the vehicles being symbols (or in some usages, signs), a symbol being anything that denotes, describes, represents, exemplifies, labels, indicates, evokes, depicts, expresses – anything that somehow or other signifies. And anything that somehow or other signifies is intersubjective, thus public, thus accessible to overt and corrigible *plein air* explication. Arguments, melodies, formulas, maps, and pictures are not idealities to be stared at but texts to be read; so are rituals, palaces, technologies, and social formations. (Geertz, 1980, p. 135)

Geertz's work shows how the sort of dialectical understanding of the interrelationship of action to cultural consciousnes that Berger and Luckmann advocate can be fruitfully employed to analyse the history of objective structures. The history of society must always be seen as the outcome of human structuring power but power that is always socio-culturally conditioned and mediated, often in the form of meaningful dramas. The task is to study the history of social and cultural structures *as structures*.

Therefore, social science must wage, as Geertz wrote in *Islam Observed*, a 'struggle for the real' (Geertz, 1968, ch. 4). This struggle is waged, first of all, by every individual person within their daily lives, and secondly by the social scientist. The latter, wishing to describe and analyse the ways in which different individuals and cultures come to their own conclusions, is faced with the second-order problem of the reality of the world itself (and hence of the validity of culturally determined understandings), and then the third-order problem of the validity of his understanding of their understandings.

Geertz rightly holds that all systems of culture – religion, art, history, philosophy, science – are attempts to go beyond common-sense understandings of the world because common sense is felt to be inadequate in some way. There is a movement to break with the 'incrustation' of common sense, and there is also an attempt to correct it in the light of what has been learned by transcending it. Common sense is refashioned through culture and the two have a dialectical relationship. We have to live in both worlds – the common-sense daily world with its felt imperfections, and the cultural world through which we try to understand and overcome imperfections (Geertz, 1968, pp. 94–5).

The greatest significance of Geertz's work for social historians lies not so much in his methodological pronouncements or use of models and theories, although they are always interesting and often illuminating, but in his *example*. Like Ladurie, he does social history in such a richly intelligent, albeit eclectic, manner that it prompts immediate admiration. But to try to abstract and generalise his approach is certainly worthwhile because it can be an aid to the improvement of all our work.

14

Relational Structurism

The fundamental problem of many approaches in the symbolic-realist tradition is their lack of a well-developed conceptualisation of macro social structure. This lack springs from their ambivalence about its real existence. On the other hand, each of them does have a well-developed concept of the personality/consciousness/culture/social action interrelationship (or complex of dialectic moments) at the micro-social level. At the heart of each of their approaches is a concept of human persons as the agents of their social world, but the nature of the social world lacks a clear specification because of their phenomenological concept of 'reality'. The writers in the systemic-evolutionary and structuralist traditions, on the other hand, have no ambivalence about the existence of macro structure. But, as we have seen, they go too far in the holistic and objectivist direction so that humans become the determined fungibles of powerful systemic mechanisms.

The individualists, reacting against systemic determinacy, postulate persons as freely moving monads, creating fleeting social situations and networks as they go but not structuring the social or geographical world in any permanent sense. Such humans, in fact, are not social agents at all but only psychologically determined individual actors. Society does not exist in a real sense for these theorists. There are only patterns of behaviour. But, as we have also seen, their concept of human rationality is too narrow and they cannot fully account for action without saying much more than they do about the structural context of action and the unobservable intentions of actors.

It remains, then, to discuss the tradition which, I believe, can overcome the inadequacies of the others by giving a full and explicit place to *all* the

279

real moments of the interacting, structuring, and changing world of society: i.e. personality, consciousness, action, culture, macro social structure, and social change. Furthermore, these theorists are very aware of the necessity for explicit models and theories in order to make explanations of structural change because much of the intentionality of actors and their real structural situations are unobservable.

COMPONENTS OF THE RELATIONAL-STRUCTURIST TRADITION

The relational-structurist tradition is the most diffuse of all the five I have examined in these chapters. Indeed, some of the writers that I shall examine may not, at first glance, appear to belong to the same category as some of the others, and the existing quasi-institutionalised arrangement of 'schools' of theory may not appear to be the same as I have identified here. But I want to argue using the criteria (identified in chapter 9) of model of social structure, mode of explanation, and general theory of social change, that all these writers share three basic similarities. They are all ontological realists about structuree; structurists about methodology; and agentialists about the explanation of change. But these criteria allow for many differences of emphasis in their general theories and many differences of detail in their concrete historical explanations.

By far the most important influences on the members of this tradition are Marx and Weber. Their explicit influences are felt constantly and their work is constantly invoked or criticised by these contemporary writers. But of course the significant differences between Marx and Weber are one of the main causes for the differences among the currents in this tradition, just as their very important similarities are also influential. And there are significant differences among self-styled Marxists and Weberians as well.

Realist-relational concept

Perhaps the most basic component of this tradition is its realist-relational conception of social structure, which is viewed as being *relatively autonomous* of individual actions and understandings but not of the structuring agency of collective action. The systemic-evolutionary and structuralist traditions are also realists of different sorts but only the present tradition adopts a conception of macro structure that employs a truly *structurist* conception of social relations. (See the discussion of such relations in chapter 8). The other two strongly realist traditions are holistic in that they see social relations as more or less wholly internal such that the individuals within them have their being only within those objective relations. The relational structurists retain an important element of externality in their specification of social relations so that human individuality in the senses of selfhood, freedom, and agency is therefore retained. Individuals can move in and out of some social relations without jeopardising their very existence every time they do so. However, there are important differences, especially between Weberians and Marxists, as to the degree of autonomy of structures from action and understanding and therefore of the objectivity of knowledge about structures.

Social-levels model

The second component that is shared by all those in this tradition is a social-levels model of society: an infrastructure/superstructure/consciousness model or something similar. This model is also employed by structuralists, mainly under Marx's influence. Some thinkers in the symbolic-realist conception also have a superficially similar model, such as Harré's practical/expressive dichotomy, but in their cases these are not really 'levels' but 'moments' in a dialectical relationship. The idea of 'levels' implies a causal or at least explanatory relationship between the (relatively autonomous?) levels. The specification of the levels, their degree of abstraction, and their interrelationship are all serious problems.

The social-levels model contrasts with the systemic-functionalist model which divides society into integrated functional subsystems, all of which play a vital role in maintaining the system in equilibrium. It also contrasts with the individualist model which sees society simply as institutionalised patterns of behaviour which are the context of individual behaviour.

Human agency

The third component is the place given to human agency, rationality, and praxis, and their close interrelationship. A model of the person is adopted that sees him or her as characterised by self-activating powers of intentionality, rationality, reflexivity, and freedom of choice. These are real capacities which may not be constantly activated or present in every action – i.e. they are not determining traits or fixed dispositions. Action is partly motivated and structured by the actor's experience of the world and knowledge of it, and particularly by the actor's perception of his or her interests, whether personal, institutional, or class interests. Action is therefore also structured by the social context. Hence agency is never completely free but always constrained and enabled by its structural and ideological situation and the experience of the actor. As both Marx and Weber saw: it is people who make history but always in particular enabling and disabling conditions. In this way a general solution to the micro/macro problem is posed.

Social classes

The importance given to the concept and role of social classes is the fourth central component of the tradition. Ontologically, class is conceived as one of the main components of social structure in the sense of being (perhaps at different times) a set of both external and internal relations. That is, class is taken to be at various times both a merely taxonomic category and a causally conditioning social relation. Theoretically, class as a social relation plays an important role in causal theories of ideology, social action, rationality, and social change, and in histories of society. (This is the case not just in Marxism, where it is obviously central, but in Weberian theories as well.) Class interests, class consciousness, and class action are seen by all the theorists as important manifestations of and contributing causes of structural change.

Ideology and critique

The fifth component is the importance given to the role of ideology and critique in society, action, and change. The concept of ideology is a problematic one and is taken to include many things. At the very least it has two related but distinct meanings: (1) system of ideas (including culture), and (2) false consciousness. We saw in previous chapters the central place given to systems of ideas by the functionalists, Annales historians, and the symbolic-realist theorists. For the Parsonian functionalists, culture is dominant in the cybernetic hierarchy of subsystems of society, and the modernisation theorists argued, under the influence of Weber and Parsons, for the priority of culture in the modernisation process. Some Annales historians believe that mentalities played an important role in history as relatively autonomous levels. For the symbolic-realist theorists, action, social interaction, and social structure are patterned and structured according to systems of ideas which serve as the motivations for, templates of, and legitimations of social behaviour and institutions. Society is constituted through and made meaningful by symbol systems. The relational structurists also usually accord an important place to ideas in forming the social world but, furthermore, and unlike all the others, they also wish to develop a critique of ideas for their adequacy as understandings and explanations of relatively objective social reality. They want to draw a distinction between social structures and symbolic universes such that the relationships between them are not necessarily one of correspondence or simple resemblance. Indeed, their relationship is fundamentally problematical. In short, systems of ideas, in so far as they are about society, can be false and hence misleading.

The idea of a perfect dialectical symmetry between ideas, action, and society, which tends to pervade the work of some symbolic theorists, is rejected by the relational structurists. Each of these moments can be seriously out of phase, leading to social conflict, a failure of social reproduction, and ultimately to social disintegration and transformation. So, ideology must be studied for its social effects and criticised for those effects as well as for its conceptual and explanatory adequacy. (This in turn raises the problem of the role of science *vis-à-vis* other forms of social knowledge.)

Unintended consequences

The previous point leads into the sixth component – the significance of unintended consequences of action and unrealised results of intentions for social structure and social change. If there are significant gaps between unconscious psychological propensities, conscious understandings, rational motivations, and individual action, then the possibility, in fact necessity, of unintended and unrealised structural and social behavioural consequences arises. This problem cannot be adequately dealt with by approaches that see understandings, motivations, actions, and structures as being in mutually reinforcing (dialectical, behaviourist, or functional) relationships.

Society as historical structure

Finally, we come to the seventh, and in some ways most fundamental, aspect of the tradition – the idea that all society is inherently changing and is therefore historical. The writers in this tradition conceive of society as a historical structure in a way that many of the writers in other traditions do not. The *structurist* idea is essentially the idea of *structural production, reproduction, and change* because it refers to the process of continual *structuring* of the social world by agential actors. The idea of structuration comes ultimately from Marx and it was very influential in the work of Weber and Piaget. Versions of it were adopted by those in the symbolic-realist tradition (notably Harré and Geertz) and some of those in the structuralist tradition (notably Ladurie) but only the relational structurists give it its rightful place because only they have as central all the ideas of consciousness, agency, action, macro structure, and structural history. According to the structurist tradition, the three moments of historical experience and the historical process are:

1 Given circumstances, which are enabling and disabling of action
2 Conscious action that is historically significant
3 The intended and unintended consequences of action, which turn into objective and seemingly unalterable conditions of action and thought.

These conditions are taken, by most structurists, to be the various *levels* of structure. Indeed, so important have the base/superstructure/ideology and analogous models or metaphors become that virtually all macrosociologists now have to take a stand regarding their usefulness. Certainly all the writers discussed below do. In fact, there have been heated debates among Marxists, in particular, about their meaning and usefulness.

Outside the Marxist debate, as critical bystanders, have been the Weberians who, while professing allegiance to a more vaguely defined levels model, have on the whole not been historical materialists. In fact they have usually accorded the primary causal role in history to culture in one form or another. And in recent years some writers from the systemic-functionalist tradition, strongly influenced by Weber, have argued for a synthesis between their approach and Marxism. Also standing outside but close to the debate are Norbert Elias, Anthony Giddens, and Alain Touraine. They have recently offered synthetic attempts to transcend the debate while retaining some commitment to the levels model.

There are, then, four identifiable streams of theorising within this broad relational-structurist tradition: Marxist and Weberian (which are the main ones); Elias's figurationism; and structurationism, which includes Giddens and Touraine.

MARXIST APPROACHES TO HISTORICAL STRUCTURAL CHANGE

Marxism is not the only form of historical materialism.[1] Indeed, historical materialism predates Marx by a century because the Scottish historical sociologists of the late eighteenth century, notably Adam Smith, Adam Ferguson, and John Millar, had an underdeveloped technological materialist approach to the stages of history and they were a strong influence on Marx. The German historical school of economists such as Roscher, Knies, and Hildebrand, who were contemporaneous with Marx, and later Schmöller and Sombart, also had a version of socio-economic materialism. Max Weber was influenced by them and Marx when he wrote his sociological materialist works on the history of capitalism. The British radical labour historians of the late nineteenth and early twentieth centuries, such as the Hammonds, the Webbs, and Tawney, were vaguely historical materialists in their outlook but not much influenced by Marxism. Similarly, the early British economic historians of the late nineteenth century, such as Toynbee, Ashley, Rogers, Cunningham, and Hobson, were also making a radical proposal to study the history of society from the bottom up, as it were, and so

---

[1] On the history of historical materialism, see Anderson (1976), E. Seligman (1907), Weber (1903–6).

reactivating the old Scottish materialist tradition in a new form. We saw in chapter 12 that the Annales School (notably Fèbvre, Bloch, and Braudel) are historical materialists of a geopolitical as well as quasi-Weberian kind, and that Lévi-Strauss believed he had located his structural enquiries into cultures on the superstructure of Marx's infrastructure. And in anthropology there is now a developing ecological (sometimes called cultural) materialist approach to explanation, epitomised by Sahlins, Goody, and Harris.

All forms of historical materialism share two fundamental premises:

1 They see long-term history as a progressive development of human mastery of nature and, hence, material productivity, and a corresponding development of the scale and complexity of social organisation and culture.
2 They locate the basic force for social development within the material level of society.

But how they define 'material', how the material level causes history, and what the relationship is between the historical materialist model and historical evidence are not at all agreed. Vulgar historical materialism, which has virtually no adherents today, postulates a simple mechanical model in which the superstructure of politics and ideology is a reflection of the technological/economic base, but all other forms of materialism postulate some causal feedback relationships and quite often tacitly posit a functionalist explanatory relationship between the levels of a social totality (see the next section).

The structuralist Marxist approach, which was discussed in chapter 12, tries to marry Marxism with the structuralist concepts of causation and science. It therefore concentrates on establishing an *a priori* nomological-deductive system of concepts of modes of production, social totalities, and world systems, from which can be derived the correct concepts of particular societies and their supposedly necessary laws of change. That approach therefore offers what is in effect an ahistorical foundation for explanations, although in practice some structuralists have not always followed such precepts, as of course they are unable to do if wishing actually to explain history.

The approaches discussed here do history in an empirical and comparative mode, refusing to write purely theoretical histories, retaining a place for the relative autonomy of empirical evidence and the variability of historical experience. Moreover, unlike the structuralists who see the fundamental force for change originating somehow in the structure itself, these empirical historians retain a central place for the structring and transforming power of individual and collective conscious action, which often leads to unintended consequences. Moreover, Marxist social history at its best tries to be a *totalising* study of society and in a manner superior to the Braudelian structuralist kind, partly because it does retain a central place for structuring individual and collective action and partly because it has a general theoretical orientation that guides (but does not determine) the analyses of the interrelationship of all the moments and levels of the social totality.

Eric Hobsbawm is perhaps the best known and most wide ranging of Marxist historians. He has done a good deal to try to articulate what he sees as the methodological basis of Marxist history, and the very large corpus of his work exemplifies what a totalising Marxist approach to the history of society can achieve. (See the quotation in my five themes for a summary of his totalising view of the task of social history.) For him, Marxist history and social history should be seen as synonymous because it is Marxism that provides the best foundation for a history of society. In a series of important articles,[2] he has delineated the framework for a science of history, a science which should be the foundation for all social science.[3] He wrote (in 1981a) that history as a discipline is concerned with 'very complex forms of social change, interaction and synthesis'. In order to achieve this,

> History requires both general theories and, for analytical purposes, techniques analogous to experimental isolation, such as the systematic comparison of cases and certain statistical phenomena, such as the transition from pre-capitalist to capitalist societies or the tendencies of development of capitalism, it must also and primarily operate at less general levels of theory. As Marx knew, it is not enough to formulate the mechanism of human social evolution in its most general form, man's increasing capacity to control his natural environment by means of the social process of labour (the combined material forces and social relations of production), but these must also be analysed and specified for particular stages of development, societies and situations. Moreover, there are considerable limits to the possibility of isolating phenomena for the purpose of analysis. History might almost be defined as the discipline which deals with things which are never equal and cannot be supposed to be equal. Furthermore, it requires not merely mechanisms of general change and within the limits of the particular stage of development, but explanations of the specific outcomes of change, i.e. answers to the question why situation A was followed by situation B and not C, D, or any other. (Hobsbawm, 1981a, p. 633)

This passage gives an indication of what Hobsbawm means by the vexed concept 'scientific history'. This was stated more clearly elsewhere when he said that a social science must have a structural-functionalist orientation to its subject matter (1968, 1971b). But Marxism's particular

---

[2] Hobsbawm (1968, 1971a, 1971b, 1972, 1978, 1979a, 1980, 1981a, 1981b, 1984).
[3] For good overviews of Hobsbawm's work, see Cronin (1978) and Genovese (1984).

form of such an approach insists on a *hierarchy* of social phenomena and the existence of *internal contradictions* that counteract the equilibrium. These allow the explanation of social change and social transformation, unlike other forms of structural-functional analysis (see chapter 10) which are either ahistorical or reduce history to an over-simplified traditional/ modern dichotomy (Hobsbawm, 1968, pp. 273–4).

The basic question for Hobsbawm's approach to history is that of the development of human society from paleolithic to industrial: 'Why did some human societies proceed in this direction along different routes, and for different distances?' (1981a, p. 630) For Hobsbawm it was Marx who made the most systematic and serious attempt to answer this question. He took Marx's approach to structural historical transformation to contain three main elements. The first was a mechanism of transformation – the contradiction between the forces and relations of production. The second was a model of all the levels of society – economic structure, superstructure, and forms of consciousness. Moreover, this model posits the analytical primacy of the mode of material production. The third element was an underdeveloped conception of the relationship between conscious human action and objective structural history.

Hobsbawm's big books – *Industry and Empire, The Age of Revolution, The Age of Capital,* and *Captain Swing* – exemplify this approach. They are constructed on levels and the levels are examined as being relatively autonomous, but always his starting place – the capitalist economy – informs the analysis. His version of historical materialism is certainly non-determinist in the sense that there is no strong structural causality or inevitability about transformations, and economic and social development is always combined and uneven. Moreover, the role of class consciousness and class struggle is vital. Just as Marx both theorised and showed in his works of contemporary analysis, such as *The Eighteenth Brumaire of Louis Bonaparte* and *The Class Struggles in France,* that class struggle is the 'locomotive' of history, so Hobsbawm and other Marxist historians have concentrated on its significance for social change.

Many contemporary Anglophone Marxist historians share Hobsbawm's central concern to investigate the historically arisen and changing relationship between the moments of collective action, consciousness, culture, and socio-economic structure.[4] However, the main divisions between them are over socio-economic and cultural perspectives and the role and type of theory used. They are not necessarily in opposition and in fact some writers are in more than one camp (such as Hobsbawm and Moore), but these distinctions indicate that the approaches emphasise

---

[4] For general discussions of Anglophone Marxist historiography, see Hobsbawm (1978), Johnson (1976, 1978, 1979a, 1979b), McLennan (1981), Samuel (1980a).

different 'levels' of the social totality and carry out analyses primarily on these different 'levels' and see differing roles for theory. They all agree that the dialectical relationship between the 'levels' is not predetermined but is a matter for empirical investigation in particular cases. Individual and class struggle, of both the aggregate kind over surpluses and the politically conscious, collective kind over the relations of class domination and the power of state apparatuses, is the decisive realm of human action from the point of view of both structural change and contemporary politics. The political dimension should never be forgotten; it is the politics of their own society and milieu that is perhaps the fundamental motivation for these Marxists to pursue historical enquiries.

Contemporary Marxist socio-economic history, exemplified by some of the writings of Hobsbawm, Rodney Hilton, Perry Anderson, Robert Brenner, and Immanuel Wallerstein (see bibliography) concentrates on explaining the history of economic structures as sets of forces and social relations of production by reference primarily to the dialectical interplay and contradictions between the forces and relations and how this structures class struggle and cultural expression. They are all explicitly and strongly theoretical in their approach. Their theoretical orientation is elaborately *a priori* but this is not to say that they therefore write theoretical histories in the way that Parsons and Smelser tended to do. They still attach great importance to the relative autonomy of evidence and to deriving inductive generalisations. But evidence is organised and interpreted through the framework of various versions of historical materialist theory.

The particular historical problem for these writers is the origins and history of capitalism as a mode of material production and international exchange, and as the fundamental structural force which has transformed the world during the last four centuries through its impact on other modes of production. Capitalism is defined by Marxists as a mode of production which is given its specificity by its particular *relations* of production. Capitalist relations are essentially ones of private property.[5]

The property relations/class conflict perspective (as Holton, 1981, has aptly called it), which is the basis of Marx's account of the origins of capitalism,[6] is now found at its strongest in the work of Maurice Dobb (1946), Rodney Hilton (1952, 1978, 1984), and Robert Brenner (1976, 1977, 1982). There is thus a case for saying they are the most 'orthodox' Marxist historians of the origins of capitalism as a mode of production. Hobsbawm's (1954) work also employs this perspective. The basic idea

---

[5] There has been an extensive debate among Marxists on the origins of capitalism. See, e.g., Anderson (1974a, 1974b), Brenner (1976, 1977, 1982), Frank (1975), Hilton (1952, 1976, 1978, 1984), Ladurie (1978), B. Moore (1966), Wallerstein (1974); and for an overview of the debate see Foster-Carter (1976, 1978).

[6] It is possible to extract several slightly different theories of the origins of capitalism out of Marx's work, as Holton (1981) has clearly demonstrated.

here is that struggle in the countryside between peasants, tenants, and landlords destroyed the feudal manorial fetters and allowed a progressive development of the forces of production through the institutionalisation of capitalist relations (see Holton, 1981, pp. 842–54).

The approaches of Wallerstein, Anderson, and Moore all move away from this 'orthodox' Marxism to varying degrees. Wallerstein (1974) stresses, as shown in chapter 12, the role of the international division of labor and exchange within an emerging world system based on the original emergence of capitalism in the north-west European core. It was the conscious activities of the erstwhile feudal, turned capitalist, class that supposedly 'created' the new system of capitalist agriculture at a favourable historical moment.

Perry Anderson employs (in 1974a and 1974b) theories and insights drawn from non-Marxists, such as Weber, Hintze, and Postan, to supplement his Marxist theory. Moreover, like Hobsbawm, he is strongly opposed to a simple application of the base/superstructure/consciousness model, particularly the ideas that the mode of production is a more or less autonomous level, and that the model applies to all societies, not just the capitalist. Furthermore, Anderson has tried to show in his two books what was unique about Western European feudalism that enabled it to give rise to capitalism from within while nowhere else did so (1974a, part III). The crucial aspect was its politico-legal system – the fusion of vassalage, benefice, and immunity – which produced a *sui generis* pattern of sovereignty and dependence. The feudal ideological code 'rendered compatible pride of rank and humility of homage, legal fixity of obligations and personal fidelity of allegiance' (1974a, pp. 409–10).

In this he shows an affinity for Weber's account, which stresses the role of ideology and culture in feudal society. But he is strongly critical of Weber's methodology because Weber's account is vitiated by the use of ideal types. These have the effect of treating feudalism and patrimonialism as 'detachable and atomic "traits" rather than as unified structures; consequently they can be distributed and mixed at random by Weber, who lacked any *historical* theory proper after his pioneering early work on Antiquity.' (Anderson, 1974a, p. 410) Against such a methodology Anderson defended the necessity for retaining general concepts, but they must be allied with particular descriptions. His premise was that there is no divide between necessary historical laws and short-run contingency. Both are equally amenable to adequate knowledge of their causality (Anderson, 1974a, p. 8).[7]

Barrington Moore studied, in *The Social Origins of Dictatorship and Democracy* (1966), the political roles of landed upper classes and the peasantry in the process of industrialisation and modernisation in England, France, United States, China, Japan, and India. His approach is

---

[7] For a discussion of Anderson's work see Runciman (1981).

at once historical materialist, general theoretical, anti-empiricist, and empirically comparative. Historical materialism was defended against culturalist and Parsonian static functionalist approaches. But it is not a slavishly Marxist materialist interpretation of history in the sense of always seeking for the correct formulation of the relationship between forces and relations, modes of production, base and superstructure. Rather, it is a very general and weak materialist thesis that he defends. His general view is that it is the socio-economic structural situation that is crucial for the explanation of political action but, nevertheless, he does not wish to deny the role of culture either.

> There is always an intervening variable, a filter, one might say, between people and an 'objective' situation, made up from all sorts of wants, expectations, and other ideas derived from the past. This intervening variable, which it is convenient to call culture, screens out certain parts of the objective situation and emphasises other parts. There are limits to the amount of variations in perception and human behavior that can come from this source. Still the residue of truth in the cultural explanation is that what looks like an opportunity or a temptation to one group of people will not necessarily seem so to another group with a different historical experience and living in a different form of society. The weakness of the cultural explanation is not in the statement of such facts, though there is room for a debate over their significance, but in the way they are put into the explanation. Materialist efforts to exorcise the ghost of idealism in cultural explanations are chanting at the wrong spook. (B. Moore, 1966, p. 484)

And in *Injustice: the Social Bases of Obedience and Revolt* (1978) he wrote that

> the Marxist position is open to serious criticism when it asserts, as Marx himself occasionally did, that economic changes necessarily *cause* intellectual and social changes. Sometimes they may and sometimes not, and the causation can also run in the opposite direction. Economic institutions have often been adapted to military, political, and even religious considerations. Systems of ideas and cultural meanings also display a dynamic of change quite on their own that may have very significant consequences for economic institutions. That changes in economic arrangements are a necessary condition for successful change in, say, law, morals, and religious beliefs is not the same thing as asserting that economic changes are always the causes for the latter. Universal propositions about the primacy of economic changes, even when qualified by the useful escape clause 'in the long run', are to be rejected out of hand. (B. Moore, 1978, pp. 468–9)

Both books are therefore strongly empirically oriented. Moore is opposed to the testing of abstract models (1978, p. xvi). But this does not mean that he is an empiricist. General theoretical concepts about hidden structures were employed throughout his work and he was rightly critical of the kind of mindless empiricism that cliometricians engage in. He believed that counting makes it necessary sooner or later to ignore structural distinctions.

> The more definitions the investigator makes in order to catch up with structural changes, the smaller and less useful and trustworthy become the statistical piles with which he works. At bottom the sizes of the different piles are consequences of structural changes. They are not the changes themselves. (B. Moore, 1966, p. 520)

Moore's work in *Social Origins* and *Injustice* contains (like that of Hobsbawm) a form of the structurationist approach to society and change because he attempts to link, especially in the latter book, theories and studies of personality, the motivations of collective action, the universal features of action, theory of social structure, and a theory of ideology in order to explain historical collective actions and processes of structural change.[8]

The socio-cultural historians, such as Edward Thompson, Christopher Hill, Eugene Genovese, and Raymond Williams are in fact not opposed to the socio-economic historians whom I have just discussed. But they deserve separate treatment because they have concentrated on problems of explanation of cultural change. Moreover, many of them, like Moore, have been rather hostile towards strongly theoretical, sociological, and what they see as over-generalising, approaches to social historical explanation. And their version of materialism is sometimes so weak that the distinctions between them and some Weberians and some symbolic realists, such as Geertz and Ladurie, is virtually non-existent.

Edward Thompson epitomises this hostility and the corresponding defence of history in a determinedly empirical and inductive mode.[9] In *The Making of the English Working Class* (1963) he wrote that:

> By class I understand a historical phenomenon, unifying a number of disparate and seemingly unconnected events, both in the raw material of experience and in consciousness. I emphasize that it is a *historical* phenomenon. I do not see class as a 'structure', or even as a 'category', but as something which in fact happens (and can be shown to have happened) in human relationships. (Thompson, 1963, p. 9)

[8] Barrington Moore's work has been sympathetically discussed by D. Smith (1983a, 1984a) and J. M. Wiener (1975).

[9] On Thompson, see Johnson (1976, 1978, 1979b, 1981), Kaye (1984), B. Palmer (1981), G. Williams (1979).

Thompson's concept of 'social class' is identical to that of 'class experience' and 'class consciousness'. Furthermore, it falsely juxtaposes historical and sociological forms of enquiry as if sociology is necessarily static in its approach. Thompson claims Marx's authority for his concept of class but this is unsustainable. Marx made an important distinction, which underlies many of his writings, between a class in itself – an unconscious objective economic relation – and a class for itself. Thompson has collapsed the two together, something that Hobsbawm (1971a) strongly counselled against.

In keeping with Thompson's suspicion of general concepts, he did not develop precise analytical concepts of 'culture' or 'society' in *The Making*. But this problem has been further discussed (and remedied somewhat) in later works (see 1977a, 1977b, 1978a, 1978b) where he has analysed the relationship of historical enquiry to anthropology and sociology and in so doing made clearer his own methodology. In 'Folklore, Anthropology and Social History' (1978b) he averred that he was not opposed to the use of theory *tout court*. He defined social history as the 'systematic examination of norms, expectations, values' (p. 16) and said that it must draw upon anthropology and sociology. But the question is: how? It cannot do so, in his view, in the way that socioeconomic history draws upon economics because those two disciplines (at least the Marxist variants) developed in close association and so the theory used is already historically oriented. The problem with much anthropological and social theory is its ahistorical character. And it is also often anti-economic (pp. 16–17).

He objected to the use of the base/superstructure metaphor because of its supposed effect of arbitrarily reifying these concepts. Therefore, he believed, the metaphor has an 'inbuilt tendency to lead the mind towards reductionism or a vulgar economic determinism', and so moves towards utilitarianism and positivist thought – i.e. 'bourgeois ideology' (p. 18). Furthermore, giving even an interpretive, heuristic priority to the 'economic' (as Hobsbawm does) is also false, in his estimation.

Hence the question of Thompson's allegiance to Marxism arises. He answered this by arguing that Marx did not equate 'mode of production' with 'economic', or the institutions, ideology, and culture of a ruling class with all culture and morality. Rather, Marx's 'mode of production' 'gives' also the attendant relations of production which, Thompson said, are also relations of dominance and subordination. The mode of production 'provides' the 'general illumination in which all other colours are plunged and which modifies their general tonalities' (as Marx wrote in the Introduction to the *Grundrisse*). Relations of production 'find expression in' class formations and their struggles in modern society. But class is not a static category; it describes 'people in relationship over time'. Therefore class for Thompson is both an 'economic' and a 'cultural' formation and neither has priority (pp. 20–1). In brief, then,

Thompson's proposal for the relationship between 'social being' and 'social consciousness' is the following:

> In any given society, in which social relations have become set in class ways, there is a cognitive organization of life which corresponds to the mode of production and the historically evolved class formations. This is the 'common sense' of power; it saturates everyday life; it is expressed, more or less consciously, in the overarching hegemony of the ruling class and in its forms of ideological domination. The 'theatre' of power is only one form of this domintion.
>
> But within and beneath this arch there are innumerable contexts and locations in which men and women, confronting the necessities of their existence, derive their own values and create their own culture, intrinsic to their own mode of life. In these contexts we cannot conceive of social being apart from social consciousness and norms: it is meaningless to ascribe priority to one over the other. Historians can recover the distinct ways of life, and attendant values, of particular groups and occupations: the 'independence' of the artisan, the different communal values of the villager, the forester, the weaving community. At points the culture and the values of these communities may be antagonistic to the overarching system of domination and control.
>
> The presure upon social consciousness of social being reveals itself now, not so much along a horizontal basis/superstructure cleavage, as in (a) *congruities*, (b) *contradiction*, and (c) *involuntary change*. (Thompson, 1978b, pp. 21–2)

Notice, firstly, about this summary of Thompson's framework that there is an ambivalence about his avowed rejection of the base/superstructure model but at the same time his retention of quasi-causal concepts such as 'gives', 'provides', 'finds expression in', 'corresponds to'. Secondly, he has not shown why the base/superstructure metaphor cannot remain as an abstract metaphor – a general source model rather than being reified and reductionist. Hobsbawm's use of it, for example, is not reductionist. Thirdly, if the base/superstructure metaphor is rejected, what is the force of 'historical materialism' as an explanatory model or theory? Surely, the fundamental claim of Marxism is as historical *materialism*, which must imply some form of causal or functional relationship between material production and the other moments of the social totality, or else it is just a form of interactionism between the levels of society or even a culturalist approach like that of Weber. If that causal relation is entirely abandoned, as Thompson seems to wish, then the core of Marxism is abandoned.

Thompson ultimately stops short of outright rejection and does reaffirm a Marxist position when he concludes his discussion in the 'Folklore, Anthropology, and Social History' paper with the statement that involuntary changes in material life resulting from changes in technology, demography, new trade routes, raw material discovery, epidemics, affect production relations but do not spontaneously re-structure a mode of production (1978b, p. 21).

Thompson's obvious anguish over trying to retain historical material-ism while avoiding reductionism, which has given rise to all his quibbling over the idea of causation, could be avoided by paying more attention to the concept of causation and, in particular, by adopting the notions of natural powers and emergence that I argued for in chapter 8. This would avoid equating causation with mechanical connection and so allow for politics and culture to be emergent levels, not having mechanically causal links with material production.

This desire to avoid both reification and reductionism but remain a materialist has been extensively discussed by Raymond Williams (1977, 1980, 1981) who has subjected the base/superstructure metaphor to a detailed analysis. He rightly argues that it is not the concepts of 'base' and 'superstructure' that need to be studied but 'specific and indissoluble real processes, within which the decisive relationship, from a Marxist point of view, is that expressed by the complex idea of "determination"' (1977, p. 82). He believed that the idea must refer to a social process of agency and its social limits rather than to some external compulsion. Therefore,

> the key question is the degree to which the 'objective' conditions are seen as *external*. Since, by definition, within Marxism, the objective conditions are and can only be the result of human actions in the material world, the real distinction can be only between *historical* objectivity – the conditions into which, at any particular point in time, men find themselves born, thus the 'accessible' conditions into which they enter – and *abstract* objectivity. . . . But 'society', or 'the historical event', can never in such ways be categorically abstracted from 'individuals' and 'individual wills'. Such a separation leads straight to an alienated, objectivist 'society', working 'unconsciously', and to comprehension of individuals as 'pre-social' or even anti-social. 'The individual' or 'the genotype' then become positive extra-social forces.
>
> This is where the full concept of determination is crucial. For in practice determination is never only the setting of limits; it is also the exertion of pressures. . . . 'Society' is then never only the 'dead husk' which limits social and individual fulfilment. It is always also a constitutive process with very powerful pressures which are both expressed in political, economic, and cultural formations and, to

take the full weight of 'constitutive', are internalized and become 'individual wills'. (Williams, 1977, pp. 85-7)[10]

This is a helpfully clear statement of the basic structurationist idea that society is both the enabling condition for and result of collective action over time. Nevertheless, it still does not make a case for rejection of the social-levels metaphor as an *abstract* source model. Reification and reductionism can be avoided while retaining the model if the model is seen not as a mechanical causal one but a heuristic device that directs attention to certain general relationships and, perhaps, *functional* connections. This, at least, was the view of Hobsbawm and, latterly, of G. A. Cohen in his attempt to rehabilitate an 'old-fashioned' form of Marxism, to which I shall return in a moment.

RECENT DEBATES OVER MARXIST EXPLANATION

There have been three main debates in Anglophone countries during the past two decades concerning the explanatory foundations of Marxist historiography. The fundamental issues in all three concern the nature of *causation* (as both an epistemological and empirical problem) and the *relationship of theory to empirical evidence* in explanation, i.e. the sorts of issues I have been discussing in the previous section.

The first debate centred on what was taken by Perry Anderson and Tom Nairn (see Anderson, 1964, 1966, 1968, 1980; Nairn, 1964, 1970) to be a deplorable lack of totalising, structural theory in British Marxist historiography at that time (1964) and the corresponding complete lack of a totalising history of modern British society (Anderson, 1964, p. 12). Anderson proposed the use of the Gramscian theory of hegemony and the Lukacsian theory of class consciousness to develop a new account of British history.

In a long and powerful reply, Edward Thompson (1965) attacked their account of English history, their attempt to import European theory, and moreover, what he saw as their overdeterministic use of theory and lack of empirical orientation. He averred that Marx, like Darwin and like all true empirical historians, had a respect for 'grand facts'. In their work can be seen, he said,

> that exciting dialectic of making-and-breaking, the formation of conceptual hypotheses and the bringing of empirical evidence to enforce or to break down these hypotheses, that friction between 'molecular' research and 'macroscopic' generalization to which

---

[10] The approach of Raymond Williams is analysed by Neale (1984).

Wright Mills often referred. In any vital intellectual tradition this dialectic, this abrasion between models and particulars, is always evident. (Thompson, 1965, p. 64)

Thompson's objections to the use of models were that they petrify into axioms and are too selective with regard to evidence because they direct attention only to certain phenomena (p. 78). But he conceded that models must be used, for to try to do without them is either to cease to be a historian or to 'become the slaves of some model scarcely known to ourselves in some inaccessible ara of prejudice' (p. 78). Models must be used sceptically, to establish a delicate equilibrium between synthesising and empirical modes; 'this is the creative quarrel at the heart of cognition.' (p. 78)[11]

The major impetus for the second debate came from French structuralism, especially from Althusser who, as we saw in chapter 12, attempted to solve the problem of the general relationship of the economy to politics and culture by arguing that Marx had a Spinozist notion of structural causality. The social totality, as a structure of contradictions, supposedly structures all the possibilities within it such that society is a 'natural-human' holistic system. Individual and class action is determined by the structure as instanes of structural causality. The structure is said to be immanent in its effects. Therefore the relationship of theory to evidence is one of the priority of theory and its determination of data. Structures have to be constructed within theory and cannot be arrived at by induction. The particular historical events and processes are read off, or deduced, from the ahistorical theory.

Edward Thompson has also been the most vigorous opponent of structuralist Marxism on grounds broadly similar to his opposition to the Anderson/Nairn thesis. He rightly accused Althusser and the British post-Althusserians (notably Hindess and Hirst) of being ahistorical, theoreticist, and idealist and therefore of being a threat not only to historical materialism but to reason itself (Thompson, 1978d, p. 196)! Thompson's most fundamental and telling criticism of the Althusserians is that they have no category or way of understanding *experience* – 'social being's impingement upon social consciousness' – and therefore falsify the 'dialogue' with empirical evidence that knowledge production, including Marxism, has inherent within it. They confuse the empirical with empiricism and reject both. Furthermore, Althusserian structuralism is one of *stasis*, unable to account for history (pp. 196–7).[12]

---

[11] For discussions of this debate see Anderson (1980), Nield (1980).

[12] The relationship of structuralism to empirical historical research has been the subject of an extensive, sometimes acrimonious debate among British Marxists, much of it carried on in *History Workshop*. See the contributions by Anderson (1980), Clarke (1979), Hall (1981), Hirst (1979), Johnson (1978, 1981), McClelland (1979), McLennan (1981), Nield (1980), Nield and Seed (1979), Samuel (1980b, 1981a), Selbourne (1980), O'Neill (1982), G. Williams (1979).

Against idealism and stasis, Thompson proposed his concept of 'historical logic' as the philosophical basis of all historical enquiry. This is a very valuable contribution by Thompson – one of the very few places where a practising Marxist historian has reflected at length about the philosophical foundations of his discourse. By 'historical logic' he means a method which is appropriate to historical materials,

> designed as far as possible to test hypotheses as to structure, causation, etc., and to eliminate self-confirming procedures ('instances', 'illustrations'). The disciplined historical discourse of the proof consists in a dialogue between concept and evidence, a dialogue conducted by successive hypotheses, on the one hand, and empirical research on the other. The interrogator is historical logic; the interrogative a hypothesis (for example, as to the way in which different phenomena acted upon each other); the respondent is the evidence, with its determinate properties. (Thompson, 1978d, p. 231)

Thompson's historical 'logic' exhibits several important features. Firstly, in so far as it states an epistemological doctrine there is nothing about that doctrine that makes it peculiar to history. What Thompson is defending, in a slightly muddled way perhaps, is a version of the social realist epistemology that I argued for in chapters 7 and 8 and, in particular, the convergence idea of truth and the realist social ontology. Secondly, his defence of the historicity of the historical discipline is an argument not for the uniqueness of historical logic but for the merging of historical and sociological modes of enquiry. Thirdly, his argument does not imply the rejection of the scientific nature of history but rather affirms it, given the account of science I have developed in chapters 7 and 8.

The problem that Thompson has been wrestling with, as have Althusser, Godelier, Williams, and all the others who have worried about the base/superstructure relationship, is that of *causation*. Does the base cause the superstructure in some sense? This problem has been discussed in a much more rigorous, analytical, and clear manner by the participants in the third debate who are essentially analytical philosophers, as well as Marxists, notably G. A. Cohen and Jon Elster.

Cohen defends a *functionalist/teleological* reading of Marx (based on very careful textual exegesis) which is similar to but goes well beyond that of Hobsbawm, and a construal of Marx as a *theoretician* of history as well as a practitioner. It is important that the issue of what Marx might have said or meant should be separated from what a viable historical materialism might be. There is no doubt that Marx's work and that of many Marxists (e.g. Hobsbawm, Althusser, Godelier, and Moore) does contain consequence-type explanations (see chapter 8 for a discussion of their structure) in which actions and structural changes are explained by their final consequences. Cohen demonstrates clearly that the famous 'Preface' of 1859 rests on such an argument:

> To say that an economic structure *corresponds* to the achieved level
> of the productive forces means: the structure provides maximum
> scope for the fruitful use and development of the forces, and
> obtains *because* it provides such scope. To say that being *deter-
> mines* consciousness means, at least in large part: the character of
> the leading ideas of a society is explained by their propensity, in
> virtue of that character, to sustain the structure of economic roles
> called for by the productive forces. (G. A. Cohen, 1978, pp. 278–9)

Moreover, he interprets and defends Marx as arguing that the forces of
production, particularly technology, are primary in history and that the
forces of production develop through history. These two claims go
together:

> (a) The productive forces tend to develop throughout history (The
> Development Thesis.
> (b) The nature of the production relations of a society is explained
> by the level of development of its productive forces (The Primacy
> Thesis proper). (G. A. Cohen, 1978, p. 134)

It is important to note that neither of these theses asserts claims of
mechanical causality. The first is a claim about a tendency only, not a law
of necessary evolution. The second is also an explanatory claim, not a
law of invariable association of events. The two theses were expressed in
a later article by the following formulation: 'I say, and Marx says, that
history is, fundamentally, the growth of human productive power, and
that forms of society rise and fall according as they enable and promote,
or prevent and discourage, that growth.' (G. A. Cohen, 1982b, p. 483)
That is, in Elster's terminology, there is an objective teleology in history.

While certainly agreeing that the work of Marx and many later
Marxists does contain functionalist explanations, Jon Elster has vigor-
ously attacked such putative explanations, as we saw in chapter 8. For
him the only legitimate explanations in social science are rationalist/
intentionalist at the level of individual actions, and causal at the level of
structures and collectivities. For him it is game theory that ties the two
together by showing how rational/intentional action is strategically
oriented towards and made possible by the existence of other intentional
actors in a situation of mutual interaction (Elster, 1982b, p. 463).[13]

The heart of this dispute is what is meant by 'explain' in the social

---

[13] The main contributions to this recent debate have been by Cohen (1978, 1980, 1982a,
1982b), Elster (1980, 1982b, 1983), Giddens (1982b), Lukes (1983), Mandelbaum (1982),
Miller (1981), Offe and Berger (1982), Roemer (1982), Shaw (1978), Van Parijs (1982a).
See the excellent survey of the debate by Lash and Urry (1984). For earlier discussions of
Marxism and functionalism, see van den Berghe (1963), Godelier (1977, 1978), Hobsbawm
(1968), Lipset (1976), Merton (1976).

sciences. For Elster, explanations have to be by reference to causal mechanisms or their analogues, such as intentions and rationality. For Cohen, explanations can be by reference to subsequent consequences but, obviously, that is not a causal relation because it would violate the order of time. Rather, in Cohen's words, if a cause *e* produces an effect *f* then it can be said that '*e* occurred because the situation was such that an event of type *E* would cause an event of type *F*' (1982b, p. 486) Thus to say that the productive forces explain the nature of the economic structure and the economic structure explains the nature of the super-structure, is to say that the superstructure is functional for the economic structure because it stabilises it and the economic structure is functional for the level of the forces of production because it promotes their development (p. 488).

The only way in which such a dispute can ever be ultimately resolved is by empirical results, and the fundamental empirical problem for all structural historians is, as Hobsbawm pointed out, why there has been technological, economic, and political development in the long run of human history, as well as, within that general movement, a lack of development or regression in certain places and certain times. As Cohen has seen very clearly (1982b, p. 489) and contrary to Elster, game theory and methodological individualism offer no assistance in this quest because the outcomes of episodes of *class* conflicts have to be explained and that can only be done in terms of the relationship of class actions to *structural* conditions. It is the structural conditions that are vital and methodological individualism cannot deal with them adequately.

WEBERIAN APPROACHES TO HISTORICAL STRUCTURAL CHANGE

Certain themes are shared by all those in the Weberian tradition, as is the case with Marxists. Many of these themes were formed through Weber's encounter with Marxism, a Marxism it must be remembered of late nineteenth-century Germany and the Second International and so being more positivist, reductionist, and determinist than that which has been articulated in recent decades. Weber's basic aim was to try to explain the content and genesis of modern Western rationalism, a rationalism of culture and economy, but at the same time he rejected the older approaches of historical materialism and positivist evolutionism. He constructed a new methodology which established a division of labour between history and sociology.

Society, for Weber, was not a holistic deterministic entity, as some positivists and some early Marxists portrayed it. Elements of subjectiv-ism, phenomenology, and hermeneutics were central to his social theory. Three of the methodological implications of this were a relativistic theory of truth, an individualistic methodology, and a culturalist theory of action. However, it is essential to realise that these methodological tenets were all expressed against the prevailing positivist holism. When Weber came to wrote structural histories (e.g. 1896, 1909, 1923), he often presented much more realist and structurist explanations, which are surprisingly similar to Marx's (cf. Roth, 1976; B. Turner, 1981). There is, therefore, an ambiguous Weberian legacy arising from the gap between his methodological pronouncements and his actual practice. But what is not at issue is his use of abstract ideal-type concepts and models in historical explanation, his emphases upon the role of cultures in structural transformations, and his rejection of determinist historical explanations. The individual/society, material/cultural, and subjective/objective dialectical interactions are all central to his work and to that of those influenced by him, such as Reinhard Bendix, Albert Hirschman, Peter Berger, Roland Robertson, Ernest Gellner, S. N. Eisenstadt, W. G. Runciman, J. Baechler, and Bryan Turner. But the differing emphases placed upon these moments can give somewhat different approaches to explaining structural change. In particular I believe it is possible to divide contemporary Weberian macro-sociological approaches into those that concentrate on culture, ideology, and politics, and those that offer more materialist explanations. But just as is the case with Marxist historians, this is a somewhat arbitrary divide. All Weberians do hold, to some extent, that ideology and culture, rather than material interests, labour, or production, is the decisive realm for explaining structuring and transformative social action.

Weberian culturalist modernisation theory is epitomised by Reinhard Bendix's four major books (1959, 1977, 1978, 1984).[14] He defends a 'historicist' approach to social change in opposition to what he calls a 'rationalistic' one. By the latter he meant an objectivist and ahistorical approach (whether idealist or materialist) which searches for the supposedly objective forces in history that are beyond human intentionality and control. He mistakenly includes all Marxism in this camp, although his citation of Braudel and Wallerstein as examples are apt. The historicist approach, on the other hand, sees truth as relative to historical conditions, to particular methods, and to the interests of the enquirer (Bendix, 1984, p. 9). Bendix's historicism does not abandon the search for truth but it sees sociological truth as conditional and relatively non-cumulative. This is basically because (*pace* Weber) it respects the interplay between subjective and objective understandings and therefore assumes that people act with a good awareness of what they are doing and that what they do has meaning for them and for others. In turn, interpretations of meanings by the actors and by external observers can change these meanings and hence their actions (1984, pp. 30–1). However, actions are not wholly internally motivated by subjective meanings.

---

[14] For a discussion of the work of Bendix, see Stinchcombe (1978).

They are also motivated and constrained by external situations. This is widely agreed, as Bendix pointed out. The problem, then, as Berger, Geertz, Bendix, and many other Weberians have seen very clearly, is to bridge the subjective/objective and freedom/determinism gaps in order to show how people do indeed make their own history but also how particular circumstances, which are the result of people having made history in the past, condition that history-making. The structural conditions of action include ideologies and cultures. As Geertz has rightly said, these are not just mental structures and processes but exist in the world, so to study their power and influence is not to adopt idealism as some mistaken critics of the Weberians seem to believe.

Bendix's main concern has been with the roles of cultural systems, ideologies, and beliefs in setting the context for, dominating, and being the motivation for human structuring action and in legitimating social structures. But he has also been concerned to show how structures have influenced the development and articulation of ideologies, including philosophical systems about society. In *Work and Authority in Industry* (1959) he studied the rise and influence of managerial ideologies in the process of industrialisation in England, Russia, and America. In *Nation Building and Citizenship* (1977) he studied authority relations and the movements towards democracy during the process of industrialisation in Western Europe, Japan, Russia, and India. And in *Kings or People* (1978) he studied the relationship between political orders and cultural relations that originated in medieval societies. Looking back at this large body of work he wrote in his 1984 book that ideologies must be studied for their effects upon the social structure because

the ideas developed for the many by or on behalf of the few are a clue to an understanding of industrial societies. For such ideas can promote the social cohesion of a class, justify their good fortune in their own eyes, facilitate communication, help resolve the dilemmas of organization with which men in command must deal on a daily basis, and also actually help persuade workers that the distribution of rewards in society is fair.

Ideas may do any of these things only proximately, or not at all. The legitimacy of an industrial society depends, at least in part, on the persuasiveness of these ideologies. Entrepreneurs – managers and others who direct the organizations of industrial societies – have made use of managerial ideologies time and again. These people, who play an important role in modern society, may be deceived by ideas, but they also think they know what they are doing. These are the reasons why I believe such ideas are worth examining over time and in a comparative perspective. (Bendix, 1984, p. 75)

In spite of his opposition to Marxism, Bendix's theory of the relationship of ideologies to action and the social structure was quite similar to that of the cultural materialists, such as Moore and Thompson. They hold, as he does, that while ideologies are legitimations and rationalisations they are also the result of 'historically cumulative response patterns amongst groups'. Accordingly,

> ideologies of management can be explained *only in part* as a means to an end and as rationalizations of self-interest; they also result from the legacy of institutions and ideas which is 'adopted' by each generation much as a child 'adopts' the grammar of its native language. Historical legacies are a part of the social structure: they should not be excluded from the social sciences, which focus attention upon the persistence of group structures and the unanticipated consequences of conscious social action. (Bendix, 1984, p. 80)

For the Weberian culturalists the neo-evolutionary approach to the origins of modern society is also inadequate on several grounds. Firstly, they reject the systemic-functionalist model of society and adopt instead a version of the social-levels model which sees ideologies, political systems, and socio-economic structures as relatively autonomous. Secondly, they reject the evolutionary idea of a universal and simple dichotomy of traditional and modern stages. Thirdly, they reject the psycho-dynamic and rationalistic concepts of evolutionary mechanisms and adopt instead a comparative historical approach to empirically examining the causes of particular historical processes located in the dialectical interaction of personality, culture, and innovative entrepreneurial activity. Accordingly, fourthly, they have an agency theory of personality and action.

They are also strongly opposed to the individualist/economistic approach to economic and social change on the general grounds that the motivations of individual and group actions are much more complex than the 'rational economic man' model allows (cf. Hirschman, 1981, ch. 14, p. 303, and 1970, 1977, 1982). That approach greatly devalues the roles of culture, ideology, and politics in the process of modernisation, as D. C. North saw from within the paradigm. From a position originally just outside the tradition and increasingly influenced by Weber, Albert Hirschman has cogently criticised the idea of rationality that it contains and its inability to give a proper place to these other motivations of economic actions or the unintended and unrealised consequences of actions for structural change. He saves the idea of rationality while showing the inadequacies of economistic rationality, as well as the necessity for a political approach to economic change.

The socio-materialist/class conflict reading of Weber is well supported by his writings on the social history of ancient civilizations, of feudalism, and of capitalism in texts such as *The Agrarian Sociology of Ancient*

Civilizations and *General Economic History*. However, one of the fundamental differences with Marxism is not so much over the role of culture in transformation but with the *sources* of Western rationalist culture. For Weber rationalism not only plays a decisive role in the advance of the West instead of the East but rationalism is somehow *inherent* in Western societies ever since its spark struck root in the soil of classical Greece. From then on it was the *telos* of Western society. That idea allowed Weber and later Weberians (as well as Braudel) to see capitalism as present in antiquity and early Renaissance Europe simply because there was large-scale trade.

This rational exchange approach to the history of capitalism has recently been defended by W. G. Runciman (1983a; see also 1982 and 1984) who has directly confronted and rejected the (vulgar) Marxist claim that all societies are class societies by arguing that ancient Rome was both capitalist and classless. He invokes the Weberian notion of 'status' (rather than economic relations) to help explain Roman social structure, social conflict, and social change.

By 'capitalism' Runciman meant 'a system based on the private ownership of property in which the relations between its members are normally transacted through the market by way of a cash nexus' (Runciman, 1983a, p. 157). And ancient Rome was clearly capitalist in this sense, as he demonstrates. But he argues that it did not give rise to social classes in the Marxian sense of the relationship of individuals to the means of production because these differences did not exist. However, Runciman is contradictory on this point because he also points out (pp. 164–5) that the mass of people in the classical period owned no land, which was the major means of production, and that there was an artisanate and proletariat (p. 167), so in the ownership sense there were at least two classes – landed and landless. His argument is that classes in the politically conscious sense did not form, although one could, by *a priori* reasoning, have expected them to do so given the capitalist nature of the society. This was because, he conjectures,

> economic power and the sanctions attaching to it are less funda-
> mental to its organisation than either social-cum-ideological or
> political-cum-military power (or both of them). This assertion is,
> no doubt, open to argument by those who hold either that all
> relations of power are reducible to one kind only, or that there is
> some other form of power and therefore dimension of social
> structure not reducible to any of the three. But ... both of these
> objections can be met ... because they are particularly implausible
> in the case of classical Rome. Not only does the problem ... arise
> precisely because of the evident difficulty of reducing all other
> relationships of power to class relationships in the Roman case, but
> the independent importance both of social exclusiveness, status-

consciousness and ideological hegemony on the one hand and of violence, usurpation and physical coercion on the other are readily demonstrable. . . . The mixture of coercive and ideological sanctions . . . [was] so strong and pervasive . . . that the changes in the social structure which would otherwise have followed from the workings of the market and the influx of new wealth were subordinated to the pre-existing modes of power. (Runciman, 1983a, p. 169)

It was legitimacy and prestige more than economic interests that motivated private and political action (p. 174). Such an ideology, the coercive apparatus of powerful individuals and the state, and a lack of social mobility, reinforced each other. Runciman argues that if there had been less mobility, class consciousness might have arisen among the *déclassés*, but limited opportunity for mobility probably absorbed their potential leaders (p. 178). Without classes and class conflict the Roman social structure, based upon kinship, status, and stable strata, remained remarkably unchanged for centuries despite great economic changes wrought by capitalism (pp. 176–7). If this is so, then it is a striking counter-example for historical materialism to come to terms with. I believe it probably can do so by reasserting its basic concept of 'relations of production' to argue that Rome was in fact *not* capitalist in the sense of capitalist *production* and so never revolutionised the relations of production to sweep away the ties of kinship and status. But that would require a long discussion for which there is no space here.

FIGURATIONS AND CIVILISATIONS

We have seen how the influences of Marx and Weber gave rise to two broad overlapping streams within the relational-structurist tradition. But in addition to these two main streams there are two others, as yet not so strong or influential. The first of these has been single-handedly invented by Norbert Elias and the importance of his work has begun to be appreciated only in the last decade or so.

Elias is a historical sociologist *par excellence* who has written at length about problems of explanation as well as producing three very important works of historical sociological analysis (1978a, 1982, 1983). He has strongly opposed behaviourism, holism, and functionalism and has done much to articulate a new and powerful concept of social structure and its relationship to individuals. The heart of his approach is the concept of 'figuration'. A figuration is a web of interdependencies of persons which is characterised by power balances, such as a school, a town, a social stratum, or a state, as in figure 12 (Elias, 1978b, p. 15).

This shows that Elias's figuration is a process of mutual interweaving

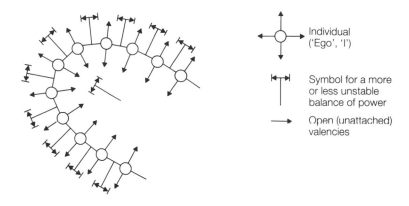

Figure 12 Elias's concept of figuration

such that the actions of persons within it are inextricably interdependent. On the micro level, the constituents are individual persons, such as the participants in a game, but the figuration is constituted wholly by the players. It is not, as Elias emphasised, an ideal type constructed by an observer by abstracting from the behaviour of individuals. Rather, it is a real concrete structure, constituted by the totality of the relationships between the individuals. A figuration forms a 'flexible lattice-work of tensions' (1978b, p. 130. See also 1983, pp. 13–14). The concept is not restricted to the micro level. It is applicable to whole societies and even international systems. Figurations can have great stability and continuity and so sometimes seem to be almost unchanging. The medieval European figuration of knight/page/priest/bondsman endured for centuries. Today figurations such as worker/employee/manager relationships seem very durable (1983, p. 13).

He saw the task of historical sociology as being 'to bring the unstructured background of much previous historical research into the foreground and to make it accessible to systematic research as a structured weft of individuals and their actions' (1983, p. 26). His underlying model of social change was therefore succinctly expressed in the following way. Sociology has to solve the problem, as he said and as I argued in chapters 8 and 9, of how social order and social change are neither planned nor random. His general answer was the following:

> Plans and actions, the emotional and rational impulses of individual people, constantly interweave in a friendly or hostile way. *This basic tissue resulting from many single plans and actions of men*

can give rise to changes and patterns that no individual person has planned or created. From this interdependence of people arises an order sui generis, an order more compelling and stronger than the will and reason of the individual people composing it. It is this order of interweaving human impulses and strivings, this social order, which determines the course of historical change; it underlies the civilizing process.

This order is neither 'rational' – if by 'rational' we mean that it has resulted intentionally from the purposive deliberation of individual people; nor 'irrational' – if by 'irrational' we mean that it has arisen in an incomprehensible way.... Only if we see the compelling force with which a particular social structure, a particular form of social intertwining veers through its tensions to a specific change and so to other forms of intertwining, can we understand how those changes arise in human mentality, in the patterning of the malleable psychological apparatus, which can be observed over and again in human history from earliest times to the present. (Elias, 1982, pp. 230–2)

Elias believed that the concept of figuration and his model of social change helped to explain, among other processes, European industrialisation (see 1978b, pp. 140–2), the origins of the absolutist state (see 1982), the court society of Louis XIV's Versailles (see 1983), and the history of the origins of courtly manners (see 1978a). Furthermore, as *What is Sociology?* (1978a) clearly shows, he was strongly opposed to employing a social-levels model as anything more than a a heuristic device, and to any form of structuralist explanation. The intertwining and interaction of social agents (whether persons, groups, classes, or states) was the decisive force in history.[15]

STRUCTURATIONISM

Structurationist approaches to the explanation of action and/or structure and structural change are implicit in the work of several theorists in this relational-structurist tradition, for example, Hobsbawm, Moore, Thompson, Bendix, and Elias, and also in the work of some of those in the symbolic-realist tradition, such as Harré, Geertz, and Ladurie. Eric Hobsbawm, in fact, in his 1981 article, gave what is a convenient summary of it, as quoted in my five themes. Figure 13 attempts to give a schematic outline of the approach, but such a diagram cannot, of course, do justice to the fundamentally important aspect of time.

Structurationism has its roots in Marx's work and not just his early so-

---

[15] For helpful discussions of Elias's work, see D. Smith (1984), Mennell (1977).

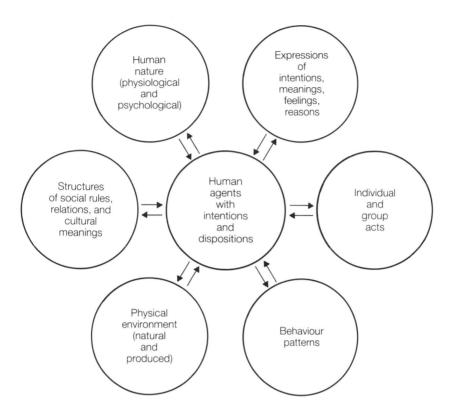

Arrows show directions of possible causative influence. In general, the agent is the producer of structural and observable products, but the strength and relationships of causes will vary with social-environmental context and over time.

Figure 13   The structurationist paradigm

called humanist writings, but also in his mature work as evidenced particularly strongly in the *Grundrisse* (see, e.g., Marx, 1857–8, p. 712). Furthermore, Marx's approach was predicated on his desire to cut through the misleading, or fetishised, character of social appearances in order to grasp the real, historically developed, relations beneath, so that, for example, it could be understood that the alienation of labour in capitalist society is only a transitory phase (see Marx, 1857–8, pp. 831–2).

Versions of structurationism (but only labelled that by Giddens) have recently been systematised by Anthony Giddens, Alain Touraine, and Philip Abrams as consciously synthetic attempts to transcend the weaknesses of existing methodologies of socio-historical explanation by incorporating (or rejecting) elements from many existing approaches and combining them into an approach that builds upon the accumulated insights of a century of theorising. In fact, many thinkers have begun to converge upon this synthetic point from apparently completely independent points of view, notably from Francophone post-structuralism, English post-Marxist social theory, French action sociology, and German post-Marxist and post-Weberian hermeneutic philosophy (see Hoy, 1979).

The fundamental claim of structurationism is to be a framework for linking action, consciousness, and structure, to study how intentional and unintentional action structures the world and how social structures enable and disable action and consciousnes. Jean Piaget wrote that in his view

> the subject's activity calls for a continual 'decentring' without which he cannot become free from his spontaneous intellectual egocentricity. This 'decentring' makes the subject enter upon, not so much an already available and therefore external universality, as an uninterrupted process of coordinating and setting in reciprocal relations. It is the latter process which is the true 'generator' of structures as constantly under construction and reconstruction. The subject exists because, to put it very briefly, the being of structures consists in their coming to be, that is, their being 'under construction'. . . .
>
> *There is no structure apart from construction*, either abstract or genetic. (Piaget, 1971b, pp. 139–40)

This passage shows the importance given to the notion of *agency* by structurationists. We saw in chapters 7 and 12 that Piaget emphasised the role of the epistemological subject in structuring the world and his knowledge of it through interaction with it.

Giddens has done more than most to develop a framework for studying how human agency relates to structure. Summarising his approach, we get the following archetypal account of structurationist methodology (Giddens, 1982b, pp. 8–11):[16]

> 1 The approach must contain a theory of the conscious subject. The subject must be recovered as a reasoning, acting being, otherwise any approach is too objectivist. But the subject must be decentred and so consciousness is not seen as a given starting point of analysis.

[16] Structurationism has been extensively discussed in the last few years. See, for example, Archer (1982), Bhaskar (1979, 1980, 1982a), Dallmayr (1982), Gane (1983), Gross (1983), Hirst (1983), Lash and Urry (1984), Shotter (1980b, 1983), B. Smart (1982), D. Smith (1983b), Urry (1983), Wright (1983).

2 Subjectivism must be avoided. Neither the human agent, nor society, has primacy.

Each is constituted in and through recurrent practices. The notion of human 'action' presupposes that of institution and vice versa. Explication of this relation thus comprises the core of an account of how it is that the structuration (production and reproduction across time and space) of social practices takes place. (Giddens, 1982b, p. 8)

3 'Action' refers to two components of conduct: 'capability' and 'knowledgeability'. By the first is meant that the agent 'could have acted otherwise'. The agent is therefore a being with individual and social *power*. 'Knowledgeability' refers to the practical consciousness of ordinary actors about their own society and the conditions of their own activities. It is not equatable with knowing consciously in the sense of 'held in mind' but is, rather, the modes of tacit knowing about how to 'go on' in social life. Neither is it equatable with the ability to make decisions in the game-theroetic sense because it is less conscious and less rational than that.

4 Institutions are structured social practices that have a broad spatial and temporal extension. In the structurationist approach

'structure' refers to rules and resources instantiated in social systems but having only a 'virtual' existence. The structured properties of society, the study of which is basic to explaining the long-term development of institutions, 'exist' in only their instantiation in the structuration of social systems and in the memory traces (reinforced or altered in the continuity of daily social life) that constitute the knowledgeability of social actors. But institutionalised practices 'happen' and are 'made to happen' through the application of resources in the continuity of daily life. Resources are structured properties of social systems, but 'exist' only in the capability of actors, in their capacity to 'act otherwise'.... [Therefore] an essential element of the theory of structuration [is] the thesis that the organisation of social practices is fundamentally *recursive*. Structure is both the medium and the outcome of the practices it recursively organises. (Giddens, 1982b, pp. 9–10)

5 A further central aspect of Giddens's structurationism is the *time–space relation*. He rejects the synchronic/diachronic and change/stability dichotomies of many social theories. Social conduct and social structure are fundamentally temporal and all societies have a sense of themselves as historic, although this has very different meanings in different societies. They are also

located in a geographic space which is integral to their being. So, any good theory should make no reified distinctions between time and timelessness and structure and environment (1979a, ch. 6).

6 This leads to the final aspect of his approach – *social change*. The approach gives rise not to a general theory but, rather, to the general methodological position that the forces for change have to be looked for in the relations between action, consciousness, institutions, and structures.

> First we have to show how, in the context of the rationalis-ation of action, definite practices are reproduced: how actors' penetration of the institutions which they reproduce in and through their practices, makes possible the very reproduction of these practices. This necessarily involves applying the theorem ... that all social actors know a great deal about what they are doing in processes of interaction; and yet at the same time there is a great deal which they do not know about the conditions and consequences of their activities, but which none the less influences their course. Second, we have to investigate the effects of the 'escape' of activity from the intentions of its initiators upon the reproduction of practices, through processes which relate the practices in question to other features of broader social systems of which they are part. (Giddens, 1979, pp. 215–16)

Unfortunately, Giddens has not yet applied his framework to the analysis of processes of social history. This contrasts with Alain Touraine who has been developing for the past two decades what he has called 'the sociology of action' and which received its canonical formulation in *The Self-Production of Society* (1977b). His approach is based on three main concepts:

> *historicity*, which defines the instruments of society's self-production; the *system of historical action*, meaning that totality composed of social and cultural orientations, by means of which historicity exercises its domination over society's functioning; and *class relations*, struggles for the control of historicity and of the system of historical action. (Touraine, 1977b, p. 6)

He is opposed to both objectivist and subjectivist sociology. Society is, rather, the product of action and social relations and is capable of both reproduction and transformation but not in some holistic/intentional/ systemic sense. Society possesses a capacity for 'symbolic creation' which enables meaning – the orientation of conduct – to arise out of the relationship of conduct to its social situation. That is, it has a capacity for self-action – to form and transform its functioning – on the basis of its investments (the situation) and its own self-image. This distance that exists between society and action Touraine calls 'historicity'.

> *Society is not what it is but what it makes itself to be*: through *knowledge*, which creates a state of relations between society and its environment; through *accumulation*, which subtracts a portion of available product from the cycle leading to consumption; through the *cultural model*, which captures creativity in forms dependent upon the society's practical domination over its own functioning. It creates the totality of its social and cultural orientations by means of a historical action that is both work and meaning.
>
> The image that takes shape, then, is that of a society which is not solely a system of internal and external exchanges but first and foremost an agent of its own self-production, an agent in the creation of orientations of social action on the basis of practice and consciousness of the production of work. (Touraine, 1977b, p. 4)

Furthermore historicity is directed and organised by the power of class relations and, in essence, the division of society into two opposing classes. The ruling class becomes responsible for historicity by appropriating it and so attempts to go beyond mere self-reproduction to knowledge. The 'popular' class defends itself and seeks, in turn, to gain control of historical action by overthrowing the ruling class. Class struggle for Touraine is thus over the management and control of historical action (p. 5).

Touraine's approach to structural change is therefore one that concentrates on social interaction, culture, and class, and not on the consciousness of individual actors.[17]

Drawing upon the structurationism of Giddens, Philip Abrams has made the most extended and impressive argument for merging history and sociology into a single discourse (1982, especially ch. 10), something that Edward Thompson had (mistakenly) believed should not be done and some others, notably cliometricians, mistakenly believed should be achieved on the basis of massive counting. A viable historical sociology has indeed to be based on a structurationist approach, as, for example, Ladurie, Geertz, Hobsbawm, Moore, Bendix, and Elias have actually achieved. They have done so by showing how individuals and their actions relate to other individuals and to social structures, as sets of relations, over time. Individualist historians (e.g. Macfarlane, 1978;

---

[17] Touraine has recently applied his action sociology to the analysis of several contemporary social movements (see, for example, 1981, 1983).

Laslett, 1971) fail to take account of such structures and of how individuals and groups structure the world *as a process* of constituting society. And qualitative, deliberately non-sociological historians, such as Thompson in *The Making of the English Working Class* (1963), run a severe risk of failing to *explain* in any coherent consistent and publicly shared way. The importance of theory is crucial. What we have to do is, as Abrams put it,

> find a way of living with the fact of the mutual interdependence and contamination of theory and evidence without resorting to either the anti-theoretical fetishism of history-as-evidence towards which the History Workshop sometimes seemed to slide or the a-historical fetishism of theory-as-knowledge which some structuralists in their more extreme moments seem to espouse. Either retreat pulls the core, reality-apprehending, project to pieces. (Abrams, 1982, p. 333)

Therefore the way forward for social historians is not rigorously to apply some *a priori* method, abstracted from historical time, but to seek always to find the dialectical relationships between the moments of the social totality and the levels of structure. They can do no better than to follow the examples of Eric Hobsbawm and Emmanuel Le Roy Ladurie, who epitomise the achievement of scientific social history.

Conclusion

Social history can become a science if it founds itself on realism and methodological structurism. This is not to claim, as has been shown at length, that it should or can become an empiricist science in the way that physics is taken to be by many who practise it or observe it. Physics, however it is characterised by philosophers, is not a model for all science, let alone other types of discourse. To be a science a discourse must attempt to make progress towards providing objective accounts of structural mechanisms. These accounts are always constructed within theoretical frameworks; but the possibility of gradual convergence on increasingly truthful accounts of causation is a powerful regulator of scientific practice. The structure of reasoning in a scientific social history should be as defended in chapter 8 and summarised in figure 6 on page 157.

One of the main consequences of methodological structurism for the social sciences is to provide a basis for the unification of sociology and history. Social historians have a peculiar problem of disciplinary delineation, as many of them have recognised, since they wish to be both historians and social scientists. They wish both to distinguish themselves from action historians by enquiring into the social totality and to transcend and supersede the explanatory practices of traditional historians; thus their aim has to be not just to explain the relationship between social structures and actions and events but also to uncover and account for the history of real structures themselves. If their practice were to be based upon the structurationist paradigm it would provide a framework for *simultaneously* explaining particular acts, events, patterns of behaviour, and structural change. Such a paradigm is thus well suited to be the basis for social history. Traditional historians avoid using such a framework, at the loss of a good deal of explanatory power, because they see themselves as explaining 'unique' individual acts, events, and processes largely by reference to 'unique' dispositions, pruposes, and

313

reasons, and not to general social and psychological imperatives. But I believe they are largely mistaken in this, or at least incomplete in their explanations; although intentions and reasons are certainly necessary to such explanation. It is because of the deeper relationship of partly intentional individual behaviour to both the given structural conditions of behaviour and the production, reproduction, and transformation of structures, that action-oriented and structure-oriented history can be united on a more fundamental level. Such a unified science would then incorporate all the existing empirical and theoretical social and historical studies.

Within this last perspective, the structurationist paradigm has the virtues of providing all-encompassing coherence, without reduction. Furthermore, it makes it possible to retain a temporal dimension as intrinsic to any study of society since structure, action, and behaviour are interrelated in a dynamic, transforming, manner.

This approach does attempt to argue that particular acts and events can only be investigated for their causation, significance, and meaning within a structural context. However, it does not deny that there is merit in making a division of labour between the explanation of particular individual acts and events and the explanation of patterns of behaviour and structures, since, on one level, every act and event is different from every other and the precise mix of mechanisms or imperatives will vary in every case. Nevertheless, on another level, all acts and events do fall under general descriptions and into general patterns and, furthermore, no particular act is the outcome of a truly unique set of mechanisms. The two kinds of history must be methodologically united on this deeper level, and thus able to take account of the relationship of particular acts and events to patterns of behaviour and social structures over time.

I am proposing, then, a basis for a new division of labour within a unified social science. At present the socio-historical studies are officially or institutionally divided primarily between history on the one hand, and the social studies on the other. This division is derived from the idea that history is concerned with change, with the 'past', and with uniqueness or particularity; and social studies with structural continuities and generalities, usually in the 'present'. But of course this division completely fails to grasp the existing situation, especially in regard to economic and social history. Historians do generalise and social scientists do particularise. While historians usually do try to restrict themselves to the 'past', social scientists, especially when conducting concrete enquiries, deal with both the 'past' and the 'present' (so-called), as well as being intimately concerned with change. This division has not always existed, having arisen and become institutionalised only since the second half of the nineteenth century.

In fact, any methodological distinction between supposedly past- and present-oriented enquiries is completely false since there is no real present separate from that which has already occurred. All phenomena are by definition past, since they must already have happened for us to be aware of them. Of course there are processes which continue to occur and have not yet run their full course, and which are contemporaneous with our own personal experience of the world. But the distinction sometimes made between historical and present-oriented studies on the basis of personal experience as opposed to recorded experience is misleading, since our modes of experiencing past and contemporary events are in fact not different. Sensational experience can be of our immediate surroundings only and all information comes to us through our senses. Apart from the small part of the world that we are able to experience directly, all our information about it comes to us in the form of the *recorded* reports, impressions, and interpretations of others, whether of events contemporaneous with our own lives or not. Thus nearly all socio-historical explanation relies upon recorded information, including even our own memories. Whether we compile and record information ourselves or rely upon the recordings of others makes no methodological difference; nor does the age of the records.

Similarly, any division between static and dynamic studies has validity only as a heuristic device. Since all societies are in a constant if gradual state of change, both internally and in their connections with their natural environment, any attempt to study them in isolation from either their changing material foundations or relational transformations must be abstract and one sided. Such abstractions do, however, have their uses but are not confined to any of the existing sub-branches of the historical and social studies. While societies are constantly changing it is often helpful to postulate them theoretically as fixed entities; and, in any case, the fact that structures gradually change does not rule out the possibility of scientific enquiry since they do have a relative continuity as structures. Without such continuity scientific enquiry would be impossible, and so would all social understanding since language and meaning themselves would be impossible.

The existing divisions between the social sciences such as sociology, economics, and politics, are perhaps more firmly based since they deal with what seem to be relatively natural levels or subsystems within society. But I believe they too may be ill founded if these divisions disguise what are really only reified theoretical constructions. The economic and the political, for instance, are often treated by those who study them as if they were relatively self-contained levels or structures or types of behaviour, rather than merely as abstractions. If, however, they were not even relatively independent then much academic work in economics and politics would have to be modified radically. If forms of behaviour are not really 'economic' or 'political', and if actors do not themselves perceive their actions in this way, then perhaps some social science took a wrong turning in the late nineteenth and early twentieth centuries. Many social scientists do now believe this and wish to reunite the various strands, just as Marx and Weber did. But clearly there must be some division of labour within a unified social science. How is it to be based?

My first proposal is for a division of labour simply between theoretical and concrete enquiries. Let me hasten to add that I do not mean either that the two should be done separately, using different discourses, or that there should be a simple distinction between theory and observation. I envisage a situation analogous to that in some natural sciences, such as particle physics or cosmology, where theory and experimentation and observation react dialectically with each other, constantly employing the findings of the other to produce new problems, new techniques, and new solutions. But the amount of expertise required and the complexity of the subject necessitate a division of labour.

We should view the whole domain of human consciousness, action, behaviour, culture, and social structure as one field of entities existing on a single plane without the possibility of reduction to biology or psychology. This is the domain of the social. Theoretical work within this domain would be concerned with constructing *general* theories of the nature, causation, and history of human behaviour and social structures and of their interconnections. It would be abstract and philosophical. Concrete enquiry would be concerned with examining the causation, meaning, and effects of *particular* beliefs, actions, patterns of behaviour, structures, and transformations.

My second proposal is for a further division of labour at the concrete level between enquiries into actions on one hand, and enquiries into patterns of behaviour and structures on the other. Although both must use the work of the other, it is possible to study social structures relatively independently of particular actions and the lives of particular persons because they are not reducible to individuals, although they would not exist if the *totality* of humans expired. Whenever there are numbers of people existing together they form families, institutions, social networks, languages, cultures, and so on, which then take on a life of their own and exert influence over action.

The structurationist research paradigm ties the three aspects together through theory and shows how they relate over time. Concrete enquiry must employ theory and necessarily produces results which affect theory. Theory must draw upon both philosophy and concrete results but does not attempt to explain the particularity of actions and structures. The best social scientific work, such as that now being done under the aegis of social history and historical sociology embodies these dialectical relationships between abstract generalities and concrete particularities and between action and structure. Of course there will always be a problem of the adequacy of social theory to grasp all the complexities of particular situations and actions since there is undoubtedly a degree of indeterminacy in social life. But social science can live with that just as natural science does.

Thus I am advocating a threefold division of labour, within a unified science of society (which should be properly called 'sociology'), between social theory, structural history, and action history. 'Social history', properly so-called, should then be seen, if it is to have meaning as a concept, as the history of society as an entity. Economic history is at present the chief form of structural history, but its concentration on a rather narrow conception of the economy limits its explanatory potential. It should be incorporated into and superseded by structural history, which would then be similar to the political economy of the eighteenth and nineteenth centuries, and which has revived in recent years.

The term 'historical sociology' is also much used nowadays by social scientists who wish to emphasise the particular and dynamic nature of their object of enquiry. But attempts such as by Laslett (1977) and Cahnman (1976) to see it as a new type of discourse separate from sociology and history have been confused. Sociology has always had some interest in social change; and social history, properly so-called, in fact attempts to do what the historical sociologists say they wish to do. I believe the term 'structural history' captures better the essence of the discourse and should be seen as synonymous with 'social history', 'historical sociology', 'social change', and 'cultural change' – all terms referring basically to the one kind of process of *structural* change.

Bibliography

Abrams, Philip (1980), 'History, Sociology, Historical Sociology', *Past and Present*, no. 87.
—— (1982), *Historical Sociology*, Somerset: Open Books.
Achinstein, Peter (1968), *Concepts of Science*, Baltimore: Johns Hopkins Press.
—— (1969), 'Approaches to the Philosophy of Science', in Achinstein, P. and Barker, S.F. (eds) (1969), *The Legacy of Logical Positivism*, Baltimore: Johns Hopkins Press.
Addis, Laird (1981), 'Dispositions, Explanations, and Behaviour', *Inquiry*, vol. 24.
Adorno, Theodor W. (1976), 'Introduction', 'Sociology and Empirical Research', and 'On the Logic of the Social Sciences', in Adorno, T. et al., *The Positivist Dispute in German Sociology*, London: Heinemann.
—— et al. (1976), *The Positivist Dispute in German Sociology*, London: Heinemann.
Agassi, Joseph (1960), 'Methodological Individualism', reprinted in O'Neill, J. (ed.) (1973), *Modes of Individualism and Collectivism*, London: Heinemann.
—— (1964), 'The Nature of Scientific Problems and their Roots in Metaphysics', reprinted in Agassi, J. (1975), *Science in Flux*, Dordrecht: Reidel.
Albert, Hans (1978), 'Science and the Search for Truth', in Radnitzky, S. and Andersson, S. (eds) (1978), *Progress and Rationality in Science*, Dordrecht: Reidel.
Alexander, Jeffrey C. (1984), 'Social-Structural Analysis: Some Notes on its History and Prospects', *Sociological Quarterly*, vol. 25.
Allport, G. W. (1962), 'The General and the Unique in Psychological Science', reprinted in Reason, P. and Rowan, J. (eds) (1981), *Human Inquiry*, Chichester: John Wiley.
Alston, William P. (1974), 'Conceptual Prolegomena to a Psychological Theory of Intentional Action', in Brown, S. C. (ed.) (1974), *Philosophy of Psychology*, London: Macmillan.

—— (1976), 'Traits, Consistency, and Conceptual Alterntives for Personality Theory', reprinted in Harré, R. (ed.), (1976), *Personality*, Oxford: Basil Blackwell.

—— (1978), 'Yes, Virginia, There is a Real World', *American Philosophical Association Proceedings and Addresses*, vol. 52.

Althusser, Louis (1969), *For Marx*, Harmondsworth: Penguin.

—— (1971), *Lenin and Philosophy*, London: New Left Books.

—— (1972), *Politics and History*, London: New Left Books.

—— (1973), 'The Conditions of Marx's Scientific Discovery', *Theoretical Practice*, no. 7/8.

—— (1976), *Essays in Self-Criticism*, London: New Left Books.

—— and Balibar, Etienne (1970), *Reading Capital*, 2nd edn, London: New Left Books.

Anderson, Perry (1964), 'Origins of the Present Crisis', reprinted in Anderson, P. and Blackburn, R. (eds) (1966), *Towards Socialism*, Ithaca: Cornell University Press.

—— (1966), 'Socialism and Pseudo-Empiricism', *New Left Review*, no. 35.

—— (1968), 'Components of the National Culture', *New Left Review*, no. 50.

—— (1974a), *Lineages of the Absolutist State*, London: New Left Books.

—— (1974b), *Passages from Antiquity to Feudalism*, London: New Left Books.

—— (1976), *Considerations on Western Marxism*, London: New Left Books.

—— (1980), *Arguments within English Marxism*, London: New Left Books.

—— (1983), *In the Tracks of Historical Materialism*, London: Verso.

Anscombe, G. E. M. (1979), *Intention*, 2nd edn, Oxford: Basil Blackwell.

Antoni, Carlo (1959), *From History to Sociology*, London: Merlin Press.

Apel, Karl-Otto (1976), 'Causal Explanation, Motivational Explanation, and Hermeneutical Understanding', in Ryle, G. (ed.) (1976), *Contemporary Aspects of Philosophy*, Stocksfield: Oriel Press (Routledge and Kegan Paul).

Archer, Margaret S. (1982), 'Morphogenesis vs Structuration', *British Journal of Sociology*, vol. 33.

Argyle, Michael (1967), 'The Social Psychology of Social Change', in Burns, T. and Saul, S. B. (eds) (1967), *Social Theory and Social Change*, London: Tavistock.

——, Furnham, Adrian and Graham, Jean Ann (1981), *Social Situations*, Cambridge: Cambridge University Press.

Armstrong, D. M. (1968), *A Materialist Theory of the Mind*, London: Routledge and Kegan Paul.

—— (1970), 'The Nature of Mind', reprinted in Block, N. (ed.) (1980), *Readings in Philosophy of Psychology*, London: Methuen.

—— (1972), 'Materialism, Properties, and Predicates', *The Monist*, vol. 56.

—— (1973), 'Epistemological Foundations for a Materialist Theory of the Mind', reprinted in Armstrong, D. M. (1981), *The Nature of Mind and Other Essays*, Brighton: Harvester.

—— (1977), 'The Causal Theory of the Mind', reprinted in Armstrong, D. M. (1981), *The Nature of Mind and Other Essays*, Brighton: Harvester.

—— (1978a), 'Naturalism, Materialism, and First Philosophy', *Philosophia*, vol. 8.

—— (1978b), *Nominalism and Realism*, Cambridge: Cambridge University Press.

—— (1978c), *A Theory of Universals,* Cambridge: Cambridge University Press.

—— (1979), 'Perception, Sense-Data and Causality', in Macdonald, G. F. (ed.) (1979), *Perception and Identity,* London: Macmillan.

Aron, Raymond (1938), *Introduction to the Philosophy of History,* Boston: Beacon Press, 1961.

Arrow, Kenneth J. (1967), 'Values and Collective Decision Making', in Laslett, P. and Runciman, W. G. (eds) (1967), *Philosophy, Politics, and Society,* third series, Oxford: Basil Blackwell; also reprinted in Hahn, F. and Hollis, M. (eds) (1979), *Philosophy and Economic Theory,* Oxford: Oxford University Press.

—— (1977), 'Current Developments in the Theory of Social Choice', *Social Research,* vol. 44; also reprinted in Barry, B. and Hardin, R. (eds) (1982), *Rational Man and Irrational Society?,* Beverly Hills: Sage.

Atkinson, R. F. (1978), *Knowledge and Explanation in History,* London: Macmillan.

Aune, Bruce (1977), *Reason and Action,* Dordrecht: Reidel.

Ayer, A. J. (1946), *Language, Truth and Logic,* Harmondsworth: Penguin.

—— (ed.) (1959), *Logical Positivism,* NY: Free Press.

—— (1967), 'Man as a Subject for Science', in Laslett, P. and Runciman, W. G. (eds) (1967), *Philosophy, Politics, and Society,* Third Series, Oxford: Basil Blackwell.

Baechler, Jean (1975), *The Origins of Capitalism,* Oxford: Basil Blackwell.

Balibar, Etienne (1978), 'From Bachelard to Althusser: the Concept of "Epistemological Break"', *Economy and Society,* vol. 7.

Barnes, Barry (1974), *Scientific Knowledge and Sociological Theory,* London: Routledge.

—— (1977), *Interests and the Growth of Knowledge,* London: Routledge and Kegan Paul.

—— (1981), 'On the Conventional Character of Knowledge and Cognition', *Philosophy of Social Sciences,* vol. 11.

—— (1982), *T. S. Kuhn and Social Science,* London: Macmillan.

—— and Bloor, David (1982), 'Relativism, Rationalism, and the Sociology of Knowledge', in Hollis, M. and Lukes, S. (eds) (1982), *Rationality and Relativism,* Oxford: Basil Blackwell.

Barry, Brian (1970), *Sociologists, Economists, and Democracy,* Chicago: University of Chicago Press.

—— and Hardin, Russell (eds) (1982), *Rational Man and Irrational Society?,* Beverly Hills: Sage.

Bauman, Zygmunt (1978), *Hermeneutics and Social Science,* London: Hutchinson.

Beauchamp, Tom L. and Rosenberg, Alexander (1981), *Hume and the Problem of Causation,* NY: Oxford University Press.

Becker, Gary S. (1974), 'A Theory of Social Interactions', *Journal of Political Economy,* vol. 82.

—— (1976a), 'Altruism, Egoism, and Genetic Fitness: Economics and Sociobiology', *Journal of Economic Literature,* vol. 14.

—— (1976b), *The Economic Approach to Human Behavior,* Chicago: University of Chicago Press.

—— (1979), 'Economic Analysis and Human Behaviour', in Levy-Laboua, L. (ed.) (1979), *Sociological Economics,* London: Sage.

Bekker, Konrad (1952), 'The Point IV Program of the United States', in Hoselitz,

B. (cd.) (1952), *The Progress of Underdeveloped Areas*, Chicago: University of Chicago Press.

Bellah, Robert N. (1959), 'Durkheim and History', reprinted in Cahnman, W. J. and Boskoff, A. (eds) (1964), *Sociology and History*, Glencoe: Free Press.

Bendix, Reinhard (1959), *Work and Authority in Industry*, NY: Harper Torchbooks.

—— (1967), 'The Comparative Analysis of Historical Change', in Burns, T. and Saul, S. B. (eds) (1967), *Social Theory and Economic Change*, London: Tavistock.

—— (1970), 'Culture, Social Structure, and Change', in Bendix, R. (1970), *Embattled Reason*, NY: Oxford University Press.

—— (1977), *Nation-Building and Citizenship*, 2nd edn, Berkeley: University of California Press.

—— (1978), *Kings or People: Power and the Mandate to Rule*, Berkeley: University of California Press.

—— (1984), *Force, Fate, and Freedom*, Berkeley: University of California Press.

—— and Roth, Guenther (1971), *Scholarship and Partisanship: Essays on Max Weber*, Berkeley: University of California Press.

Benn, S. I. and Mortimore, G. W. (eds) (1976), *Rationality and the Social Sciences*, London: Routledge and Kegan Paul.

Bennett, Johnathan (1979), 'Analytic Transcendental Arguments', in Bieri, P. et al. (eds), *Transcendental Arguments and Science*, Dordrecht: Reidel.

Benton, Ted (1977), *Philosophical Foundations of the Three Sociologies*, London: Routledge and Kegan Paul.

—— (1984), *The Rise and Fall of Structural Marxism*, London: Macmillan.

Berger, Peter L. (1963), *Invitation to Sociology*, Harmondsworth: Penguin.

—— (1977), *Facing up to Modernity*, Harmondsworth: Penguin.

—— (1978), 'The Problem of Multiple Realities: Alfred Schutz and Robert Musil', in Luckmann, T. (ed.) (1978), *Phenomenology and Sociology*, Harmondsworth: Penguin.

—— and Berger, Brigitte (1976), *Sociology: a Biographical Approach*, Harmondsworth: Penguin.

—— Berger, Brigitte and Kellner, Hansfried (1973), *The Homeless Mind*, Harmondsworth: Penguin.

—— and Kellner, Hansfried (1981), *Sociology Reinterpreted*, Harmondsworth: Penguin.

—— and Luckmann, Thomas (1966), *The Social Construction of Reality*, Harmondsworth: Penguin.

Berghe, Pierre L. van den (1963), 'Dialectic and Functionalism: towards a Synthesis', reprinted in Demerath, N. J. and Peterson, R. A. (eds) (1967), *System, Change, and Conflict*, NY: Free Press.

Bergmann, Gustav (1967), *The Metaphysics of Logical Positivism*, 2nd edn, Madison: University of Wisconsin Press.

Berkhofer, Robert F. (1969), *A Behavioral Approach to Historical Analysis*, NY: Free Press.

Berlin, Isaiah (1960), 'The Concept of Scientific History', reprinted in Dray, W. H. (ed.) (1966), *Philosophical Analysis and History*, NY: Harper and Row.

—— (1962), 'The Purpose of Philosophy', reprinted in Berlin, I. (1978), *Concepts and Categories* (ed. H. Hardy), London: Hogarth Press.

—— (1969), 'Historical Inevitability', in *Four Essays on Liberty*, London: Oxford University Press.

Bernstein, Richard J. (1976), *The Restructuring of Social and Political Theory*, London: Methuen.

—— (1983), *Beyond Objectivism and Relativism*, Oxford: Basil Blackwell.

Bershady, Harold (1973), *Ideology and Social Knowledge*, Oxford: Basil Blackwell.

Bertalanffy, Ludwig von (1955), 'General Systems Theory', reprinted in Demerath, N. J. and Peterson, R. A. (eds) (1967), *System, Change, and Conflict*, NY: Free Press.

Betti, Emilio (1980), 'Hermeneutics as the General Methodology of the *Geistesswissenschaften*', in Bleicher, J. (1980), *Contemporary Hermeneutics*, London: Routledge and Kegan Paul.

Bhaskar, Roy (1975), *A Realist Theory of Science*, Leeds: Leeds Books.

—— (1978), 'On the Possibility of Scientific Knowledge and the Limits of Naturalism', *Journal for the Theory of Social Behaviour*, vol. 8.

—— (1979), *The Possibility of Naturalism*, Sussex: Harvester.

—— (1980), 'Scientific Explanation and Human Emancipation', *Radical Philosophy*, no. 26.

—— (1982a), 'Emergence, Explanation, and Emancipation', in Secord, P. F. (ed.) (1982), *Explaining Human Behavior*, Beverly Hills: Sage.

—— (1982b), 'Realism in the Natural Sciences', in Cohen L. J. et al. (eds) (1982), *Logic, Methodology, and Philosophy of Science*, VI, Amsterdam: North-Holland.

Birnbaum, Pierre (1976), 'Power Divorced from its Sources: a Critique of the Exchange Theory of Power', in Barry, B. (ed.) (1976), *Power and Political Theory*, London: John Wiley.

Black, Max (1954), 'Metaphor', reprinted in Black, M. (1962), *Models and Metaphors*, Ithaca: Cornell University Press.

—— (1960), 'Models and Archetypes', reprinted in Black, M. (1962), *Models and Metaphors*, Ithaca: Cornell University Press.

—— (1979), 'More About Metaphor', in Ortony, A. (ed.) (1979), *Metaphor and Thought*, Cambridge: Cambridge University Press.

Blau, Peter M. (1964), *Exchange and Power in Social Life*, NY: John Wiley.

—— (1968), 'Interaction: Social Exchange', *International Encyclopaedia of the Social Sciences*, vol. 7.

—— (1970), ' "Comment" on Homans', in Borger, R. and Cioffi, F. (eds) (1970), *Explanation in the Behavioural Sciences*, Cambridge: Cambridge University Press.

—— (1971), 'Justice in Social Exchange', in Turk, H. and Simpson, R. L. (eds) (1071), *Institutions and Social Change*, Indianopolis: Bobbs-Merrill.

—— (1974), 'Parameters of Social Structure', in Blau, P. (ed.) (1976), *Approaches to the Study of Social Structure*, London: Open Books.

—— (1975), 'Structural Constraints of Status Complements', in Coser, L. (ed.) (1975), *The Idea of Social Structure*, NY: Harcourt, Brace, Jovanovich.

—— (ed.) (1976a), *Approaches to the Study of Social Structure*, London: Open Books.

—— (1976b), 'Parallels and Contrasts in Structural Inquiries', in Blau, P. (ed.), *Approaches to the Study of Social Structure*, London: Open Books.

—— (1977), *Inequality and Heterogeneity*, NY: Free Press.

—— (1978), 'A Macrosociological Theory of Social Structure', *American Journal of Sociology*, vol. 83.

—— (1981), 'Diverse Views of Social Structure and their Common Denominator', in Blau, P. and Merton, R. (eds) (1981), *Continuities in Structural Inquiry*, London: Sage.

—— (1982), 'Structural Sociology and Network Analysis: an Overview', in Marsden, P. and Lin, N. (eds) (1982),*Social Structure and Network Analysis*, Beverly Hills: Sage.

—— (1983), 'Comments on the Prospects for a Theory of Social Structure', *Journal for the Theory of Social Behaviour*, vol. 13.

—— and Merton, Robert K. (eds) (1981), *Continuities in Structural Inquiry*, London: Sage.

Blaug, Mark (1980), *The Methodology of Economics*, Cambridge: Cambridge University Press.

Bleicher, Josef (1980), *Contemporary Hermeneutics*, London: Routledge and Kegan Paul.

—— (1982), *The Hermeneutic Imagination*, London: Routledge and Kegan Paul.

Bloch, Marc (1954), *The Historian's Craft*, Manchester: Manchester University Press.

—— (1962), *Feudal Society*, two vols, 2nd edn, London: Routledge.

—— (1966), *French Rural History*, London: Routledge and Kegan Paul.

Block, Ned (1981), 'Psychologism and Behaviourism', *Philosophical Review*, vol. XC.

—— (1982), 'Functionalism', in Cohen, L. J.et al. (eds) (1982), *Methodology and Philosophy of Science*, VI, Amsterdam: North-Holland.

Bloor, David (1976), *Knowledge and Social Imagery*, London: Routledge and Kegan Paul.

—— (1981), 'The Strengths of the Strong Programme', *Philosophy of Social Sciences*, vol. 11.

Blumer, Herbert (1969), *Symbolic Interactionism*, Englewood Cliffs: Prentice-Hall.

Bock, K. E. (1963), 'Evolution, Function and Change', reprinted in Eisenstadt, S. N. (ed.) (1970), *Readings in Social Evolution and Development*, Oxford: Pergamon.

—— (1964), 'Theories of Progress and Evolution', in Cahnman, W. J. and Boskoff, A. (eds) (1964), *Sociology and History*, Glencoe: Free Press.

—— (1979), 'Theories of Progress, Development and Evolution', in Bottomore, T. and Nisbet, R. (eds) (1979), *A History of Sociological Analysis*, London: Heinemann.

Boden, Margaret A. (1977), *Artificial Intelligence and Natural Man*, Hassocks: Harvester.

—— (1979a), 'The Computational Metaphor in Psychology', in Bolton, N. (ed.) (1979), *Philosophical Problems in Psychology*, London: Methuen.

—— (1979b), *Piaget*, Glasgow: Fontana.

Bohm, David (1980), *Wholeness and the Implicate Order*, London: Routledge and Kegan Paul.

Boissevain, Jeremy (1974), *Friends of Friends*, Oxford: Basil Blackwell.

Bonnell, Victoria E. (1980), 'The Uses of Theory; Concepts and Comparisons in Historical Sociology', *Comparative Studies in Society and History*, vol. 22.

Børst, C. V. (ed.) (1970), *The Mind/Brain Identity Theory*, London: Macmillan.

Bottomore, Tom (1976), 'Structure and History', in Blau, P. (ed.) (1976), *Approaches to the Study of Social Structure*, London: Open Books.

—— and Nisbet, Robert (1979), 'Structuralism', in Bottomore, T. and Nisbet, R. (eds) (1979), *History of Sociological Analysis*, London: Heinemann.

Boudon, Raymond (1971), *The Uses of Structuralism*, London: Heinemann.

—— (1981b), 'Undesired Consequences and Types of Structures of Systems of Interdependence', in Blau, P. and Merton, R. (eds) (1981), *Continuities in Structural Inquiry*, London: Sage.

—— (1983), 'Individual Action and Social Change', *British Journal of Sociology*, vol. 34.

Boyd, Richard N. (1973), 'Realism, Underdetermination, and a Causal Theory of Evidence', *Nous*, vol. 7.

—— (1979), 'Metaphor and Theory Change: What is 'Metaphor' a Metaphor for?', in Ortony, A. (ed.) (1979), *Metaphor and Thought*, Cambridge: Cambridge University Press.

—— (1980), 'Materialism without Reductionism: what Physicalism does not Entail', in Block, N. (ed.) (1980), *Readings in Philosophy of Psychology*, London: Methuen.

—— (1983), 'On the Current Status of the Issue of Scientific Realism', *Erkenntnis*, vol. 19.

Bradie, Michael (1972), 'Is Scientific Realism a Contingent Thesis?', in Schaffner, K. F. and Cohen, R. S. (1974), *PSA 1972*, Dordrecht: Reidel.

Braithwaite, R. B. (1953), *Scientific Explanation*, Cambridge: Cambridge University Press.

Braudel, Fernand (1973), *The Mediterranean and the Mediterranean World in the Age of Philip II*, two vols, NY: Harper and Row.

—— (1977), *Afterthoughts on Material Civilization and Capitalism*, Baltimore: Johns Hopkins University Press.

—— (1980), *On History*, London: Weidenfeld and Nicolson.

—— (1981), *Civilization and Capitalism, 15th–18th century. Vol. I: The Structures of Everyday Life*, London: Collins.

—— (1982), *Civilization and Capitalism, 15th–18th century. Vol. II: The Wheels of Commerce*, London: Collins.

—— (1984), *Civilization and Capitalism, 15th–18th century. Vol.III: The Perspective of the World*, London: Collins.

Bredemeier, Harry C. (1979), 'Exchange Theory', in Bottomore, T. and Nisbet, R. (eds), *History of Sociological Analysis*, London: Heinemann.

Brenner, Robert (1976), 'Agrarian Class Structure and Economic Development in Pre-Industrial Europe', *Past and Present*, no. 70.

—— (1977), 'The Origins of Capitalist Development: a Critique of Neo-Smithian Marxism', *New Left Review*, no. 104.

—— (1982), 'The Agrarian Roots of European Capitalism', *Past and Present*, no. 97.

Brodbeck, May (1954), 'On the Philosophy of the Social Sciences', reprinted in O'Neill, J. (ed.) (1973), *Modes of Individualism and Collectivism*, London: Heinemann.

—— (1958), 'Methodological Individualisms: Definition and Reduction', reprinted in O'Neill, J. (ed.) (1973), *Modes of Individualism and Collectivism*, London: Heinemann.

—— (1962), 'Explanation, Prediction, and Imperfect Knowledge', *Minnesota Studies in Philosophy of Science*, vol. III.

Brown, Richard Harvey (1978), 'Symbolic Realism and Sociological Thought: Beyond the Positivist-Romantic Debate', in Brown, R. H. and Lyman, S. (eds) (1978), *Structure, Consciousness, and History*, Cambridge: Cambridge University Press.

—— and Lyman, Standford M. (1978), 'Symbolic Realism and Cognitive Aesthetics: an Invitation', in Brown, R. H. and Lyman, S. (eds) (1978), *Structure, Consciousness, and History*, Cambridge: Cambridge University Press.

Buchdahl, Gerd (1980), 'Neo-Transcendental Approaches Towards Scientific Theory Appraisal', in Mellor, D. H. (ed.) (1980), *Science, Belief, and Behaviour*, Cambridge: Cambridge University Press.

Buckley, Walter (1957), 'Structural-Functional Analysis in Modern Sociology', in Becker, H. and Boskoff, A. (eds) (1957), *Modern Sociological Theory in Continuity and Change*, NY: Dryden Press.

—— (1967), *Sociology and Modern Systems Theory*, Englewood Cliffs: Prentice-Hall.

Bunge, Mario (1980), *The Mind–Body Problem*, Oxford: Pergamon.

—— (1981), *Scientific Materialism*, Dordrecht: Reidel.

Burger, Thomas (1977), 'Talcott Parsons, the Problem of Order in Society, and the Program of an Analytical Sociology', *American Journal of Sociology*, vol. 83.

Burke, Kenneth (1968), 'Interaction: Dramatism', *International Encyclopaedia of the Social Sciences*, vol. 7.

—— (1973), *The Philosophy of Literary Form*, 3rd edn, Berkeley: University of California Press.

Burke, Peter (ed.) (1973), *A New Kind of History: From the Writings of Fèbvre*, London: Routledge and Kegan Paul.

—— (1978), 'Reflections on the Historical Revolution in France: the Annales School and British Social History', *Review*, vol. 1.

—— (1980), *Sociology and History*, London: George Allen and Unwin.

—— (1981), 'People's History or Total History?', in Samuel, R. (ed.) (1981), *People's History and Socialist Theory*, London: Routledge and Kegan Paul.

Burrow, J. W. (1966), *Evolution and Society*, Cambridge: Cambridge University Press.

Bury, J. B.(1932), *The Idea of Progress*, NY: Dover Publications.

Cahnman, Werner J. (1976), 'Historical Sociology: What it is and What it is not', in Varma, B. N. (ed.) (1976), *The New Social Sciences*, Westport: Greenwood Press.

—— and Boskoff, Alvin (1964), 'Sociology and History: Reunion and Rapprochement', in Cahnman, W. J. and Boskoff, A. (eds) (1964), *Sociology and History*, Glencoe: Free Press.

Callinicos, Alex (1976), *Althusser's Marxism*, London: Pluto Press.

Callon, M. and Latour, B. (1981), 'Unscrewing the Big Leviathan: How Actors Macro Structure Reality and How Sociologists Help Them to do so', in Knorr, K. and Cicourel, A. (eds) (1981), *Advances in Social Theory and Methodology*, London: Routledge and Kegan Paul.

Campbell, Donald T. (1965), 'Variation and Selective Retention in Socio-

Cultural Evolution', in Barringer, H. R. et al. (eds) (1965), *Social Change in Developing Areas*, Cambridge, Mass.: Schenken.
—— (1974), 'Evolutionary Epistemology', in Schilpp, P. A. (ed.) (1974), *The Philosophy of Karl Popper*, La Salle: Open Court.
—— (1975), 'On the Conflicts between Biological and Social Evolution and between Psychology and Moral Tradition', *American Psychologist*, vol. 30.
Campbell, Norman (1921), *What is Science?*, NY: Dover Publications.
Cancian, Francesca M. (1968), 'Varieties of Functional Analysis', *International Encyclopaedia of the Social Sciences*, vol. 6.
Carnap, Rudolf (1932), 'The Elimination of Metaphysics through Logical Analysis', reprinted in Ayer, A. J. (ed.) (1959), *Logical Positivism*, NY: Free Press.
—— (1934), *The Unity of Science*, excerpts reprinted in Hanfling, O. (ed.) (1981), *Essential Readings in Logical Positivism*, Oxford: Blackwell.
—— (1938), *Foundations of the Unity of Science*, excerpts reprinted in Hanfling, O. (ed.) (1981), *Essential Readings in Logical Positivism*, Oxford: Basil Blackwell.
—— (1946), 'Truth and Confirmation', reprinted in Alston, W. P. and Nahknikian, G. (eds) (1963), *Readings in Twentieth Century Philosophy*, Glencoe: Free Press.
—— (1950a), 'Empiricism, Semantics, and Ontology', reprinted in Carnap, R. (1956), *Meaning and Necessity*, 2nd edn, Chicago: University of Chicago Press.
—— (1950b), 'Probability and Inductive Logic', reprinted in Shapere, D. (ed.) (1965), *Philosophical Problems of Natural Science*, NY: Macmillan.
—— (1956a), *Meaning and Necessity*, 2nd edn, Chicago: Unversity of Chicago Press.
—— (1956b), 'The Methodological Character of Theoretical Concepts', in Feigl, H. and Scriven, M. (eds) (1956), *Minnesota Studies in Philosophy of Science*, vol. I.
—— (1966), *An Introduction to the Philosophy of Science* (originally *The Philosophical Foundations of Physics*) (ed. Martin Gardner), NY: Basic Books.
Carr, E. H. (1961), *What is History?*, Harmondsworth: Penguin.
Chirot, Daniel (1976), 'Thematic Controversies and New Developments in the Uses of Historical Materials by Sociologists', *Social Forces*, vol. 55.
—— (1981), 'Changing Fashions in the Study of the Social Causes of Economic and Political Change', in Short, J. F. (ed.) (1981), *The State of Sociology*, Beverly Hills: Sage.
Chisholm, Roderick M. (1980), 'The Agent as Cause', in Brand, M. and Walton, D. (eds) (1980), *Action Theory*, Dordrecht: Reidel.
Chodak, Szymon (1973), *Societal Development: Five Approaches with Conclusions from Comparative Analysis*, NY: Oxford University Press.
Chomsky, Noam (1972), *Language and Mind*, enlarged edn, NY: Harcourt Brace Jovanovich.
Cicourel, A. V. (1981), 'Notes on the Integration of Micro and Macro Levels of Analysis', in Knorr-Cetina, K. and Cicourel, A. V. (eds) (1981), *Advances in Social Theory and Methodology*, London: Routledge and Kegan Paul.
Clark, Priscilla P. and Clark, Terry Nicholas (1982), 'The Structural Sources of

French Structuralism', in Rossi, I. (ed.) (1982), *Structural Sociology*, NY: Columbia University Press.

Clark, T. N. (1972), 'Structural-Functionalism, Exchange Theory, and the New Political Economy: Institutionalisation as a Theoretical Linkage', *Sociological Inquiry*, vol. 42.

Clarke, S. (1979), 'Socialist Humanism and the Critique of Economism', *History Workshop*, no. 8.

—— (1981), *The Foundations of Structuralism*, Sussex: Harvester.

Clubb, J. M. (1980), 'The "New" Quantitative History: Social Science or Old Wine in New Bottles', in Clubb, J. M. and Scheuch, E. M. (eds) (1080), *Historical Social Research*, Stuttgart: Klctt-Cotta.

—— (1981), 'History as a Social Science', *International Social Science Journal*, vol. 32.

Cohen, G. A. (1978), *Karl Marx's Theory of History: a Defence*, Oxford: Clarendon Press.

—— (1980), 'Functional Explanation: Reply to Elster', *Political Studies*, vol. 28.

—— (1982a), 'Functional Explanation, Consequence Explanation, and Marxism', *Inquiry*, vol. 25.

—— (1982b), 'Reply to Elster on Marxism, Functionalism and Game Theory', *Theory and Society*, vol. 11.

Cohen, Jon S. (1978), 'The Achievements of Economic History: the Marxist School', *Journal of Economic History*, vol. 38.

Coleman, James S. (1966), 'Foundations for a Theory of Collective Decisions', *American Journal of Sociology*, vol. 71.

—— (1971a), 'Collective Decisions', in Turk, H. and Simpson, R. L. (eds) (1971), *Institutions and Social Change*, Indianopolis: Bobbs-Merrill.

—— (1971b), 'Community Disorganisation and Conflict', in Merton, R. K. and Nisbet, R. (eds) (1971), *Contemporary Social Problems*, 3rd edn, NY: Harcourt Brace Jovanovich.

—— (1971c), *Resources for Social Change*, NY: John Wiley.

—— (1972a), 'Collective Decisions and Collective Action', in Laslett, P. et al. (1972), *Philosophy, Politics and Society*, fourth series, Oxford: Blackwell.

—— (1972b), 'Systems of Social Exchange', reprinted in Leinfellner, W. and Kohler, E. (eds) (1974), *Developments in the Methodology of Social Science*, Dordrecht: Reidel.

—— (1973), 'Conflicting Theories of Social Change', in G. Zaltman (ed.) (1973), *Processes and Phenomena of Social Change*, NY: Wiley.

—— (1974), *Power and the Structure of Society*, NY: W. W. Norton.

—— (1975), 'Legitimate and Illegitimate Uses of Power', in Coser, L. (ed.) (1975), *The Idea of Social Structure*, NY: Harcourt Brace Jovanovich.

—— (1976), 'Social Structure and a Theory of Action', in Blau, P. M. (ed.) (1976), *Approaches to the Study of Social Structure*, London: Open Books.

—— (1979a), 'The Measurement of Societal Growth', in Hawley, A. H. (ed.) (1979), *Societal Growth*, NY: Free Press.

—— (1979b), 'Purposive Actors and Mutual Effects', in Merton, R. K. et al. (eds) (1979), *Qualitative and Quantitative Social Resarch*, NY: Free Press.

—— (1979c), 'Rational Actors in Macrosociological Analysis', in Harrison, R. (ed.) (1979), *Rational Action*, Cambridge: Cambridge University Press.

—— (1979d), 'Sociological Analysis and Social Policy', in Bottomore, T. and Nisbet, R. (eds) (1979), *History of Sociological Analysis*, London: Heinemann.

—— (1982a), *The Asymmetrical Society*, Syracuse: Syracuse University Press.

—— (1982b), 'Policy, Research, and Political Theory', in Kruskal, W. H. (ed.) (1982), *The Social Sciences*, Chicago: University of Chicago Press.

—— et al. (1970), *Macrosociology: Research and Theory*, Boston: Allyn and Bacon.

Collingwood, R. G. (1946), *The Idea of History*, London: Oxford University Press.

Collins, R. (1981a), 'Micro-Translation as a Theory-building Strategy', in Knorr-Cetina, K. and Cicourel, A. V. (eds) (1981), *Advances in Social Theory and Methodology*, London: Routledge and Kegan Paul.

—— (1981b), 'On the Microfoundations of Macrosociology', *American Journal of Sociology*, vol. 86.

Connerton, P. (1980), *The Tragedy of Enlightenment*, Cambridge: Cambridge University Press.

Craib, I. (1984), *Modern Social Theory*, Sussex: Harvester.

Cranach, M. von (1982), 'The Psychological Study of Goal-Directed Action: Basic Ideas', in von Cranach, M. and Harré, R. (eds) (1982), *The Analysis of Action*, Cambridge: Cambridge University Press.

Cronin, J. (1978), 'Creating a Marxist Historiography: the Contribution of Hobsbawm', *Radical History Review*, no. 19, 1978–9.

Curd, M. (1980), 'The Logic of Discovery: an Analysis of Three Approaches', in Nickles. T. (ed.) (1980), *Scientific Discovery, Logic, and Rationality*, Dordrecht: Reidel.

Dahrendorf, R. (1959), *Class and Class Conflict in Industrial Society*, London: Routledge and Kegan Paul.

Dallmayr, F. R. (1982), 'Agency and Structure', *Philosophy of Social Science*, vol. 12.

Danto, A. C. (1963), 'The Historical Individual', reprinted in Dray, W. (ed.) (1966), *Philosophical Analysis and History*, NY: Harper and Row.

—— (1968), *Analytical Philosophy of History*, Cambridge: Cambridge University Press.

Davidson, D. (1963), 'Actions, Reasons, and Causes', reprinted in Davidson, D. (1980), *Essays on Actions and Events*, Oxford: Clarendon Press.

—— (1967a), 'Causal Relations', reprinted in Davidson, D. (1980), *Essays on Actions and Events*, Oxford: Clarendon Press.

—— (1969), 'The Individuation of Events', reprinted in Davidson, D. (1980), *Essays on Actions and Events*, Oxford: Clarendon Press.

—— (1970a), 'Events as Particulars', reprinted in Davidson, D. (1980), *Essays on Actions and Events*, Oxford: Clarendon Press.

—— (1970b), 'Mental Events', reprinted in Davidson, D. (1980), *Essays on Actions and Events*, Oxford: Clarendon Press.

—— (1971), 'Agency', reprinted in Davidson, D. (1980), *Essays on Actions and Events*, Oxford: Clarendon Press.

—— (1973), 'The Material Mind', reprinted in Davidson, D. (1980), *Essays on Actions and Events*, Oxford: Clarendon Press.

—— (1974a), 'On the Very Idea of a Conceptual Scheme', reprinted in Davidson, D. (1984), *Inquiries into Truth and Interpretation*, Oxford: Clarendon Press.

—— (1974b), 'Psychology as Philosophy', reprinted in Davidson, D. (1980), *Essays on Actions and Events*, Oxford: Clarendon Press.

—— (1978a), 'Intending', reprinted in Davidson, D. (1980), *Essays on Actions and Events*, Oxford: Clarendon Press.

—— (1978b), 'What Metaphors Mean', reprinted in Davidson, D. (1984), *Inquiries into Truth and Interpretation*, Oxford: Clarendon Press.

—— (1979), 'The Method of Truth in Metaphysics', reprinted in Davidson, D. (1984), *Inquiries into Truth and Interpretation*, Oxford: Clarendon Press.

—— (1980), *Essays on Actions and Events*, Oxford: Clarendon Press.

—— (1984), *Inquiries into Truth and Interpretation*, Oxford: Clarendon Press.

Davis, K. (1959), 'The Myth of Functional Analysis as a Special Method in Sociology and Anthropology', reprinted in Demerath, N. J. and Peterson, R. A. (eds) (1967), *System, Change, and Conflict*, NY: Free Press.

Davis, L. E. and North, D. C. (1971), *Institutional Change and American Economic Growth*, Cambridge: Cambridge University Press.

Davis, L. H. (1979), *Theory of Action*, Englewood Cliffs: Prentice-Hall.

Dawe, A. (1970), 'The Two Sociologies', *British Journal of Sociology*, vol. 21.

—— (1979), 'Theories of Social Action', in Bottomore, T. and Nisbet, R. (eds) (1979), *A History of Sociological Analysis*, London: Heinemann.

Day, J. (1980), 'Fernand Braudel and the Rise of Capitalism', *Social Research*, vol. 47.

Demerath, N. J. and Peterson, R. A. (eds) (1967), *System, Change, and Conflict*, NY: Free Press.

Dilthey, W. (1961), *Pattern and Meaning in History*, NY: Harper and Row.

—— (1976), *Selected Writings*, Cambridge: Cambridge University Press.

Dobb, M. (1946), *Studies in the Development of Capitalism*, London: Routledge and Kegan Paul.

Donagan, A. (1964), 'Historical Explanation: the Popper-Hempel Theory Rediscovered', reprinted in Dray, W. (ed.) (1966), *Philosophical Analysis and History*, NY: Harper and Row.

Doppelt, G. (1981), 'Laudan's Pragmatic Alternative to Positivist and Historicist Theories of Science', *Inquiry*, vol. 24.

Downs, A. (1957), *An Economic Theory of Democracy*, NY: Harper and Row.

Dray, W. (1957), *Laws and Explanation in History*, London: Oxford University Press.

—— (1959), ' "Explaining what" in History', in Gardiner, P. (ed.) (1959), *Theories of History*, NY: Free Press.

—— (1963), 'The Historical Explanation of Actions Reconsidered', reprinted in Gardiner, P. (ed.) (1974), *The Philosophy of History*, London: Oxford University Press.

—— (1964), *The Philosophy of History*, Englewood Cliffs: Prentice-Hall.

—— (1967), 'Singular Hypotheticals and Historical Explanation', in Gross, L. (ed.) (1967), *Sociological Theory: Inquiries and Paradigms*, NY: Harper and Row.

Dreyfus, H. L. (1980), 'Holism and Hermeneutics', *Review of Metaphysics*, vol. 34.

—— and Haugeland, J. (1974), 'The Computer as a Mistaken Model of the Mind', in Brown, S. C. (ed.) (1974), *Philosophy of Psychology*, London: Macmillan.

—— and Rabinow, P. (1982), *Michel Foucault: Beyond Structuralism and Hermeneutics*, Sussex: Harvester.

Dummett, M. (1979), 'Common Sense and Physics', in Macdonald, G. (ed.) (1979), *Perception and Identity*, London: Macmillan.

—— (1982), 'Realism', *Synthese*, vol. 52.

Durkheim, E. (1938), *The Rules of Sociological Method*, NY: Free Press.

Eade, S. (1976), 'Social History in Britain in 1976: a Survey', *Labour History*, no. 31.

Eisenstadt, S. N. (1957), 'Sociological Aspects of Political Development in Underdeveloped Countries', *Economic Development and Cultural Change*, vol. 5.

—— (1963), 'Modernization: Growth and Diversity', reprinted in Eisenstadt, S. N. (1973), *Tradition, Change, and Modernity*, NY: John Wiley.

—— (1964), 'Social Change, Differentiation, and Evolution', reprinted in Demerath, N. J. and Peterson, R. A. (eds) (1967), *System, Change and Conflict*, NY: Free Press.

—— (1965), 'Transformation of Social, Political and Cultural Orders in Modernization', *American Sociological Review*, vol. 30.

—— (1966), *Modernization: Protest and Change*, Englewood Cliffs: Prentice-Hall.

—— (1973), *Tradition, Change and Modernity*, NY: John Wiley.

—— (1974), 'Studies of Modernization and Sociological Theory', *History and Theory*, vol. XIII.

—— (1981a), 'Cultural Traditions and Political Dynamics', *British Journal of Sociology*, vol. 32.

—— (1981b), 'Some Observations on Structuralism in Sociology, with Special and Paradoxical Reference to Max Weber', in Blau, P. and Merton, R. (eds) (1981), *Continuities in Structural Inquiry*, Beverly Hills: Sage.

—— (1982), 'Symbolic Structures and Social Dynamics', in Rossi, I. (ed.) (1982), *Structural Sociology*, NY: Columbia University Press.

Ekeh, P. (1974), *Social Exchange Theory*, London: Heinemann.

Eley, G. (1979), 'Some Recent Tendencies in Social History', in Iggers, G. G. and Parker, H. T. (eds) (1979), *International Handbook of Historical Studies*, London: Methuen.

Elias, N. (1978a), *The History of Manners*, Oxford: Basil Blackwell.

—— (1978b), *What is Sociology?*, London: Hutchinson.

—— (1982), *State Formation and Civilization*, Oxford: Basil Blackwell.

—— (1983), *The Court Society*, Oxford: Basil Blackwell.

Ellis, A. and Kumar, K. (1983), *Dilemmas of Liberal Democracies*, London: Tavistock.

Ellis. D. P. (1971), 'The Hobbesian Problem of Order: a Critical Appraisal of the Normative Solution', *American Sociological Review*, vol. 36.

Elster, J. (1978), *Logic and Society*, Chichester: John Wiley.

—— (1979a), 'Anomalies of Rationality: some Unresolved Problems in the Theory of Rational Behaviour', in Lévy-Garboua, L. (ed.) (1979), *Sociological Economics*, London: Sage.

—— (1979b), *Ulysses and the Sirens*, Cambridge: Cambridge University Press.

—— (1980), 'Cohen on Marx's Theory of History', *Political Studies*, vol. 28.

—— (1982a), 'Belief, Bias, and Ideoogy', in Hollis, M. and Lukes, S. (eds) (1982), *Rationality and Relativism*, Oxford: Basil Blackwell.

—— (1982b), 'Marxism, Functionalism, and Game Theory: the Case for Methodological Individualism', *Theory and Society*, vol. 11.

—— (1982c), 'Sour Grapes – Utilitarianism and the Genesis of Wants', in Sen, A. and Williams, B. (eds), *Utilitarianism and Beyond*, Cambridge: Cambridge University Press.

—— (1983), *Explaining Technical Change*, Cambridge: Cambridge University Press.

—— (1984), 'The Contradictions of Modern Societies', *Government and Opposition*, vol. 19.

Elton, G. R. (1967), *The Practice of History*, Glasgow: Fontana.

Etzioni-Halevy, E. (1981), *Social Change*, London: Routledge and Kegan Paul.

Eyerman, R. (1982), 'Consciousness and Action: Alain Touraine and the Sociological Intervention', *Thesis Eleven*, no. 5/6.

Fales, E. (1980), 'Uniqueness and Historical Laws', *Philosophy of Science*, vol. 47.

Fèbvre, L. (1932), *A Geographical Introduction to History*, London: Kegan Paul, Trench, Trubner.

—— (1973), *A New Kind of History* (ed. P. Burke), London: Routledge.

—— (1977), *Life in Renaissance France*, Cambridge, Mass: Harvard University Press.

—— (1982), *The Problem of Unbelief in the Sixteenth Century*, Cambridge, Mass.: Harvard University Press.

Feigl, H. (1956), 'Some Major Issues and Developments in the Philosophy of Science of Logical Empiricism', *Minnesota Studies in Philosophy of Science*, vol. I.

—— (1958), *The Mental and the Physical*, reprinted with a postscript (1967), Minneapolis: University of Minnesota Press.

—— (1960), 'Mind–Body, Not a Pseudoproblem', in Hook, S. (ed.) (1960), *Dimensions of Mind*, NY: Collier.

—— (1969), 'The Origin and Spirit of Logical Positivism', in Achinstein, P. and Barker, S. (eds) (1969), *The Legacy of Logical Positivism*, Baltimore: Johns Hopkins Press.

—— (1970), 'The Orthodox View of Theories: Remarks in Defence as well as Critique', *Minnesota Studies in Philosophy of Science*, vol. IV.

—— (1971), 'Research Programmes and Induction', in Buck, R. and Cohen, R. (eds) (1971), *PSA 1970*, Dordrecht: Reidel.

—— (1974), 'Empiricism at Bay?', in Cohen, R. S. and Wartofsky, M. (eds) (1974), *Methodological and Historical Essays in the Natural and Social Sciences*, Dordrecht: Reidel.

Feinman, S. (1980), 'The Utility of Evolutionary Theory for the Social Sciences', *Current Perspectives in Social Theory*, vol. 1.

Feldman, A. S. (1965), 'Evolutionary Theory and Social Change', in Barringer, H. R. et al. (eds) (1965), *Social Change in Developing Areas*, Cambridge, Mass: Schenken.

Feyerabend, P. K. (1963), 'How to be a Good Empiricist – a Plea for Tolerance in Matters Epistemological', reprinted in Nidditch, P. H. (ed.) (1968), *The Philosophy of Science*, Oxford: Oxford University Press.

—— (1964), 'Realism and Instrumentalism', reprinted in Feyerabend, P. K. (1981, *Philosophical Papers*, vol. 1, Cambridge: Cambridge University Press.

Feyerabend, P. K. (1975a), *Against Method*, London: New Left Books.

—— (1975b), 'Popper's Objective Knowledge', reprinted in Feyerabend, P. K. (1981), *Philosophical Papers*, vol. 2, Cambridge: Cambridge University Press.

—— (1978), *Science in a Free Society*, London: New Left Books.

—— (1980), 'Democracy, Elitism, and Scientific Method', *Inquiry*, vol. 23.

—— (1981a), 'Historical Background: Some Observations on the Decay of Philosophy of Science', in Feyerabend, P. K. (1981), *Philosophical Papers*, vol. 2, Cambridge: Cambridge University Press.

—— (1981b), 'More Clothes from the Emperor's Bargain Basement', *British Journal for the Philosophy of Science*, vol. 32, reprinted in Feyerabend, P. K. (1981), *Philosophical Papers*, vol. 2, Cambridge: Cambridge University Press.

Field, H. (1972), 'Tarski's Theory of Truth', reprinted in Platts, M. (ed.) (1980), *Reference, Truth, and Reality*, London: Routledge and Kegan Paul.

—— (1973), 'Theory Change and the Indeterminacy of Reference', *Journal of Philosophy*, vol. 70.

Fisher, B. M. and Strauss, A. L. (1979), 'Interactionism', in Bottomore, T. and Nisbet, R. (eds) (1979), *A History of Sociological Analysis*, London: Heinemann.

Fisk, M. (1970), 'Are There Necessary Connections in Nature?' *Philosophy of Science*, vol. 37.

—— (1971), 'Capacities and Natures', in Buck, R. C. and Cohen, R. S. (eds) (1971), *PSA 1970*, Dordrecht: Reidel.

Fodor, Jerry A. (1983), *The Modularity of Mind*, Cambridge, Mass: MIT Press.

Fogel, R. W. (1975), 'The Limits of Quantitative Methods in History', *American Historical Review*, vol. 80.

—— (1982), 'Scientific History and Traditional History', in Cohen, L. J. et al. (eds) (1982), *Logic, Methodology and Philosophy of Science VI*, Amsterdam: North-Holland.

Forster, R. (1978), 'Achievements of the Annales School', *Journal of Economic History*, vol. 38.

Foster-Carter, A. (1976), 'From Rostow to Gunder Frank: Conflicting Paradigms in the Analysis of Underdevelopment', *World Development*, vol. 4.

—— (1978), 'The Modes of Production Controversy', *New Left Review*, no. 107.

Foucault, M. (1970), *The Order of Things*, London: Tavistock.

—— (1971), *Madness and Civilization. A History of Insanity in the Age of Reason*, London: Tavistock.

—— (1972), *The Archaeology of Knowledge*, London: Tavistock.

—— (1976), *The Birth of the Clinic*, London: Tavistock.

—— (1977), 'The Political Function of the Intellectual', *Radical Philosophy*, no. 17.

—— (1978), 'Politics and the Study of Discourse', *Ideology and Consciousness*, no. 3.

—— (1979a), *Discipline and Punish*, Harmondsworth: Penguin.

—— (1979b), *The History of Sexuality, Vol. I: An Introduction*, London: Allen Lane.

—— (1980), *Power/Knowledge*, Sussex: Harvester.

—— (1982), 'The Subject and Power', in Dreyfus, H. L. and Rabinow, P. (1982), *Michel Foucault: Beyond Structuralism and Hermeneutics*, Brighton: Harvester.

Frankfurt, H. G. (1971), 'Freedom of the Will and the Concept of a Person', reprinted in Watson, G. (ed.) (1982), *Free Will*, Oxford: Oxford University Press.

Friedman, M. (1953), 'The Methodology of Positive Economics', in Friedman, M. (1953), *Essays in Positive Economics*, Chicago: Chicago University Press.

Gadamer, H.-G. (1975a), 'Hermeneutics and Social Science', *Cultural Hermentics*, vol. 2.

—— (1975b), *Truth and Method*, London: Sheed and Ward.

—— (1976), 'The University of the Hermeneutical Problem', reprinted in Bleicher, J. (1976), *Contemporary Hermeneutics*, London: Routledge and Kegan Paul.

—— (1977), 'Theory, Technology, Practice: the Task of the Science of Man', *Social Research*, vol. 44.

—— (1979), 'The Problem of Historical Consciousness', reprinted in Rabinow, P. and Sullivan, W. M. (eds) (1979), *Interpretive Social Science: a Reader*, Berkeley: University of California Press.

—— (1981), *Reason in the Age of Science*, Cambridge, Mass: MIT Press.

Gallie, W. B. (1964), *Philosophy and the Historical Understanding*, NY: Schocken.

Gane, M. (1983), 'Anthony Giddens and the Crisis of Social Theory', *Economy and Society*, vol. 12.

Gardiner, P. (1952), *The Nature of Historical Explanation*, London: Oxford University Press.

—— (1966), 'Historical Understanding and the Empiricist Tradition', in Williams, B. and Montefiori, A. (eds) (1966), *British Analytical Philosophy*, London: Routledge and Kegan Paul.

Geertz, C. (1959), 'Ritual and Social Change: A Javanese Example', reprinted in Demerath, N. J. and Peterson, R. A. (eds) (1967), *System, Change and Conflict*, NY: Free Press.

—— (1963a), *Agricultural Involution; the Process of Ecological Change*, Berkeley: University of California Press.

—— (1963b), *Pedlars and Princes; Social Development and Economic Change in Two Indonesian Towns*, Chicago: Chicago University Press.

—— (1964), 'Social Change and Economic Modernisation in Two Indonesian Towns: a Case in Point', in Hagen, E. E. (1964), *On the Theory of Social Change*, London: Tavistock.

—— (1965), *The Social History of an Indonesian Town*, Cambridge, Mass: MIT Press.

—— (1968), *Islam Observed*, New Haven: Yale University Press.

—— (1972), 'Deep Play: Notes on the Balinese Cockfight', reprinted in Rabinow, P. and Sullivan, W. M. (eds) (1972), *Interpretive Social Science: a Reader*, Berkeley: University of California Press.

—— (1975), *Interpretation of Cultures*, London: Hutchinson.

—— (1977), 'Centers, Kings and Charisma: Reflections on the Symbolics of Power', in Ben-David, J. and Clark, T. N. (eds) (1977), *Culture and its Creators*, Chicago: Chicago University Press.

—— (1980), *Negara: the Theatre State in Nineteenth Century Bali*, Princeton: Princeton University Press.

—— (1983), *Local Knowledge*, NY: Basic Books.

Gellner, E. (1956), 'Explanations in History', reprinted in O'Neill, J. (ed.) (1973),

Modes of Individualism and Collectivism, London: Heinemann.

—— (1962), 'Concepts and Society', reprinted in Wilson, B. (ed.) (1970), *Rationality*, Oxford: Basil Blackwell.

—— (1964), *Thought and Change*, London: Weidenfeld and Nicolson.

—— (1974), *Legitimation of Belief*, Cambridge: Cambridge University Press.

—— (1979a), 'Introduction' to Gellner, E. (1979), *Spectacles and Predicaments*, Cambridge: Cambridge University Press.

—— (1979b), 'Pragmatism and the Importance of Being Ernest', reprinted in Gellner (1979), *Spectacles and Predicaments*, Cambridge: Cambridge University Press.

—— (1981), 'Relativism and Universals', in Hollis, M. and Lukes, S. (eds) (1982), *Rationality and Relativism*, Oxford: Blackwell.

—— (1983), *Nations and Nationalism*, Oxford: Blackwell.

Genovese, E. D. (1984), 'The Politics of Class Struggle in the History of Society: an Appraisal of the Work of Eric Hobsbawm', in Thane, P. et al. (eds) (1984), *The Power of the Past*, Cambridge: Cambridge University Press.

Genovese, E. F. and Genovese, E. (1976), 'The Political Crisis of Social History: a Marxian Perspective', *Journal of Social History*, vol. 10.

Gergen, K. J. (1977), 'Social Exchange Theory in a World of Transient Fact', in Hamblin, R. and Kunkel, J. (eds) (1977), *Behavioural Theory in Sociology*, New Brunswick: Transaction Books.

Gerth, H. and Mills, C. W. (1954), *Character and Social Structure*, London: Routledge and Kegan Paul.

Ghiselin, M. T. (1981), 'Categories, Life and Thinking', *Behavioral and Brain Sciences*, vol. 4.

Giddens, A. (1979), *Central Problems in Social Theory*, London: Macmillan.

—— (1981a), 'Agency, Institution, and Time–Space Analysis', in Knorr-Cetina, K. and Cicourel, A. (eds) (1981), *Advances in Social Theory and Methodology*, London: Routledge and Kegan Paul.

—— (1981b), *A Contemporary Critique of Historical Materialism*, vol. 1, London: Macmillan.

—— (1982a), 'Commentary on the Debate', *Theory and Society*, vol. 11.

—— (1982b), *Profiles and Critiques in Social Theory*, London: Macmillan.

—— (1983a), 'A Reply to my Critics', *Theory, Culture and Society*, vol. 1.

—— (1983b), 'Comments on the Theory of Structuration', *Journal for the Theory of Social Behaviour*, vol. 13.

Giere, R. N. (1974), 'History and Philosophy of Science: Intimate Relationship or Marriage of Convenience?', *British Journal for Philosophy of Science*, vol. 24.

Ginsburg, M. (1961), 'Evolution, Development and Progress', in Ginsburg, M. (1961), *Evolution and Progress*, London: Heinemann.

Glucksmann, A. (1972), 'A Ventriloquist Structuralism', *New Left Review*, no. 72.

Glucksmann, M. (1974), *Structuralist Analysis in Contemporary Social Thought: A Comparison of the Theories of Claude Lévi-Strauss and Louis Althusser*, London: Routledge and Kegan Paul.

Godelier, M. (1967), 'Structure and Contradiction in *Capital*' in Blackburn, R. (ed.) (1972), *Ideology in Social Science*, London: Fontana.

—— (1972a), 'Functionalism, Structuralism, and Marxism', in Godelier, M.

(1972), *Rationality and Irrationality in Economics*, NY: Monthly Review Press.

—— (1972b), *Rationality and Irrationality in Economics*, NY: Monthly Review Press.

—— (1976), 'Anthropology, Society and History' (with C. Lévi-Strauss and M. Augé), *Critique of Anthropology*, no. 6.

—— (1977), *Perspectives in Marxist Anthropology*, Cambridge: Cambridge University Press.

—— (1978), 'Infrastructures, Societies and History', *Current Anthropology*, vol. 19.

—— (1982a), 'The Ideal and the Real', in Samuel, R. and Jones, G. S. (eds) (1982), *Culture, Ideology and Politics*, London: Routledge and Kegan Paul.

—— (1982b), 'The Problem of the "Reproduction" of Socioeconomic Systems: a New Epistemological Context', in Rossi, I. (ed.) (1982), *Structural Sociology*, NY: Columbia University Press.

Goffman, Erving (1959), *The Presentation of Self in Everyday Life*, Harmondsworth: Penguin.

—— (1974), *Frame Analysis*, Harmondsworth: Penguin.

Goldman, A. I. (1970), *A Theory of Human Action*, Princeton: Princeton University Press.

Goldmann, L. (1977), *Cultural Creation*, Oxford: Blackwell.

Goldstein, L. J. (1956), 'The Inadequacy of the Principle of Methodological Individualism', reprinted in O'Neill, J. (ed.) (1973), *Modes of Individualism and Collectivism*, London: Heinemann.

—— (1958), 'The Two Theses of Methodological Individualism', reprinted in O'Neill, J. (ed.) (1973), *Modes of Individualism and Collectivism*, London: Heinemann.

Goody, J. (1976), *Production and Reproduction*, Cambridge: Cambridge University Press.

Gould, M. (1976), 'Systems Analysis, Macrosociology, and the Generalised Media of Social Action', in Loubser, J. et al. (eds) (1976), *Explorations in General Theory in Social Science*, NY: Free Press.

Gouldner, A. (1959), 'Reciprocity and Autonomy in Functional Theory', in Gross, L. (ed.) (1959), *Symposium on Sociological Theory*, NY: Harper and Row.

—— (1962), 'Anti-Monotaur: the Myth of a Value-free Sociology', reprinted in Gouldner, A. (1975), *For Sociology*, Harmondsworth: Penguin.

—— (1971), *The Coming Crisis of Western Sociology*, London: Heinemann.

Gregory, R. L. (1974), 'Perceptions as Hypotheses', in Brown, S. C. (ed.) (1974), *Philosophy of Psychology*, London: Macmillan.

—— (1981), *Mind in Science*, Harmondsworth: Penguin.

Gross, D. (1983), 'Time-Space Relations in Giddens' Social Theory', *Theory, Culture, and Society*, vol. 1.

Gruber, H. E. (1982), 'Piaget's Mission', *Social Research*, vol. 49.

—— and Vonèche, J. J. (eds) (1977), *The Essential Piaget*, London: Routledge and Kegan Paul.

Gusfield, J. R. (1966), 'Tradition and Modernity: Misplaced Polarities in the Study of Social Change', *American Journal of Sociology*, vol. LXXII.

Habermas, J. (1971), *Toward a Rational Society*, London: Heinemann.
—— (1972), *Knowledge and Human Interests*, London: Heinemann.
—— (1974), *Theory and Practice*, London: Heinemann.
—— (1976), 'The Analytical Theory of Science and Dialectics' and 'A Positivistically Bisected Rationalism', in Adorno, T. et al. (1976), *The Positivist Dispute in German Sociology*, London: Heinemann.
—— (1977), 'Review of Gadamer's Truth and Method', in Dallmayr, F. and McCarthy, T. (eds) (1977), *Understanding and Social Enquiry*, Notre Dame: University of Notre Dame Press.
—— (1979), *Communication and the Evolution of Society*, London: Heinemann.
—— (1980), 'The Hermeneutic Claim to Universality', in Bleicher, J. (1980), *Contemporary Hermeneutics*, London: Routledge and Kegan Paul.
Hacking, I. (1979a), 'Lakatos's Philosophy of Science', reprinted in Hacking, I. (ed.) (1981), *Scientific Revolutions*, Oxford: Oxford University Press.
—— (1979b), 'Michel Foucault's Immature Science', *Nous*, vol. 13.
Hagen, E. E. (1957), 'The Process of Economic Development', *Economic Development and Cultural Change*, vol. 5.
—— (1962), *On the Theory of Social Change*, London: Tavistock.
—— (1963), 'How Economic Growth Begins: a Theory of Social Change', reprinted in Kilby, P. (ed.) (1971), *Entrepreneurship and Economic Development*, NY: Free Press.
—— (1967), 'British Personality and the Industrial Revolution', in Burns, T. and Saul, S. B. (eds) (1967), *Social Theory and Economic Change*, London: Tavistock.
Hahn, H., Neurath, O. and Carnap, R. (1929), 'The Scientific Conception of the World: the Vienna Circle', reprinted in Neurath, O. (1973), *Empiricism and Sociology*, Dordrecht: Reidel.
Halfpenny, P. (1982), *Positivism and Sociology: Explaining Social Life*, London: George Allen and Unwin.
Hall, S. (1977a), 'The Political and the Economic in Marx's Theory of Classes', in Hunt, A. (ed.), *Class and Class Structure*, London: Lawrence and Wishart.
—— (1977b), 'Rethinking the Base-and-Superstructure Metaphor', in Bloomfield, J. (ed.) (1977), *Class, Hegemony, and Party*, London: Lawrence and Wishart.
—— (1981), 'In Defence of Theory', in Samuel, R. (ed.) (1981), *People's History and Socialist Theory*, London: Routledge and Kegan Paul.
Hanfling, O. (1981), *Logical Positivism*, Oxford: Basil Blackwell.
Hanson, N. R. (1958), *Patterns of Discovery*, Cambridge: Cambridge University Press.
Hardin, R. (1971), 'Collective Action as an Agreeable *n*-Prisoners' Dilemma', reprinted in Barry, B. and Hardin, R. (eds) (1982), *Rational Man and Irrational Society?*, Beverly Hills: Sage.
—— (1980), 'Rationality, Irrationality, and Functionalist Explanation', *Social Science Information*, vol. 19.
Harré, R. (1970), *The Principles of Scientific Thinking*, London: Macmillan.
—— (1972), *The Philosophies of Science*, London: Oxford University Press.
—— (1975), 'Images of the World and Societal Icons', in Knorr, K. D., Strasser, H. and Zillian, H. G. (eds) (1975), *Determinants and Controls of Scientific Development*, Dordrecht: Reidel.

—— (1976), 'The Constructive Role of Models', in Collins, L. (ed.) (1976), *The Use of Models in the Social Sciences*, London: Tavistock.

—— (1977a), 'The Ethogenic Approach: Theory and Practice', in Berkowitz, L. (ed.) (1977), *Advances in Experimental Social Psychology*, NY: Academic Press.

—— (1977b), 'Rules in the Explanation of Social Behaviour', in Collett, P. (ed.) (1977), *Social Rules and Social Behaviour*, Oxford: Basil Blackwell.

—— (1978), 'Architectonic Man: On the Structuring of Lived Experience', in Brown, R. H. and Lyman, S. M. (eds) (1978), *Structure, Consciousness and History*, Cambridge: Cambridge University Press.

—— (1979), *Social Being*, Oxford: Basil Blackwell.

—— (1980a), 'The Assessment of Explanatory Frameworks', typescript, Oxford.

—— (1980b), 'Man as Rhetorician', in Chapman, A. and Jones, D. (eds) (1980), *Models of Man*, Leicester: British Psychological Society.

—— (1980c), 'Social Being and Social Change', in Brenner, M. (ed.) (1980), *The Structure of Social Action*, Oxford: Basil Blackwell.

—— (1981), 'Philosophical Aspects of the Micro–Macro Problem', in Knorr-Cetina, K. and Cicourel, A. (eds) (1981), *Advances in Social Theory and Methodology*, London: Routledge and Kegan Paul.

—— (1982a), 'Psychological Dimensions', in Secord, P. (ed.) (1982), *Explaining Human Behavior*, Beverly Hills: Sage.

—— (1982b), 'Theory Families, Plausibility and Scientific Realism', typescript, Oxford.

—— (1983a), 'Commentary from an Ethogenic Standpoint', *Journal for the Theory of Social Behaviour*, vol. 13.

—— (1983b), *An Introduction to the Logic of the Sciences*, 2nd edn, London: Macmillan.

—— (1983c), *Personal Being*, Oxford: Basil Blackwell.

—— and Madden, E. H. (1975), *Causal Powers: a Theory of Natural Necessity*, Oxford: Blackwell.

—— and Secord, P. (1972), *The Explanation of Social Behaviour*, Oxford: Basil Blackwell.

Harsanyi, J. C. (1977a), 'Advances in Understanding Rational Behaviour', in Butts, R. E. and Hintikka, J. (eds) (1977), *Historical and Philosophical Dimensions of Logic, Methodology, and Philosophy of Science*, Dordrecht: Reidel.

—— (1977b), 'Morality and the Theory of Rational Behaviour', *Social Research*, vol. 44.

Harsgor, M. (1978), 'Total History: the Annales School', *Journal of Contemporary History*, vol. 13.

Harvey, D. (1969), *Explanation in Geography*, London: Edward Arnold.

Hayek, F. A. (1942–3), 'Scientism and the Study of Society', reprinted in O'Neill, J. (ed.) (1973), *Modes of Individualism and Collectivism*, London: Heinemann.

—— (1967), 'The Results of Human Action but not of Human Design', in *Studies in Philosophy, Politics, and Economics*, London: Routledge and Kegan Paul.

Healey, R. (1978), 'Physicalist Imperialism', *Proceedings of the Aristotelian Society*, vol. LXXIX, 1978–9.

Heath, A. (1971), 'Exchange Theory', *British Journal of Political Science*, vol. 1.

—— (1974), 'The Rational Model of Man', *European Journal of Sociology*, vol. 15.

—— (1976), *Rational Choice and Social Exchange*, Cambridge: Cambridge University Press.

Held, D. (1980), *Introduction to Critical Theory*, London: Hutchinson.

Hempel, C. G. (1942), 'The Function of General Laws in History', reprinted in Gardiner, P. (ed.) (1959), *Theories of History*, NY: Free Press.

—— (1950), 'Empiricist Criteria of Cognitive Significance: Problems and Changes', reprinted in Hempel, C. G. (1965), *Aspects of Scientific Explanation*, NY: Free Press.

—— (1952), 'Typological Methods in the Social Sciences', reprinted in Hempel, C. G. (1965), *Aspects of Scientific Explanation*, NY: Free Press.

—— (1959), 'The Logic of Functional Analysis', in Gross, L. (ed.) (1959), *Symposium on Sociological Theory*, Evanston: Row Peterson.

—— (1962a), 'Explanation and Prediction by Covering Laws', reprinted in Krimerman, L. I. (ed.) (1959), *The Nature and Scope of Social Science*, NY: Appleton-Century-Crofts.

—— (1962b), 'Explanation in Science and in History', reprinted in Dray, W. (ed.) (1966), *Philosophical Analysis and History*, NY: Harper and Row.

—— (1963), 'Reasons and Covering Laws in Historical Explanation', reprinted in Gardiner, P. (ed.) (1974), *Philosophy of History*, Oxford: Oxford University Press.

—— (1965a), 'Aspects of Scientific Explanation', in Hempel, C. G. (1965), *Aspects of Scientific Explanation*, NY: Free Press.

—— (1965b), *Aspects of Scientific Explanation*, NY: Free Press.

—— (1966a), *Philosophy of Natural Science*, Englewood Cliffs: Prentice-Hall.

—— (1966b), 'Recent Problems of Induction', in Colodny, R. G. (ed.) (1966), *Mind and Cosmos*, Lanham: University Press of America.

—— (1969), 'Logical Positivism and the Social Sciences', in Achinstein, P. and Barker, S. (eds) (1969), *The Legacy of Logical Positivism*, Baltimore: Johns Hopkins Press.

—— (1970), 'On the Standard Conception of Scientific Theories', *Studies in Philosophy of Science*, vol. IV.

—— (1973), 'The Meaning of Theoretical Terms: a Critique of the Standard Empiricist Construal', in Suppes, P. et al. (eds) (1973), *Logic, Methodology, and Philosophy of Science, IV*, Amsterdam: North-Holland.

Henretta, J. A. (1979), 'Social History as Lived and Written', *American Historical Review*, vol. 84.

Hesse, M. (1961), 'The Role of Models in Scientific Theory', reprinted in Shapere, D. (ed.) (1965), *Philosophical Problems of Natural Science*, NY: Macmillan.

—— (1965), 'The Explanatory Function of Metaphor', reprinted in Hesse, M. (1980), *Revolutions and Reconstructions in Philosophy of Science*, Sussex: Harvester.

—— (1966), *Models and Analogies in Science*, Notre Dame: University of Notre Dame Press.

—— (1969), 'Positivism and the Logic of Scientific Theories', in Achinstein, P. and Barker, S. (eds) (1969), *The Legacy of Logical Positivism*, Baltimore: Johns Hopkins Press.

—— (1973a), 'In Defence of Objectivity', reprinted in Hesse, M. (1980), *Revolutions and Reconstructions in the Philosophy of Science*, Sussex: Harvester.

—— (1973b), 'Models of Theory Change', reprinted in Hesse, M. (1980),

Revolutions and Reconstructions in Philosophy of Science, Sussex: Harvester.
—— (1974), *The Structure of Scientific Inference*, London: Macmillan.
—— (1975), 'Models of Method in the Natural and Social Sciences', reprinted in Hesse, M. (1980), *Revolutions and Reconstructions in the Philosophy of Science*, Sussex: Harvester.
—— (1976), 'Truth and the Growth of Scientific Knowledge', reprinted in Hesse, M. (1980), *Revolutions and Reconstructions in the Philosophy of Science*, Sussex: Harvester.
—— (1978a), 'Habermas's Consensus Theory of Truth', reprinted in Hesse, M. (1980), *Revolutions and Reconstructions in the Philosophy of Science*, Sussex: Harvester.
—— (1978b), 'Theory and the Value in the Social Sciences', in Hookway, C. and Pettit, P. (eds) (1978), *Action and Interpretation*, Cambridge: Cambridge University Press.
—— (1980), *Revolutions and Reconsructions in the Philosophy of Science*, Sussex: Harvester.
—— (1982), 'Science and Objectivity', in Thompson, J. and Held, D. (eds) (1982), *Habermas: Critical Debates*, London: Macmillan.
Hexter, J. H. (1961), 'A New Framework for Social History', in Hexter, J. H. (1961), *Reappraisals in History*, London: Longmans.
—— (1972), 'Fernand Braudel and the Monde Braudellian . . .', reprinted in Hexter, J. H. (1979), *On Historians*, London: Collins.
Heydebrand, Wolf V. (1981), 'Marxist Structuralism', in Blau, P. and Merton, R. (eds) (1981), *Continuities in Structural Inquiry*, Beverly Hills: Sage.
Hill, C. (1964), *Society and Puritanism in Pre-Revolutionary England*, London: Secker and Warburg.
—— (1975), *The World Turned Upside Down*, Harmondsworth: Penguin.
Hilton, R. H. (1952), 'Capitalism – What's in a Name?', reprinted in Hilton, R. H. (ed.) (1976), *The Transition from Feudalism to Capitalism*, London: New Left Books.
—— (ed.) (1976), *The Transition from Feudalism to Capitalism*, London: New Left Books.
—— (1978), 'Agrarian Class Structure and Economic Development in Pre-Industrial Europe; a Crisis of Feudalism', *Past and Present*, no. 80.
—— (1984), 'Feudalism in Europe: Problems for Historians', *New Left Review*, no. 147.
Hindess, B. (1977), 'Humanism and Teleology in Sociological Theory', in Hindess, B. (ed.) (1977), *Sociological Theories of the Economy*, London: Macmillan.
—— and Hirst, P. Q. (1975), *Pre-Capitalist Modes of Production*, London: Routledge and Kegan Paul.
—— and Hirst, P. Q. (1977), *Mode of Production and Social Formation: an Auto-Critique of 'Pre-Capitalist Modes of Production'*, London: Macmillan.
Hirsch, F. (1976), *Social Limits to Growth*, London: Routledge and Kegan Paul.
Hirschman, A. O. (1958), *The Strategy of Economic Development*, New Haven: Yale University Press.
—— (1963), *Journeys toward Progress*, NY: W. W. Norton.
—— (1970), *Exit, Voice, and Loyalty*, Cambridge, Mass: Harvard University Press.

—— (1977), *The Passions and the Interests*, Princeton: Princeton University Press.

—— (1981), *Essays in Trespassing; Economics to Politics and Beyond*, Cambridge: Cambridge University Press.

—— (1982), *Shifting Involvements*, Oxford: Martin Robertson.

Hirst, P. Q. (1975), 'The Uniqueness of the West', *Economy and Society*, vol. 4.

—— (1976), *Social Evolution and Sociological Categories*, London: George Allen and Unwin.

—— (1979), 'The Necessity of Theory', *Economy and Society*, vol. 8.

—— (1983), 'The Social Theory of Anthony Giddens: a New Syncretism?', *Theory, Culture and Society*, vol. 3.

Hobsbawm, E. J. (1954), 'The Crisis of the Seventeenth Century', reprinted in Aston, T. (ed.) (1965), *Crisis in Europe: 1560–1660*, London: Routledge.

—— (1962), *The Age of Revolution, Europe 1789–1948*, London: Weidenfeld and Nicolson.

—— (1968), 'Karl Marx's Contribution to Historiography', reprinted in Blackburn, R. (ed.) (1972), *Ideology in Social Science*, London: Fontana.

—— (1969), *Industry and Empire*, Harmondsworth: Penguin.

—— (1971a), 'Class Consciousness in History', in Meszaros, I. (ed.) (1971), *Aspects of History and Class Consciousness*, London: Routledge and Kegan Paul.

—— (1971b), 'From Social History to the History of Society', reprinted in Flinn, M. W. and Smout, T. C. (eds) (1974), *Essays in Social History*, Oxford: Oxford University Press.

—— (1971c), *Primitive Rebels*, 3rd edn, Manchester: Manchester University Press.

—— (1972), 'The Social Function of the Past', *Past and Present*, no. 55.

—— (1975), *The Age of Capital, 1848–1875*, London: Weidenfeld and Nicolson.

—— (1978), 'The Historians' Group of the Communist Party', in Cornforth, M. (ed.), *Rebels and their Causes*, London: Lawrence and Wishart.

—— (1979a), 'An Interview', *Radical History Review*, no. 19.

—— (1979b), 'The Development of the World Economy', *Cambridge Journal of Economics*, vol. 3.

—— (1980), 'The Revival of Narrative: Some Comments', *Past and Present*, no. 86.

—— (1981a), 'The Contribution of History to Social Science', *International Social Science Journal*, vol. 32.

—— (1981b), 'Looking Forward: History and the Future', *New Left Review*, no. 125.

—— (1984), 'Marx and History', *New Left Review*, no. 143.

—— and Rudé, G. (1973), *Captain Swing*, Harmondsworth: Penguin.

Hollis, M. (1977), *Models of Man*, Cambridge: Cambridge University Press.

—— and Lukes, S. (eds) (1982), *Rationality and Relativism*, Oxford: Basil Blackwell.

—— and Nell, E. (1975), *Rational Economic Man*, Cambridge: Cambridge University Press.

Holton, R. J. (1981), 'Marxist Theories of Social Change and the Transition from Feudalism to Capitalism', *Theory and Society*, vol. 10.

Homans, G. C. (1951), *The Human Group*, London: Routledge and Kegan Paul.

—— (1958), 'Social Behavior as Exchange', reprinted in Homans, G. C. (1962), *Sentiments and Activities*, NY: Free Press.

—— (1961), *Social Behaviour: Its Elementary Forms*, London: Routledge and Kegan Paul.

—— (1962), *Sentiments and Activities*, NY: Free Press of Glencoe.

—— (1964a), 'Bringing Men Back In', reprinted in Ryan, A. (ed.) (1973), *Philosophy of Social Science*, Oxford: Oxford University Press.

—— (1964b), 'Contemporary Theory in Sociology', reprinted as 'Structural-Functional and Psychological Theories' in Demerath, N. J. and Peterson, R. A. (eds) (1967), *System, Change and Conflict*, NY: Free Press.

—— (1967a), 'Fundamental Social Processes', in Smelser, N. (ed.) (1967), *Sociology: an Introduction*, NY: John Wiley.

—— (1967b), *The Nature of Social Science*, NY: Harcourt Brace and World.

—— (1970), 'The Relevance of Psychology to the Explanation of Social Phenomena', in Borger, R. and Cioffi, F. (eds) (1970), *Explanation in the Behavioural Sciences*, Cambridge: Cambridge University Press.

—— (1976), 'What do we Mean by Social "Structure"?', in Blau, P. (ed.) (1976), *Approaches to the Study of Social Structure*, London: Open Books.

—— (1982), 'The Present State of Sociological Theory', *The Sociological Quarterly*, vol. 23.

Hooker, C. A. (1975), 'Philosophy and Meta-Philosophy of Science: Empiricism, Popperianism, and Realism', *Synthese*, vol. 32.

—— (1978), 'An Evolutionary Naturalist Realist Doctrine of Perception and Secondary Qualities', *Minnesota Studies in Philosophy of Science*, vol. IX.

Hookway, C. (1978), 'Indeterminacy and Interpretation', in Hookway, C. and Pettit, P. (eds) (1978), *Action and Interpretation*, Cambridge: Cambridge University Press.

Hornstein, N. (1982), 'Foundationalism and Quine's Indeterminacy of Translation Thesis', *Social Research*, vol. 49.

Horwich, P. (1982), 'Three Forms of Realism', *Synthese*, vol. 51.

Hoselitz, B. F. (1952a), 'Entrepreneurship and Economic Growth', reprinted in Hoselitz, B. F. (1960), *Sociological Aspects of Economic Growth*, NY: Free Press.

—— (1952b), 'Non-Economic Barriers to Economic Development', *Economic Development and Cultural Change*, vol. I.

—— (ed.) (1952c), *The Progress of Underdeveloped Areas*, Chicago: University of Chicago Press.

—— (1953a), 'The Role of Cities in the Economic Growth of Underdeveloped Countries', reprinted in Hoselitz, B. F. (1960), *Sociological Aspects of Economic Growth*, NY: Free Press.

—— (1953b), 'The Scope and History of Theories of Economic Growth', reprinted in Hoselitz, B. F. (1960), *Sociological Aspects of Economic Growth*, NY: Free Press.

—— (1953c), 'Social Structure and Economic Growth', reprinted in Hoselitz, B. F. (1960), *Sociological Aspects of Economic Growth*, NY: Free Press.

—— (1955a), 'Patterns of Economic Growth', reprinted in Hoselitz, B. F. (1960), *Sociological Aspects of Economic Growth*, NY: Free Press.

—— (1955b), 'A Sociological Approach to Economic Development', reprinted in Hoselitz, B. F. (1960), *Sociological Aspects of Economic Growth*, NY: Free Press.

—— (1957), 'Economic Growth and Development: Non-Economic Factors in Economic Development', reprinted in Finkle, J. L. and Gamble, R. W. (eds) (1971), *Political Development and Social Change*, 2nd edn, NY: Wiley.

—— (1960a), 'The Market Matrix', in Moore, W. E. and Feldman, A. S. (eds) (1960), *Labor Commitment and Social Change in Developing Areas*, NY: Social Science Research Council.

—— (1960b), *Sociological Aspects of Economic Growth*, NY: Free Press.

—— (1961), 'Tradition and Economic Growth', in Braibanti, R. and Spengler, J. J. (eds) (1961), *Tradition, Values, and Socio-Economic Development*, Durham: Duke University Press.

—— (1964), 'Economic Development and Change in Social Values and Thought Patterns', in Zollschan, G. K. and Hirsch, W. (eds) (1976), *Explanations in Social Change*, 2nd edn, London: Routledge and Kegan Paul.

—— (1965), 'The Use of Historical Comparisons in the Study of Economic Development', in Aron, R. and Hoselitz, B. F. (eds) (1965), *Social Development*, Paris: Mouton.

—— (1972), 'Development and the Theory of Social Systems', in Stanley, M. (ed.) (1972), *Social Development*, NY: Basic Books.

—— and Moore, W. E. (eds) (1963), *Industrialisation and Society*, Paris: UNESCO, Mouton.

Hoy, D. C. (1979), 'Taking History Seriously: Foucault, Gadamer, Habermas', *Union Seminary Quarterly Review*, vol. 34.

—— (1980), 'Hermeneutics', *Social Research*, vol. 47.

Hughes, H. S. (1960), 'The Historian and the Social Scientist', *American Historical Review*, vol. 66.

Hutton, P. H. (1981), 'The History of Mentalities: the New Map of Cultural History', *History and Theory*, vol. XX.

Inkeles, A. and Smith, D. H. (1974), *Becoming Modern*, London: Heinemann.

Jardine, N. (1980), 'The Possibility of Absolutism', in Mellor, D. (ed.) (1980), *Science, Belief and Behaviour*, Cambridge: Cambridge University Press.

Jarvie, I. C. (1983a), 'Rationality and Relativism', *British Journal of Sociology*, vol. 34.

—— (1983b), 'Realism and the Supposed Poverty of Sociological Theories', in Cohen, R. S. and Wartofsky, M. (eds) (1983), *Epistemology, Methodology, and the Social Sciences*, Dordrecht: Reidel.

Joergensen, J. (1951), *The Development of Logical Empiricism*, Chicago: University of Chicago Press.

Johnson, R. (1976), 'Barrington Moore, Perry Anderson, and English Social Development', *Working Papers in Cultural Studies*, no. 9.

—— (1978), 'Thompson, Genovese, and Socialist-Humanist History', *History Workshop*, no. 6.

—— (1979a), 'Culture and the Historians', in Clarke, J. et al. (eds) (1979), *Working-Class History*, London: Hutchinson.

—— (1979b), 'Histories of Culture/Theories of Ideology: Notes on an Impasse', in Barrett, M. et al. (eds) (1979), *Ideology and Cultural Production*, London: Croom Helm.

—— (1981), 'Against Absolutism', in Samuel, R. (ed.) (1981), *People's History and Socialist Theory*, London: Routledge and Kegan Paul.

Jones, G. S. (1976), 'From Historical Sociology to Theoretic History', *British Journal of Sociology*, vol. 27.

—— (1983), *Languages of Class*, Cambridge: Cambridge University Press.

Judt, T. (1979), 'A Clown in Regal Purple: Social History and the Historians', *History Workshop*, no. 7.

Keat, R. and Urry, J. (1975), *Social Theory as Science*, London: Routledge and Kegan Paul.

Kekes, J. (1980), *The Nature of Philosophy*, Oxford: Basil Blackwell.

Kellner, H. (1979), 'Disorderly Conduct: Braudel's Mediterranean Satire', *History and Theory*, vol. 18.

Kim, J. (1978), 'Supervenience and Nomological Incommensurables', *American Philosophical Quarterly*, vol. 15.

—— (1979), 'Causality, Identity, and Supervenience', *Midwest Studies in Philosophy*, vol. IV.

Knapp, P. (1984), 'Can Social Theory Escape from History? Views of History in Social Science', *History and Theory*, vol. 23.

Knorr, K. (1980), 'Social and Scientific Method or What do we Make of the Distinction between the Natural and the Social Sciences?', in Brenner, M. (ed.) (1980), *Social Method and Social Life*, London: Academic Press.

Knorr-Cetina, K. (1981), 'The Micro-Sociological Challenge of Macro Sociology: towards a Reconstruction of Social Theory and Methodology', in Knorr-Cetina, K. and Cicourel, A. (eds) (1981), *Advances in Social Theory and Methodology*, London: Routledge and Kegan Paul.

—— and Cicourel, A. V. (eds) (1981), *Advances in Social Theory and Methodology*, London: Routledge and Kegan Paul.

Kolakowski, L. (1972), *Positivist Philosophy*, Harmondsworth: Penguin.

Körner, S. (1974), *Categorical Frameworks*, Oxford: Basil Blackwell.

Kousser, J. M. (1980), 'Quantitative Social-Scientific History', in Kammen, M. (ed.) (1980), *The Past Before Us*, Ithaca: Cornell University Pres.

Krader, L. (1974), 'Beyond Structuralism: the Dialectics of the Diachronic and Synchronic Methods in the Human Sciences', in Rossi, I. (ed.) (1974), *The Unconscious in Culture*, NY: E. P. Dutton.

Kripke, S. (1971), 'Identity and Necessity', reprinted in Honderich, T. and Burnyeat, M. (eds) (1979), *Philosophy as it is*, Harmondsworth: Penguin.

—— (1980), *Naming and Necessity*, rev. edn, Oxford: Basil Blackwell.

Kuhn, T. S. (1970a), 'Logic of Discovery or Psychology of Research', in Lakatos, I. and Musgrave, A. (eds) (1970), *Criticism and the Growth of Knowledge*, Cambridge: Cambridge University Press.

—— (1970b), 'Reflections on my Critics', in Lakatos, I. and Musgrave, A. (eds) (1970), *Criticism and the Growth of Knowledge*, Cambridge: Cambridge University Press.

—— (1970c), *The Structure of Scientific Revolutions*, 2nd edn, Chicago: University of Chicago Press.

—— (1971), 'The Relations between History and History of Science', *Daedalus*, vol. 100.

—— (1974), 'Second Thoughts on Paradigms', in Suppe, F. (ed.) (1977), *The Structure of Scientific Theories*, 2nd edn, Urbana: University of Illinois Press.

—— (1977a), 'Objectivity, Value Judgement, and Theory Choice', in Kuhn, T. S. (1977), *The Essential Tension*, Chicago: University of Chicago Press.

—— (1977b), 'The Relations between the History and the Philosophy of Science', in Kuhn, T. S. (1977), *The Essential Tension*, Chicago: University of Chicago Press.

—— (1977c), 'Theory Change as Structure-Change: Comments on the Sneed Formalism', in Butts, R. E. and Hintikka, J. (eds) (1977), *Historical and Philosophical Dimensions of Logic, Methodology, and Philosophy of Science*, Dordrecht: Reidel.

—— (1979), 'Metaphor in Science', in Ortony, A. (ed.) (1979), *Metaphor and Thought*, Cambridge: Cambridge University Press.

—— (1980), 'The Halt and the Blind: Philosophy and History of Science', *British Journal for Philosophy of Science*, vol. 31.

Kunkel, J. H. (1970), *Society and Economic Growth*, NY: Oxford University Press.

—— (1977), 'The Behavioral Perspective of Social Dynamics', in Hamblin, R. and Kunkel, J. (eds) (1977), *Behavioral Theory in Sociology*, New Brunswick: Transaction Books.

Kurzweil, E. (1980), *The Age of Structuralism*, NY: Columbia University Press.

Ladurie, E. L. R. (1959), 'History and Climate' reprinted in Burke, P. (ed.) (1972), *Economy and Society in Early Modern Europe*, NY: Harper Torchbooks.

—— (1972b), *Times of Feast, Times of Famine: a History of the Climate Since the Year 1000*, London: George Allen and Unwin.

—— (1974), *The Peasants of Languedoc*, Urbana: University of Illinois Press.

—— (1977), 'Occitania in Historical Perspective', *Review*, vol. I.

—— (1978), 'Agrarian Class Structure and Economic Development in Pre-Industrial Europe: a Reply to Robert Brenner', *Past and Present*, no. 79.

—— (1979), *The Territory of the Historian*, Sussex: Harvester.

—— (1980), *Montaillou*, Harmondsworth: Penguin.

—— (1981a), *Carnival in Romans*, Harmondsworth: Penguin.

—— (1981b), *The Mind and Method of the Historian*, Brighton: Harvester.

—— (1984), *Love, Death and Money in the Pays d'Oc*, Harmondsworth: Penguin.

Lakatos, I. (1970), 'Falsification and the Methodology of Scientific Research Programmes', in Lakatos, I. and Musgrave, A. (eds) (1970), *Criticism and the Growth of Knowledge*, Cambridge: Cambridge University Press.

—— (1971a), 'History of Science and its Rational Reconstructions', in Buck, R. C. and Cohen, R. S. (eds) (1971), *PSA 1970*, Dordrecht: Reidel.

—— (1971b), 'Replies to Critics', in Buck, R. C. and Cohen, R. S. (eds) (1971), *PSA 1970*, Dordrecht: Reidel.

—— (1974), 'Popper on Demarcation and Induction', in Schilpp, P. A. (ed.) (1974), *The Philosophy of Karl Popper*, La Salle: Open Court.

—— (1978), 'The Problem of Appraising Scientific Theories: Three Approaches', in Lakatos, I. (1978), *Philosophical Papers*, vol. 2, Cambridge: Cambridge University Press.

—— and Musgrave, A. (eds) (1970), *Criticism and the Growth of Knowledge*, Cambridge: Cambridge University Press.

Lakoff, G. and Johnson, M. (1980), *Metaphors We Live By*, Chicago: University of Chicago Press.

Lash, S. and Urry, J. (1984), 'The New Marxism of Collective Action: A Critical Analysis', *Sociology*, vol. 18.

Laslet, P. (1968), 'History and the Social Sciences', *International Encyclopaedia of the Social Sciences*, vol. 6.

—— (1971), *The World We Have Lost*, 2nd edn, London: Methuen.

—— (1976), 'The Wrong Way through the Telescope', *British Journal of Sociology*, vol. 27.

—— (1977), 'The Necessity of a Historical Sociology', in Laslett, P. (1977), *Family Life and Illicit Love in Earlier Generations*, Cambridge: Cambridge University Press.

Latsis, S. J. (1972), 'Situational Dterminism in Economics', *British Journal for Philosophy of Science*, vol. 23.

—— (1983), 'The Role and Status of the Rationality Principle in the Social Sciences', in Cohen, R. S. and Wartofsky, M. (eds) (1983), *Epistemology, Methodology, and the Social Sciences*, Dordrecht: Reidel.

Laudan, L. (1976), 'Two Dogmas of Methodology', *Philosophy of Science*, vol. 43.

—— (1977a), *Progress and its Problems*, London: Routledge and Kegan Paul.

—— (1977b), 'The Sources of Modern Methodology', in Butts, R. E. and Hintikka, J. (eds) (1977), *Historical and Philosophical Dimensions of Logic, Methodology, and Philosophy of Science*, Dordrecht: Reidel.

—— (1980), 'Why was the Logic of Discovery Abandoned?', in Nickles. T. (ed.) (1980), *Scientific Discovery, Logic, and Rationality*, Dordrecht: Reidel.

—— (1981a), 'A Confutation of Convergent Realism', *Philosophy of Science*, vol. 48.

—— (1981b), 'A Problem-Solving Approach to Scientific Progress', in Hacking, I. (ed.) (1982), *Scientific Revolutions*, Oxford: Oxford University Press.

—— (1981c), 'The Pseudo-Science of Science?', *Philosophy of Social Sciences*, vol. 11.

—— (1982), 'Problems, Truth, and Consistency', *Studies in the History and Philosophy of Science*, vol. 13.

Leach, E. (1973), 'Structuralism in Social Anthropology', in Robey, D. (ed.) (1973), *Structuralism: an Introduction*, Oxford: Oxford University Press.

—— (1974), *Lévi-Strauss*, rev. edn, Glasgow: Fontana.

—— (1981), 'British Social Anthropology and Lévi-Straussian Structuralism', in Blau, P. and Merton, R. (eds) (1981), *Continuities in Structural Inquiry*, Beverly Hills: Sage.

Lecourt, D. (1975), *Marxism and Epistemology*, London: New Left Books.

Lehrer, K. (ed.) (1966), *Freedom and Determinism*, Atlantic Highlands: Humanities Press.

Lenski, G. E. (1976a), 'Social Structure in Evolutionary Perspective', in Blau, P. (ed.) (1976), *Approaches to the Study of Social Structure*, London: Open Books.

—— (1976b), 'History and Social Change', *American Journal of Sociology*, vol. 82.

Leplin, J. (1980), 'The Role of Models in Theory Construction', in Nickles, T.

(ed.) (1980), *Scientific Discovery, Logic, and Rationality,* Dordrecht: Reidel.

Lerner, D. (1963), *The Passing of Traditional Society,* Glencoe: Free Press.

Lévi-Strauss, C. (1945), 'Structural Analysis in Linguistics and in Anthropology', reprinted in Lévi-Strauss, C. (1968), *Structural Anthropology,* Harmondsworth: Penguin.

—— (1949), 'Introduction: History and Anthropology', reprinted in Lévi-Strauss, C. (1968), *Structural Anthropology,* Harmondsworth: Penguin.

—— (1953), 'Social Structure', reprinted in Lévi-Strauss, C. (1968), *Structural Anthropology,* Harmondsworth: Penguin.

—— (1968), *Structural Anthropology,* Harmondsworth: Penguin.

—— (1972), *The Savage Mind,* London: Weidenfeld and Nicolson.

—— (1977), *Structural Anthropology,* vol. 2, Harmondsworth: Penguin.

Levy, M. J. (1952a), 'Some Sources of the Vulnerability of the Structures of Relatively Non-industrialised Societies to those of Highly Industrialised Societies', in Hoselitz, B. (ed.) (1952), *The Progress of Underdeveloped Areas,* Chicago: University of Chicago Press.

—— (1952b), *The Structure of Society,* Princeton: Princeton University Press.

—— (1953), 'Contrasting Factors in the Modernization of China and Japan', *Economic Development and Cultural Change,* vol. 2.

—— (1966), *Modernization and the Structure of Societies,* Princeton: Princeton University Press.

—— (1968), 'Structural-Functional Analysis', *International Encyclopaedia of Social Sciences,* vol. 6.

Lieberson, J. (1982), 'Karl Popper', *Social Research,* vol. 49.

Linton, R. (1952), 'Cultural and Personality Factors Affecting Economic Growth', in Hoselitz, B. (ed.) (1952), *The Progress of Underdeveloped Areas,* Chicago: Chicago University Press.

Lipset, S. M. (1968), 'History and Sociology: Some Methodological Considerations', in Lipset, S. M. and Hofstadter, R. (eds) (1968), *Sociology and History: Methods,* NY: Basic Books.

—— (1976), 'Social Structure and Social Change', in Blau, P. (ed.) (1976), *Approaches to the Study of Social Structure,* London: Open Books.

Lively, J. (1976), 'The Limits of Exchange Theory', in Barry, B. (ed.) (1976), *Power and Political Theory,* London: Wiley.

Lloyd, C. (ed.) (1983), *Social Theory and Political Practice,* Oxford: Oxford University Press.

Lockwood, D. (1964), 'Social Integration and System Integration', in Zollschan, G. and Hirsch, W. (eds) (1976), *Explorations in Social Change,* London: Routledge and Kegan Paul.

Losee, J. (1980), *A Historical Introduction to the Philosophy of Science,* 2nd edn, Oxford: Oxford University Press.

Luckmann, T. (1973), 'Philosophy, Social Sciences, and Everyday Life', reprinted in Luckmann, T. (ed.) (1978), *Phenomenology and Sociology,* Harmondsworth: Penguin.

—— (ed.) (1978), *Phenomenology and Sociology,* Harmondsworth: Penguin.

—— (1979), 'Personal Identity as an Evolutionary and Historical Problem', in Cranach, M. von et al. (eds) (1979), *Human Ethology,* Cambridge: Cambridge University Press.

—— (1981), 'Hermeneutics as a Paradigm for Social Science?', in Brenner, M. (ed.) (1981), *Social Method and Social Life*, London: Academic Press.

—— (1982), 'Individual Action and Social Knowledge', in Cranach, M. von and Harré, R. (eds) (1982), *The Analysis of Action*, Cambridge: Cambridge University Press.

Luhmann, N. (1982), *The Differentiation of Society*, NY: Columbia University Press.

Lukes, S. (1968), 'Methodological Individualism Reconsidered', reprinted in Lukes, S. (1977), *Essays in Social Theory*, London: Macmillan.

—— (1973a), *Individualism*, Oxford: Basil Blackwell.

—— (1973b), 'On the Social Determination of Truth', reprinted in Lukes, S. (1977), *Essays in Social Theory*, London: Macmillan.

—— (1978), 'The Underdetermination of Theory by Data', *Aristotelian Society*, vol. LII.

—— (1982), 'Relativism in its Place', in Hollis, M and Lukes, S. (eds) (1982), *Rationality and Relativism*, Oxford: Basil Blackwell.

—— (1983), 'Can the Base be Distinguished from the Superstructure?', in Miller, D. and Siedentop, L. (eds) (1983), *The Nature of Political Theory*, Oxford: Oxford University Press.

Lyman, S. M. (1978), 'The Acceptance, Rejection, and Reconstruction of Histories: On Some Controversies in the Study of Social and Cultural Change', in Brown, R. H. and Lyman, S. M. (eds) (1978), *Structure, Consciousness, and History*, Cambridge: Cambridge University Press.

—— and Scott, M. B. (1975), *The Drama of Social Reality*, NY: Oxford University Press.

McCarthy, T. (1978), *The Critical Theory of Jürgen Habermas*, London: Hutchinson.

McClelland, D. C. (1961a), *The Achieving Society*, NY: Free Press.

—— (1961b), 'The Achievement Motive in Economic Growth', reprinted in Kilby, P. (ed.) (1971), *Entrepreneurship and Economic Developement*, NY: Free Press.

—— (1962), 'Business Drive and National Achievement', reprinted in Etzioni, A. and Etzioni, E. (eds) (1973), *Social Change*, 2nd edn, NY: Basic Books.

—— (1963), 'The Achievement Motive in Economic Growth', in Hoselitz, B. and Moore, W. E. (eds) (1963), *Industrialisation and Society*, Paris: UNESCO, Mouton.

—— (1966), 'The Impulse to Modernization', in Weiner, M. (ed.) (1966), *Modernization*, NY: Basic Books.

McClelland, K. (1979), 'Some Comments on Richard Johnson', *History Workshop*, no. 7.

McClelland, P. D. (1975), *Causal Explanation and Model Building in History, Economics, and the New Economic History*, Ithaca: Cornell University Press.

Macfarlane, A. (1978), *The Origins of English Individualism*, Oxford: Blackwell.

McGinn, C. (1979), 'An *a priori* Argument for Realism', *Journal of Philosophy*, vol. LXXVI.

—— (1982a), *The Character of Mind*, Oxford: Oxford University Press.

Mackie, J. L. (1967), 'Fallacies', in Edwards, P. (ed.) (1967), *Encyclopaedia of Philosophy*, vol. 3, NY: Macmillan.

—— (1974), *The Cement of the Universe*, Oxford: Oxford University Press.

MacKinnon, E. (1979), 'Scientific Realism: the New Debates', *Philosophy of Science*, vol. 46.

McLennan, G. (1981), *Marxism and the Methodologies of History*, London: New Left Books.

McMullin, E. (1970), 'The History and Philosophy of Science: a Taxonomy', *Minnesota Studies in Philosophy of Science*, vol. V.

—— (1971), 'Capacities and Natures: an Exercise in Ontology', in Buck, R. C. and Cohen, R. S. (eds) (1971), *PSA 1970*, Dordrecht: Reidel.

—— (1974), 'Empiricism at Sea', in Cohen, R. S. and Wartofsky, M. (eds) (1974), *Methodological and Historical Essays in the Natural and Social Sciences*, Dordrecht: Reidel.

—— (1978a), 'Philosophy of Science and its Rational Reconstructions', in Radnitzky, G. and Andersson, G. (eds) (1978), *Progress and Rationality in Science*, Dordrecht: Reidel.

—— (1978b), 'Structural Explanation', *American Philosophical Quarterly*, vol. 15.

—— (1979), 'Laudan's Progress and its Problems', *Philosophy of Science*, vol. 46.

Magee, B. (1973), *Popper*, London: Fontana.

Makler, H. et al. (1982), 'Recent Trends in Theory and Methodology in the Study of Economy and Society', in Bottomore, T. et al. (eds) (1982), *Sociology: the State of the Art*, Beverly Hills and London: Sage.

Mandelbaum, M. (1938), *The Problem of Historical Knowledge*, NY: Harper Torchbooks.

—— (1955), 'Societal Facts', reprinted in O'Neill, J. (ed.) (1973), *Modes of Individualism and Collectivism*, London: Heinemann.

—— (1957), 'Societal Laws', *British Journal for the Philosophy of Science*, vol. 8, reprinted in O'Neill, J. (ed.) (1973), *Modes of Individualism and Collectivism*, London: Heinemann.

—— (1961), 'Historical Explanation: the Problem of Covering Laws', reprinted in Gardiner, P. (ed.) (1974), *Philosophy of History*, Oxford: Oxford University Press.

—— (1964), *Philosphy, Science, and Sense Perception*, Baltimore: Johns Hopkins Press.

—— (1977), *The Anatomy of Historical Knowledge*, Baltimore: Johns Hopkins Press.

—— (1982), 'G. A. Cohen's Defence of Functional Explanation', *Philosophy of Social Science*, vol. 12.

Manicas, P. T. (1983), 'Reduction, Epigenesis and Explanation', *Journal for the Theory of Social Behaviour*, vol. 13.

Margolis, J. (1984), 'Relativism, History and Objectivity in the Human Studies', *Journal for the Theory of Social Behaviour*, vol. 14.

Marx, K. (1850), *The Class Struggles in France: 1848–1850*, in Marx, K., *Surveys from Exile* (ed. D. Fernbach) (1973), Harmondsworth: Penguin.

—— (1852), *The Eighteenth Brumaire of Louis Bonaparte*, in Marx, K., *Surveys from Exile* (ed. D. Fernbach) (1973), Harmondsworth: Penguin.

—— (1857–8), *Grundrisse* (1973), Harmondsworth: Penguin.

—— (1859), *A Contribution to the Critique of Political Economy* (ed. M. Dobb) (1973), Moscow: Progress Publishers.

—— (1867), *Capital*, vol. I (1976), Harmondsworth: Penguin.

—— (1871), *The Civil War in France*, in Marx, K., *The First International and After* (ed. D. Fernbach) (1974), Harmondsworth: Penguin.

—— and Engels, F. (1846), *The German Ideology* (ed. C. J. Arthur) (1970), NY: International Publishers.

—— and Engels, F. (1848), *Manifesto of the Communist Party*, in Marx, K., *The Revolutions of 1848* (ed D. Fernbach) (1973), Harmondsworth: Penguin.

Masterman, M. (1970), 'The Nature of a Paradigm', in Lakatos, I. and Musgrave, A. (eds) (1970), *Criticism and the Growth of Knowledge*, Cambridge: Cambridge University Press.

Maxwell, G. (1962), 'The Ontological Status of Theoretical Entities', *Minnesota Studies in Philosophy of Science*, vol. III.

—— (1968), 'Scientific Methodology and the Causal Theory of Perception', in Lakatos, I. and Musgrave, A. (eds) (1968), *Problems in Philosophy of Science*, Amsterdam: North-Holland.

—— (1970a), 'Structural Realism and the Meaning of Theoretical Terms', *Minnesota Studies in Philosophy of Science*, vol. IV.

—— (1970b), 'Theories, Perception, and Structural Realism', in Colodny, R. (ed.) (1970), *The Nature and Function of Scientific Theories*, Pittsburgh: University of Pittsburgh Press.

Maxwell, N. (1974), 'The Rationality of Scientific Discovery: Parts I and II', *Philosophy of Science*, vol. 41.

Mayhew, B. H. (1980), 'Structuralism versus Individualism, Parts I and II', *Social Forces*, vol. 59.

—— (1982), 'Structuralism and Ontology', *Social Science Quarterly*, vol. 63.

—— (1983), 'Causality, Historical Particularism and Other Errors in Sociological Discourse', *Journal for the Theory of Social Behaviour*, vol. 13.

Mead, G. H. (1934), *Mind, Self and Society*, Chicago: University of Chicago Press.

Meehl, P. E. (1970), 'Psychological Determinism and Human Rationality: a Psychologist's Reaction to Popper's "Of Clouds and Clocks"', *Minnesota Studies in Philosophy of Science*, vol. IV.

—— and Sellars, W. (1956), 'The Concept of Emergence', *Minnesota Studies in Philosophy of Science*, vol. I.

Megill, A. (1979), 'Foucault, Structuralism, and the Ends of History', *Journal of Modern History*, vol. 51.

Mennell, S. (1977), '"Individual" Action and its "Social" Consequences in the work of Norbert Elias', in Gleichmann, P. R. et al. (eds) (1977), *Human Figurations*, Amsterdam: Amsterdam Sociological Tijdschrift.

Mepham, J. (1973), 'The Structuralist Sciences as Philosophy', in Robey, D. (ed.) (1973), *Structuralism: an Introduction*, Oxford: Oxford University Press.

Merleau-Ponty, M. (1960), 'The Philosopher and Sociology', reprinted in Luckmann, T. (ed.), *Phenomenology and Sociology*, Harmondsworth: Penguin.

Merrill, G. H. (1980), 'Three Forms of Realism', *American Philosophical Quarterly*, vol. 17.

Merton, R. K. (1968), *Social Theory and Social Structure*, enlarged edn, NY: Free Press.

—— (1976), 'Structural Analysis in Sociology', in Blau, P. (ed.) (1976), *Approaches to the Study of Social Structure*, London: Open Books.

Meyer, J. R. and Conrad, A. H. (1957), 'Economic Theory, Statistical Inference, and Economic History', *Journal of Economic History*, vol. 17.

Miller, R. W. (1978), 'Methodological Individualism and Social Explanation', *Philosophy of Science*, vol. 45.

—— (1981), 'A Review of Cohen's "Karl Marx's Theory of History"', *Philosophical Review*, vol. XC.

Mink, L. O. (1965), 'The Autonomy of Historical Understanding', reprinted in Dray, W. (ed.) (1966), *Philosophical Analysis and History*, NY: Harper and Row.

—— (1973), 'The Divergence of History and Sociology in Recent Philosophy of History', in Suppes, P. et al. (eds) (1973), *Logic, Methodology, and Philosophy of Science*, IV, Amsterdam: North-Holland.

—— (1979), 'Philosophy and Theory of History', in Iggers, G. and Parker, H. (eds) (1979), *International Handbook of Historical Studies*, London: Methuen.

Mises, L. von (1960), *Epistemological Problems of Economics*, Princeton: D. van Nostrand.

Mitchell, J. N. (1978), *Social Exchange, Dramaturgy, and Ethnomethodology*, NY: Elsevier.

Moore, B. (1966), *Social Origins of Dictatorship and Democracy*, Harmondsworth: Penguin.

—— (1978), *Injustice*, London: Macmillan.

Moore, W. E. (1960), 'A Reconsideration of Theories of Social Change', reprinted in Eisenstadt, S. N. (ed.) (1970), *Readings in Social Evolution and Development*, Oxford: Pergamon.

—— (1961), 'The Social Framework of Economic Development', in Braibanti, R. and Spengler, J. J. (eds) (1961), *Tradition, Values and Socio-Economic Development*, Durham: Duke of University Press.

—— (1963), 'Industrialization and Social Change', in Hoselitz, B. and Moore, W. E. (eds) (1963), *Industrialization and Society*, Paris: Mouton, UNESCO.

—— (1970), 'Toward a System of Sequences', in McKinney, J. C. and Tiryakian, E. A. (eds) (1970), *Theoretical Sociology*, NY: Appleton-Century-Crofts.

—— (1974), *Social Change*, 2nd edn, Englewood Cliffs: Prentice-Hall.

—— (1977), 'Modernization as Rationalization: Processes and Restraints', in Nash, M. (ed.) (1977), *Essays in Honor of Hoselitz*, Chicago: Chicago University Press.

—— (1979), 'Functionalism', in Bottomore, T. and Nisbet, R. (eds) (1979), *A History of Sociological Analysis*, London: Heinemann.

Mueller, D. C. (ed.) (1983), *The Political Economy of Growth*, New Haven: Yale University Press.

Mulkay, M. J. (1971), *Functionalism, Exchange, and Theoretical Strategy*, London: Routledge and Kegan Paul.

Murdock, G. P. (1949), *Social Structure*, NY: Free Press.

Murphey, M. G. (1973), *Our Knowledge of the Historical Past*, Indianapolis: Bobbs-Merrill.

Nagel, E. (1960), 'Determinism in History', reprinted in Dray, W. (ed.) (1966), *Philosophical Analysis and History*, NY: Harper and Row.

—— (1961), *The Structure of Science*, London: Routledge and Kegan Paul.

Nairn, T. (1964), 'The English Working Class', *New Left Review*, no. 24.

—— (1970), 'The Fateful Meridian', *New Left Review*, no. 60.

Neale, R. S. (1981), *Class in English History 1680–1850*, Oxford: Basil Blackwell.

—— (1984), 'Cultural Materialism: a Critique', *Social History*, vol. 9.

Neurath, O. (1931), 'Empirical Sociology', reprinted in Neurath, O. (1973), *Empiricism and Sociology*, Dordrecht: Reidel.

—— (1932), 'Protocol Sentences', reprinted in Hanfling, O. (ed.) (1981), *Essential Readings in Logical Positivism*, Oxford: Basil Blackwell.

—— (1944), 'Foundations of the Social Sciences', *International Encyclopaedia of Unified Science; Foundations of the Unity of Science*; vol. II, no. 1, Chicago: University of Chicago Press.

—— (1973), *Empiricism and Sociology*, Dordrecht: Reidel.

Newton-Smith, W. (1978), 'The Underdetermination of Theory by Data', *The Aristotelian Society*, supplementary vol. LII.

—— (1981), *The Rationality of Science*, London: Routledge and Kegan Paul.

Nickles, T. (1980), 'Scientific Discovery and the Future of Philosophy of Science', in Nickles, T. (ed.) (1980), *Scientific Discovery, Logic and Rationality*, Dordrecht: Reidel.

Nield, K. (1980), 'A Symptomatic Dispute? Notes on the Relation between Marxian Theory and Historical Practice in Britain', *Social Research*, vol. 47.

—— and Seed, J. (1979), 'Theoretical Poverty or the Poverty of Theory: British Marxist Historiography and the Althusserians', *Economy and Society*, vol. 8.

Nisbet, R. E. (1969), *Social Change and History*, London: Oxford University Press.

—— (1970), 'Developmentalism: a Critical Analysis', in McKinney, J. C. and Tiryakian, E. A. (eds) (1970), *Theoretical Sociology*, NY: Appleton-Century-Crofts.

—— (1972), 'The Problem of Social Change', in Nisbet, R. E. (ed.) (1972), *Social Change*, Oxford: Basil Blackwell.

Nolte, E. (1975), 'The Relationship between Bourgeois and Marxist Historiography', *History and Theory*, vol. XIV.

North, D. C. (1971), 'Institutional Change and Economic Growth', *Journal of Economic History*, vol. 31.

—— (1979), 'A Framework for Analysing the State in Economic History', *Explorations in Economic History*, vol. 16.

—— (1981), *Structure and Change in Economic History*, NY: W. W. Norton.

—— (1984), 'Government and the Cost of Exchange in History', *Journal of Economic History*, vol. 44.

—— and Thomas, R. P. (1970), 'An Economic Theory of the Growth of the Western World', *Economic History Review*, vol. 23.

—— and Thomas, R. P. (1971), 'The Rise and Fall of the Manorial System: a Theoretical Model', *Journal of Economic History*, vol. 31.

—— and Thomas, R. P. (1973), *The Rise of the Western World*, Cambridge: Cambridge University Press.

Oakeshott, M. (1933), *Experience and its Modes*, Cambridge: Cambridge University Press.

Offe, C. and Berger, J. (1982), 'Functionalism vs Rational Choice: Some Questions Concerning the Rationality of Choosing One or the Other', *Theory and Society*, vol. 11.

—— and Wiesenthal, H. (1980), 'Two Logics of Collective Action: Theoretical Notes on Social Class and Organizational Form', in Zeitlin, M. (ed.) (1980), *Political Power and Social Theory*, vol. I. Greenwich: Jai Press.

O'Hear, A. (1982), *Karl Popper,* London: Routledge and Kegan Paul.

Olson, M. (1965), *The Logic of Collective Action,* Cambridge, Mass.: Harvard University Press.

—— (1982), *The Rise and Decline of Nations,* New Haven: Yale University Press.

—— (1983), 'The South will Fall Again: the South as Leader and Laggard in Economic Growth', *Southern Economic Journal,* vol. 49.

O'Neill, J. (1972), *Sociology as a Skin Trade,* London: Heinemann.

—— (ed.) (1973a), *Modes of Individualism and Collectivism,* London: Heinemann.

—— (1973b), 'Scientism, Historicism, and the Problem of Rationality', in O'Neill, J. (ed.) (1973), *Modes of Individualism and Collectivism,* London: Heinemann.

—— (1982), *For Marx, Against Althusser,* Washington, DC: Center for Advanced Research in Phenomenology and University Press of America.

Opp, K.-D. (1979), 'Group Size, Emergence, and Composition Laws: Are there Macroscopic Theories *sui generis?*', *Philosophy of Social Science,* vol. 9.

Outhwaite, W. (1975), *Understanding Social Life; the Method called 'Verstehen',* London: George Allen and Unwin.

Palmer, B. D. (1981), *The Making of E. P. Thompson: Marxism, Humanism, and History,* Toronto: New Hogtown Press.

Palmer, R. E. (1969), *Hermeneutics,* Evanston: Northwestern University Press.

Parsons, T. (1937), *The Structure of Social Action. Vol. I: Marshall, Pareto, Durkheim; Vol. II: Weber,* paperback edn, NY: Free Press.

—— (1951), *The Social System,* NY: Free Press.

—— (1954), *Essays in Sociological Theory,* revised edn, NY: Free Press.

—— (1960), 'Pattern Variables Revisited: a Response to Robert Dubin', reprinted in Parsons, T. (1967), *Sociological Theory and Modern Society,* NY: Free Press.

—— (1961), 'Some Considerations on the Theory of Social Change', reprinted in Eisenstadt, S. N. (ed.) (1970), *Readings in Social Evolution and Development,* Oxford: Pergamon.

—— (1963), 'On the Concept of Political Power', reprinted in Parsons, T. (1969), *Politics and Social Structure,* NY: Free Press.

—— (1964), 'Evolutionary Universals in Society', reprinted in Parsons, T. (1967), *Sociological Theory and Modern Society,* NY: Free Press.

—— (1966), *Societies,* Englewood Cliffs: Prentice-Hall.

—— (1970a), 'On Building Social System Theory: a Personal History', *Daedalus,* vol. 99.

—— (1970b), 'Some Problems of General Theory in Sociology', in McKinney, J. C. and Tiryakian, E. A. (eds) (1970), *Theoretical Sociology,* NY: Appleton-Century-Crofts.

—— (1975), 'The Present Status of Structural-Functional Theory in Sociology', in Coser, L. (ed.) (1975), *The Idea of Social Structure,* NY: Harcourt Brace Jovanovich.

—— (1976), 'Social Structure and the Symbolic Media of Interchange', in Blau, P. (ed.) (1976), *Approaches to the Study of Social Structure,* London: Open Books.

—— (1977), *The Evolution of Societies,* Englewood Cliffs: Prentice-Hall.

—— (1982), 'Action, Symbols, and Cybernetic Control', in Rossi, I. (ed.) (1982), *Structural Sociology*, NY: Columbia University Press.

—— and Shils, E. A. (1951), 'Values, Motives, and Systems of Action', part 2 of Parsons, T. and Shils, E. A. (eds) (1951), *Toward a General Theory of Action*, NY: Harper and Row.

—— and Smelser, N. J. (1956), *Economy and Society*, London: Routledge and Kegan Paul.

Passmore, J. (1966), *A Hundred Years of Philosophy*, 2nd edn, Harmondsworth: Penguin.

Perkin, H. (1962), 'Social History', in Finberg, H. P. R. (ed.) (1962), *Approaches to History*, London: Routledge and Kegan Paul.

—— (1972), *The Origins of Modern English Society, 1780–1880*, London: Routledge and Kegan Paul.

—— (1976), 'Social History in Britain', *Journal of Social History*, vol. 10.

Perrot, M. (1976), 'The Strengths and Weaknesses of French Social History', *Journal of Social History*, vol. 10.

Pettit, P. (1978), 'Rational Man Theory', in Hookway, E. and Pettit, P. (eds) (1978), *Action and Interpretation*, Cambridge: Cambridge University Press.

—— (1979), 'Rationalization and the Art of Explaining Action', in Bolton, N. (ed.) (1979), *Philosophical Problems in Psychology*, London: Methuen.

Piaget, J. (1971a), *Insights and Illusions of Philosophy*, London: Routledge and Kegan Paul.

—— (1971b), *Structuralism*, London: Routledge and Kegan Paul.

—— (1972a), *The Principles of Genetic Epistemology*, London: Routledge and Kegan Paul.

—— (1972b), *Psychology and Epistemology*, Harmondsworth: Penguin.

—— (1977a), *The Development of Thought*, Oxford: Basil Blackwell.

—— (1977b), *The Essential Piaget* (ed. H. E. Gruber and J. J. Voneche), London: Routledge and Kegan Paul.

Platts, M. (1979), *Ways of Meaning*, London: Routledge and Kegan Paul.

—— (ed.) (1980), *Reference, Truth and Reality*, London: Routledge and Kegan Paul.

Polanyi, M. (1962), *Personal Knowledge*, London: Routledge and Kegan Paul.

Polkinghorne, D. (1983), *Methodology for the Human Sciences*, Albany: State University of New York Press.

Popper, K. R. (1961), *The Poverty of Historicism*, 2nd edn, London: Routledge and Kegan Paul.

—— (1966), *The Open Society and its Enemies. Vol. 1: Plato; Vol. 2: Hegel and Marx*, 5th edn, London: Routledge and Kegan Paul.

—— (1970), 'Normal Science and its Dangers', in Lakatos, I. and Musgrave, A. (eds) (1970), *Criticism and the Growth of Knowledge*, Cambridge: Cambridge University Press.

—— (1972a), *Conjectures and Refutations*, 4th edn, London: Routledge and Kegan Paul.

—— (1972b), *The Logic of Scientific Discovery*, revised edn, London: Hutchinson.

—— (1972c), *Objective Knowledge*, Oxford: Oxford University Press.

—— (1976), 'The Logic of the Social Sciences' and 'Reason or Revolution?', in Adorno, T. et al. (1976), *The Positivist Dispute in German Sociology*, London: Heinemann.

Porpora, D. V. (1983), 'On the Prospects for a Nomothetic Theory of Social Structure', *Journal for the Theory of Social Behaviour*, vol. 13.

Poster, M. (1982), 'Foucault and History', *Social Research*, vol. 49.

Putnam, H. (1973), 'Philosophy and our Mental Life', reprinted in Putnam, H. (1975), *Mind, Language and Reality*, Cambridge: Cambridge University Press.

—— (1974), 'The "Corroboration" of Theories', in Schilpp, P. A. (ed.) (1974), *The Philosophy of Karl Popper*, La Salle: Open Court.

—— (1975a), *Mathematics, Matter and Method: Philosophical Papers Vol. I*, Cambridge: Cambridge University Press.

—— (1975b), 'The Meaning of Meaning', reprinted in Putnam, H. (1975), *Mind, Language and Reality*, Cambridge: Cambridge University Press.

—— (1975c), 'Language and Reality', in Putnam, H. (1975), *Mind, Language and Reality*, Cambridge: Cambridge University Press.

—— (1975d), *Mind, Language and Reality: Philosophical Papers Vol. 2*, Cambridge: Cambridge University Press.

—— (1976), 'What is Realism?', *Proceedings of the Aristotelian Society*, vol. LXXVI.

—— (1978), *Meaning and the Moral Sciences*, London: Routledge and Kegan Paul.

—— (1981), *Reason, Truth and History*, Cambridge: Cambridge University Press.

—— (1982a), 'Three Kinds of Scientific Realism', *The Philosophical Quarterly*, vol. 32.

—— (1982b), 'Why Reason Can't be Naturalized', *Synthese*, vol. 52.

—— (1982c), 'Why There isn't a Ready-Made World', *Synthese*, vol. 51.

Quine, W. V. (1951), 'Two Dogmas of Empiricism', reprinted in Quine, W. V. (1980), *From a Logical Point of View*, 3rd edn, Cambridge, Mass.: Harvard University Press.

—— (1960), *Word and Object*, Cambridge, Mass.: MIT Press.

—— (1969), *Ontological Relativity and Other Essays*, NY: Columbia University Press.

—— (1970), 'On the Reasons for Indeterminacy of Translation', *Journal of Philosophy*, vol. LXVII.

—— (1980), *From a Logical Point of View*, 3rd edn, Cambridge, Mass.: Harvard University Press.

Rabinow, P. (1983), 'Humanism as Nihilism: the Bracketing of Truth and Seriousness in American Cultural Anthropology', in Haan, N. et al. (eds) (1983), *Social Science as Moral Inquiry*, NY: Columbia University Press.

—— and Sullivan, W. M. (eds) (1979), *Interpretive Social Science: a Reader*, Berkeley: University of California Press.

Radcliffe-Brown, A. R. (1952), *Structure and Function in Primitive Society*, London: Routledge and Kegan Paul.

Radnitzky, G. (1979), 'Justifying a Theory versus Giving Good Reasons for Preferring a Theory: On the Big Divide in the Philosophy of Science', in Radnitzky, G. and Anderson, G. (1979), *The Structure and Development of Science*, Dordrecht: Reidel.

—— (1981), 'Progress and Rationality in Research: Science from the Viewpoint of Popperian Methodology', in Grmek, M. D. et al. (eds) (1981), *On Scientific Discovery*, Dordrecht: Reidel.

Revel. J. (1978), 'The Annales: Continuities and Discontinuities', *Review*, vol. 1.

Ricoeur, P. (1978), 'History and Hermeneutics', in Yovel, Y. (ed.) (1978), *Philosophy of History and Action*, Dordrecht: Reidel.

—— (1980), *The Contribution of French Historiography to the Theory of History*, Oxford: Oxford University Press.

—— (1981), *Hermeneutics and the Human Sciences*, Cambridge: Cambridge University Press.

Robertson, R. (1978), *Meaning and Change*, Oxford, Basil Blackwell.

Rocher, G. (1974), *Talcott Parsons and American Sociology*, London: Nelson.

Roemer, J. E. (1982), 'Methodological Individualism and Deductive Marxism', *Theory and Society*, vol. 11.

Rogowski, R. (1983), 'Structure Growth and Power: Three Rationalist Accounts', *International Organization*, vol. 37.

Rorty, R. (1975), 'Realism and Reference', *The Monist*, vol. 59.

—— (1979a), 'Pragmatism, Relativism, and Irrationalism', reprinted in Rorty, R. (1982), *Consequences of Pragmatism*, Sussex: Harvester.

—— (1979b), 'Transcendental Arguments, Self-Reference, and Pragmatism', in Bieri, P. et al. (eds) (1979), *Transcendental Arguments and Science*, Dordrecht: Reidel.

—— (1980), *Philosophy and the Mirror of Nature*, Oxford: Basil Blackwell.

Roseberry, W. (1982), 'Balinese Cockfights and the Seduction of Anthropology', *Social Research*, vol. 49.

Rosenberg, M. (1979), 'Disposition Concepts in Behavioral Science', in Merton, R. et al. (eds) (1979), *Qualitative and Quantitative Social Research*, NY: Free Press.

Rossi, I. (1974), 'Structuralism as Scientific Method', in Rossi, I. (ed.) (1974), *The Unconscious in Culture*, NY: E. P. Dutton.

—— (1981), 'Transformational Structuralism: Lévi-Strauss's Definition of Social Structure', in Blau, P. and Merton, R. (eds) (1981), *Continuities in Structural Inquiry*, Beverly Hills: Sage.

—— (1982), 'Relational Structuralism as an Alternative to the Structural and Interpretive Paradigms of Empiricist Orientation', in Rossi, I. (ed.) (1982), *Structural Sociology*, NY: Columbia University Press.

Rostow, W. W. (1971), *The Stages of Economic Growth*, 2nd edn, Cambridge: Cambridge University Press.

Roth, G. (1971), 'Sociological Typology and Historical Explanation', in Bendix, R. and Roth, G. (1971), *Scholarship and Partisanship*, Berkeley: University of California Press.

—— (1976), 'History and Sociology in the work of Max Weber', *British Journal of Sociology*, vol. 27.

—— (1979), 'Duration and Rationalization: Fernand Braudel and Max Weber', in Roth, G. and Schluchter, W. (eds) (1979), *Max Weber's Vision of History*, Berkeley: University of California Press.

Roth, M. S. (1981), 'Foucault's "History of the Present"', *History and Theory*, vol. 20.

Runciman, W. G. (1969), 'What is Structuralism?', reprinted in Ryan, A. (ed.) (1973), *Philosophy of Social Explanation*, Oxford: Oxford University Press.

—— (1981), 'Comparative Sociology or Normative History? A Note on the Methodology of Perry Anderson', *European Journal of Sociology*, vol. 21.

—— (1982), 'Origins of States: the Case of Archaic Greece', *Comparative Studies in Society and History*, vol. 24.

—— (1983a), 'Capitalism without Classes', *The British Journal of Sociology*, vol. 34.

—— (1984), 'Accelerating Social Mobility: the Case of Anglo-Saxon England', *Past and Present*, no. 104.

Ryan, A. (ed.) (1973), *The Philosophy of Social Explanation*, Oxford: Oxford University Press.

Ryle, G. (1949), *The Concept of Mind*, NY: Barnes and Noble.

—— (1954), *Dilemmas*, Cambridge: Cambridge University Press.

—— (1968), 'Thinking and Reflecting', in Vesey, G. (ed.) (1968), *The Human Agent*, London: Macmillan.

Samuel, R. (1980a), 'British Marxist Historians: 1880–1980, Part One', *New Left Review*, no. 120.

—— (1980b), 'History Workshop Methods', *History Workshop*, no. 9.

—— (1981a), 'History and Theory', in Samuel, R. (ed.) (1981), *People's History and Socialist Theory*, London: Routledge and Kegan Paul.

—— (1981b), 'People's History', in Samuel, R. (ed.) (1981), *People's History and Socialist Theory*, London: Routledge and Kegan Paul.

Santamaria, U. and Bailey, A. M. (1984), 'A Note on Braudel's Structure as Duration', *History and Theory*, vol. 23.

Savage, S. P. (1981), *The Theories of Talcott Parsons*, London: Macmillan.

Sayer, D. (1979), *Marx's Method*, Sussex: Harvester.

Scheuch, E. K. (1980), 'Quantitative Analysis of Historical Material as the Basis for a New Co-operation Between History and Sociology', in Clubb, J. M. and Scheuch, E. K. (eds) (1980), *Historical Social Research*, Stuttgart: Klett-Cotta.

Schlick, M. (1930), 'The Turning Point in Philosophy', reprinted in Ayer, A. J. (ed.) (1959), *Logical Positivism*, NY: Free Press.

—— (1932a), 'On the Foundation of Knowledge', reprinted in Hanfling. O. (ed.) (1981), *Essential Readings in Logical Positivism*, Oxford: Basil Blackwell.

—— (1932b), 'Positivism and Realism', reprinted in Hanfling, O. (ed.) (1981), *Essential Readings in Logical Positivism*, Oxford: Basil Blackwell.

—— (1938), 'Structure and Context' and 'Meaning and Verification', reprinted in Hanfling, O. (ed.) (1981), *Essential Readings in Logical Positivisn*, Oxford: Basil Blackwell.

Schutz, A. (1940), 'Phenomenology and the Social Sciences', reprinted in Luckmann, T. (ed.) (1978), *Phenomenology and Sociology*, Harmondsworth: Penguin.

—— (1945) 'On Multiple Realities', *Philosophy and Phenomenological Research*, vol. 5.

—— (1960), 'The Social World and the Theory of Social Action', *Social Research*, vol. 27.

—— (1967), *The Phenomenology of the Social World*, London: Heinemann.

Schwartz, S. P. (ed.) (1977), *Naming, Necessity and Natural Kinds*, Ithaca: Cornell University Press.

Scott, K. J. (1961), 'Methodological and Epistemological Individualism', reprinted in O'Neill, J. (ed.) (1973), *Modes of Individualism and Collectivism*, London: Heinemann.

Scriven, M. (1956), 'A Possible Distinction between Traditional Scientific Disciplines and the Study of Human Behaviour', *Minnesota Studies in Philosophy of
Science,* vol. I.
—— (1959), 'Truisms as the Grounds for Historical Explanations', in Gardiner,
P. (ed.) (1959), *Theories of History,* NY: Free Press.
—— (1963), 'New Isues in the Logic of Explanation', in Hook, S. (ed.) (1963),
Philosophy and History: a Symposium, NY: New York University Press.
—— (1966), 'Causes, Connections and Conditions in History', in Dray, W. H.
(ed.) (1966), *Philosophical Analysis and History,* NY: Harper and Row.
—— (1969), 'Logical Positivism and the Behavioral Sciences', in Achinstein, P.
and Barker, S. (eds) (1969), *The Legacy of Logical Positivism,* Baltimore:
Johns Hopkins Press.
—— (1975), 'Causation as Explanation', *Nous,* vol. 9.
Searle, J. R. (1983), *Intentionality,* Cambridge: Cambridge University Press.
Secord, P. F. (1977), 'Making Oneself Behave: a Critique of the Behavioural
Paradigm and an Alternative Conceptualisation', in Mischel, T. (ed.) (1977),
The Self, Oxford: Basil Blackwell.
Selbourne, D. (1980), 'On the Methods of History Workshop', *History Work-
shop,* no. 9.
Seligman, B. B. (1971), *Main Currents in Modern Economics,* vols 1, 2, 3,
Chicago: Quadrangle Paperbacks.
Seligman, E. R. A. (1907), *The Economic Interpretation of History,* 2nd edn,
NY: Columbia University Press.
Sellars, W. (1962), 'Philosophy and the Scientific Image of Man', reprinted in
Sellars, W. (1963), *Science, Perception and Reality,* London: Routledge and
Kegan Paul.
—— (1963), *Science, Perception, and Reality,* London: Routledge and Kegan
Paul.
—— (1965), 'Scientific Realism or Irenic Instrumentalism', in Cohen, R. S. and
Wartofsky, M. (eds) (1965), *Boston Studies in Philosophy of Science,* vol. II,
Dordrecht: Reidel.
—— (1966), 'Fatalism and Determinism', in Lehrer, K. (ed.) (1966), *Freedom and
Determinism,* Atlantic Highlands: Humanities Press.
—— (1968), *Science and Metaphysics,* London: Routledge and Kegan Paul.
—— (1973), 'Conceptual Change', in Pearce, G. and Maynard, P. (eds) (1973),
Conceptual Change, Dordrecht: Reidel.
—— (1973), 'Actions and Events', *Nous,* vol. VII.
—— and Meehl, P. E. (1956), 'The Concept of Emergence', *Minnesota Studies in
Philosophy of Science,* vol. I.
Semmel, B. (1976), 'H. T. Buckle: the Liberal Faith and the Science of History',
British Journal of Sociology, vol. 27.
Sen, A. K. (1976), 'Rational Fools: A Critique of the Behavioural Foundations of
Economic Theory', *Philosophy and Public Affairs,* vol. 6.
—— (1983), 'Accounts, Actions, and Values: Objectivity of Social Science', in
Lloyd, C. (ed.) (1983), *Social Theory and Political Practice,* Oxford: Oxford
University Press.
Shapere, D. (1964), 'The Structure of Scientific Revolutions', *Philosophical
Review,* vol. LXXIII.

—— (1966), 'Meaning and Scientific Change', reprinted in Hacking, I. (ed.) (1981), *Scientific Revolutions*, Oxford: Oxford University Press.

—— (1969), 'Notes Towards a Post-Positivistic Interpretation of Science', in Achinstein, A. and Barker, S. (eds) (1969), *The Legacy of Logical Positivism*, Baltimore: Johns Hopkins Press.

—— (1974a), 'Discovery, Rationality, and Progress in Science: a Perspective in the Philosophy of Science', in Schaffner, K. F. and Cohen, R. S. (eds) (1974), *PSA 1972*, Dordrecht: Reidel.

—— (1974b), 'Natural Science and the Future of Metaphysics', in Cohen, R. S. and Wartofsky, M. (eds) (1974), *Methodological and Historical Essays in the Natural and Social Sciences*, Dordrecht: Reidel.

—— (1974c), 'On the Relations between Compositional and Evolutionary Theories', in Ayala, F. J. and Dobzhansky, T. (eds) (1974), *Studies in the Philosophy of Biology*, London: Macmillan.

—— (1974d), 'Scientific Theories and their Domains', in Suppe, F. (ed.) (1977), *The Structure of Scientific Revolutions*, 2nd edn, Urbana: University of Illinois Press.

—— (1977), 'What can the Theory of Knowledge learn from the History of Knowledge?', *The Monist*, vol. 60.

—— (1980), 'The Character of Scientific Change', in Nickles, T. (ed.) (1980), *Scientific Discovery, Logic, and Rationality*, Dordrecht: Reidel.

—— (1982a), 'The Scope and Limits of Scientific Change', in Cohen, L. J. et al. (eds) (1982), *Logic, Methodology, and Philosophy of Science VI*, Amsterdam: North-Holland.

—— (1982b), 'Reason, Reference, and the Quest for Knowledge', *Philosophy of Science*, vol. 49.

Shapiro, G. (1976), 'Prospects for a Scientific Social History', *Journal of Social History*, vol. 10.

Shaw, W. H. (1978), *Marx's Theory of History*, London: Hutchinson.

Sheridan, A. (1980), *Michel Foucault: the Will to Truth*, London, Tavistock.

Shiner, L. E. (1975), 'Tradition/Modernity: an Ideal Type Gone Astray', *Comparative Studies in Society and History*, vol. 17.

Shotter, J. (1976), 'Acquired Powers: the Transformation of Natural into Personal Powers', reprinted in Harré, R. (ed.) (1976), *Personality*, Oxford: Basil Blackwell.

—— (1980a), 'Action, Joint Action, and Intentionality', in Brenner, M. (ed.) (1980), *The Structure of Action*, Oxford: Basil Blackwell.

—— (1980b), 'Men the Magicians: the Duality of Social Being and the Structure of Moral Worlds', in Chapman, A. J. and Jones, D. M. (eds) (1980), *Models of Man*, Leicester: British Psychological Society.

—— (1983), 'Duality of Structure and Intentionality in an Ecological Psychology', *Journal for the Theory of Social Behaviour*, vol. 13.

Silverman, H. J. (1980), 'Phenomenology', *Social Research*, vol. 47.

Simon, H. A. (1976), 'From Substantive to Procedural Rationality', in Latsis, S. (ed.) (1976), *Method and Appraisal in Economics*, Cambridge: Cambridge University Press.

—— (1983), *Reason in Human Affairs*, Oxford: Basil Blackwell.

Skinner, B. F. (1953), *Science and Human Behavior*, NY: Collier-Macmillan and the Free Press.

—— (1963), 'Behaviorism at Fifty', reprinted in Wann, T. W. (ed.) (1964), *Behaviorism and Phenomenology*, Chicago: University of Chicago Press.

Skinner, Q. (1975), 'Hermeneutics and the Role of History', *New Literary History*, vol. VII.

Skocpol, T. (1977), 'Wallerstein's World Capitalist System: a Theoretical and Historical Critique', *American Journal of Sociology*, vol. 82.

—— and Somers, M. (1980), 'The Uses of Comparative History in Macrosocial Inquiry', *Comparative Studies in Society and History*, vol. 22.

Smart, B. (1982), 'Foucault, Sociology, and the Problem of Human Agency', *Theory and Society*, vol. 11.

Smart, J. J. C. (1959), 'Sensations and Brain Processes', reprinted in Børst, C. V. (ed.) (1970), *The Mind/Brain Identity Theory*, London: Macmillan.

—— (1963), *Philosophy and Scientific Realism*, London: Routledge and Kegan Paul.

—— (1965), 'Conflicting Views About Explanation', in Cohen, R. S. and Wartofsky, M. (eds) (1965), *Boston Studies in Philosophy of Science*, vol. II, Dordrecht: Reidel.

—— (1982), 'Difficulties for Realism in the Philosophy of Science', in Cohen, L. J. et al. (eds) (1982), *Logic, Methodology, and Philosophy of Science*, VI, Amsterdam: North-Holland.

Smelser, N. J. (1959), *Social Change in the Industrial Revolution*, London: Routledge and Kegan Paul.

—— (1962), *Theory of Collective Behavior*, London: Routledge and Kegan Paul.

—— (1963), 'Mechanisms of Change and Adjustments to Change', in Hoselitz, B. and Moore, W. E. (eds) (1963), *Industrialisation and Society*, Paris: Mouton, UNESCO.

—— (1966), 'The Modernization of Social Relations', in Weiner, M. (ed.) (1966), *Modernization*, NY: Basic Books.

—— (1967a), 'Processes of Social Change', in Smelser, N. J. (ed.) (1967), *Sociology: an Introduction*, NY: John Wiley.

—— (1967b), 'Sociological History: the Industrial Revolution and the British Working-Class Family', reprinted in Flinn, M. and Smout, T. C. (eds) (1974), *Essays in Social History*, Oxford: Oxford University Press.

—— (1968a), 'Social and Psychological Dimensions of Collective Behaviour', in Smelser, N. J. (1968), *Essays in Sociological Explanation*, Englewood Cliffs: Prentice-Hall.

—— (1968b), 'Toward a General Theory of Social Change', in Smelser, N. J. (1968), *Essays in Sociological Explanation*, Englewood Cliffs: Prentice-Hall.

—— (1976), *The Sociology of Economic Life*, 2nd edn, Englewood Cliffs: Prentice-Hall.

Smith, A. D. (1973), *The Concept of Social Change*, London: Routledge and Kegan Paul.

Smith, D. (1978), 'Domination and Containment: an Approach to Modernisation', *Comparative Studies in Society and History*, vol. 20.

—— (1982), 'Social History and Sociology – More than Just Good Friends', *Sociological Review*, vol. 30.

—— (1983a), *Barrington Moore: Violence, Morality, and Political Change*, London: Macmillan.

—— (1983b), ' "Put not your Trust in Princes" – a Commentary upon Anthony

Giddens and the Absolute State', *Theory, Culture and Society,* vol. 1.

—— (1984a), 'Morality and Method in the Work of Barrington Moore', *Theory and Society,* vol. 13.

—— (1984b), 'Norbert Elias: Established or Outsider?', *The Sociological Review,* vol. 32.

Spengler, J. J. (1955), 'Social Structure, the State, and Economic Growth', in Kuznets, S. et al. (eds) (1955), *Economic Growth: Brazil, India, Japan,* Durham: Duke University Press.

—— (1960), 'Economic Development: Political Preconditions and Political Consequences', *Journal of Politics,* vol. 22.

—— (1961), 'Theory Ideology, Non-Economic Values, and Politico-Economic Development', in Braibanti, R. and Spengler, J. J. (eds) (1961), *Tradition, Values, and Socio-Economic Development,* Durham: Duke University Press.

—— (1965), 'Social Evolution and the Theory of Economic Development', in Barringer, H. R. et al. (eds) (1965), *Social Change in Developing Areas,* Cambridge, Mass.: Schenken.

Sperber, D. (1979), 'Claude Lévi-Strauss', in Sturrock, J. (ed.) (1979), *Structuralism,* Oxford: Oxford University Press.

Stearns, P. N. (1976), 'Coming of Age', *Journal of Social History,* vol. 10.

—— (1980), 'Toward a Wider Vision: Trends in Social History', in Kammen, M. (ed.) (1980), *The Past Before Us,* Ithaca: Cornell University Press.

Sternberg, R. J. et al. (1979), 'Metaphor, Induction and Social Policy', in Ortony, A. (ed.) (1979), *Metaphor and Thought,* Cambridge: Cambridge University Press.

Stinchcombe, A. L. (1978), *Theoretical Methods in Social History,* NY: Academic Press.

Stoianovich. T. (1976), *French Historical Method: the Annales Paradigm,* Ithaca: Cornell University Press.

—— (1978), 'Social History: Perspective of the Annales Paradigm', *Review,* vol. 1.

Stone, L. (1976), 'History and the Social Sciences in the Twentieth Century', reprinted in Stone, L. (1981), *The Past and the Present (essays),* London: Routledge and Kegan Paul.

—— (1979), 'The Revival of Narrative', *Past and Present,* no. 85.

Stout, H. S. (1975), 'Culture, Structure and the "New" History: a Critique and an Agenda', *Computers and the Humanities,* vol. 9.

Strawson, P. F. (1979), 'Perception: its Objects', in Macdonald, G. (ed.) (1979), *Perception and Identity,* London: Macmillan.

Strong, T. B. (1978), 'Dramaturgical Discourse and Political Enactments: Toward an Artistic Foundation for Political Space', in Brown, R. H. and Lyman, S. M. (eds) (1978), *Structure, Consciousness and History,* Cambridge: Cambridge University Press.

Sturrock, J. (1979), 'Introduction' to Sturrock, J. (ed.) (1979), *Structuralism and Since,* Oxford: Oxford University Press.

Suchting, W. A. (1972), 'Marx, Popper, and Historicism', *Inquiry,* vol. 15.

Suppe, F. (1977a), 'The Search for Philosophic Understanding of Scientific Theories', in Suppe, F. (ed.) (1977), *The Structure of Scientific Theories,* 2nd edn, Urbana: University of Illinois Press.

—— (1977b), 'Afterword', in Suppe, F. (ed.) (1977), *The Structure of Scientific Theories,* 2nd edn, Urbana: University of Illinois Press.

—— (ed.) (1977c), *The Structure of Scientific Theories,* 2nd edn, Urbana: University of Illinois Press.

Taylor, C. (1964), *The Explanation of Behaviour,* London: Routledge and Kegan Paul.

—— (1970), 'The Explanation of Purposive Behaviour', in Borger, R. and Cioffi, F. (eds) (1970), *Explanation in the Behavioural Sciences,* Cambridge: Cambridge University Press.

—— (1971), 'Interpretation and the Sciences of Man', reprinted in Rabinow, P. and Sullivan, W. M. (eds) (1979), *Interpretive Social Science: a Reader,* Berkeley: University of California Press.

—— (1977), 'What is Human Agency?', in Mischel, T. (ed.) (1977), *The Self,* Oxford: Basil Blackwell.

—— (1978), 'The Validity of Transcendental Arguments', *Proceedings of the Aristotelian Society,* vol. LXXIX.

—— (1979), 'Sense Data Revisited', in Macdonald, G. (ed.) (1979), *Perception and Identity,* London: Macmillan.

—— (1980), 'Understanding in Human Science', *Review of Metaphysics,* vol. 34.

—— (1981), 'Understanding and Explanation in the *Geisteswissenschaften*', in Holtzman, S. and Leich, C. (eds) (1981), *Wittgenstein: To Follow a Rule,* London: Routledge and Kegan Paul.

—— (1983), 'Political Theory and Practice', in Lloyd, C. (ed.) (1983), *Social Theory and Political Practice,* Oxford: Oxford University Press.

—— (1984), 'Foucault on Freedom and Truth', *Political Theory,* vol. 12.

Taylor, J. G. (1979), *From Modernization to Modes of Production,* London: Macmillan.

Thalberg, I. (1980), 'How Does Agent Causality Work?', in Brand, M. and Walton, D. (eds) (1980), *Action Theory,* Dordrecht: Reidel.

Thomas, K. (1963), 'History and Anthropology', *Past and Present,* no. 24.

Thompson, E. P. (1963), *The Making of the English Working Class* (1968), Harmondsworth: Penguin.

—— (1965), 'The Pecularities of the English', reprinted in Thompson, E. P. (1978), *The Poverty of Theory,* London: Merlin.

—— (1967), 'Time, Work, Discipline, and Industrial Capitalism', reprinted in Flinn, M. and Smout, T. C. (eds) (1974), *Social History,* Oxford: Oxford University Press.

—— (1973), 'Patrician Society, Plebeian Culture', *Journal of Social History,* vol. 7.

—— (1976), 'On History, Sociology, and Historical Relevance', *British Journal of Sociology,* vol. 27.

—— (1977a), 'The Crime of Anonymity', in Hay, D. et al. (1977), *Albion's Fatal Tree,* Harmondsworth: Penguin.

—— (1977b), *Whigs and Hunters,* Harmondsworth: Penguin.

—— (1978a), 'Eighteenth-Century English Society: Class Struggle Without Class?', *Social History,* vol. 3.

—— (1978b), 'Folklore, Anthropology, and Social History', *Indian Historical Review,* vol. 3, reprinted as a Studies in Labour History pamphlet, Brighton, 1979.

—— (1978c), *The Poverty of Theory, and Other Essays,* London: Merlin.

—— (1978d), 'The Poverty of Theory: or an Orrery of Errors', in Thompson, E. P. (1978), *The Poverty of Theory and Other Essays,* London: Merlin.

—— (1981), 'The Politics of Theory', in Samuel, R. (ed.) (1981), *People's History and Socialist Theory*, London: Routledge and Kegan Paul.

Thompson, J. B. (1981), *Critical Hermeneutics; a Study in the thought of Paul Ricoeur and Jürgen Habermas*, Cambridge: Cambridge University Press.

Tilly, C. (1970), 'Clio and Minerva', in McKinney, J. C. and Tiryakian, E. A. (eds) (1970), *Theoretical Sociology*, NY: Appleton-Century-Crofts.

—— (1978), 'Anthropology, History, and the Annales', *Review*, vol. 1.

—— (1980a), 'Historical Sociology', *Current Perspectives in Social Theory*, vol. 1.

—— (1980b), 'Two Callings of Social History', *Theory and Society*, vol. 9.

Tilly, L. A. (1980), 'Social History and its Critics,', *Theory and Society*, vol. 9.

Tipps, D. C. (1973), 'Modernization Theory and the Comparative Study of Societies: a Critical Perspective', *Comparative Studies in Society and History*, vol. 15.

Tolman, E. C. (1951), 'A Psychological Model', in Parsons, T. and Shils, E. A. (eds) (1951), *Toward a General Theory of Action*, NY: Harper and Row.

Topolski, J. (1973), 'Lévi-Strauss and Marx on History', *History and Theory*, vol. XII.

Toulmin, S. (1953), *The Philosophy of Science*, London: Hutchinson.

—— (1970), 'Reasons and Causes', in Borger, R. and Cioffi, F. (eds) (1970), *Explanation in Behavioural Sciences*, Cambridge: Cambridge University Press.

—— (1972), *Human Understanding*, vol. 1, Oxford: Oxford University Press.

—— (1974), 'Rules and their Relevance for Understanding Human Behaviour' in Mischel, T. (ed.) (1974), *Understanding Other Persons*, Oxford: Basil Blackwell.

Touraine, A. (1964), 'Towards a Sociology of Action', reprinted in Giddens, A. (ed.) (1974), *Positivism and Sociology*, London: Heinemann.

—— (1966), 'The Raison d'Être of a Sociology of Action', reprinted in Giddens, A. (ed.) (1974), *Positivism and Sociology*, London: Heinemann.

—— (1970), 'Sociology of Development', reprinted in Eisenstadt, S. N. (ed.) (1970), *Readings in Social Evolution and Development*, Oxford: Pergamon.

—— (1971), *The Post-Industrial Society*, London: Wildwood House.

—— (1976), 'Eight Ways to Eliminate the Sociology of Action', reprinted in Freiberg, J. (ed.) (1979), *Critical Sociology*, NY: Irvington.

—— (1977a), 'Introduction' and 'Crisis of Transformation', in Birnbaum, N. (ed.) (1977), *Beyond the Crisis*, NY: Oxford University Press.

—— (1977b), *The Self-Production of Society*, Chicago: University of Chicago Press.

—— (1981), *The Voice and the Eye*, Cambridge: Cambridge University Press.

—— et al. (1983), *Solidarity; Poland 1980–81*, Cambridge: Cambridge University Press.

Trevelyan, G. M. (1942), *English Social History*, London: Longmans.

Trevor-Roper, H. R. (1972), 'Fernand Braudel, the Annales, and the Mediterranean', *Journal of Modern History*, vol. 44.

—— (1980), *History and Imagination*, Oxford: Oxford University Press.

Turner, B. S. (1981), 'Weber and the Sociology of Development', in Turner, B. S. (1981), *For Weber*, London: Routledge and Kegan Paul.

Turner, J. H. (1983), 'Idiographic vs Nomothetic Explanation: a Comment on Porpora's Conclusions', *Journal for the Theory of Social Behaviour*, vol. 13.

Urry, J. (1983), 'Duality of Structure: Some Critical Issues', *Theory, Culture, and Society*, vol. 1.

Utz, P. J. (1973), 'Evolutionism Revisited', *Comparative Studies in Society and History*, vol. 15.

Vann, R. T. (1976), 'The Rhetoric of Social History', *Journal of Social History*, vol. 10.

Van Parijs, P. (1981), *Evolutionary Explanation in the Social Sciences*, London: Tavistock.

—— (1982a), 'Functionalist Marxism Rehabilitated: a Comment on Elster', *Theory and Society*, vol. 11.

—— (1982b), 'Perverse Effects and Social Contradictions', *British Journal for Sociology*, vol. 33.

Veblen, T. (1970), *The Theory of the Leisure Class*, London: Unwin Books.

Veltmeyer, H. (1974), 'Towards an Assessment of the Structuralist Interrogation of Marx: Claude Lévi-Strauss and Louis Althusser', *Science and Society*, vol. 38.

Vernon, R. (1979), 'Unintended Consequences', *Political Theory*, vol. 7.

Vesey, G. N. A. (1968), *The Human Agent*, Royal Institute of Philosophy Lectures, vol. 1, 1966–7, London: Macmillan.

Vico, G. (1970), *The New Science* (abridged and edited by T. G. Bergin and M. H. Fisch), Ithaca: Cornell University Press.

Vilar, P. (1973), 'Marxist History; a History in the Making: Towards a Dialogue with Althusser', *New Left Review*, vol. 80.

Viner, J. (1952), 'America's Aims and the Progress of Undeveloped Countries', in Hoselitz, B. (ed.) (1952), *The Progress of Underdeveloped Areas*, Chicago: University of Chicago Press.

Wallace, W. L. (1969), 'Overview of Contemporary Sociological Theory', in Wallace, W. (ed.) (1969), *Sociological Theory*, London: Heinemann.

—— (1981), 'Hierarchic Structure in Social Phenomena', in Blau, P. and Merton, R. (eds) (1981), *Continuities in Structural Inquiry*, London: Sage.

Wallerstein, I. (1974), *The Modern World-System*, vol. 1, NY: Academic Press.

—— (1977), 'The Tasks of Historical Social Science', *Review*, vol. I.

—— (1979), *The Capitalist World-Economy*, Cambridge: Cambridge University Press.

—— (1980), *The Modern World-System*, vol. II, NY: Academic Press.

—— (1983), *Historical Capitalism*, London: Verso.

—— (1984), *The Politics of the World-Economy*, Cambridge: Cambridge University Press.

Walsh, W. H. (1942), 'The Intelligibility of History', *Philosophy*.

—— (1967a), 'Colligatory Concepts in History', reprinted in Gardiner, P. (ed.) (1974), *The Philosophy of History*, Oxford: Oxford University Press.

—— (1967b), *An Introduction to Philosophy of History*, 3rd edn, London: Hutchinson.

Walters, R. G. (1980), 'Signs of the Times: Clifford Geertz and Historians', *Social Research*, vol. 47.

Walton, P. and Gamble, A. (1972), *From Alienation to Surplus Value*, London: Sheed and Ward.

Warrinder, C. K. (1981), 'Levels in the Study of Social Structure', in Blau, P. and Merton, R. (eds) (1981), *Continuities in Structural Inquiry*, Beverly Hills: Sage.

364 Bibliography

Wartofsky, M. W. (1980), 'Scientific Judgement: Creativity and Discovery in Scientific Thought', in Nickles, T. (ed.) (1980), *Scientific Discovery: Case Studies*, Dordrecht: Reidel.

Watkins, J. W. N. (1953), 'Ideal Types and Historical Explanation', reprinted in O'Neill, J. (ed.) (1973), *Modes of Individualism and Collectivism*, London: Heinemann.

—— (1955), 'Methodological Individualism: a Reply', reprinted in O'Neill, J. (ed.) (1973), *Modes of Individualism and Collectivism*, London: Heinemann.

—— (1957), 'Historical Explanation in the Social Sciences', reprinted in O'Neill, J. (ed.) (1973), *Modes of Individualism and Collectivism*, London: Heinemann.

—— (1958), 'The Alleged Inadequacy of Methodological Individualism', reprinted in Krimerman, L. (ed.) (1969), *The Nature and Scope of Social Science*, NY: Appleton-Century-Crofts.

—— (1970), 'Imperfect Rationality', in Borger, P. and Cioffi, F. (eds) (1970), *Explanation in the Behavioural Sciences*, Cambridge: Cambridge University Press.

—— (1974), 'The Unity of Popper's Thought', in Schilpp, P. A. (ed.) (1974), *The Philosophy of Karl Popper*, book 1, La Salle: Open Court.

—— (1976), 'The Human Condition: Two Criticisms of Hobbes', in Cohen, R. S. et al. (1976), *Essays in Honour of Lakatos*, Dordrecht: Reidel.

—— (1978a), 'Corroboration and the Problem of Content Comparison', in Radnitzky, G. and Andersson, G. (eds) (1978), *Progress and Rationality in Science*, Dordrecht: Reidel.

—— (1978b), 'The Popperian Approach to Scientific Knowledge', in Radnitzky, G. and Andersson, G. (eds) (1978), *Progress and Rationality in Science*, Dordrecht: Reidel.

Watnick, M. (1952), 'The Appeal of Communism to the Underdeveloped Peoples', in Hoselitz, B. (ed.) (1952), *The Progress of Underdeveloped Areas*, Chicago: University of Chicago Press.

Watson, G. (1975), 'Free Agency', reprinted in Watson, G. (ed.) (1982), *Free Will*, Oxford: Oxford University Press.

Weber, M. (1896), 'The Social Causes of the Decline of Ancient Civilizations', translation in Weber, M. (1976), *Agrarian Sociology of Ancient Civilizations*, London: New Left Books.

—— (1903–6), *Roscher and Knies: the Logical Problems of Historical Economics* (1975), NY: Free Press.

—— (1904–5), *The Protestant Ethic and the Spirit of Capitalism* (trans. T. Parsons) (1930), London: George Allen and Unwin.

—— (1909), *The Agrarian Sociology of Ancient Civilizations* (1976), London: New Left Books.

—— (1921), *Economy and Society* (1978), Berkeley: University of California Press.

—— (1923), *General Economic History* (1961), NY: Collier Books.

—— (1949), *The Methodology of the Social Sciences* (ed. E. A. Shils and H. A. Finch) (1949), NY: Free Press.

Weeks, J. (1982), 'Foucault for Historians', *History Workshop*, no. 14.

Weingartner, R. H. (1961), 'The Quarrel about Historical Explanation', *Journal of Philosophy*, vol. LVIII.

Wellman, B. (1983), 'Network Analysis: Some Basic Principles', in Collins, L. (ed.) (1983), *Sociological Theory*, San Francisco: Josey Bass.

White, H. V. (1973), 'Foucault Decoded: Notes from Underground', *History and Theory*, vol. XII.

—— (1979), 'Michel Foucault', in Sturrock, J. (ed.) (1979), *Structuralism and Since*, Oxford: Oxford University Press.

White, M. (1943), 'Historical Explanation', reprinted in Gardiner, P. (ed.) (1959), *Theories of History*, NY: Free Press.

Wiener, J. M. (1975), 'The Barrington Moore Thesis and its Critics', *Theory and Society*, vol. 2.

Wiener, M. J. (1981), *English Culture and the Decline of the Industrial Spirit, 1850–1980*, Cambridge: Cambridge University Press.

Wilden, A. (1972), *System and Structure*, London: Tavistock.

Williams, G. (1979), 'In Defence of History', *History Workshop*, no. 7.

Williams, R. (1961), *Culture and Society, 1780–1950*, Harmondsworth: Penguin.

—— (1965), *The Long Revolution*, Harmondsworth: Penguin.

—— (1977), *Marxism and Literature*, Oxford: Oxford University Press.

—— (1980), *Problems in Materialism and Culture*, London: New Left Books.

—— (1981), *Culture*, Glasgow: Fontana.

Winch, P. (1958), *The Idea of Social Science and its Relation to Philosophy*, London: Routledge and Kegan Paul.

—— (1964), 'Understanding a Primitive Society', reprinted in Wilson, B. (ed.) (1974), *Rationality*, Oxford: Basil Blackwell.

Windelband, W. (1980), 'History and Natural Science', *History and Theory*, vol. 19.

Wisdom, J. O. (1970), 'Situational Individualism and the Emergent Group Properties', in Borger, P and Cioffi, F. (eds) (1970), *Explanation in the Behavioural Sciences*, Cambridge: Cambridge University Press.

Wittgenstein, L.(1921), *Tractatus Logico-Philosophicus*, London: Routledge and Kegan Paul.

—— (1967), *Philosophical Investigations*, 3rd edn, Oxford: Basil Blackwell.

Wright, E. O. (1983), 'Giddens's Critique of Marxism', *New Left Review*, no. 138.

Wrong, D. H. (1961), 'The Oversocialized Conception of Man in Modern Sociology', *American Sociological Review*, vol. 26.

Zeldin, T. (1976), 'Social History and Total History', *Journal of Social History*, vol. 10.

Index